THE INTERPRETATION OF LANGUAGE

VOLUME I:
UNDERSTANDING THE SYMBOLIC
MEANING OF LANGUAGE

THE
INTERPRETATION
OF LANGUAGE

VOLUME I:
UNDERSTANDING THE SYMBOLIC
MEANING OF LANGUAGE

THEODORE THASS-THIENEMANN

JASON ARONSON, INC. NEW YORK

There is no eye like understanding,
There is no blindness like ignorance,
There is no enemy like sickness,
Nothing dreaded like death.
Alexander Csoma de Körös
Translated from the Tibetan language

Library of Congress Catalog Card Number: 73-79984

Complete Set: **ISBN** 0-87668-086-4
Volume I: **ISBN** 0-87668-087-2
Volume II: **ISBN** 0-87668-088-0

Manufactured in the United States of America

PREFACE

These two books were written at the time three philosophical revolutions met and collided with one another. The first was Freud's psychoanalysis that unveiled an image of man never envisaged before. The second was Husserl's phenomenology culminating in existentialism. The third force was logical positivism, with variations that still dominate our academic life.

These three movements had different preconceptions and widely different goals. Yet, despite their differences, they were all children of the same age. They all agreed in their radical turn toward language; each tried in its own way to break the language barrier, to reach beyond the surface of everyday, conventional speech, to find the hidden language beyond or beneath it. For the first time the interpretation of language had the unique opportunity to unite these divergent trends.

The Interpretation of Language was conceived in the awareness of the "linguistic conjunction" in philosophy that had never happened before and perhaps never will happen again.

The first volume, *Understanding the Symbolic Meaning of Language,* is based on the conviction that understanding verbal symbolism is a basic knowledge. Verbal symbolism is like arithmetic for all the physical-mathematical sciences: it is not linguistics as a specialized science, nor psychology as pursued in laboratories, nor even philosophy as a super-science of sciences, but the foundation of all humanistic disciplines.

Being a root science, verbal symbolism explores root meanings of concepts encased in language. This was also Freud's credo about psychoanalysis. He said, "Symbolism is certainly not the whole of psychology, but its substructure and perhaps its entire foundation. The possibility of its application to medical purposes must not lead us astray."

v

The fundamentalist design of psychoanalysis is the language-centered psychotherapy: it is a radical turn away from the logical-mathematical construct of man toward the here and now of the individual person and his actual sensory experience.

Freud proclaimed the dignity of the human body at a time when the vital functions were excused as subhuman necessities of life. He singlehandedly challenged contemporary prejudices by pleading for proper understanding of the sexual side of human nature. He destroyed the illusion of man as a wholly rational, conscious being. He declared the human body to be clean, white as snow, and innocent.

The recognition of the natural dignity of the body-self with all its sensory experiences may be the most wholesome trend of our days. We do not drink "H_2O" but water. To Newton and his followers, an apple falling from a tree became a highly abstract physical-mathematical problem of gravity. To the newly recovered trust in sensual reality, the answer to this event may also be: the apple fell from the tree because it had grown ripe, tasty, and colored in the ever-mysterious process of organic maturation. This is not a "scientific" answer, if "scientific" means something apart from factual reality, yet it represents the incontestable truth of everyday experience incorporated in language.

The interpretation of language as the *scientia prima* is, by its very nature, open to everyone. It appeals to all who work in the field of psychology or deal professionally with spoken or written verbal material; it is addressed to psychoanalysts, psychiatrists, and social workers. It also concerns the writer, the teacher of English and linguistics, the preacher of the Bible, and the copywriter in marketing and advertising.

In my second volume, *Understanding the Unconscious Meaning of Language,* I apply the fundamental principles elaborated in the first to verbal material selected out of the wealth of the English vocabulary. I want to demonstrate here that universals, generally thought to be located in the logical formulas of abstract syntactic structures, are also in evidence in the concrete reality. Words like *day* and *night, fire* and *water, sun* and *moon, man* and *woman, life* and *death, right* and *left,* refer to invariable human experiences. I choose for interpretation the events of separation and reunification, a small segment of invariant experience that is both archaic and common, repeated by so many individuals through the millenia that it could be interpreted as a collective dream of the whole language community. I apply the general principles Freud used in interpreting dreams and neurotic symptoms. Freud, not a linguist, discovered the linguistic truth that the body as a whole with all its organs and functions speaks a language. He introduced the distinction between the conscious surface of speech and the latent language that dwells in the preconscious, subconscious, and unconscious part of the mental organization. The manifest surface is registered in grammars and vocabularies. The repressed language beneath, however, may interfere with normal speech, and may even break out in neurotic symptoms.

Exploring the background of behavior became the rallying point where the otherwise discrepant philosophies met, revealing a new dimension of the mind, an anti-rational view of the world that was as true and real as the rational one. The logical analysis of language started from similar premises. Bertrand Russell defined his philosophy as logical atomism, and came to the conclusion that the apparent verbal form of a sentence might just cover up the real proposition. Wittgenstein, influenced by Russell as well as by Freud, also maintained that "language disguises thought." He realized that the word is "like a film on a deep water": "The older a word, the deeper it reaches." Husserl would have preferred to call phenomenology "archaeology," if this term had not been occupied by another science. The same was true of Freud, when he compared his work with the excavation of Pompei. This desire to expand consciousness beyond the limits of everyday speech was also the program of William James, Freud's wisest philosopher-psychologist contemporary. The whole analytical trend culminated in Heidegger's essentialist philosophy, which he called "the road toward language." He insisted upon the requirement of philosophy that the tools of mental operations, the words, should be as transparent and as clean as the instruments of surgical operations. But there will remain always some dark spot in the mind covering even the most important terms, if one does not know why they mean just what they actually mean. The interpretation of language wants to remove these blind spots of the mind. Freud's most comprehensive dictum says: "Where Id was there Ego shall be." This is also the aim of *Understanding the Unconscious Meaning of Language*.

It is to the credit of good dictionaries that they provide information about the background of lexical meanings, "in the conviction that a detailed care accorded to the etymologies will have been justified if they succeed in helping students to achieve a deeper understanding of their language," in the words of *Webster's New World Dictionary*. However, dictionaries are primarily interested in the material aspect of language; they cannot engage in psychological-linguistic interpretations. As a rule they list in numerical order the various meanings attached to one word. What comes first and what last is mostly decided arbitrarily. For instance the word *spring* may mean 1. a "jump"; 2. a "fountain"; 3. a "coil of wire"; 4. a "season." But how and why have such disparate meanings become attached to one and the same sound pattern? If fragments of a Greek vase were unearthed, one would not just number the fragments, but would instead reconstruct the lost whole that once existed that could impart meaning to the disparate fragments. Meaning supposes the grasp of the whole. Truth is always the whole truth. Such work implies reconstruction, the restoration of the hypothetical original. This is, as all reconstructions, an act of creative imagination, and as such will remain conjectural. But this does not mean that reconstructions are not scientific, since all means of linguistics, psychology, anthropology, and archaeology can be mobilized for achieving it.

Some reviewers of my books have asked why, since the material is selected as universally human, it is restricted to the Western heritage. Universal concepts are true in theory, but seldom valid in the empirical human reality. We are bound to a specific linguistic-cultural reality. One would have to be born again in order to shed all the imprints of Western heritage. Even if one studies with anthropological thoroughness the idiom of some aboriginal tribe, the Western man or woman will remain a foreigner in the realm of aboriginal meanings, unless he or she becomes initiated as a member of the tribe and is actually absorbed by the tribal culture. Otherwise one may faithfully record which word means what, but inevitably will still just scratch the surface of language and not grasp the real meaning, remaining an outsider to the whole realm of fantasies and magic belief connected to it. For such reasons I preferred to stay within the familiar boundaries of our old Western cultural heritage.

1973, West Roxbury,   Th. Th.
        Mass. 02132

CONTENTS

INTRODUCTION: FACTS AND THEORIES

The verbal facts presented in the following chapters are generally known and familiar to everyone who speaks English.
We take everyday English for granted. Why, then, question
it if it functions well and serves our needs perfectly? One
occasionally consults a dictionary if one stumbles upon some
strange expression in reading or writing, but that is no reason
to study English as if it were a foreign language. Why waste
time and energy on a mental operation that one learned to
perform with utmost economy? It is as if, while running down-
stairs, someone should ask us to stop and think about every
step and every stair. The normal speaker internalized his
language in early childhood. He has grown up in it and grown
together with it. It has become a part of his personality. He
has developed a basic trust in his mother tongue. He might
feel rather irritated if someone questions facts that are obvious
in any case. Surely it will strike the normal speaker as indicative of a rather paranoid streak if someone asks again and
again: "Why did you say it? What does it mean?"—thus
expressing suspicion when there is no justification for doubt
and no other way in which to say it. Our sense perceptions
are exposed to an incessant flow of messages informing us
about the affairs of the world, but most of them are not worth
any attention. Why, then, should one pay attention to routine
functions which work best automatically? Why should one
observe one's heartbeat, pulse rate, or respiration when there
is no reason to worry about them? If someone worries about
swallowing, he may develop a "lump in the throat."

Some parents may feel irritated when their small child

1

asks questions about facts that are obvious to the adult mind. I would like to recover something of this wondering of the child while looking at the endless columns of our good dictionaries as they unfold, define, describe, and classify the empirical facts that constitute our everyday language. Some facts which seemed to be obvious may turn out, on closer inspection, to be far from self-evident. They raise complicated questions of interpretation and understanding. It depends largely on one's theoretical orientation which of the many facts appear as important, which of the data will be selected and observed out of the "buzzing confusion" of daily experiences. We select the best and discard the rest. It is well known that progress in knowledge results not from accumulating more and more data, but from an overall shift in the frame of reference. A change of viewpoint may bring about a re-evaluation of what is known and shed new light upon phenomena which never attracted attention. The falling of an apple from a tree was not much of a problem until Newton raised a question which may have struck his contemporaries as paranoid. Facts receive meaning and significance through theoretical preconceptions. Man is not always conscious of his preconceptions when he faces the obvious which he takes for granted.[1]

I wish to keep the following confrontation with verbal material as free from theoretical preconceptions as possible. Just as it is the practice in clinical training to reduce all theoretical constructs to the minimum in order to achieve the fresh immediacy and accuracy of observation, so let us accept the verbal facts as they speak for themselves and forget the preconceptions that we are accustomed to attach to them.

The basic assumptions, which are maintained in the following presentation, refer to language as a specifically human attribute, to be understood in terms of organic life and development.

The thesis maintained is that language is human, and human alone. Animals do not speak. No man, however low in culture, was ever found to be without language. No animal, however high in the evolutionary scale, was ever found to possess a language. If an animal could ask an intelligent question, it would have crossed the language barrier and would not be an animal anymore.

The world that man perceives is not a prefabricated reality. It is not the world that a fish, a peacock, or a dog perceives. It is the human world, which man tries to know, explore, understand, and control.

Symbolic behavior is directed toward knowledge. This distinguishes man from animal.

Man does not simply perceive things, but also perceives the meaning of things. Meaning precedes perception. That which does not mean anything is not, as a rule, perceived. Perception and retention are vital adaptive functions. They are not aimed at meaningless events.

Symbolic behavior is creative. Man does not react mechanically to physical stimuli, but acts in thought and fantasy by using and creating symbols. Man is not limited to the physical reality, but transcends it into the dimension of its symbolic representations.

Language is the preeminent field of symbolic representation and creativity. The study of symbolism entails the study of language.

The study of symbolic behavior is the solid foundation and the common source out of which the sciences of psychology and linguistics have drawn their best insights into human behavior.

Psychology and linguistics deal with an identical material— symbolic behavior. For this reason the two sciences are inseparable from one another. Linguistics without psychology is as blindfolded as is psychology without an understanding of symbolic verbal behavior.

Even though the realm of symbolic behavior is the focal point of behavioral sciences, the intensive study of verbal symbolism is a rather new field of scientific investigation. Why it is so should be explained. It is a strange phenomenon that two sciences, which are interdependent in their research material and closely related to one another's methods and principles, developed in independence, if not in indifference, to one another's efforts. Both sciences were founded on realistic principles at about the same time, the end of the last and the beginning of the present centuries. The age of the great linguists was also the age of the great psychologists.[2] The exploration of the prehistory of our languages materialized in the classic works of linguistics at about the same time that the discovery and first exploration of meanings and unconscious mental operations were made by Sigmund Freud. Both sciences became alienated from one another for many reasons.[3] They cooperated with one another, however, in one specific field—sound engineering. The ideal goal, which both sciences approached successfully through common efforts, was the speaking machine, the high-speed electronic computer, which can perform complicated mental operations, can even translate a text from one language into another.[4] But mechanical engineering, however perfect, did not lead to a better understanding of symbolic creativity as the distinguishing mark of man.[5] Machines can translate but cannot write a text.

The discovery of symbolism was made not in the laboratories of experimental psychology, but in the clinical practice of psychiatry. The whole discovery and the "new key" which opened up a new understanding in philosophy, logic, psychology, and linguistics, and which proved to be useful even in biology, was first ridiculed and misrepresented and is still often caricatured by the term "Freudian symbol." The whole field of research in symbolism, which Freud opened up for psychology and linguistics, has been discredited by those who felt the impact and the consequences of the newly found insight into mental functioning.

It was a turning point indeed in the history of psychology when Joseph Breuer, not Freud, in the years 1880–1882, applied the "cathartic" method for the "abreaction" of symptoms which we would no longer call "hysterical."[6] It was not really Breuer himself, but his famous patient, Anna O., who discovered the surprising fact, not understood at that time, by stating that the "talking cure" under hypnosis, a kind of "chimney sweeping," relieved her symptoms, of which she had many. It seems to be paradoxical to observe, in retrospect, that neither Breuer nor Freud, in their joint publication, became aware of their radical departure from the solid ground of medical science, especially from the schools of Helmholtz and Brücke, two physiologists to whom they both were faithfully dedicated.[*] Breuer, perhaps in a more skeptical mood,

---

[*] Peter Amacher, "Freud's Neurological Education and Its Influence on Psychoanalytic Theory," *Psychological Issues* (New York: International Universities Press, 1965), Vol. 4.

said that his finding 'makes the least claim of originality."
Freud, more assertively, perhaps with a dim vision of the
great future ahead, spoke about far-reaching consequences
and how superior this new method was compared with others.
However, he subscribed, as did Breuer, without reservations
to the medical creed of causation, to the belief in the *cessante
causa cessat effectus* (extinguishing the cause means extinguishing the effect). He did not realize that he had hit upon
the fountainhead of a new understanding of human nature. He
discovered the realm of symbols, meaning, and understanding. The new method revealed the healing power of speech—
alleviating symptoms by channeling them into verbal expressions. Freud admitted that this cathartic method was only "a
symptomatic and not a causal therapy."

It was quite a while before Freud realized that words can
mean more in therapy than medicine. Even though the "talking cure" was considered as symptomatic, it implied the conclusion that the strange symptoms, which at that time were
termed "hysterical," represent symbolic behavior. They hide
a secret meaning. Such symbolically expressed meanings can
be deciphered. Bodily symptoms are a kind of expression, an
awkward substitute for speech.

Skeptical as the discoverers were in the days of their breakthrough, they initiated, nevertheless, the study of symbolic
behavior and the language-centered psychotherapy. The
medical sciences of those days relied on objective tests, on
biological facts, and not on words. A new type of medical
therapist emerged from the hypnotic "talking cure"—a therapist who wanted to understand language, a listener who
observed his patients' expressive behavior, verbal or otherwise, and tried to unravel his patients' symbolic thought
processes. Every word, however senseless or inappropriate,
that the patient uttered became clinical material and called
for interpretation and understanding. Language and linguistics
entered through Breuer's method into the field of medicine.

When language became the substratum with which the
clinician had to deal, the medical concept of cause became
replaced by the concept of meaning. Cause and meaning are
not the same. The cause is anchored in the objective sphere,
while meaning is personal, an individual variable. If there is
an infection, the medical internist asks for its cause, not for

its meaning. The same view prevailed in psychotherapy. It was against the accepted logic of sound medical philosophy to replace hydrotherapy, electrotherapy, drug therapy with words, but it seemed even more bizarre to postulate that the bodily symptoms of a patient had meaning, were symbolic gestures, and could be understood. By proclaiming that the cure for some mental derangements had to be sought in the dimension of symbolic representation and meaning, Freud arrived at the point of no return. He found himself outside of the boundaries of the accepted natural sciences. He was declared to be "nonscientific." He confessed later in his general lectures that if anyone breaks through the chain of causation at one single point, "he has thrown overboard the whole *Weltanschauung* of science."[7] He did it and never really became aware of it.

A new psychology of symbolism emerged out of his discovery. This new psychology needed new concepts which were not to be found in the vocabulary of physical or medical sciences. The quality of symbolic behavior that stood out most prominently was its personal and subjective meaning which derived from the past experiences of the patient. Consequently, the biography of the individual became the focus of research as never before in the history of psychology or medicine. However, the meaning soon revealed another feature, namely, that it could be shifted from the object of direct reference to another one, to any part of the body; thus the expression becomes metaphorical. The symbol, just as the sound pattern of a word, can refer to many different meanings. Freud said first that the meaning can be "transposed." Later on, he used the term "converted." These symbolic meanings may attach themselves to any organ or to any specific situation; thus they can become fixated. They also can be fused with other meanings and "condensed." Symbolic meanings can grow autonomous and independent from their primary reference; they can turn into "complexes." They can reflect upon one another and multiply into the "meaning of meaning" and transcend into the infinite. The understanding of meaning supposes a common ground, a degree of sympathy between the speaker and listener, thus supposing "transference." All such concepts were never heard of in clinics or laboratories of natural sciences. Freud said hard words in his popular general lectures, words which bespeak some of his disillusions in the biological ideals of his youth. He said that he could not make any use of the "descriptive psychology" nor of the "experimental psychology" which concentrates on the physiology of the sense organs and is so taught in schools. He went even further and declared that psychology has to liberate itself from every foreign preconception deduced from anatomy, physiology or chemistry. It must be founded on concepts of "purely psychological order."[8] He searched for ways and means of understanding symbolic behavior.

As Freud progressed on the road of understanding and interpreting symbolic behavior, as he studied the meaning of symptoms, the lapses of neurotic memory, the slightest malfunctions in speech or writing, or the misplacing of objects, he tried to unravel the meanings in the language of dreams, he was even eager to find out the symbolic processes which became objectified in religion, ritual, custom and folklore—yet he never undertook the task of exploring the most archaic and fertile soil of symbolic creativity which is the field of language. He stated that we would understand the language of the dream better if we knew and had an adequate analysis of language.[9] He contributed himself to the fabulous expansion of psychoanalytical insight into the various fields of art and literature—only language itself remained exempt from intensive analytical interpretation.

Because language remained in the blind spot of analytical interpretation, the misconception grew up that symbolism is the undesirable result of the morbid function of a sick mind; thus, the sound mind can do without it. Such misgivings are still lingering on in the literature otherwise interested in "semantics." It is true that Freud discovered symbolic behavior first in compulsive bodily reactions which he understood as expressive gestures of the unconscious. Then he investigated the symbolism of dream imagery and came to the conclusion that unconscious wishes seeking satisfaction often create nonsensical substitutes for the real objects which they cannot attain. He also demonstrated that compulsive actions and rituals lead to utterly senseless performances which are useless from the pragmatical or practical viewpoints of common sense, yet they imply meaning, they satisfy a need which is rooted in man's symbol-creating capacity. It appealed to the common sense to contradict and to say: symbolism has nothing to do with the sound mind; it is just as dream fantasies and other nonsensical unconscious malfunctions—not worthy of much attention, it does not belong to reality, and to thought processes geared toward this pragmatic reality which is the only subject matter of scientific investigation.

It was some time before it was recognized that the often ridiculed "Freudian symbol" held the key to the truth which since has become a trite axiom.* This is the thesis that man is the "symbolic animal" (*animal symbolicum*), that the creation of symbols is a fundamental activity of the sound human mind. Not only the lowest, but also the highest mental activities of man are symbolic. The primitive mind, the infantile mind, and the schizophrenic mind expose with distinct clarity just this capacity of man which leads to his best and highest creative achievements.

---

* Georg Groddeck, the only analyst who influenced Freud, grasped first and independently man's innate capacity for creating symbols. See *The Book of the It,* introduction by Lawrence Durrell (New York: Random House, Inc., Vintage Books, 1961). The original German *Das Buch vom Es* was published in 1923. See also: Martin Grotjahn, "Georg Groddeck and His Teaching about Man's Innate Need for Symbolization," *Psychoanalytic Review* (1945), 32:9–24. An equally outstanding work of the immense post-Freudian literature on dream symbolism is the book of Calvin S. Hall, *The Meaning of Dreams: Their Symbolism and Their Sexual Implications* (New York: Dell Publishing Co., Inc., 1959). First published in 1953, this work, based on extensive empirical material, illustrates well the spontaneous symbol-creating activity of the normal mind and integrates dream research in the field of general psychology. It also demonstrates convincingly, in contradiction to Freud, that the symbols of dreams do not conceal but reveal, they do not disguise but disclose the essentials of the meaning. This insight is of principal importance for the understanding of verbal symbolism. The age-old dream books since Artemidorus' *Oneirocritics* are dictionaries. These dictionaries are worthless to the psychologist but valuable to the linguist.

PART ONE

THE
LINGUISTIC
APPROACH

INTRODUCTION

The term "symbolic behavior" embodies the basic assumption of this book. Speech is one of the manifestations of symbolic behavior. *Behavior implies meaning.* While motion, reaction and performance can be attributed to any mechanism, one refers to "behavior" only in cases where bodily actions or changes are embedded in an organism and are aimed at the world in which the organism lives. A dead body can be moved, but it does not "behave" anymore. However operationally the description of the "verbal behavior" may proceed, it cannot avoid the final conclusion that speaking and thinking are intimately interwoven with one another. Thought processes suppose context and meaning. One cannot simply think; one has to think *something.* One does not simply "behave," but behavior is directed toward a conscious or unconscious goal. This makes the difference between the noises of a machine and verbal behavior. Thought and meaning are not part of the measurable physical reality, yet they are real and constitute the essence of any verbal behavior. "Words without thought never to heaven go," said Shakespeare correctly. It does not help much to turn this axiom around and say: "Thought without words" does not exist. If this is the case, thinking is silent speaking, a *monologue intérieur,* and as such, just an "objective type of behavior as baseball" (Watson). Another formulation holds that thinking is a case when the speaker and the listener happen to be "within the same skin."[1] Such basic identification of speaking and thinking is the characteristic of early infancy. It was also in the minds of the early Greek philosophers who termed this identity

11

Logos—"Word"—the beginning of all things. The *Word* without meaning is inconceivable. Progress in linguistic thinking was made just by overcoming acoustical-physiological phonetics and introducing the concept of meaning. The elements of languages are not phonetic sound units, but phonemes, the building blocks of morphemes—sound units which make sense and represent the smallest units of meaning, if "meaning" could be atomized at all.

Meaning cannot be cut to pieces; it cannot be counted, measured or quantified even though attempts have been made in this direction.[2] We say "It means so much to me," or "It means nothing," yet one symbol cannot be measured with another symbol. Sign, symbol, and meaning are correlative concepts. What appears as sign or symbol on the objective scale is experienced in subjective reality as meaning. There is no possibility that "meanings may be kept outside the skin"[3] because perception is inherently a subjective experience. The subjective grasp of meaning precedes its verbal formulation; it is a pre-verbal process not necessarily verbalized. There are unconscious and pre-conscious thought processes which operate on pre-verbal levels, as revealed in dreams, somnambular states, subliminal perceptions, hysterical fugues, delusions, and some post-hypnotic behavior. Verbal behavior does not refer simply to speech, but supposes language. It is a texture like all behavior of conscious and unconscious processes. Behavior is "what the organism does or *says*" (Watson), but nothing that we do or *say* is fully conscious or totally unconscious. One sphere infiltrates into the other; one interferes with the other. Verbal formulations emerge out of the paradoxical no-man's-land of the scale called pre-verbal, pre-logical or pre-conscious. I do not doubt the thesis of Gestalt psychologists that we perceive figures by some pre-programmed, inherent organization as segregated wholes separated from their background. However, this does not prove that perception precedes meaning, that we perceive first, then attach meaning to it as a label. On the contrary, the discrimination between figure and ground reveals that meaning is implied. What is felt as more important stands out as figure in distinction to the less important, which serves as background. The aspect of meaning is implied in the discrimination, expectation, organization, and projection which are inseparable from all perception; otherwise, in seeing, one might "see indeed and not perceive," in hearing, one might "hear indeed and not understand," as is said in the Bible.

Meaning, being rooted in the subjective life experience, can be understood on different levels. If two men speak to one another, one may say, with some exaggeration, that they speak two different languages because their subjective world of meanings is not the same. Each meets the other at his best if both speak the same language, but with a different accent. Everyone is wrapped up in his personal *idiom*, which means, originally, in his own private language. Accordingly, *idiotism* means "a popular or peculiar, private way of speaking" on the one hand, but it also means the behavior of a mentally deficient person. The ability to communicate and understand the other's behavior is thus considered a sign of mental health, while to remain shut up in one's own idiom appears as a sign of idiocy. The ability to grasp the meaning implied in the verbal behavior of the other person is a measure of flexibility and intelligence, while the insistence on one's own frame of reference approaches the rigidity of idiocy. Those who grew up with two mother tongues know best that there are feelings, meanings, which can be said in one language and not in the other. Great lyric poetry, for instance, defies translation. It is too deeply rooted in the meaning world of a specific idiom. If one speaks to a child, one is prepared, even within the same mother tongue, to grasp the peculiar idiom of the child. Yet, do we really understand the peculiar verbal behavior of a child? It has been proven rather conclusively, by experimenting with proverbs, that a simple sentence, on the surface a trite, hackneyed banality, can be understood on quite different levels.[4]

It shall be demonstrated that the idiom of the Bible or of Shakespeare can be understood on different levels. This obviously holds true as well for the verbal behavior in any speech situation. It can say more than the speaker intended to say; it can be misunderstood if the meanings are not translated properly from one private idiom into the other.

Accepting these premises, one will understand that the structure of language reflects the mental organization, and that linguistics and psychology are inseparable from one another. Expressed in structural terms: what we speak is the language of the Ego; it receives its dynamic power from the Id, the language of which is symbolic, pictorial and pre-verbal. The language of the Id is contradicted by the language of the Superego, represented by the social code, propriety, education, spelling, grammar. The dynamic interplay of these agencies explains that there are different levels of meanings present in every verbal utterance. Valuable unconscious material will be recovered from unchecked slang expressions and from the fantasies of earliest childhood. Such verbal material is by and large pre-verbal. Mental patients in the state of regression may fall back to such fantasies which have not yet reached the articulation of verbal expression. In harking back to these earliest stages of infancy, something short of impossible is implied because one wants to verbalize feelings and sensations which have never been expressed in verbal form before, as one does sometimes in dreams, and falls back upon pictures, symbols, and imagery which did not reach the level of verbal articulation. In such cases one speaks in terms of an individual verbal mythology, nonsensical and antirational, as are the fantasies of the Id if translated into the daylight of the Ego language. One does not speak this Id language, although one may understand it. Often, one must be satisfied with just a glimpse into the pre-verbal abyss underlying the well-controlled language of the Ego.

Man is thus basically bilingual: one language is the elaboration of his conscious Ego; the other is the forgotten language, a repressed language, the outflow of the Id. The influence of one language upon the other has been called "interference" in linguistic literature. This interference results in a strange accent, or in loan words, borrowed from another idiom, but the interference referred to here does not derive from without; it results from an internal conflict and means the breakthrough of the Id forces within the speaking subject. One does not accept thought processes of dreams at their face value and asks: What is behind them? Yet, we seem to be ready to accept the verbal production at its lexical definition and suppose that there is nothing behind it.

The postural language of the body, the bodily expressions of emotions, and the total pre-verbal behavior, such as symptomatic actions, are generally interpreted in terms of unconscious motivation. This means that the subject is not aware of what he is doing and does not understand his own overt behavior, just as he does not understand his dreams either. One is generally not prepared for this *double entendre* inherent in the structure of verbal behavior—a manifest outside surface and a latent repressed inside meaning.

The question of unconscious interference in thought processes and their verbal expression reaches beyond psychology and linguistics. It is a problem of philosophy. It raises the much more general problem of the objectivity of thinking. No one will be more prone to reject all kinds of unconscious interference than the philosophers of clear consciousness, of pure logic, ontology and epistemology. However, the question was often raised: Does anything of pure logic exist free of any unconscious organization?[5]

When Descartes said: *Cogito ergo sum*—"I think thus I am," one is reminded that he spoke the late Latin-French, and, in that language, the classic *cogitō, -āre*, "to think," has been replaced by *pensāre*, French *penser*, properly meaning "to depend"; also the French *savoir*, from the Latin *sapere*, properly means "to taste." Thus Descartes' famous dictum properly says, "I depend or taste, therefore I am." In a similar way the Latin saying *Sapere aude*—"dare to know," properly says "dare to taste." This is indeed the unconscious verbalization referring to the primary feeding-sucking experience.* The breast of the mother is the first reality, security and knowledge, indeed. Perhaps Descartes was not aware of the unconscious implication of his logical axiom.

Anyhow, it is conspicuous that philosophers who surely would object to any intrusion of unconscious fantasies into their ontological analysis, if they are completely absorbed in their abstract thought processes and want to refer to an object of undoubtful reality, will often choose an example from among hundreds of possibilities, according to their personal preference, either the "apple" or the

---

* "Descartes sets to work in a quite simple and childlike manner." Georg Wilhelm Friedrich Hegel, *Lectures on the History of Philosophy*, Vol. III, translated by E. S. Haldane and F. H. Simson (London: Kegan Paul, Trench, Trübner & Co., 1895), p. 223.

pencil—the symbol of the mother or the father. "A like apple, B like bull," the New England Primer said.[6]

The basic duality of mental operations is inherent in every utterance. Materialistic monism accepts only the surface of verbal behavior. In the following chapters the phenomenological description of symbolic behavior implied in the duality of verbal structure will be attempted.* The mechanistic information theory also deals with the duality of message and noise, thus of figure and ground, of meaningful and meaningless communication.[7] One can grasp the totality of verbal behavior by recognizing the interference in every word and every sentence. Language can be understood as sign *and* as symbol. It can be interpreted as physical *and* mental; as personal speech *and* collective language; as subjective expression *and* objective representation; as conceptual *and* emotional; as conscious production of the Ego *and* unconscious manifestations of Id forces. The inside language interferes with the outside speech. Nothing supports the monistic aspect in linguistics. The unique quality of language consists not in monism but in the awareness of its conflicting qualities. Finally, a difficult question will be faced without having a ready-made answer to offer: this is the problem of archaic heritage. The verbal heritage is archaic. The question of archaic heritage is basic for the understanding of language as well for psychology.[8]

---

* Maurice Merleau-Ponty, "On the Phenomenology of Languages," in *Signs*, translated by Richard C. McCleary (Evanston, Ill.: Northwestern University Press, 1964). Remy C. Kwant, *Phenomenology of Language* (Pittsburgh, Pa.: Duquesne University Press, 1965).

SIGN AND SYMBOL

Any verbal utterance can be understood as a sign; it can be understood as a symbol. It would be a mistake to understand a gesture or a word as a sign, when it was intended to be a symbol. The difference is in the interpretation of meanings. The proper distinction between sign and symbol is of crucial importance for the understanding and evaluation of any text, whether it is colloquial, literal, biblical, clinical, or commercial advertising.[9]

The distinction between sign and symbol is the more in order because language is unique in its function. Its uniqueness consists in its capacity of functioning both ways, on two or even more levels simultaneously. For instance, the word *fire* can be a warning signal calling for the fire department. This is function one (1). In the context of a sentence the word can mean simply "household fire," and function not as a warning sign, but as a plain denotation of a reality concept. It refers not to one or another reality experience, but to the general idea, image, or fantasy of "Fire." In such a case the word *Fire* has a communicative function, understood by everyone. This is function two (2). Beyond this communicative representation of the concept "fire," the word can carry many connotations. It can refer to the myth of "Fire." Everyone carries his own private, everyday mythology; it sometimes has little in common with the experiential reality. Let us call this mythological-symbolic meaning function three (3). Our language heritage shows, in this case, that a definite distinction is made between function two and three. The word *fire*, related to the Greek *pur*, "fire," referred to the household

17

fire on the hearth, on the one hand; and the Latin *ignis*, "fire," related to the Sanskrit *Agni*, "god of fire," referred to the mythical fire on the other hand. If one speaks about a "burning passion," one obviously does not refer simply to the household fire, but to a fantasy about this reality, to the devouring quality of fire, mostly described in oral terms. This third function of "fire" does not define the reality concept, but suggests meanings, sometimes "surplus meanings," connotations, which may have a great reality value in subjective experiences. This mythological subjective fantasy of "fire" is not simply an individual fantasy, but an image shared by many people.

When Shakespeare's Cleopatra says: "I am fire and air; my other elements I give to baser life," one is well aware, while grasping the symbolic meaning of fire, also of the communicative lexical concept of fire; thus one is uniting in one act two different meanings of "fire." Only the human mind can perform this creative synthesis of the communicative denotation and the evocation of a representative image—all this in one act similar to binocular vision. No wonder that functions are overlapping and often confused in the pertinent literature.

However concise a one-sentence definition might be, it hardly will account for the essential features which unite and which distinguish signal behavior and symbolic behavior. For this reason I prefer the descriptive method. Phenomenological description permits one to point out first the common characteristics, then the distinctive qualities which separate the sign function from the symbolic one.

The common feature of both consists of the obvious fact that the sign is a vehicle of meaning and the symbol is also one. Meaning is implied in or projected upon the sign as well as the symbol. Both are not simply physical entities, but mean something beyond their physical existence. They are thus not only concepts of objects, but also concepts of functions. They are not what they appear to be, but transcend their reality reference. They refer to something else beyond their physical existence. Both "say" something, but this is the end of their common function. What they say and how they say it is different.

The examples at hand are the road signs. They give direc-

of history. No individual can make them, change them or destroy them according to a personal whim because it is a part of history. In other words, the historical process is irreversible and unique and never can be repeated like an experiment in a laboratory. The symbol is inseparable from its embeddedness in the real historical time, while the time which a stimulus needs to produce a reaction refers to an abstract concept of time. It does not make any difference whether the salivation of a dog to the red light happened yesterday or years ago. The symbolic meaning, on the contrary, depends on the concrete historical date. It is not certain that the symbolic meaning valid today will be valid in the years to come. Let this be made clear: the symbolic meanings carried by verbal forms are part of a historical-social context. If one wants to understand symbolic behavior, one cannot assume the ahistoric attitude of physical sciences. Physics, chemistry or mathematics have no relationship to history. Linguistics and psychology, on the contrary, cannot divest themselves of the historicity of the symbolic material at their disposal. Ahistoric approaches to verbal behavior are as much amiss as asymbolic psychology would be, which does not recognize the specific socio-historical space-time setting of the individual in question. Symbols do not emerge and flourish in the abstract. In the spheres of physics and chemistry, one deals with the asymbolic cause and effect, stimulus and response, or with physical laws which are valid always and everywhere and can therefore be predicted. The emergence of a symbol is the result of a creative act. It is as unpredictable as the future is in history.

A third characteristic of the symbol consists of the fact that the symbolic meaning permeates, sometimes consciously, mostly unconsciously, the physical vehicle which is its carrier. There exists an unconscious hidden correspondence between the meaning and its vehicle; this vehicle might be a phonemic pattern of a word, a picture or a gesture. In the case of signs, the intended meaning and its physical carrier have nothing in common. They became coupled together by chance either by classic or by operant conditioning. In the case of the symbol, the physical representation participates in the meaning. Let us return to the previously mentioned example of the red traffic light. There exists a phenomenon called color

symbolism, which can be tested in various cultural settings.*
Colors were chosen to carry distinct connotations. The red
color is connected with specific associations in the symbolic
language of flowers. The "red carnation" shall be interpreted
later in terms of flower symbolism (p. 179). The color "red"
means "blood" in some languages. In the same way the color
green is associated, as the English background of the word
reveals, with the noun *grass* and the verb *to grow,* and also
with the Latin verb *crescō, -ere,* "to grow." These instances
indicate that man normally does not perceive abstract colors,
but the color of "something." This "something," whether
"blood" or "grass," interferes with the meanings of red and
green. In other words: the symbolic carrier participates in
the meaning which it carries. The colors of the flag participate
in the complex meaning of "nation," which it consciously
carries. The cross is inseparable from the meaning of Christianity. They have grown together. For this reason a sign can
be ignored. One can even act contrariwise to the expected
behavior. But such transgression within the signal behavior
stands on another plane than the offense against the flag,
against the name of a person, or against a religious symbol
which is felt as sacrilege.

This observation leads to a fourth distinctive quality of the
symbol. This is the function of representation, directed toward
knowledge. The symbol has a cognitive function. A sign
demands a reaction in the sensory-motor sphere of the physical
reality; the symbol addresses man who wants to see, observe,
contemplate, and asks not for the cause but for the meaning
of a phenomenon. The symbol is the tool of thinking. It does
not simply react to the physical reality, but presents its meaning and demands understanding. It creates an intermediary
sphere between the objective physical and the subjective
reality. Language is the most elaborate realization of this
intermediary sphere. While the subhuman creatures live
within the limitations of the here and now of concrete fac-
tuality, the human mind transcends the boundaries of the
sensory immediacy through its capacity of creating symbols.
Man does not live simply in the physical world of action, but
in the world of language and symbols as well. The reality

---

* See p. 291.

of language and symbolic representations is often felt to be more factual, concrete and real than the facts of the sensory world. Man lives, thinks and acts therefore in a world of meanings. The reality of language is felt so strongly because it interposed itself between man and reality. Could one dismiss it or feel antagonistic toward its ambiguities, as some of its critics do, because it relates not simply to reality in a one-to-one pairing, or because it is no simulacrum, not even an imitation of sensory experiences but the representation of meanings? Without the representational function of symbols, man would ever have remained on the subhuman level of intelligence.

A fifth quality results from the distance between symbol and reality. The normal adult mind is aware of the difference between the name and the person so named, or between the word, its intended meaning, and the thing called by the word. Primitive mentality, as it appears in early childhood or in regressed mental states, does not differentiate in the same way. "Word magic" or "word realism" supposes the original fusion between the perception of the thing and its symbolic representation. According to this magic thinking, the name *is* the person. By calling out a word, one can "call into existence" the thing. This strange fusion between word and thing is the result, primarily, of the magic perception of reality. "All things are full of god," Thales said. Primitive perception does not primarily grasp the objective qualities which we perceive in things, but projects subjective meanings, human qualities and relationships into the relationship of objects. For instance, the nicknames with which small children tease one another are often cruelly exact and to the point. They perceive one another with the eyes of a caricaturist, calling their playmates "Fatso," "Skinny," "Gorilla," "Duck," "Sheep," "Fish." There is no name for the unique subjective perception, so they create one out of their resources. This shows the creative aspect in the cognitive function of symbolic representations.

In the course of development the distances between word-meaning, thing-meaning and symbolic meaning grow, and man becomes more and more aware of the tension between the general discursive content and the nondiscoursive ineffable connotations of the intended meaning. The pre-verbal perception, never verbalized before, contains an element of new organization which can be represented only through the figurative extension of conventional meanings. For such reasons symbolism is in its deepest layer figurative. The metaphor expresses the new meaning through old forms. Languages can present the new and the old, the figurative and the literal meaning in one act and let the figure stand out by making the old meaning transparent. For instance, in this sentence: "I have set before thee an open door, and no man can shut it" (Revelations 3:8), every word is known by its literal definition, yet the sentence as a whole can be understood within the biblical context on the level of figurative symbolism. Does the symbolic interpretation and understanding obfuscate the literal understanding by their extension to ever new meanings? It does not seem to. The literal meaning becomes, through this interpretation, "deeper," which means it stands out in high relief and assumes the qualities of a "good form," called *prägnanz* in psychology.

The symbolic behavior implies a further characteristic: it supposes organization, interdependence, structures which reflect or translate the structures and relationships perceived in the physical reality. No symbol can remain isolated without context, as no word stands alone as it appears described in the dictionary. However, this does not prove that words exist only in dictionaries, or grammar exists only in books. The grammatical structures of a language are as much carriers of symbolic meanings as words, but the psychological interpretation of syntactic structures is only in its beginnings.

Efforts have been made to eliminate the symbolic qualities of language from its cognitive function in organizing thought processes, as if a metaphor or a figure of speech were a logical nonsense, an artistic exaggeration or decoration which belongs to poetry and not to discoursive propositional thinking. The novelty of a thought or concept always will resort to the figurative extension, thus for metaphorical transformation of discoursive meanings.

One cannot eliminate symbolic thinking by calling all signs symbols or all symbols signs. Such watering down of opposite concepts does not reduce the creative metaphorical quality of symbolism to the well-established discoursive-literal usage. The negative attitude, rejecting any interpretation of behavior in terms of symbolism, is reflected in the various efforts which try to reduce symbols into sign-elements, for instance, describing symbolic behavior as stimulus generalization or multiple choice reaction. By insisting that the difference of sign and symbol is simply the difference of one-to-one and one-to-many meanings (Joseph R. Royce),[10] one does not account for the fact that the difference is not one of quantity, but one of quality. Similar to this reductionism is the statement that there are simple, primary signs and there are signs of signs, meaning of meanings, and these are the symbols. One sign can be replaced, of course, by another sign; the second sign can also be replaced even by a third one, but the third would carry the same meaning as the first one. In the case of symbols a cumulative reaction will develop because the new symbol will participate in the meaning of the old one. Most words have changed their symbolic meaning in the course of history. If the meaning of one word became objectionable, for some reason, a symbolic cover word, a euphemism was used instead, but the fate of the cover word was almost the same, after a while, as that of the original cruder meaning which it was supposed to replace.

> The Old English used a verb referring to "birth" which became repressed because the concept of *cennan*, "beget," was charged with a tabooed meaning. The original verb became replaced by the verb *to bear* a child, which properly meant "to carry" the child. However, this verb again became infected, sooner or later, with the original meaning, so we use "lying-in," "bring to life."

Meanings change their vehicles, as vehicles change their meanings. The process of symbol formation is an ever-creative activity implied in all thought processes. The symbolic extension and transposition of meanings are not as has sometimes been inferred—a neurotic or pathological process. The primary stage of symbol development is indicated by the so-called primary symbols, pre-symbols, or proto-symbols. Bodily symptoms belong to this group. They unite the discoursive and nondiscoursive meaning. For instance, in the case of blushing the bodily reaction and the meaning implied are both grasped in one act, just as in the case of the flag, whosoever grasps its meaning is also fully aware that it is a piece of cloth, or that the cross, besides its religious significance, is a material thing.

The word as a symbol is a complex phenomenon.[11] It may be used as a signal, it may designate an idea or indicate a concept, but it may also carry connotations which are not explicit but implied in its representational function loaded with conceptual overtones. It may also have an evocative and expressive intensity in a given context. It is far from being simply an "artificial sign." One cannot be sure as to the artificial or arbitrary character of word symbols. It is true that various languages denote one and the same concept by such different words as Greek *pur*, Latin *ignis*, Italian *fuoco*, French *feu*, Spanish *fuego*, Swedish *old*, Germanic *Feuer*, Russian *ogon*, and so forth, all meaning the same as the English *fire*. It is an essential characteristic of the symbol word that it was not made by an individual whim, but emerged out of an historic development. Our languages differ in this point from Esperanto and other artificial signal systems. It is a matter of fact that we have no insight any longer into the prehistoric process which has matched the physical sound pattern and meaning into one perfect unity.[12] It is equally true that man, when he has lost the insight into the true process of gradual development of existing things, is always inclined to suppose that these things were made by an individual artisan or demiurgic craftsman in arbitrary fashion. Small children think in the same way.[13] The more man progresses in knowledge and insight, the less room will be left for explanations supposing arbitrary decisions or chance happenings.

The Greek philosophers once hotly discussed the problem of whether language, like moral laws, is set by arbitrary statutes and thus is a humanly controlled institution (*thesei*) or originates in the ever-unchanging nature (*phusei*). Can one make the sophistic claim of the arbitrary setting of language an axiom of scientific research? I do not think so. In doing so, one would contradict another axiom of scientific thinking, which is: nothing understandable is arbitrary. If one cannot understand any longer the connection between sound pattern and meaning, because this association lies beyond the memories accessible to our minds, then the dissatisfied researcher finds some solace in the thesis that, after all, this connection was brought about by an individual, arbitrary whim.

The deepest layer of symbolism (as has been clearly formulated by Ernest Jones) represents ideas of the "self and the immediate blood relations and of the phenomena of birth, life, and death."[14] In the following chapters a more detailed phenomenological description of language shall be presented. It will be demonstrated that the own body is the primary reality which is the reason for the immediacy and autonomy of body symbolism. It is invariably the own self which is reflected in the verbal expressions concerning the reality of the outside world, birth, life, death, or the closest family relationship. The insight into the symbolic representation of the body and its functions became fundamental for the interpretation of language. It is difficult to understand why man uses such different sections of reality for projecting his noncognitive internal sensations. There is no answer to it, just as there is no real answer or insight in the choice of neurosis.[15]

Many unanswered questions remain even there. Symbol and meaning still describe the central problems of psychology and linguistics. The reader should be aware of the resistance to the concept of symbol and meaning in present psychological and linguistic literature. The protagonist of operant conditioning (B. F. Skinner) asserted that, in his view, the only scientific solution is "to reject the traditional formulation of verbal behavior in terms of meaning."[16] A noted biologist (L. von Bertalanffy), who is well aware of the fact that symbolism makes the difference between human and subhuman behavior, wonders how it is possible that recent textbooks on general psychology do not even mention, do not list in their index, the terms "symbol" or "meaning." Another outstanding authority, an expert in mathematical biology, who is deeply involved in semantic studies (Anatol Rapoport), mentions, almost in an apologetic tone, the name of Carl Jung, who was a pioneer in research in symbolism. "In mentioning the latter I plead not guilty in advance to any accusation of an inclination to mysticism. I am only taking a cue from biology."[17] Another expert on the "Development of the Perceptual World" (Charles M. Solley)[18] speaks of the "professional suicide" which a psychologist would commit nowadays by dealing with such concepts as "consciousness" or "meaning." He says that consciousness and meaning are the two problems that he would prefer to avoid. If he were to discuss them, he would quite likely be charged by fellow psychologists "with being mentalistic, anachronistic or tenderminded."* The same prejudice infested behavioristic linguistics. "For many linguistic students the word 'meaning' itself has almost become an anathema" (C. C. Fries).[19] The most elaborate presentation of behavioristic theories of perception (by Floyd H. Allport) deals almost as if it were an appendix with "the unsolved problem of meaning" from a behavioristic viewpoint. He also comes to the conclusion that meaning has "long been a neglected stepchild in psychology. Or perhaps it is like Cinderella. . . ."[20] Such confessions could be multiplied. They prove that extra-scientific forces interfere with the only objective of science: to seek and speak the truth, and nothing but the truth.

The strongest searchlight on symbolism and meaning is shed by psychopathology on language and behavior.† There exists a strange form of verbal behavior—behavior without

---

* By way of contrast I quote a few words of the Russian psychologist Lev Semenovich Vygotsky, who cannot be accused of being idealistic or "mentalistic." He says: "The view that sound and meaning in words are separate elements leading separate lives has done much harm to the study of both the phonetic and the semantic aspects of language. . . . This separation of sound and meaning is largely responsible for the barrenness of classical phonetics and semantics . . . " He says that "the focal issue of human psychology" is uncovering the problem of thought and language. The unit of verbal thought "can be found in the internal aspect of the word, in *word meaning* . . . it is the word meaning that thought and speech unite into verbal thought. . . . Clearly, then, the method to follow in our exploration of the nature of verbal thought is semantic analysis—the study of the development, the functioning, and the structure of this unit, which contains thought and speech interrelated." *Thought and Language*, edited and translated by Eugenia Hanfmann and Gertrude Vakar (Cambridge, Mass.: The M.I.T. Press, 1962), pp. 4–5.

† The "meaning of meaning" is perhaps best exposed by its opposite, by the ultimate "meaninglessness" of the existentialist philosophy of "Nothingness." This is the main topic of the so-called "absurd" art, literature, and drama. In Ionescoe's *The Chairs* a hired lecturer explains the ultimate wisdom of humanity to empty chairs, to a non-existent audience in an unintelligible language.

meaning. It is generally called psychopathic behavior, or personality disorder. There exists, also, a kind of aphasia called "semantic aphasia." When people speak correctly, but do not say anything, their words have no meaning. They declare "eternal love," propose, even contract marriage, but without any meaning. Love, hatred, loyalty, decency, honor, or duty are, to them, phonetic patterns void of meaning. Their behavior is clearly diagnosed as a "mask of sanity," a case of psychopathology.[21] In contradistinction to semantic aphasia, the behavior which is still considered as normal is symbolic and imbued with meaning. The following chapter will describe language as the most elaborate system of symbolic behavior.

We have lost the symbol-creating capacity which is alive in poets, in dreams, in young children, and in regressed mental cases. The perception of reality gradually disperses the magic which covered the perceived reality like a fog in an age when mythical fantasies were still creative. This profound change in man's relationship to his setting is not understood without accepting the symbolic foundation of our verbal heritage. There are plenty of evidences which prove that the child, the regressed patient, and pre-literate people have an altogether different attitude toward reality. They display an endowment of "physiognomic perception," of the fusion of sense perceptions, of the loss of distance between meaning and vehicle, object and its name, between the speaker and his language, between subject and object, between internal sensation and cognitive perception. Developmental psychology did everything to convince the skeptics that our square pegs of the conceptual language do not fit into the round holes of the early ages. The formative forces operating in our verbal heritage are rooted in this pre-verbal symbolic soil which man deserted while growing up, when he started to translate the representational symbols of the early ages into denotative concepts. What appears now as a lexical term with a clear-cut definition may have once been a symbol loaded with emotions and unconscious fantasies.[22]

See on the "absurd" Albert Camus, *The Myth of Sisyphus,* translated by Justin O'Brien (New York: Random House, Inc., Vintage Books, 1959).

This translation from the figurative symbol language into the discoursive language can be illustrated by clinical instances.

Lauretta Bender and Allison Montague described the psychotherapy of a little girl who grew up in a brothel where her mother was employed. When she was brought to the attention of the children's psychotic ward she drew over and over again pictures of houses, trees, churches. These pictures were in her fantasies sexual symbols, and for this reason taboo objects—"and don't you say nothing against it," she explained. In the course of her successful therapy she gradually regained contact with reality and the frightening shadows of sexual connotations receded. Finally the "house" became nothing but a house, the "tree" became just an ordinary apple tree, and the "church" became the picture of a church and nothing else. When the symbolic perception vanished, the child was ready to leave the hospital.[23]

Another illustrative example of the language behavior of a schizophrenic patient in the therapeutic situation: he came in blushing and giggling and throughout the session would not talk. Prior to the interview with the female therapist he was working in carpentry, making a chair, but the chair was not simply a chair. The word *stool* meant both "chair" and "excrement." The two meanings interfered with one another. Their identification was completely unconscious.[24]

The two aspects of reality, the repressed symbolic and the cognitive conscious aspect, are best contrasted with one another by the mental patients themselves who were for a long time submerged in the dreamlike unreality of the world of symbols, then gradually regained their balance and grasp of reality. They seemed to discover a new world with which they had lost contact.

An outstanding example of this transition from one perceptual world into another is the case of Renée, the schizophrenic girl who has been analyzed and cured through "symbolic realization" by Marguerite Sechehaye.[25] Symbolic realization means just this leading the patient step by step through "transitory symbols" out of her autistic symbol-world into the bright daytime of realities. Renée described the nonreality of her fantasies after she regained health:

"When, for example, I looked at a chair or a jug, I thought not of their use or function—the jug not as something to be used for holding water or milk, a chair not as something to sit on—but as having lost their names, their functions and meanings; they became things and began to take on life, to exist. . . . The stone jar . . . was there facing me, defying me with its presence, with its existence. . . . My eyes met a chair, then a table, they were alive, too, asserting their presence. I attempted to escape their hold by calling out their names. But the words echoed hollowly, deprived of all meaning. . . ."

When Renée progressed in her cure, she discovered a new contact with reality.

"I realized that my perception of things had completely changed. . . . It was the same with things. They were useful things, having sense. Here was an automobile to take me to the hospital, cushions I could rest on. With the astonishment that one views a miracle, I devoured with my eyes everything that happened. This is it, this is it, I kept repeating, this is it—Reality."

The question will be raised: What can linguistics do for the better understanding of the symbolic language of dreams and infantile fantasies? What kind of help can the therapist expect from the work of the linguist in his clinical practice? The answer to these questions strikes at the core of the understanding of verbal communications. I insert some concrete instances.

The case history of a schizophrenic patient (female) has been described. The outstanding feature of her behavior is her relationship to a teapot. She says she hears voices out of the teapot. Her therapist, Roland Kuhn, commenting on this hallucination says that we ". . . must be satisfied to learn that the patient hears voices out of the teapot not as we may hear voices simply from an adjoining room, but that the teapot talks to her just as a human being and only a human being will talk to us."[26]

Languages reveal best how "things" have been perceived symbolically for countless generations. In order to understand the symbolic meaning of the teapot, one must be aware of the fact that the human head had been used as a drinking vessel since cannibalistic ages. For this reason the identification of skull and drinking vessel is implied in almost all Indo-European languages.[27] Limiting the linguistic material to the patient, if she spoke German, the German *Kopf*, "head," is a derivative of the late Latin *cupa*, meaning "head" and "vessel," also continued in the English *cup*. If the patient was French-speaking, the French *tête*, "head," derives from the late Latin *testa*, meaning "tile, brick, an earthen pot, pitcher, jug, urn." The teapot, even in present, everyday mythology, has kept many of the human attributes. Nursery rhymes also make use of this identification. A whole world of archaic fantasies opens up by looking into the origin of the pertinent verbal expressions. In terms of scoring Rorschach responses, the perception of the "thing teapot," the drinking vessel as a human head, seems to be a rare response, indeed, indicative of schizophrenia; yet looking at it in the light of the millennia of language responses, it is a popular response, a very popular one indeed.[28]

The "head-vessel" association is, as it were, a recurrent dream. I quote another clinical example:

A patient, female, twenty-eight, suffering from social anxiety, made various drawings of a juglike shape with holes; then the jug shape itself became facelike. "In fact something very intense, full of complex human feeling is beginning to shine through," her therapist says. And, finally, she gave the drawing a name. She said: "It is my mother."[29]

What is the clinical use of the linguistic understanding of the symptom now? The therapist is supposed to grasp a hidden meaning which did not enter the conscious mind of the patient. One may surmise that the patient speaks this symbol language, although he is not aware of it. For the time being there is no answer to the questions when did the patient acquire this symbol language, how and why are schizophrenics sometimes like creative poets, able to revive dead metaphors out of the cemetery of forgotten associations and rediscover pathways of associations which once were common, but have been abandoned in the course of history. Yet, the emergence of such archaic fantasies can be evaluated in clinical practice as an indication of anxiety. The patient, projecting upon the teapot, tries to externalize that part of her personality which she is afraid of, which is morbid. The therapist may enter into the world of her private mythology by realizing that, as a woman, she is one of the "weaker vessels," her *health* is not *whole* at all (both words derived from the same form), as a pot may be; her health is *frail* (a derivative of the Latin *fragilis*), as a pot may be; it is perhaps broken, *crazy* (which originally meant "full of cracks," cracked up), as a pot may be. The therapist, in grasping the fantasies of his patient, might be able to speak on the level of her symbolic language.

The trend of associations can be pursued even further. The "weaker vessel" refers not only to the head, but also to the female organ. The "talking teapot" has its parallel in the Latin saying *Vulva loquitur,* the "womb spoke." The term *teapot* is known in this meaning in English slang.

In order to expose this implication of "jug" with more clarity, one can refer to other verbal instances. There is an old saying that "The jug goes to the well till it breaks." Piaget, in his well-known experiments, presented this saying to children of the ages of nine to eleven in order to test their understanding. One child, ten, commented: "Because the jug is not so hard, because it is getting old."[30] College students, when confronted with the same question, also gave the same childish answer: "When the jug is growing old, well, sooner or later it will crack up." Behind this interpretation looms the fantasy, once more, that the "weaker vessel," by growing old, becomes *frail, fragile.* If it is not obvious anyhow, the analysis of the key words will make the latent meaning of the saying transparent. First, it happens that *jug* is actually a pet name for *Joan, Joanna*. One can observe in other instances that in a case where a pet name becomes a common noun, more often than not there is a "common" idea implied; a highly delicate meaning has to be covered up. *Jug*, as a pet name, carried a special connotation; it referred to easy virtue. "Whoop Jug! I love thee," Shakespeare said. The original meaning of the "jug" is quite transparent if one supposes that the jug goes, indeed, to the well, which is an absurdity. It is, of course, on the conceptual level nonsense that "pitchers have ears," or that the jug has a *neck, foot, lid, handle,* a *belly* as do *pot-bellied* persons. In Greek *gastra* means the "belly of the jug"; it is related to *gastēr,* "stomach," just as *mētra,* "womb," is related to *mētēr,* "mother." The *well* to which this jug-Joan is going is not just water. It is at least a "boiling water," as indicated by the relationship of the noun *well* and the verb *to well up,* meaning "to boil." Job says, praising the Lord: "He maketh the deep to boil like a pot" (Job 41:31). The well seems to contain such boiling water, fire-water. The whole relationship is indicated in the German language in which *Brunnen* means "well" and the verb *brennen,* "to burn," *Brunst,* "fire, sexual heat," "estrus," and *brunzen,* "urinate." The breaking of the vessels is an integral part of wedding ceremonies in Eastern and Western cultures, so there can be little doubt as to the meaning of the accident which may happen to the jug-Joan at the well. However, if the jug is not simply a jug, but a lady, a lady-Joan, it will be protected and not break at the burning fountain. Therefore, the jug, which is carefully covered up by wickerwork, is called *demijohn,* from *Dame Joan.* It will not break at the dangerous well. The proverb offers, on the manifest surface, a trite banality, but looking into the origin of the key words, it says something like "go slow with petting, sooner or later you will become a broken vessel, deflowered." The "talking teapot" perhaps has much to say about the "boiling water," "cracking up," "crazy," and broken vessel.

THE PSYCHOSOMATIC QUALITY
OF LANGUAGE

The interpretation of verbal expressions reflects the specific scientific climate of the age. Actually, it is the climate of physics, mathematics and chemistry. Medical sciences, psychology and linguistics proceeded under the spell of classic Newtonian mechanics, with the assumption: the more they can approach quantitative physico-chemical formulations, the more "scientific" they will become. This meant, for the medical practitioner, an ever greater effort to "localize" the pathogenic cause in an ever smaller segment of the organism until the cellular pathology proclaimed through the authority of Virchow that all sickness can be reduced to the sickness of the cells. Psychology and linguistics followed the general trend along these same lines.

Even though the cellular pathological concepts did not apply to language in the same way as to the human organism, changes occurred in both, desirable or undesirable, and had to be explained in scientific terms. Linguists also tried to "localize" the causes of changes, possibly in the smallest attainable physical units of sound forms, and considered the "infection," through contact of one sound form with another, as the most satisfactory explanation. "Contamination" is a medical concept as well as a linguistic concept. It is also general knowledge that even the most orthodox pathologist will, in actual practice, advise his hypertension patient to "take it easy, relax," and resort to some similar reassuring suggestions out of an undefined, nonscientific philosophy, implying that in the final analysis psychological motives have triggered the physiological changes in the organism. Experienced practitioners often feel that they better not tell the patient that the reason for his complaint is "emotional." The patient might feel offended by such a diagnosis and feel exposed as a hypochondriac, when he expected a helpful medication. He cannot accept the fact that the symptom about which he complained is not the result of "something wrong" in his system, but, instead, is the consequence of a conflicting emotional relationship with his environment, with his profession, or with his mate, mother-in-law, or even with his own ideal self. The physical reason is felt as honorific, but mental reason as disgrace, because it shows that the person is not in proper control of his own health. In a similar way verbal expressions change, or rather, were changed by the language community because something went wrong in the total organism. The old forms needed to be repaired, exchanged, or replaced by new ones. The common-sense interpretation of such changes asks for some physical reasons. It wants to localize some tangible evidence within the physical condition of the word, within the sound pattern. It will protest vigorously against any reference to the emotional attitudes or conflicts within the language community. The man on the street is as realistically minded as the scientist. The only failure of their sound philosophy is that they accept only the physical existence as real and forget about the reality of inside experiences, which sometimes can become a very painful reality indeed. They do not perceive that body and mind, *soma* and *psyche,* exist together as an inseparable unity. This dual unity is the most elementary fact of human existence.

One does not know how and when this dual unity of body-mind began. There is no proper explanation, either, for the fact that the chimpanzee lacks "the gift of tongues," which is inherent in the human nervous system. The capacity for symbolism, language, and speech must be founded on a layer of the organism in which body and mind are still one. Neural operations, such as those working on the circulatory, glandular, alimentary, or respiratory system in sleep, as well as during the waking state, belong to an undifferentiated unity. Body processes in such states are registered in dreams sometimes, but not by the conscious awareness. It is generally assumed that the less differentiated the functions of the body are from their subjective perception, the more unconscious they remain.

This observation leads to the proper understanding of language. It is psychosomatic in character. It implies a simultaneous physical and mental activity. The activity of the vocal apparatus and the sound produced belong to the physical reality, while the work of the mental apparatus which makes the uttered sound meaningful and understood by others belongs to the psychical reality. Language, therefore, is a psychophysical phenomenon; one part cannot be separated from the other without destroying the whole. Phonemics and semantics cannot be separated from one another. One will understand that, despite all efforts to the contrary, the science of language cannot be exclusively the science of phonemics. It is also the science of meanings. Linguistics cannot avoid being "mentalistic," or otherwise it would miss the essential point of its very purpose.

The new perspective for medical therapy as well as for linguistics was opened up through the experiments with verbal hypnosis by Breuer and the young Freud. They discovered that words can heal. General practitioners were too prejudiced by their cellular doctrines to accept the fact that bodily conditions can be relieved, changed, eliminated, and also aggravated by words. The pioneers did not at first understand this healing effect of language. They called it "magic." When verbal hypnosis could produce bodily symptoms, bring about changes in the cardiovascular functions, influence the work of the vegetative system, control eye reflexes, and make one shiver and tremble in response to softly spoken words, then there must be some unknown capacity inherent in the use of language, and such psychological motives may have been influential on the functions of the speech organs during the long history of the development of language. Verbal hypnosis can influence one's speech habits, make one lisp or stutter, compel one to avoid the usual word, and repetitiously use a strange expression.

Emotions are inseparable from the simultaneous bodily changes. The slightest alterations of the emotional balance are registered instantly as a change in the biophysical and biochemical state of the body. This means, in other terms, that the body as a whole is expressive of the emotional state of the organism.[31] The speech organs are no exception. The vocal utterances are gestures of the vocal apparatus. The voice in which a word or a sentence is said, its tonal quality and intensity belong to the whole context of the bodily manifestations of emotions. Vocal language, however, differs from the other forms of emotional reactions because it is conscious in its intention, while skin reactions, metabolic symptoms, or disturbances in the vegetative system are not under the control of the conscious Ego. Psychoanalysis started with the assumption that there exist "pent-up" or "strangulated" emotions which did not find the verbal channels for expression. If the verbal outlet, or the acting out, became blocked, for some reason, to an unconscious wish or need, the conflicting feeling may explode in bodily symptoms, functional disorders, or into other forms of an "organ language." The choice of a specific organ as an outlet for emotional tension is still an unexplained phenomenon. It raises the problem of "organ inferiority," the Achilles heel or the weakest point of any given organism.[32] Psychoanalysis started from the basic assumption of "catharsis," which means that bodily symptoms which are the outgrowth of unrelieved emotional tension can be resolved by expressing them in terms of the conscious verbal language. Verbal expression has a healing effect.

The psychosomatic approach cut across the borderlines of medicine, psychology and linguistics. First, it turned the attention away from the localizing aspect of biophysical-chemical pathology and encompassed the total behavior of the human organism. From this viewpoint psychoanalysis asserted the idea of behaviorism; it considered the human organism as an indivisible totality. It demonstrated that man is more than the summary or assembly of various cells and organs, even more than the bearer of speech organs. A stomach ulcer could be treated locally by medical means; the new approach, on the contrary, suggested the question: What does the ulcer mean within the organic reactions of the vegetative system, what specific emotional conflicts are expressed by it? Body symptoms thus imply meaning and often say what words could not express. Whereas the conscious ego speaks through the rational verbal language, the observable behavior of the body speaks an expressive language of its own. It may even say "no" when the verbal language asserts "yes." We understand this language of facial expression, posture, gesture, or involuntary bodily changes first and best. The small child understands the facial expression of his mother long before he understands the verbal language.[33] This seems to be paradoxical because the child does not see his own emotional reactions, but only can feel the muscular tonus by which they are produced. The coordinated, voluntary behavior, as manifested by speech or action, has to be understood in its embeddedness in the involuntary, expressive innervations such as blushing, smiling, eye blinking. The voluntary verbal utterance is perceived on the background of the tonal quality, the high or low key, the tempo, speed, and loudness of the voice produced by the speech organs, which is characteristic of the muscular tension of the total organism. The rhythm and the melody are the most subtle conveyance of discrete meanings. One can say, "Please do as you like," with the most friendly or the most unfriendly accent. The so-called Alzheimer's disease, especially Parkinson's disease, are surely organic diseases of the nervous system. As the face loses its expressibility, the voice, too, becomes a monotonous clatter, without rhythm, melody, or other tonal qualities of normal intonation. The observation of such pathological cases makes one really aware of the rhythmic-tonal quality of speech. However, this rhythmic-melodious flow of speech is not produced by the speech organs. The muscular tension of the whole body participates in it. If one wants to refer to "speech organs," it could be stated without exaggeration that the body, as a whole, is an expressive organ of speech.

The question might be raised whether bodily symptoms are signs or symbols. A symptom might function as a warning signal; it may "indicate" an inside event, just as smoke indicates fire, or lightning indicates thunder. The mental state and the bodily expression are perceived as two sides of one and the same act, thus we find the fixed one-to-one relationship which is characteristic of signs. On the other hand, this fixed connection of inside and outside events in the organism is just the opposite of any arbitrary sign system. The bodily changes in emotions appear to be a much more universal system of expression and communication than any verbal language. It can be understood across and beyond the barriers of various languages. Cultural differences do not affect it as the spoken languages. One may even state that the gesture language of the body, the somatic expression, is the only universal language.

However, this universal somatic language is more than a sign language; it is, in its deepest essence, symbolic. Symptom formation does not necessarily reveal a fixed one-to-one relationship. It is well known that "hysterical" symptoms may speak a most peculiar, individual jargon. It is a characteristic symptom of the abnormal mind that it does not correlate emotion and expression in the same way as the normal mind. Schizophrenics may laugh when there is nothing funny to laugh about; they may weep and cry when there is no reason for grief; they may grow angry and express it when one cannot see any commensurate cause or object of such anger.

Bodily symptoms, as expressive movements of the total organism, thus represent the most elementary layer of symbolism which is still close to "natural" signs. They are called "proto-symbols" (H. Werner), or "primary symbols" (E. Fromm) because they serve as the foundation of all the higher forms of symbolic expression.[34] All vocal language, in a general sense, is somatic expression. The psychosomatic identity of body and mind is still rooted in the biological needs and their subjective perception, out of which all higher, and more abstract, forms of symbolization developed. This psychosomatic cooperation concerns medicine as well as psychology and linguistics. The body symbolism of the vocal language cannot be deciphered any more, in most cases, because its origins lie hidden in the prehistoric past. It appears, in our mental apparatus, as unconscious, and for this reason it is open to analytical interpretation. The second part of the present study will concentrate just on this most elementary form of symbolism—the psychosomatic symbolism of the body—because it is the thesis maintained that man perceives, thinks, and speaks in terms of his own body and bodily functions.

THE PERSONAL AND THE INTERPERSONAL
QUALITY OF LANGUAGE

Distinction is made in English, as in many other languages, between "speech" and "language." By "speech" we mean the individual and actual use of language. By "language" we mean a system of symbols which exists prior to any individual "speech." The individual cannot make it; he cannot change it; he can only learn to make use of it because language belongs to the whole community. "Speech" refers to the "verbal behavior" of the individual, while "language" is essentially a trans-individual phenomenon.[35] The individual uses the common system of symbols if he wants to make himself understood. This is a rather trite truism; however, it calls attention to the fact that "language" exists only in the "mind" of a community. It is "mental" by its nature, a dormant complicated system of symbols which can be actualized and turned from an inside potentiality into an outside reality. This materialization of language is called speech. For this reason speech can be subjected to material analysis; it can be recorded, measured, quantified; but this is not possible with language. Language is more than what is factually transformed into physical reality by one or another speaker. Speaking is a continuous interpersonal process of selecting and rejecting in order to find out, among an almost unlimited choice of expressions, just the right one which the speaker feels will best fit the actual situation. There are good reasons why in Greek, Latin, and the Germanic languages the idea of "select" or "pick up" is used to denote the concept of "to speak" and "to write." The speaker is, in fact, confronted with an abundance of verbal forms stored in his mother

41

tongue. By selecting and rejecting he must decide which expression he feels is the best; but every decision is a personal act, made by the individual alone. The way a man speaks is, therefore, the most revealing manifestation of his personality.

However, even this engagement of the whole personality does not restrict speaking to one person, to the speaker, alone. Man always speaks to someone. If he speaks to himself, he speaks to an imaginary someone who is identical with himself. When he speaks, his words are aimed; he wants to be understood; he wants to question, inform, convince another person. The speaking person therefore transcends his own self. This fact is of psychological significance. The consciousness of the self transcends its own being. The I is aware of the non-I— it is filled with the world. Transcendence is its essence. An empty consciousness is as much an absurdity as speaking would be without a partner. The interpersonal moment is present even in the most individual manifestation of language. It supposes the other person and a situation in which both speaker and hearer agree on a common system of symbolism. This agreement in the meaning of language is presupposed, although there is more meant, and otherwise meant than understood. The individual A is understood by B, if B is able to translate into his own world what has been said by A. If B does not succeed, then he does not understand A, even if they speak the same language. This results in the "shut-up-ness" of the individual (Kierkegaard). A remains shut up in his A-world, B in his B-world, just as a dog is shut up in his dog-world and a peacock in his peacock-world. The criterion of the abnormal personality is this withdrawal from the common ground of communication and understanding. The psychotic person is shut up in his own lonely world. It is called abnormal because people find it strange and perplexing. They cannot understand it even though the psychotic speaks the same language as the others do.

How can one cross the bridge between the personal symbol language of the one and the common language of the others? One point is obvious: one has to learn to understand the other's language, and not the other way around, insisting that the other should learn to speak my language. The problem is to find a "transitory symbol" which may serve as a bridge and permit some preliminary communication between the two language entities.

Refer once more to Marguerite Sechehaye, who introduced the symbolic realization in psychotherapy. She described the case of her patient Renée, a schizophrenic girl, nineteen, who suffered feeding frustrations in her early childhood. "On my observation that she need only eat the beautiful apples I gave her, she stopped me abruptly and pointing to my bosom, said, 'Renée doesn't want the apples of grown-ups, she want real apples, mama's apples.' For me this was a shaft of light. I perceived the deep symbolism of the apples and the course I must adopt to relieve the patient. I at once gave her a piece of apple (no more apples in quantity) saying, 'It's time to drink the good milk from mama's apples; mama is going to give it herself to her little Renée.' And Renée, her head resting on my shoulder, ate her piece of apple with all the concentration and contentment of a nursing baby."[36]

In order to recognize the personal and interpersonal qualities of language, one has to consider the symbolism by which language discloses its own being, and also distinguishes itself from "speech" and separates "speaking" from "saying." How the meaning of "language," "speaking" and "saying" was grasped by different people and different generations is best illustrated by the pertinent verbal expressions.

The concept of "language" does not exist for the small child or for the infantile mind. Only "speech" is real or factual to them. They do not realize that speech supposes language. If one does not know the language, one cannot speak. Mythical thinking still perceives "speech" and "language" in a hazy, undifferentiated unity. "Thinking" also is included. For instance, in the biblical story of Babel the confusion of minds is depicted as the confusion of speech. We do not consider mental disturbances as speech disturbances any more. By the same token, harmony and peace among men are described in the Bible as "the whole earth was of one language, and of one speech" (Genesis 11:1). Thus, it is said: "let us go down, and there confound their language, that they may not understand one another's speech." Man has since learned that peace and understanding are not simply the matter of a universal language. If people become "mixed up" and do not understand one another, the confused speech is not the primary reason, but rather the consequence of the trouble.

The unitary concept of "language," "speaking," and "thinking" is brought into focus by the Greek comprehensive term *logos*. The meaning of this concept is rooted in the unconscious identification of "word" and "seed." The seed represents potentialities, future, growth, and becoming. The seed is also the carrier of the life-substance, *psychē*, which flies away with the last exhalation, thus, "speaking," "ejaculation," and being alive by breathing are interrelated concepts. The noun *logos* derives from the Greek verb *legō*, "to pick out, to gather," as seeds were gathered by the early food gatherers. It also means "to say, to speak." It describes, in material symbolism, the spoken word as the seed picked up, but at the same time it points out in the seed-word the creative potentialities of language. The Greek *spermo-logos* means one who is picking up seeds, then it denotes "gossiping," perhaps implying that someone picked up only a few words or scraps of information. In the New Testament the term is rendered as "babbler" (Acts 17:18), thus describing speech on the infantile level. In the Latin translation the "babbler" is called *verbum seminator*, "sower of words"; in the Old English translation *word-seawere*, "word-sower," scatterbrain. The *logos* "seed-word" represented in Stoic philosophy the generative principle, the "Seminal Logos," *Logos Spermatikos*. It still referred to the primary unitary concept, not to the "word" as an element of speech as defined in grammar. They used different terms for the grammatical word: *epos, rhēma, onoma*. The *logos* is the creative word. It participates in the transpersonal spirit. It is the vehicle of the becoming of all created things. It is congruent with truth and reality, thus, with true "being" itself. To the Greek mind reason reflects truth and reality, thus *logos* meant reasoning, reckoning, counting, accounting. This was a complex unitary idea of the word; it also included the act of "saying," but in the course of history it disintegrated into the various aspects of "language," "speaking," "saying," "thinking," "counting."

The general Western concept of "language" is symbolized by the voice or by the organs of speech such as "tongue," "lips" and "mouth." The identification of "language" with the tongue reaches beyond the Indo-European unity. For instance in Japanese *kotoba* means "tongue, speech, language"; in Hungarian *nyelv* means both "tongue" and "language." The Hebrew knows this concept as *lāshōn* or *leshōnah,* "tongue, speech, language," but generally uses the "lips," *sāphāh,* to represent "language." To the Western mind the tongue is the symbol of language.* It obviously implies that language is identical with speech. So the Greek *glōssa,* the Latin *lingua,* the obsolete English *tongue,* as in *mother-tongue,* the obsolete German *Zunge* denote "language" by the "tongue."

One can observe, in verbal expressions, the gradual differentiation of "speech" and "language." The German language still preserved the undifferentiated unity of *sprechen,* "to speak," and *Sprache,* "language." In the English Bible it is said, when Moses refers to his speech inhibition: "I am slow of speech and of a slow tongue" (Exodus 4:10). The Old English version says simply: *habbam laetran tungan,* "I have a late tongue." In this case the tongue refers to a difficulty in articulation, not to a disturbance in language.

I chose some examples from Shakespeare's vocabulary. It often coincides with and perhaps is often influenced by classical Greek and by biblical usage. The "tongue" is opposed, in Shakespeare's fantasies, by the "heart." He says, for instance: "Her tongue cannot obey her heart nor can her heart inform her tongue"; or "What my tongue darest not, that my heart shall say." In these, as in many similar instances, the "tongue" means "speech," the external materialization of a more subtle internal pre-

* See pp. 248–250.

verbal process. The speaking of the "tongue" appears as a rather poor representation of the much richer idea of *logos* represented by the "heart." The "tongue," as every living symbol, developed its own secondary symbols. The "tongue" speaks, and the Ego is a passive observer, sometimes too weak to control it. This is the symptom of depersonalization and disintegration of the Ego. In such cases the person feels: "Not *I* speak, but something else; *it* speaks through me." Shakespeare's Falstaff says: "I have a whole school of tongues in this belly of mine and not a tongue of them all speaks any other word but my name." By the same token, some children say that they think "with the tongue." They identify speaking and thinking. The tongue thus holds a double function: it is external and internal, the mediator between the inside and outside personality. It is felt as external if it is contrasted by "heart," then it is felt to be an inappropriate, clumsy tool, often a disobedient servant of internal sensations. Yet, the tongue participates also in the internal personality. It is the incorporation of the very essence of man. "Speech," not "language," was in Shakespeare's mind when he attributed to the tongue qualities as "good," "sweet," "princely," "gentle," "learned," "soft-slow," "subduing," "chattering," "unreverend," "slander-ous," "wagging," "riotous," "rattling," "rude," "poisonous," "base," "bitter," "forked," "lying," "killing," and many more individual qualities. This individualized tongue can be the "serpent's tongue," "the woman's tongue," "the sugar tongue," "the slander's tongue," a "golden tongue," a "false-speaking tongue." There is "power in the tongue of man." No wonder that the tongue seems to have been a taboo in accordance with the magic numinous quality of language. This might explain that, for instance, the Greek language avoided altogether the old, inherited name, which was preserved in the English *tongue* or the Latin *lingua*, and used a euphemism instead, *glōssa*, which originally meant "something pointed," "the tip" of the tongue. The next related word is *glōchis, -inos,* "any projecting point, as the point of an arrow." This seems to be an old symbol. "Their tongue is as an arrow shot out" (Jeremiah 9:8).

In the Old Testament Hebrew not the tongue, but the "lips" serve generally as the symbol of "language." Wycliff still, in 1382, translated: "For thothe the erthe was of on *lip* and of the same wordis," but later changed the text to "was of on language . . . " (Genesis 11:1). While the "tongue" absorbed in English the emotions and feelings otherwise symbolized by the "heart" as the true being, the "lips" became in contrast the appearance, the outside front of the speaking person in such terms as *lip-service, lip-comfort, lip-labor,* "empty talk." "You have a double tongue within your mask," Shakespeare says. The internal "tongue" is contrasted with the external lips. In Latin *ōs, ōris,* "mouth," *ōrāre,* "to speak, pray," emphasize the oral quality of "speech." In German *Mund-art,* properly "mouth-manner," denotes the "dialect," in distinction to *Sprache,* "language." Not the speech organs, but the voice produced is symbolic for language in Greek *phōnē,* "voice" and "language" related to *phēmi,* "to say." In Old English *reord* means "voice" and "language"; the same with the Gothic *razda,* "voice" and "language."

One could arrange a sequence of English words according to the shift from the speaker to the hearer and the increasing eagerness to be understood by others. Such a scale would start with the autistic *babble* and proceed to *blab, blabber, gabble, tattle, twaddle, prattle, prate, chatter, chat, talk, speak, say, tell,* with all the specifications of the goal-directed speech as to *explain, exhort, advise, summon, question, answer, pray,* and many more. The intransitive "speaking" is distinguished from the transitive "saying" in most languages, as in Latin *loqui* or *fāri,* "to speak," vs. *dīcere,* "to say"; in Italian *parlare,* "to speak," vs. *dire,* "to say"; in French *parler,* "to speak," vs. *dire,* "to say"; in German *sprechen,* "to speak," vs. *sagen,* "to say." The same fundamental distinction runs through many other languages. It shows that speaking was perceived in its double function. From the viewpoint of the speaking individual, it was expression, "ejaculation," a bodily sensation, but it was, at the same time on the objective plane a statement, question, answer, message, advice, gossip, threat, call, praise,

48

sermon, prayer, curse, or any other form of interpersonal communication.

The Greek *laleō* means "babble." It is a sound imitation, like many other terms, for the autistic, infantile speech. This meaning shifted in the New Testament Greek to "speak"; it also absorbed the meaning "to preach." Similar development can be found in Slavic languages, perhaps under the influence of the Greek. In English the same process of growing up from "babbling" to "speaking," or regressing by "speaking" as "babbling" can be observed in *chatter, chat*. The English *prattle, prate* refer to the infantile speech. The same word in Dutch, *praten,* means "to speak." The verb *to talk* is progressively taking over the meaning of "speech." The question will be raised: What is the reason for this general invasion of the infantile language into the speech of adults? The answer to this question is given by the fact that language discloses its own being. It discloses not a coding-decoding control mechanism, but a state of mind which is infantile and primitive.

The emphasis on the infantile mind is responsible, I suppose, for the development of the Latin *fabula,* "a narrative, a story," into the general notion of *fabulor, -āri,* "to speak." This verb is continued in the Spanish *hablar,* "to speak." This change from the "fable" to "speech" shows, again, how language perceived its own essence as emerging out of the world of fantasies. Even more instructive is, in this respect, the equation of "parable" and "speech." The Greek *para-ballō* properly means "to throw-beside." It is the twin word of *sym-ballō,* "to throw-together." The "parable" is a consciously elaborated "symbol." The noun *parabolē* properly denotes this placing of two things beside one another, "a comparison, illustration, byword, proverb." Out of the Latin *parabola,* the general notion of "word" developed in the late Latin with the same meaning. The emotional power of this *parabola* was so strong that it outcrowded and made obsolete the old term *verbum,* "word." The late Latin is continued in the Spanish *palabra,* Italian *parola,* French *parole.* The verb *parabolāre,* "to speak," became *parlare* in Italian, *parlar* in Spanish, *parler* in French. This word succeeded in replacing completely the classic term *loqui*, "to speak"; it even overtook the similar *fabulāri*, "to speak." Because language is, in the last analysis, figurative, implying the *double entendre* of two meanings, it properly reflects its own essence as *parabolic* in the mirror of symbolism. The parable "throws side by side" two meanings in such a way that they should shed light upon one another and on a third meaning implied, but not overtly expressed. Lao-tse formulated his philosophy in parabolic sayings. The Bible is a book of parables, riddles, proverbs, allegories, metaphors, and various forms of symbolic expression. Some people can grasp only one or the other meaning overtly expressed, but do not reach the third meaning implied. The "parable" is equated with "speech" in the Old Testament Hebrew. The Hebrew *māshāl* means "to liken, to speak in similes." This was the general style of speaking. Another term for this figurative speech is *chīydāh*, translated as "maxim, puzzle, dark saying, riddle, proverb, speech." This word derives from a verb *chūwd*, "to tie a knot, to propound a riddle." As strings are tied together by a knot, so are the two implied meanings tied together. The Lord also reveals His will in human language in a symbolic way. He says to Miriam and Aaron: "If there be a prophet among you, I the Lord will make myself known unto him in vision, *and* will speak unto him in a dream." But, to Moses He will speak "mouth to mouth, even apparently, and not in dark speeches" (Numbers 12:6-8). Language was perceived to be, in its essence, figurative, inviting, thinking, solving the riddles, finding out the hidden meaning implied. This attitude toward language was different from ours because we have since lost the original appeal of parabolic and symbolic expression. The prophets speak in parables. "They say of me, Doth He not speak parables?" (Ezekiel 20:49). To *speak parables* is a stereotype formula of the biblical language. Christ taught in parables. The people who were not initiated in His teaching grasped only the outward shell of His sayings, but His disciples were supposed to understand the secret meaning implied. "Unto you," said Christ to His disciples, "it is given to know the mystery . . . but unto them that are without, all these things are done in parables" (Mark 4:11). The original concept of language was still close to "vision" and "dreams." Speaking in "dark speeches" or to "speak in dreams" were not two very different communications. Both required penetrating interpretation, problem-solving, and understanding. They expose the original symbolic nature of language.

The nonrational element of language reveals itself in some other words which once were loaded with magic and mystery, but their esoteric meanings evaporated in subsequent rational ages. Language once held a sacral meaning. In Old English *spell*, "story, saying," referred to the magic power enclosed in figurative speech.* The verb *spellian* originally implied the same attitude toward "language" as the Old Testament Hebrew: "to find out, to guess, decipher, to comprehend or understand by study." The verbal expressions were shrouded by the same symbolic cover as dreams and visions, and their mystery had to be "di-spelled" in order to be fully understood. The noun *spell* means "a set of words, a formula or verse supposed to possess magical powers, charm, an occult or mysterious influence, a fascinating or enthralling charm." Shakespeare said: "She workes by charmes, by spelles, by th' figure." This primary numinous quality of *spell* and *spelling* is behind the term *gospel*, from the former *god spell*, "good spell," the translation of the Greek *evangelion*, properly "good message." The *spell* with the meaning of "a fit," as "under the spell of somebody" or "cast a spell on somebody," still supposes an alien, irresistible power intruding into the self. This word underwent the same general process of losing the numinous, mythological qualities as languages in general. It became, in realistic understanding, a term for writing and reading. The original magical content became repressed. Some authorities even contend that the verb *to spell*, with the meaning of "to write," is a completely different word from the word referring to the magic *spell*. However, children, when first confronted with writing and reading, still may feel the magical qualities of the written

* See pp. 123–124.

word and the technique of writing and reading. Every word may still appear to them as a riddle, the meaning of which has to be deciphered. The written form still preserved, to them, the primary fascination of the symbol, and it has been observed in clinical practice that inhibitions in writing and reading develop in consequence of the magic of "spelling."

A third verb, *to spell*, "to substitute for, to work in place of another," is also supposed to have developed independently, according to the best authorities, yet it is obvious that after repression of the magic of the symbol, of the tying of the two strings into a knot, the real concept emerged of one working for the other, as one word is the substitute for another in symbolic usage.

The process of "di-spelling," the magic of symbolism and reducing mysteries to realities, can be observed in other terms within the field of language. As illustrations the words *question* and *answer* may serve the purpose. The English verb *to ask*, Old English *acsian, axian*, unites two different meanings: "to ask for, to make a request," and "to ask about, to inquire." Some languages make a clear distinction between these two verbal acts; for instance, the German *bitten*, "request," and *fragen*, "to inquire, question." It is significant that other languages did not develop this differentiation. Like the English *to ask*, the Greek *erōtaō*, the Latin *rogāre*, the Italian *domandare*, the French *demander* cover both meanings. This fact shows that originally both concepts were the same. The *question* and the *request* were originally felt to be identical. In both the compelling power of magic was present. Compulsion and enforcement are prior to free decision. As in *spell* or *charm*, the speaker tries to impose upon the other a compulsive force in order to receive what he wants, either a verbal response or a gift. It seems to be the result of a long development until the speaker learned to respect the freedom of decision in the other, whether it be a divinity or a man. One can make a scale of these meanings from compulsion to freedom, thus, *compel, enforce, require, command, demand, beseech, entreat, bid, ask, pray, beg*, and so on. Even the *prayer* had, formerly, an ingredient of magic, thus enforcing the request and imposing one's own will upon the divinity. It was a turning point when it was said: "Father . . . not my will, but thine, be done" (Luke 22:42). The compulsive force was still present in the "invitation." The polite request of someone's presence contained a force of compulsion. In Latin *invītus* means "against one's will, unwilling, reluctant." The "invitation" is still worded in the Bible as "*compel* them to come in, that my house may be filled" (Luke 14:23). The meaning of *to ask for* developed under religious influence, hence, the substitute expressions *I pray you, I beg you,* and the phonetic relationship between German *bitten,* "to ask for," and *beten,* "to pray."

The verb *to answer* originally did not mean simply a "reply" to a question. In the Bible the old formula is sometimes translated "and he answered and said" when no previous question was raised. In English *to swear* strongly indicates the reference to a superior power in the verbal expression. To *answer,* Old English *andswarian,* once invoked the magic power of language as it remained preserved best in its legal use. The Latin *spondeō, -ēre* means "to promise solemnly, to bind or pledge one's self; to promise for another, to become security for a person"; and the verb *respondeō, -ēre,* "to promise a thing in return for something else." From this, the Italian *rispondere,* the French *répondre,* and the Spanish *responder* developed. In the *response* "responsibility" was once implied.

The verbal analysis of language developed, by necessity, in pairs of contrasting concepts. Mystery supposes the opposite concept of clarity of thinking; the nearness and intimacy of speech suppose publicity and distance between the speaker and hearer. The irrational invokes the rational; the supranatural solemnity stands out from the background of the natural, everyday speech; the irresponsible babbling is opposed to the responsible enunciation.

The mystic word is whispered and supposes intimacy. It is addressed to the divine or to the initiated who understands its esoteric meaning. The Old English term for "whispering" is *runian,* German *raunen,* "to whisper in the ear." The letters were called *rune,* "magic character, mystery." The secrecy assumed later on an evil connotation. The prophet says, as a curse: "thy speech shall be low out of the dust, and thy voice shall be, as of one that hath a familiar spirit, out of the ground, and thy speech shall whisper out of the dust" (Isaiah 29:4). The Psalmist defines this meaning of whisper by saying: "all that hate me whisper together against me" (Psalms 41:7). The Latin term is even more descriptive: *adversum me susurrabant omnes inimici mei.*

The opposite of "secrecy" and "whisper" is the public, loud voice of the market. In Greek *agora* means "assembly," hence, *agoreuō,* "to speak in the assembly"; it is, in the usage of Homer, the general term for speaking. The same concept, perhaps under Greek influence, appears also in Germanic languages. In Old English *maethel* means "meeting, council"; the same in Old German *mahal,* Gothic *mathl,* "market," and accordingly, the Old English *maethlan, maelan* means "to speak," in Old German *mahalan,* "to speak, to promise, to summon before court," then "to give in marriage." In German the "husband" is still called *der Gemahl,* the "wife" *die Gemahlin,* to "marry" *vermählen.* In Danish *maal, tunge-maal* means "language."

Speaking in public supposes the loud voice and the identification of speech with this voice which can be heard on the market or in the assembly. In English to *call* refers to this loud voice. In Greek the corresponding term is *kaleō,* "summon, call by name"; in Latin *calō, -āre* means to "call out, proclaim, summon"; it was a technical term of the sacral language. The word is related with the synonymous *clamō, -āre,* "to shout, cry." This aspect perceives the essence of language in the loud, publicly spoken word which implies, however, by the old magic, a promise, a legal obligation, thus, responsibility for its consequences. Accordingly, the Latin *vocō, -āre* means "to call," *vōx;* "voice," and *vocabulum,* "word." The Latin *verbum* and the related English *word* also suppose this loud publicity, as do the Greek *rhēma,* "word," and *rhētōr,* "public speaker."

When the speaker was too far removed to be heard, his message was conveyed by a messenger. The messenger "announced," which means repeated verbatim the text which was entrusted to his memory. His function was as important in the illiterate ages as is the written message in our age. The Greek symbolic language spoke about the "winged words," *epea pteroenta*. Perhaps not the words were winged, but the messenger was winged like Hermes, the messenger of the Olympians. The wings represent the speed of the birds and the speed in the transmission of the message. The Greek *angelos,* "messenger," renders the biblical Hebrew *malach,* "messenger angel." Hermes was the *angelos* of gods.

The "dark speech" of magic and mystery is opposed by the clarity of thinking and its clarification through verbal expression. Locke's formula, *homo rationale quia orationale*—"man is rational because he speaks," is founded upon the insight of the Greek and Latin languages. *To point out* a specific meaning is in English still synonymous with "speaking." In Latin *dicō, -ere,* "to speak," originally meant "to point out," as in *in-dicate; dicō, -āre* means "to announce, *dedicate."* This concept of language obviously belongs to the public juridical and religious solemnity. It is the opposite of the informal colloquial speaking expressed by *loqui,* "say." The legal aspect is emphasized by the Latin *iu-dex,* "judge," from *ius,* "law," and *dicere,* "speak." In Greek the goddess of justice is called *Dikē;* her name belongs to the verb *deiknumi,* "to show," the parallel word of the Latin *dicere.* The religious content of the verb developed in *de-dicāre,* "to proclaim the consecration of something."

The meaning "to point out" by words developed further into "counting." The mental operation of counting supposes that the individual items are singled out, one by one, and united in a category or group. The English verb *to tell* means both "to count" and "to say." The Old English *talian, tellan* also means "to think." The same relationship exists between the German *die Zahl,* "number," *zählen,* "to count," and *er-zählen,* "to relate." The Dutch *taal* means "language."

To sum up the above observations, language discloses its essence through its own symbols in its double aspect. It participates in the subjective personal and the objective transpersonal spheres of existence.

THE SUBJECTIVE AND THE OBJECTIVE
QUALITY OF LANGUAGE

Grammatical categories differentiate the substantive and the adjective. The substantive *rose* denotes the summary and interrelationship of all those qualities which belong to the invariably lasting and necessary existence of the "rose," while the adjective *red* is just "attributed"; it refers to a transient and contingent quality of the rose. These two grammatical categories express two different attitudes toward reality. One could be denoted as "substantial," the other as "attributive." In the substances, one tries to grasp reality by its objective, lasting, and necessary qualities; the adjective opens up the individual and subjective aspect. One is led by these grammatical categories to suppose that the things "have" the attributed quality. While the rose *is* a rose, it *has* the quality of being red. Expressing this in technical terms, there are primary and secondary qualities. The only problem is that what has been grasped by naïve realism to be the primary quality of the "rose"—form, shape, fragrance—is perceived in the same subjective way as the so-called secondary characteristics.*

This differentiation between the two kinds of qualities is the product of highly developed thinking. Our languages originally were not so sensitive to the substantial qualities, in distinction to the contingent or transient qualities. This distinction is not so definite in everyday life, either; therefore, one can observe the fluctuation of grammatical forms between

---

* On primary and secondary qualities, see Wolfgang Köhler, *Gestalt Psychology* (New York: Mentor Books, 1959), p. 9.

substantives and adjectives. If there exists a marked difference in man's attitude toward reality, it can be said that the
more primitive language is, the more it is inclined to perceive
reality not as the scientist would perceive it in looking for the
necessary and objective qualities of phenomena, but rather
would perceive the world in its transient relationship to man.
This implies necessarily the subjective and individual attitude;
it is loaded with emotions. This makes the whole picture of
the world, as disclosed in verbal expressions, personal, variable, and transient. It expresses not what things "are," but
what they "mean" to man. Things are denoted in language
not primarily by their physical qualities, but by their psychological meaning.

Not only words, but things have meaning. Things are
understood without words; they "speak for themselves." Things
disclose their meaning. If a thing-meaning is ambiguous,
verbal explanation may specify it. The door has an objective
thing-meaning, but an inscription can specify it as "exit" or
"entrance." If the owner of the house supposes that the door-
bell does not "speak for itself," he may apply an inscription
"Bell." If he is, for some reason, overcautious, he may apply
still another sign pointing to the "Bell," saying "Ring Here."
Sense perception need not necessarily reach the level of
verbal designation. It can remain nameless, because it is not
supposed to be conveyed; it is not destined for communication. The specific noises of an approaching airplane can readily
be perceived even though the plane cannot be seen, but these
noises are not made for the purpose of communication. What
do things finally mean? What do they "say"? One can recognize, in the realm of thing-meaning, the same duplicity just
described in terms of grammatical categories as substantive
and adjective.

The nominalism of medieval philosophy clearly distinguished between the objective existence of things and the
subjective attitude toward their existence. An object, for
instance, a machine, can be described in its "ontological
existence" as an object for itself, but there will always be a
great deal implied which belongs to the perceiving subject.
Different people have various attitudes toward the same
object; they perceive the same objective existence in their
own subjective ways. The size, the shape, the material it is

made of, its purpose, its owner, or price, or its manufacturer, or the way it works, its achievement, and many other qualities may stand out as decisive figures for the subjective perception, as well as its aesthetic appreciation. It can be agreeable or disagreeable, a source of happiness or of frustration; it may be understood as a symbol of prosperity or of catastrophe. One's vocabulary is too meager to list all the subjective occasional meanings which do not belong to the necessary essence of the thing. These subjective meanings fluctuate and emerge and fade away in the minds of the speaking individuals. People, however, are interested primarily in the objective aspect of things, which is common and implicit in all its various subjective interpretations. So, the same person can be addressed in different ways by different persons, although the same person is always meant. This distinction between the objective "ontological" aspect and the subjective attitude toward it seems to be clear as far as the thing-meanings are concerned. This distinction, however, is not so definite when it is applied to the symbolic word-meaning. The subjective moment definitely interferes with the perception of the object, just as the same person is called by various confidential, official, endearing, derogatory, "pet," or "nick" names. In the the same way various languages refer to the same object by the subjective evaluation of the ontological meaning and reveal thereby the subjective attitudes which were accepted by the community.

I chose, as an illustrative example, the word "match." This tool of lighting is a relatively new invention, so it is interesting to observe the names given to it by various language communities. Some languages have perceived it primarily by the material of which it is made. The Slavic languages simply call it "little stick"; Serbo-Croatian *sibica*, Russian *spezchka*. The sulfur is perceived as a distinctive feature in the Bohemian *sirka;* the phosphorus in the Spanish *fosforo*. The German language is more specific and indicates the use of this stick, thus adding motion, an active verbal concept, *"Streich-holz"* (from *streichen*, "to rub, strike," and *Holz*, "wood"). Other languages concentrate on the purpose of the tool. This thing is used to make fire or light and, thus, they connect it with "fire" or "light." The Greek *pureion* is a derivative from *pur,* "fire." The Italian *fiammifero,* properly "flame-bringer," is a parallel to the Greek *phōs-phoros,* "light-bringer," which has its Latin equivalent in *luci-fer.* In Dutch this is the usual name of the match. All these terms are existing words which have been applied in naming "match"; thus, they have carried over into the new concept certain previously existing ideas. This holds true for the Dutch *lucifer,* for the Spanish *fosforo,* for the New Greek *spirto* (which is a derivative of the Latin *spiritus*), and for the English *match.*

The word *match* is found with two different meanings in our vocabularies. There seems to be present a chance homophony, that is, two completely different words happen to have the same phonemic form. One *match* is the object for lighting; the other *match* refers to persons who are well suited to be married to one another; it denotes the matrimonial union. As a verb, it means "to join in marriage." This meaning may also be applied to things, meaning "to fit together."

According to dictionaries, these two words with the same sound form come from two different sources. The *match* for lighting is of French origin; it is a loan word from the Old French *mesche*; the corresponding modern French word is *mèche,* meaning "wick." However, the question will be asked as to why it was necessary to borrow from French a word for "wick" when the English already had an old genuine term for it: the Old English *weoce,* from which our word *wick* is derived. The French word came into use by English-speaking people not for its explicit lexical meaning, but because of an implication which appealed, for some reason, to unconscious fantasies. In order to find out the source of the dynamic force in the French *mèche,* the Old French *mesche,* "wick," one must look into the background of this word also. This French *mèche* is said to be a derivative of the Latin-Greek word *myxa,* which means "the discharge from the nose, mucus, a mucous discharge" and also "a lamp-nozzle." A "nozzle" properly means "a little nose." The French *mèche* obviously had some association with the "nose." However, the French word cannot be a direct derivative of the Latin-Greek *myxa* (because a former *x* does not develop into a French *ch*), but it is more than probable that it has been contaminated in the late Latin by another closely associated word, *mucca* or *muccus,* denoting "snivel," or the mucous secretion of the nose, a bodily condition characteristic of a catarrh of the respiratory system. It seems strange, perhaps, that the "wick," burning at one end, should be associated with the idea of "mucus" or catarrh of the nose. Why should a lamp have a "little nose"? Upon looking into equivalent meanings in other languages, one can discover the same association between the burning "wick" and "mucus." Thus, there can be no doubt that this association exists. It was obviously the wax dripping from the candle when its wick was burning that evoked the fantasy of a dripping nose. Bodily fantasy holds the priority. Phenomena of the objective world are perceived in the picture of bodily experiences. The candlelight seen and interpreted as a dripping nose also shows how language goes beyond the mere reality perception. It implies a fantasy, a nonsensical, absurd, almost schizophrenic illusion into an object which is, in itself, nothing but a burning candle. The part of the lamp in which the "wick" burns was perceived in the image of the oral-nasal cavity and named accordingly, in English, as "nozzle"; the burning particles dripping from the *nozzle* are called *muccus* in late Latin. Thus, one finds this association in many Romance languages, for instance, the Italian *moccolo* means "snivel," "wick," and "tip of the nose." In German, *schneuzen* denotes "to clear the nose," and *die Kerzen schneuzen,* "to clear the candles." This association has been projected upon the sky, too. In obsolete German *die Sterne schneuzen* properly says "the stars clear the nose," but this refers to the "shooting stars." The "meteor" is called *Stern-schnuppe* or *Stern-Schnupfen* in German, properly "star-catarrh." English also knows this association. While the verb *to snuff* means to draw in through the nose, the noun *snuff* means the charred end of the candlewick, and *snuffers* are a kind of shears for cropping and holding the snuff of a candle.

Even if one accepts as a matter of fact that the dripping

of the burning candlelight evoked the dripping nose, it hardly can be supposed that this imaginary picture was a pleasant one. It became forgotten and repressed. I think that the French term *mèche,* formerly *mesche,* was accepted as a loan word in English as *match* because of this repressed implication. There was no need to borrow the French word for a notion which had the proper Germanic name *wick.* The French word was propelled into our vocabulary by the force of repressed fantasies.

There are, however, much older fantasies, dating back to prehistoric ages, which have assimilated the French loan word in the English language. These fantasies are implied in the English *match* meaning "marriage." The *match* for lighting still carries a slight reference to the primary act of making fire. In the Indo-European prehistory the so-called fire drill was generally used for kindling fire: this consisted of a pointed stick of hard wood which was worked by pulling a string tied to it to drill a hole into another softer piece of wood. This drilling of fire, though not practiced in daily life, remained preserved as a ritual in kindling the sacral fire in Greek, Latin and Hindu antiquity.* There were other procedures, too, such as rubbing with a stick (just as the German *Streichholz* calls the match a "rubbing wood").[37]

The striking and rubbing of two pieces of wood, a hard and a soft one, until fire ensued, have been associated with sexual fantasies since prehistoric ages. This word means the "matrimonial union"; the verb *to match* means to marry; *love match* is even more expressive. This phrase derives from the Old English *ge-maca, ga-maecca* or *maecca,* "mate," "spouse," which is a nominal form of *macian,* "to make." One may ask, what do the mates "make" that they were so called? It is the imaginary making of fire which has been grasped as the distinctive feature. To "make fire" was the symbolic expression for "to make love."

Many examples prove that the sexual desire was perceived in the image of fire. Everything said about the mind is figurative, symbolic. The *spiritus* (alcohol) is

---

* See p. 312.

inflammable. In New Greek the "match" is called *spirto* by these associations. It is called *spirto* because in the New Greek language "fire" is the essence of "spirit."

The projection of sex upon the notion of fire connected the imaginary figure of the "bringer of fire" with the ideas of guilt and sin. Where lust is, there is guilt and anxiety. The Christian eschatology calls Satan by the name of *Lucifer*. This is a compound form from *lux, lucis,* "light," and *ferre,* "to bring"; it thus means "bringer of light." Why was Satan called by this name? According to the Hebrew tradition, Satan was originally an archangel, cast out of heaven because he revolted against the Father. "And he said unto them, I beheld Satan as lightning fall from heaven" (Luke 10:18). He was called "light-bringer." This supports the idea that his rebellious deed was just this act of bringing light prohibited by the heavenly Father. *Lucifer* is also the name of the light-bringing morning star which is otherwise called *Venus,* after the goddess of love. This association of Lucifer and Venus again suggests that some connection was made between making fire and making love. In obsolete English, as in present-day Dutch, *lucifer* is the name of the lighting "match." The word carries the forgotten implications of the other *match,* referring to love and marriage. The name of the morning star is *phōs-phoros* in Greek, properly "light-bringer." This Greek term is continued in the Spanish *fosforo,* "match." The Italian *fiammifero,* "flame-bringer," refers to "match" by a similar association. However, one must take notice of the change in the symbolic meanings: to make fire, to bring the flame, and to bring light may be one act on the reality level, but the meanings are different. While the drilling of fire was perceived in terms of sexual fantasies, the bringing of light became symbolic for the rise of consciousness, for the perception of reality, thinking and enlightenment, and the expansion of the intellect.

The myth grew out of the same fantasies that shaped the verbal expressions. There is, however, a marked difference between the verbal and the mythological expression. The pictures preserved in language preserved the immediate outlet of the underlying fantasies, whereas the myth often shows a secondary state. In this secondary state the original meaning has been forgotten and the verbal forms are no longer understood; thus, man tried to explain them in a rational way. Consequently, the mythological account may contain elements which are generally called "secondary rationalization," a common-sense elaboration of the original fantasies, the meaning of which was not immediately understood. There can be little doubt that sexual fantasies have found their secondary rationalization in the picture-language of myth. Thus, the word *match*, in the modern sense of the lighting tool, may, in its phonemic form, continue the French *mesche, mèche,* "wick," but in its meaning it has absorbed the fantasies which are implicit in *match, love match*, marriage. The *Rigveda* (III. 29:1-3) describes the two pieces of wood serving the fire drill in terms of the male and female organs, uniting all the three meanings of *match* in one: "piece of wood, marriage, and fit to one another."

Upon being confronted with a diversity of names for one and the same object, one may ask the question, what is the reason for this diversity of names? The answer to this question depends upon one's understanding of language. An answer frequently given says that the cultural situation is different. This answer does not explain anything, but merely repeats by circumlocution a fact which is known anyhow—the fact that the object meaning is the same, but that the word symbols are different. The "word" does not refer to the object as such, but refers to the *idea* of this object which exists in the mind of the speaker and hearer.

Looking into the background of verbal expressions, one may derive a fact basic for the understanding of language. The ontological meaning of things may be the same, but the subjective perception of the same thing might be very different. The word does not refer to the object which is in reach of sense perception, but refers primarily to memory images, ideas, sometimes called "notion-pictures." This is a fantasy which does not exist in space and reality, but in the mind of the speaker and his partner.

Thus, the words denoting the "match" do not refer to the

concrete object itself, but point to the idea of this object, to the notional image which exists in the mind. For this reason words do not say much about things. They do not reflect an objectively recorded reality, but represent only images of this reality, images which are sometimes fantastically unreal. Words refer to the meanings of things, not to the things as such (as is tacitly supposed in some dictionaries). The objective content of meaning, as recorded in dictionaries, is supposed to be understood by the speaker and the hearer of the same speech community, and thus needs no further elaboration by definition. The subjective component, on the other hand, is, in fact, ineffable, and eludes any objective definition. It is seldom expressed overtly; it may be implied tacitly. The question is unanswerable as to which came first—the word or the thing or perhaps an idea underlying both? One will find, in many of the following instances, a clear indication that "in the beginning was the word." In other instances the word can only be a secondary interpretation of an existing thing. And, in the third case, the fantasy image was first. Word and thing try to materialize, by various means, some preexistent image which belongs to fantasy. To set an equation mark between "word" and "thing" may result in complete misunderstanding.

For these reasons language is not like a mirror reflecting the reality, but is projecting inside images upon the outside world. This assumption does not diminish the historical value of linguistic research, but rather increases it. It does not seek to reconstruct through linguistic means the prehistory of a material culture, but seeks to find an access through language to the prehistory of thinking. This holds true especially for the discipline of "linguistic archaeology," formerly called linguistic paleontology. It was successful in bridging the gap between the science of things and the science of words. It tried to integrate into a consistent unity the findings of comparative linguistics, as well as the immense amount of material brought to light by archaeology, ethnography, and anthropology. In doing so, it attempted to attain to the plasticity of a reality-lexicon (German *Reallexikon*) in order that in the final analysis words and things would explain one another. The prehistory of language was called upon to testify on behalf of the prehistory of culture. If there ever existed anything like an Indo-European language (which seems evident, according to the findings of comparative linguistics), there must have existed also an Indo-European culture, and consequently, a people identified by this culture. "Linguistic archaeology" deals with a previously existing reality, the debris of which remained preserved in the vestiges of language, just as there have been fossil imprints preserved in relics of stones. Such investigation is of psychological interest, the more so, the more fantasies than object realities enter the picture. The words denoting "match" disclose relatively little as far as the physical properties of the "match" are concerned. They do not reveal much as to what the "match" was, but they characterize the people who used the match. The same is true for the prehistory of words and things. They reflect one upon the other. Language reveals not the prehistory of material things, but the prehistory of the human mind.

THE CONCEPTUAL AND THE EMOTIONAL
QUALITY OF LANGUAGE

Language has often been described as a barrier separating man and animal. Language makes the categorical difference that exists between the barking of a dog, an outcry of pain, on the one hand, and a propositional statement, for instance, "The weather is beautiful," on the other hand. This is, however, a rather crude distinction of the emotional and the conceptual quality of language. Language inherently carried this double character. It is emotional and conceptual at the same time. Both qualities are inseparable from one another. They represent two aspects of the same phenomenon: the conceptual aspect suggests, as it were, a horizontal look upon language; the emotional aspect, a vertical one. This is, of course, figurative speech, but everything said about the mind is figurative.[38]

The distinction between conceptual and emotional language is a rather late development of the individual as well as of thinking in general. For the primitive concepts of the *mind*, as implied in the verb *to mind*, cognition is inseparable from emotion and action. No "pure reason" existed for the Greek or Roman philosophy either. Thinking meant feeling and doing. The thoughts were "winged words." Plato therefore compared the mind to a "cage full of birds" (Theaetetus 197c). Troublesome thoughts appeared as little winged creatures in the chest, much like our "butterflies in the stomach."

The conceptual language shows the tendency to single out a denotation with clear-cut borderlines, and to indicate positively what is meant and what is not meant. This is the main objective of scientific language. Its ideal is the binary system of either true or false. It uses words as *terms*. The English word *term* is derived from the Latin *terminus*, "boundary, limit." It points to definite borderlines, exact boundaries separating the designated figure from the ground. It supposes a well-segregated "good" form. In this sense the definition of the "moon" is a question of astronomy, of the "blood," a question of hematology, that of "breast" belongs to anatomy, and the study of meanings has nothing to do with linguistics. The strict borderlines of the meanings are of primary importance in the scientific as well as the legal use of language. The words of law must have their proper delineations, otherwise the law would become ambiguous. The *Corpus Juris Secundum*, published in many volumes,[39] collects the decisions of legal instances dealing with the verbatim interpretation of the law. It is the chief American semantic vocabulary on the conceptual-denotative meaning of words. The Supreme Court has to decide, in many cases, what is included in a given situation in the meaning of the words of law and what is not included. It is interesting to observe in the legal use of language that the Supreme Court, too, comes to realize that the denotative meaning of words is never as unequivocal, clear, and plain as signs or signals are for animal and man. The very meaning depends on the person who is speaking, on the context of the sentence as a whole, and on the whole speech situation referred to.

What does the law mean when it says "clear and present danger"? The Chief Justice said the following in a carefully worded interpretation of these terms:

> "Nothing is more certain in modern society than the principle that there are no absolutes, that a name, a phrase, a standard has meaning only when associated with the considerations which gave birth to the nomenclature. See Douds 339 U.S. at 397. To those who would paralyze our government in face of impending threat by encasing it in a semantic straitjacket, we must reply that all concepts are relative." (June 5, 1951, opinion on the overthrowing of government.) Although one will not subscribe to the belief that all concepts are relative, one can understand the Chief Justice's predicament, which is that a word is never a mere designation, as a signal is supposed

to be, nor a mere denotation which can be equated with a logically correct definition. "Water" means something other than H_2O. The conceptual content is just the same whether we say *circle* or "the closed plane curve such that all of its points are equidistant from a point within, the center." The meaning of the one word *circle* is not exhausted by this "horizontal" definition of eighteen words. It carries implications which cannot be grasped by geometrical circumlocution. The difference is not in the surface extension of the meaning, but in its intensity, in the depth of implications. As to the conceptual content, there is no great difference whether one says "it is urgent" or "woods are burning"; whether one says "clear and present danger" or, as the Romans said, *Hannibal ante portas* (Hannibal before the gates). Words have an evocative power, stirring up emotions which are not included in the logical definition of the meaning. The "prägnance" of meanings does not depend simply on the clear-cut definition, but on the emotional implications. Meaning, in this sense, is not two-, but three-dimensional.

The language of the sciences, as well as that of law, tries to reach perfection in denotative meanings, and naturally the scientists will often feel that language is too fluid to convey their concepts as distinctly as they desire. Attempts have been made through all ages to pin down words to one definite nominative meaning, or to discard words altogether and use other symbols instead, as mathematics does. This is, perhaps, one of the reasons for quantifying everything in scientific discourse, for translating qualitative differences into figures and numbers, since the mathematical expression alone is felt to be exact without ambiguities. The language ideals of mathematics or of chemistry represent the "horizontal" aspect of meanings, the explicit meanings of denotations.*

The other extreme has been fathomed by poets. For their purposes the expressive, evocative, emotive, and symbolic

---

* Einstein said: "The words and the language, as they are written or spoken, do not seem to play any role in my mechanism of thought." Albert Einstein, *Ideas and Opinions* (New York: Crown Publishers, Inc., 1954), p. 25.

power of language was often felt to be inadequate. Hence, one can see the reason for all the complaints against the "husk" which encases, in the conventional expression, the intended meaning which is singular and personal. For such reasons attempts were made to discard language altogether and to replace it with music or art.

These two opposite tendencies are inherent in all verbal expressions—one pressing toward precise and strict denotation of concepts, the other rather indefinite in the extension of the meaning, but strong as to the intensity of expression. One cannot overlook the psychological implications of these opposite tendencies. They correspond to opposite types of personality. One personality is characterized by cautious, meticulous, strictly formal, perfectionistic behavior, and feels secure only within the boundaries of the clear-cut restrictions of a well-protected world which is settled in orderly fashion once and for all. The other speaks in rather loose terms; his expressions are intensive, overflowing, emotionally unbalanced, stimulated by wishful or fearful thinking, exuberant in hopes and depression, led by emotions rather than by facts, transcending his own existence beyond the borderlines of the restricted personality. The first type displays a hint of paranoia, while the latter has a streak of schizophrenia. The predominant use of either the conceptual or the emotional content of language is of characterological relevancy.

In the realm of art, just as in any verbal expression, one can discern two kinds of styles—one tending toward sharp forms, clear-cut figures standing out distinctly from the background, and the other tending toward the dissolution of all forms, the breaking down of the edge contours into the shades and colors of the background. The former style is generally termed "classic" and the latter "romantic." The language of poetry, seeking the high degree of intensity, is also characterized by these two kinds of expression: it can tend toward either the logical classic or the colorful and dynamic romantic style of expression.

The science of language shows some characteristic features inherited from the Stoic philosophy. This Latin school of philosophy developed the basic grammatical ideas. It was also, for ethical reasons, antagonistic toward emotions and even more so toward their expression. They thought that man

should be ashamed of his emotions and not display them.
This attitude contradicted the behavior described in the
Greek tragedies, where the free outlet of emotional lamenta-
tion, weeping, whining, cursing is not a shame. The rejection
of emotions by the Stoic philosophy influenced the science of
linguistics. It has resulted in the negative tendency to dismiss
not only the irrational and emotional content of language as
logic does, but also to dismiss psychology, since emotions seem
to be exempt from the rules of logic and are the seat of unpredictable elements in language which cannot be categorized
by logistic computations. There is an emotional antagonism
to the emotions which is especially apparent in the so-called
semantic literature. Even if it admits, as a matter of course,
that emotional motives cannot reasonably be excluded from
verbal expression, it considers the emotions as an undesirable
or negligible by-product, as a concomitant variable of the
propositional content that alone matters. Language exists in
this understanding as far as it is conscious in the members of
the language community; thus, all that does not appear in
consciousness has no reality and does not exist in the realm
of language.

As an illustration of the conceptual and emotional
aspects of language, the word "night" may serve as an
example. What is the denotative meaning of "night"? A
recent dictionary definition says: "The period of darkness from dusk to dawn," or "the time of darkness without
any light of the sun." Because the exact meaning of the
word is, in some legal cases, of decisive importance, the
Corpus Juris Secundum (CJS) collects the various definitions as applied by legal instances. Thus, the "night" is
defined as meaning "the time from sunset to sunrise";
"the period from the termination of daylight in the evening until earliest dawn of next morning"; "that space of
time during which the sun is below the horizon of the
earth, except that space which precedes its rising and
follows its setting"; "the time between one hour after
sunset on one day and one hour before sunrise on the
next day"; "thirty minutes after sunset until thirty minutes
before sunrise"; "where there is insufficient daylight to
discern a man's features," and so on. Needless to say, there

is much arbitrary decision in placing sharp borderlines where there are none in the reality of language. All these definitions move on the same plane I called "horizontal."

As an example of the opposite tendency, I quote some instances showing how Shakespeare used the word "night." Here are implications which are not covered by legal definitions. He says "the great cause of the night is the lack of sun" . . . "O night which ever are if day is not" . . . "The cripple tardy-gaited night who, like a foul and ugly witch, doth limp so tediously away" . . . "The deep of night is creeping upon our talk" . . . "The eye of heaven is out and misty night covers the shame that follows sweet delight" . . . "Creeping murmur and the poring dark fills the wide vessel of the universe" . . . "The foul womb of night" . . . "Dark-eyed night," and so on. The borderlines of this meaning of "night" cannot be defined in strict terms. Shakespeare gives a complete phenomenological description of "night" in the tirades "in such a night . . ." of Lorenzo and Jessica in *The Merchant of Venice*. The word "night" is charged, in these examples, with emotional intensity.

It will be one of our tasks to find out what are the reasons for this emotional power in words. The source of this intensive, evocative power is not manifest on the conceptual level described in dictionaries. The lexical meaning does not explain the emotional concentration that lies within this word. One must seek this source in another layer of language which is not obvious anymore in the conceptual meaning "per definition."

There are measurable differences in the galvanic skin responses indicative of the emotional impact of language. The emotional response is different, depending on (a) the word, (b) whether the word is uttered or heard, (c) by whom it is uttered or heard, (d) whether the same concept is denoted in Latin, French or in the English vernacular, (e) whether said or heard privately or publicly, (f) if all elements are kept constant, no emotional response can be repeated a second time. It is a unique event. However variable the emotional reactions are, they prove that no word, not even a mathematical or geometrical term, is without emotional power.

In order to show how the emotional intensity of a word can be explored, as model may serve the prize-winning essay on the psychoanalytical interpretation of the word *smug* by Jacob Arlow.[40] If similar intensive analysis would be given to various parts of our vocabulary and if our dictionaries would be illustrated by clinical material like this word *smug,* one surely would understand English better.

The adjective *smug* covers three different meanings: (a) trim, spruce, smart in dress, (b) clean, neat, correct, tidy, (c) self-satisfied, complacent. The outstanding study of the word by Jacob Arlow starts, and rightly so, from the meaning *c* and he works his way back to the meaning *b*; yet for some reason he does not start on the final stretch of research, this is the road back from meaning *b* to the meaning *a* which contains the root meaning of the word. This instance shows once more that free-associations, as described by Arlow, are in themselves not conclusive. They disclose the full meaning only if they are understood in the context of the common verbal heritage. They disclose not simply the thought processes of the individual patient but may reveal associations inherent in the common language. I want to complete Arlow's case studies with the missing linguistic material in order to come to a better understanding of the word *smug.* There is another point which remained without answer: the adjective *smug* often appears linked up or closely associated with the adjective or noun *snob.* A *snob* is *smug* and the *smug* are *snobbish.* What is the relationship of these two words? Do they mean the same? If not, what is the difference implied?

"Smug," in the meaning *c,* is generally described in terms of being complacent, satisfied with one's own existence and consequently displaying a conceited air. The term *com-placent* used mostly in this connection describes well the quiet pleasure of satisfaction. To be "smug" means to be *grati-fied,* this from *gratis* "pleasing, agreeable" and *facere,* "to make," thus indicating that the gratification is pleasing and agreeable. The "smug" is self-*satisfied,* this from *satis* "enough" and *facere* "to make," thus indicating the "com-plete" *ful-fillment,* the filling full of all desires. These terms reflect the happy unity of mother and child. While their separation is perceived as the painful sensation of emptiness and loneliness with the craving for something missing, the reunification of mother and child is expressive of the perfect, self-centered being.* Such being is complete in itself and does not care for the outside world. But "smug" also suggests the conscious awareness of such self-satisfaction and the arrogance that goes with it. The "smug" does not want anything because he already has everything. His complacency is like that of the well-fed babe drifting into sleep.

The emotional content of *smug* derives from early sibling rivalry. The meaning *c*, "self-satisfied, complacent," is the new baby on the breast of the mother while the other feels hungry and dissatisfied. One may understand that the well-fed babe is not only complacent, looks so delighted as if it had swallowed the whole world—indeed, the nipple of the mother meant to it the whole world. It is so absorbed in this relationship that the whole world did not exist for it does not need anyone, it does not care for the whole world. One will understand the negative emotional reaction implied in this word: it is the envy and the jealousy of the disinherited against the happier competitor for the breast of the mother which defines the emotional tone of the word. One may understand that the *smug* one may also appear to the other as "clean, neat, correct, tidy." These are the qualities the mother expects and which are for this reason the attributes of the favorite child.

Some points have to be cleared up in this connection. One is the association with *snob*. This word means primarily one who is cringing, admiring, imitating with superiors but deals contemptuously with inferiors. The *smug* is a *snob* because he not only takes advantage of the favors of the mother but does everything in the way of flattering in order to keep or even to increase these favors.

The word *snob* is said to be of uncertain origin; however, the above free-association brought up the essential

* See *The Subconscious Language*, pp. 19–20, 36–37, 122–123.

content of the meaning: "he looked down his nose at me." This word hardly can be separated from the verb *to snub* which is said to be of Scandinavian origin, meaning "to treat with contempt or neglect." Other related forms are *to snuff*, "to draw in through the nose," and *to sniff*, "to inhale air audibly through the nose," and *to snuff*, "express contempt." The German language also calls the "snobbish" attitude *hoch-nasig*, meaning properly "high-nosed," thus it perceives the arrogance of the snob by his body posture of being *snub-nosed*, lifting the nose high as if it were dripping, "looking down the nose."

More difficult to grasp is the primary meaning *a* of *smug*, "trim, spruce, smart in dress." The reference to dress seems to be a secondary application of the original meaning implied. One has to go back to the Old English form of the word. In Old English *smugan, smeogan* means to "creep into," thus the *smuggler* originally denoted the "creeper." This evokes once again the memories of the earliest infancy. The new babe may first appear in the sight of its siblings as an intruder. The Old English *smugan* which denoted the slipping through a narrow hole, derives from an old Indo-European basic form which originally denoted something "slippery." The Latin *mucus* belongs to it. The intruder is a "slippery, mucuous, slimy" one. The dripping nose will remind later on of the original slimy quality which was the first impression perceived with the new babe. The "smug" intruder is "close" to the mother, it crept into the lap of the mother and does not even feel guilty for taking away this privileged position from the other children.

The corresponding German word is *Schmuck*. It denotes "ornament, jewels," as an adjective *schmuck* means "neat, smart, trim, spruce." The verbal form *schmücken* "to adorn, trim" originally meant "to press oneself into or through something narrow." It is the intensive form of the verb *sich schmiegen* "to nestle." The slippery creeping in and nestling of the intruder is the basic meaning of this form in all the other Germanic languages. The dress is "smug" if it is trim. The *smock* denotes a "shirt for a woman which has only a round hole to put the head through." This primary point of reference makes the whole picture of the *smug* more positive: the "smug" is an intruder, he crept in through a hole furtively like a smuggler. He not only monopolizes the advantages of being close to the mother but is even a snob, he pleases the mother fawningly and *snubs* the others and treats them with contempt. The emotional intensity of the word derives from a situation of early infancy.

THE CONSCIOUS AND THE UNCONSCIOUS QUALITY OF LANGUAGE

Considering the facts as they present themselves for phenomenological description, one will come to the conclusion that the language of the Ego depends to a great extent upon the language of the Id. The evocative power might derive from some hidden source; however, by simply stating this, one does not explain the reason why it is so. Why are some verbal expressions charged with emotional stress, while others are not? The reason is obviously not apparent on the surface of language as described in dictionaries by common-sense definitions.

The whole meaning-complex of verbal expressions can be compared to a free-floating iceberg, to which Freud, during the early years of psychoanalysis, compared the structure of the mind. This is, of course, figurative speech, but there are good reasons why all structural descriptions are topographic. They apply equally to language and thinking and can be used in linguistics as in psychology. The lexical meaning looms on the surface of language. As used in speech, it represents only a small segment of the whole meaning complex. The implications and connotations remain in the subconscious or unconscious.* Behavioral science, with an aversion to any "myth of

---

* The great founders of scientific linguistics, contemporaries of Sigmund Freud, had no contact with the psychoanalytic movement, yet in one way or another they had a clear vision of the unconscious character of verbal phenomena. They failed, however, to recognize the impact which the psychology of the unconscious would have upon linguistics. An anticipation of Freud's concept of the unconscious can be found in the linguistic literature at the end

the unconscious" (Watson),[41] tried to wipe out these implications which are inherent in the "meaning of the meaning" and to reduce language to a "basic" vocabulary of denotations (we have the "basic" translations of some classics and the Bible). But, for instance, the word *night* carries, in Shakespeare's language, or in Homer's, a load of connotations that cannot be reduced to "basic" language and cannot be caught in the net of any logistic definition. These connotations are often irrational and they evoke absurd fantasies.* Linguistics

---

of the past century; especially in Heymann Steinthal, *Einleitung in die Psychologie und Sprachwissenschaft. Abriss der Sprachwissenschaft* (Berlin: 1888). This is a remarkable work uniting psychological and linguistic insight. A new note in understanding language was struck by Hermann Paul, *Prinzipien der Sprachwissenschaft*, 1st ed. (Halle: Niemeyer, 1880), translated as *Principles of the History of Language*, by A. Strong (London: Swan Sonnenschein, 1888). Hermann Paul said: "Perhaps the greatest progress by modern psychology consists in the acknowledgment of the fact that a great many psychological processes go on without clear consciousness, and that everything which has been in consciousness remains an effective motive in the unconscious. The acknowledgment of this as a matter of fact is of the greatest importance for linguistics, and it became utilized by Steinthal in great extent. All manifestations of speech are flowing out of this dark space of the unconsciousness of the mind" (p. 23). These and many similar statements were made before Freud's works were written. See also the chapter, "Association und Reproduktion. Bewusstes and Unbewusstes," in Berthold Delbrück, *Grundfragen der Sprachforschung: Mit Rücksicht auf W. Wundts Sprachpsychologie Erörtert* (Strassburg: Trübner, 1901).

* Benjamin Lee Whorf, *Language, Thought and Reality* (New York: John Wiley & Sons, 1956). Whorf, surely an original thinker and excellent interpreter of aboriginal languages, distinguished the "phenotype" and the "cryptotype" of each word meaning. He called "phenotype" the overt lexical meaning described by common-sense definition, and called "cryptotype" the "submerged" unconscious implications. He recognized that "the totality of meaning is a joint product of cryptotype and phenotype factors." He also came to the insight that the "dredged up" cryptotype may be an important factor in "a more pronounced consciousness and clearer understanding of the phenotype itself" (p. 109). Enlightening as these and many other of his ideas are, it should be pointed out that there is no need for calling the overt lexical meaning "phenotype" and the repressed sub- or unconscious meaning "cryptotype." This mixing the biological terms of genetics into linguistics may result

did not refer to the iceberg metaphor, but used the figurative expressions of *stem* and *root* of words. These are again similes, referring to something visible in order to explain something that is invisible. Both terms, *stem* and *root,* belong to the field of psychology or philosophy, rather than to linguistics. These terms became obsolete in linguistics because they were understood to denote the very questionable nonexistent atoms and molecules of language.* However, the underlying idea came from the correct realization of the psychological fact that there exists, as it were, an invisible root, and this root is an integral part of the whole plant. It is even the more persistent, more vital part. The subterranean life and growth are as complicated and essential to the plant as the life and growth of the visible stem. The "root," in this figurative sense, is a philosophical and psychological concept. Edward Husserl once explained that metaphysics is the "science of the roots," the science of the origin of all things.† In interpreting language, I shall refer to the pre-conscious and unconscious

---

in gross misunderstandings. Whorf is also mistaken when he thinks "I believe I am the first to point out the existence of this submerged layer of meaning which in spite of this submergence functions regularly in the general linguistic whole" (p. 111). Whorf wrote this in 1937. Freud's *Interpretation of Dreams* appeared in 1900. C. G. Jung published his *Psychology of the Unconscious* in 1912. Whorf also wrote: "The resemblance of the cryptotypes to the concept of the unconscious of Freud, and still more perhaps of Jung, will no doubt strike you, although the parallel should perhaps not be carried too far." But the parallel goes very far.

* Joshua Whatmough, a linguist, not a neurologist, just on the way to "the mathematical theory of the behavior of nerve networks," stated: "The convention of meaning is the very core and essence of language. If the root, as I see it, does not exist, then thought and meaning and linguistic expression do not exist." "The Neural Basis of Language and the Problem of the Root," *Harvard Studies in Classical Philology* (1941), 52–133.

† "Philosophy . . . by its very essence is the science of true beginnings, of origins, the *rhidzōmata pantōn*. And the method of a science concerned with the roots of things, the method of a radical science, must itself be radical and this in every respect." These were the significant words (in translation) by which E. Husserl started on the way of phenomenology. "Philosophie als strenge Wissenschaft," *Logos* (1910), 1:289–290.

qualities of verbal expressions as to the "invisible" roots and compare the "visible" stems with the conscious content.

Concerning the "root" meanings, one can observe a strange attitude toward language.[42] Man really trusts his fellowman if he knows him, if he knows his background, his origin and his destination. Man is familiar with a whole situation if he knows its origin and "roots." He feels secure in the present situation if he has an insight into it from past experiences. It is rather exceptional that only in the understanding of language does man want to forget about the past in order to understand the present.

There must be a positive reason for this attitude. The reason is the desire that something unpleasant should be wiped out or forgotten. Man wants to repress or destroy something which is present in his mind. He feels that it should not be there. Perhaps shame and guilt, or a painful humiliation may be connected with it. Language is a system of symbols based chiefly on forgetting. In many instances the original meaning of a word had first to be forgotten, repressed, stamped out of the memory, in order that the new and acceptable meaning could be established. Languages are rooted in past ages, older than any material relics can reach. They derive through an unbroken continuity from prehistoric man. Man is not proud of his ancestors and of the imprints which they left upon present-day language. He tries to wipe out the humiliating memories. He feels that the success of his progress toward a more human future depends on his ability to forget, to eradicate all the signs and marks of the past which may disturb his conscience. If one has grown together with the language in which one speaks and thinks and which is the instrument of sublime feats of spirit in philosophy and poetry, one feels disturbed if one is reminded that this, our beautiful language, appears vulgar and brutal, as it was used by our ancestors untold centuries ago. These memories are painful. The sexual implications of language are particularly disturbing. The civilized man wants to get rid of his prehistoric ancestry, but this does not change the fact that language, in its whole structure, derives from prehistoric sources. Modern man hopes to overcome the memories which he feels are subhuman and below the dignity of moral self-respect. If, now, the purpose of linguistic analysis is to be a "root science" and to dig up

facts belonging to past ages out of languages, its undertaking
may be shocking. Why should it be necessary to revive memories which, for good reasons, were repressed in the course of
history? What benefit could be expected from such undertak-
ings when a harmful effect upon the present usefulness of language seems to be obvious? Why should one know things one
does not want to know and which fall short of our moral
judgment?

The answer to these objections (which reach to the very
core of the intensive analysis of language) is not a simple
one.[43] One must take into consideration the question of what
is meant by "forgetting" and "memory." Does something which
is forgotten cease to exist anymore? The destruction of
memory is the greatest curse in Old Testament language (Job
18:17–18). But is such destruction of memories possible at
all? Memories can persist in a system as a secret source of
strength, or as a poison, or a cancerous growth. They can
return and reappear unexpectedly, just when they are supposed to be forgotten for good. Memories of childhood may
appear in dreams, for instance, the scene of the house in
which one was born and which since became completely
forgotten may reappear in dreams. What is meant, in particular, when it is said that the meaning of a word has been
forgotten by the whole language community?

Objections to these assumptions may be raised in terms of
a "functional autonomy" of motives. It is said that, "as the
individual or motive matures, the bond with the past is
broken. The tie is historical, not functional." This theory
"declines to view the energies of adults as infantile or archaic
in nature. Motivation is always contemporary."[44] I take issue
with this theory of functional autonomy because the concept
of time does not allow it, even if one wants to forget that "the
bond with the past is broken." Nothing is "contemporary"
without "past." The past is "contemporary," it is present.
Even the Acropolis and the Parthenon belong to modern
Athens. There is no present without past.*

---

* The conflict of the ahistorical-functional and the historical
attitudes is also evident in linguistic literature. Saussure tried to
separate radically the ahistorical "synchronic" viewpoint from the
historical "diachronic" viewpoint, but is such radical separation

It would be a mistake indeed to consider the forgotten meaning as being nonexistent in the language community.* It is a latent power, a potentiality which may emerge in full existence if the repressive energy is not vigilant, as in dreams, or if it is distracted in another way. Forgetting is a dynamic process. I am not satisfied with stating that the old meaning, the original etymological content of a word, just faded away or was worn out by frequent usage during the ages and needed to be exchanged for a new one. It is generally supposed that words, like coins, lose their impress in the course of such constant circulation. Such popular analogies have nothing to do with entropy, nor with the "lapse of meaning" through monotonous repetition. They miss the essential point in the dynamic understanding of changing meanings.

Oblivion came about not just through the senescence of a word. Constant and frequent usage does not make a word obsolescent or forgotten. There must be some reason for this decay. One will find, more often than not, that the original meaning did not simply fade out, but became destroyed, wiped out by an active force, by a language "Superego" which worked against it. If the new meaning of a word replaced the old one, there must be a connection between them. The new meaning is a recast of the old idea.† Though the substitute

---

possible at all? Merleau-Ponty said to this point: "No matter how strongly Saussure insisted upon the duality of the two perspectives (synchronic and diachronic), his successors have to conceive a mediating principle in the form of the *sublinguistic schema* (Gustave Guillaume). . . . We must recognize that the present diffuses in the past to the extent that the past has been present. History is the history of successive synchronies, and the contigency of the linguistic past invades even the synchronic system." Maurice Merleau-Ponty: "On the Phenomenology of Language," in *Signs*, translated by Richard C. McCleary (Evanston, Ill.: Northwestern University Press, 1964), pp. 86–87.

* Edward Sapir clearly recognized the "unconscious special pleading" in the "drift" of language: "Psychoanalysts will recognize the mechanism. The mechanism of 'repression of impulse' and of its symbolization can be illustrated in the most unexpected corners of individual and group psychology . . ." *Language: An Introduction to the Study of Speech* (New York: Harcourt, Brace & Co., Harvest Book, 1949), p. 157.

† The linguist Hermann Paul said long before Freud and psychoanalysis: "The old word-meanings have an aftereffect chiefly

appears to be new, it has something in common with the forgotten meaning whose place it has taken. The old wine was poured into new bottles. This will help to reach a better understanding of verbal symbolism. Because language is in constant change and almost every word has been substituted for a previously existing one, it follows that the symbolic meaning of a word stands for another one, for the original meaning which has been repressed. By this process of substitution, the symbol has become charged with many connotations. It denotes one thing, but means something else not overtly expressed. This is, in fact, the original implication of the word *symbol*, which is a derivative of the Greek verb *sumballein*, "to throw together" (from *sun*, "together," and *ballein*, "to throw"). What was "thrown together" in the symbolic meaning? An old meaning became united with a new one; an expressed meaning with the former repressed one, the original meaning and the substitute which stands for it have grown together into a new unity. The symbol carries a double reference in its very existence: one reference points to a reality concept, the other to a repressed fantasy. One part of the symbolic meaning is manifest, like the "stem"; the other part is its underlying unconscious "root." The mental act of grasping both is like binocular vision, the human quality of visual perception.

Having recognized this double character inherent in the symbolic nature of language, it will become impossible to understand language only in two dimensions, seeing only the manifest surface, and take no notice of the third dimension— the latent content which is repressed. The two-dimensional view would be especially misleading if one and the same phonemic pattern has developed on the manifest surface an array of different meanings. Then, though the invisible root may be one, the visible stems appear to be independent of one another. If A and B hang together by an underground communication through root C, it is a futile attempt to construct on the manifest surface some logical transition between

imperceptible, within the dark chamber of the unconscious of the soul." *Loc. cit.*, p. 25. Franz Boas, *Handbook of American Indian Languages* (Washington: Government Printing Office, 1911), also contains a remarkable, seldom-quoted chapter on "Unconscious Character of Linguistic Phenomena," pp. 67ff.

A and *B* when none exists in reality. But the real coherence can be found by accepting the fact that *A* and *B* are symbols; that they stand as substitutes for a repressed *C*. The meaning of *C* is still present as a latent possibility in both; they are associated with one another because they grew out of the same root.

The different meanings of words are listed, numbered, and defined in dictionaries. They are mostly arranged in some logical order, starting with the most general concept and proceeding toward the more specific applications. However, meanings do not develop according to such logical sequences. Each word raises anew, in its own way, the basic question: Why and how did so many, often so disparate, meanings become attached to *one* sound pattern? It would be difficult to find among the thousands of words listed in alphabetical order ten words which denote *one* thing and nothing else. In many cases one can observe the efforts on the part of the makers of dictionaries to arrange the disparate meanings in a rainbow sequence in which the first has something in common with the second, the second with the next, and so on, thus suggesting that the meanings developed in such an order. Yet, language does not play this logical domino game. If, for instance, five meanings are listed, the fifth does not depend on the previous four in the row. The meanings are independent from one another.

In order to come to a better understanding of the confusing array of disparate meanings, one is confronted with the question: How do all these meanings hang together? If they did not develop in linear sequence, the cyclic structure offers the most plausible alternative. There is always *one* central idea reflected in all and in each meaning. If there are five different meanings listed, they mirror, in five varieties, the *one* common center. They may in five different variations illustrate the process of "sublimation," the gradual de-mythologization, debiologization, the liberation from bodily fixation and references to the human organism or its functions. The five meanings might be independent from, yet related to, one another through the common center which is mostly an emotionally loaded concept, not an empty logical abstraction, but a very concrete experience of the body-self. Thus, each word raises a problem. It is for analysis to find out the *one* central idea which unfolded its latent content in the many new verbal incorporations. The central idea may still loom on the surface like any "return of the repressed." For instance, the Greek *gignomai* still means "to be born," but it is used generally with the sublimated meaning "to become." The original biological reference might have been lost in the course of history. In English, during the period of Old English, it was often lost in the previous ages of language development. Comparative linguistics rendered great service to the psychological understanding of language. It opened up a storehouse of case histories of words.

The intensive analysis of word complexes is not an accepted procedure in linguistic literature. The basic concepts of the changing meanings were not even found by linguistics, but by Freud while analyzing the "language" of hysterical symptoms. He found that hysterical symptoms, which appear so flexible and in such variety, are charged with meaning. The meaning attached to them displays a specific character. The emotional intensity of this meaning is seldom commensurate with its content. The meaning of the hysterical symptom derives its emotional power from an invisible source, from another repressed meaning for which the manifest symptoms are only substitutes. One can understand the variety of hysterical symptoms by grasping their connection with the very source of the emotional intensity; this is the repressed, seemingly long-forgotten event or fantasy which, for some reason, has been wiped out of the conscious mind.

The same holds true for the meaning of verbal expressions. They are the linguistic parallels of symptom-formation. They show the same characteristics as does symptom-formation in general. The stronger the rejected impulse is, or the more painful the forgotten episode was, the greater is the variety of symptoms which grow out of this repressed content. So it is with language. The stronger or more powerful the underlying root concept was, the more abundant are its shoots on the manifest surface of language. If a whole cluster of words with the same phonemic pattern grows out with the most different meanings, one may surmise that a strong impulse has been repressed and, in consequence, has driven a great variety of substitutes to the manifest surface of language.

In summing up these observations, the conclusions may be formulated in three points.

A. If no distinction is made between sign and symbol, the misunderstanding will prevail that words are nothing but arbitrary signs. Consequently, only the lexical meaning "per definition" can be considered as a matter of linguistic interpretation. The unconscious content of language is beyond the scope of such understanding.

B. If one accepts, in contradistinction to mechanistic theories, that the verbal symbol carries a reference to something repressed and forgotten, it follows that language offers a unique approach to unconscious fantasies. These fantasies follow the logic of emotions. They are unrealistic, nonsensical, absurd, just as is the imagery of dreams. Interpreting the various lexical meanings, which grew out of unconscious fantasies, in terms of common-sense reasoning is just as fruitless as interpreting the pictures of dreams on the logical-conceptual level of reality-perception. Moreover, for the playing child or for the neurotic, just as for nonliterate people, the world of fantasies is more real, more actual, than the world of physical realities. For these reasons the psychological interpretation of verbal forms will have a closer contact with psychopathology than with the psychology which restricts its observations to the field of the so-called normal life.

C. The science of etymology holds a completely different position within the frame of analytical interpretation of language from that which it holds on behavioristic premises. In descriptive linguistics there is no room for etymology. According to this theory etymology deals with forgotten forms and meanings which do not exist in the actual speech-community, therefore, the subject matter of etymology has no reality, no significance for those who speak the language. Thus, the study of word origins satisfies mere historical curiosity, but does not serve the end of understanding language. However, it is a matter of scientific thinking, especially in psychology, to become aware of the motivation which escapes observation. Thinking will not be safe from a logical viewpoint if one does not realize its coherence with the underlying verbal fantasies. Etymology is, in this understanding, not a historical discipline, but the study of motivation. It is the key to the understanding of unconscious fantasies which have been accepted by the language community. They underlie all speech activity. The great linguist Karl Vossler once said: "In the final instances of their science all good etymologists are fortune hunters and interpreters of dreams. Through hundredfold experiences they know that they cannot do much with their knowledge of the shifting of consonants or of meanings if fortune does not smile on them and whisper the dream that gave life to the word they are tracking. Moreover, those etymologies that are considered by the expert as well established, and as presenting no further problems, are usually the most problematical from the point of view of the philosophy of language."[45]

Let us add that they are the most problematical ones for the analytical interpretation of language, too.

In order to illustrate this point, I chose the unconscious identification of "word" and "seed." This example will demonstrate how a primary symbolic meaning, once repressed, became translated into the conceptual language. Once the "root" was a complex syncretic fantasy loaded with awe and anxiety; the stem which branched out of it developed in many disparate concepts which do not reveal their common origin anymore.

The basic identification of man, animal and plant is supposed by the words referring to *sperma* and *semen*. The Latin *semen* denotes the "seed" of plant as well as the "seed" of man. It can be used like the biblical term "seed" for "offspring," "descent," "son." In the Gothic language *mana-sēths*, properly "man-seed," is the general term for the human race, for "man-kind." The Greek word *sperma* belongs to the verb *speirō*, which means "scatter seed" or "sow," also "spray, sprinkle," "emit sparks." The sower surely emits no sparks, does not spray or sprinkle if "sowing" is understood just as what it is according to the lexical definition. The explanation is given by the meaning "to sow children, to engender, beget them." The subjective sensation of emitting semen is described by this verb, rather than the sowing of the field. No doubt will be left about the primary meaning of the agricultural sowing if one considers the verb which is the parallel form of *speirō*; this is the verb *spargaō*. This means "to be full to bursting, to swell, to be ripe," "to swell with humors"; it means that one is full with desire, one is bursting, coveting fervently with lust. The word is descriptive of the Dionysiac complex.

The same holds true for the relative Latin verb *spargō, -ere*, "to strew, throw here and there, cast, hurl or throw about, scatter; to bestrew, sprinkle, spatter, wet, to bedew, moisten." The Germanic languages developed various verbal forms from this underlying fantasy. These are the interrelated words *spring, sprinkle, spray, spark, sprawl* and *speak*. The word *spring*, with all its various meanings implied, belongs to this cluster. It is a psychological problem in itself to find out how such different meanings of *spring* ("to move, suddenly and rapidly," "to arise from a source as the plant springs from a seed," "to explode or discharge," "to rise up"; and, as a noun, "a jump or leap," "a coil of wire with elasticity," "a flow of water," "the season of the year," "any period of beginning and newness as the spring of his life") may hang together. Such fertility and differentiation of meanings are indicative of the intensity of emotions invested in the original meaning repressed. Each meaning projected upon a specific situation the overall complex of which was expressed by the Greek verbs *speirō* and *spargaō*.

The four closely related English words are *sprinkle, spray, spark* and *sprawl*. The verb *sprinkle* definitely refers not just to the agricultural scattering of seeds, but to something fluid. The word *spark*, in strange contradiction, suggests that this something fluid is an ignited substance emitted by a body. The notion of emitting sparks was included also in the Greek *speirō*. The ejaculation of semen in the generative act is the primary point of reference and, thus, responsible for the notion of "spark." The verb to *spray* refers to something in between the two former notions. It can mean on the one hand "to sprinkle" something fluid, or "to sprout" on the other hand. The relative German verbs follow the same pattern—the German *sprühen* means "to sparkle," *spriessen*, "to sprout," and *spritzen*, "to spray." The English *sprawl* also belongs to this cluster of words. It must be very disturbing for the realistic-minded interpreter to find this word in such a group of associations, and to find out some transitory meanings without resorting to unconscious fantasies. This verb means "to move when lying down, with awkward extension and motions of the limbs" and "to spread the limbs carelessly in recumbent position." This posture has little to do with the sowing of the field, but has much in common with the ejaculation of semen. These words obviously have something in common, otherwise they would not be built upon the same phonemic pattern. This common element is an unconscious fantasy which never can be found among the meanings listed in vocabularies.

In Lithuanian the according form is *sporga*, "spark." Yet, there exists a parallel form *sparginti*, denoting "to throw salt into a fluid." Such an odd transfer of meanings never can be fully understood on the grounds of historical or philological reasoning, yet one has to answer the question as to how and why the notion of "salt" entered this whole cluster of words centered around "sowing." One must recall, in this case, in answering this question, the finding which has been corroborated by many anthropological evidences that "salt" may assume the meaning of "semen." To spill salt is ominous for just such a reason. All these words suggest that man himself is always the primary point of reference, therefore, the process of sowing is perceived as the bodily function of emitting semen.

Another transfiguration of the notion of "semen" is the association between "semen" and "word," or between the agricultural act of "sowing" and "speaking."

This equation of "word" and "seed," or "speaking" and "sowing" may sound strange for the first moment, but this equation will be understood better in reference to the phallic meaning of the tongue. "The body as phallus" is the known fantasy[46] which becomes conspicuous by the association of "blushing" and "erection." The foundation of these fantasies, which appear in various forms in regressed delusions, is the primitive concept which considers the head as the seat not of the intellectual capacities, but of the generative power of man. The gradual shift from the sexual potency to the capacity of thinking, speaking, reading, counting, and knowing is reflected in the pertinent terms in *gignō*, *gen-erate*, *know*, and *knee*. The same change from the physiological to the intellectual may explain the association of "seed" and "word."

The ideas of "seed" and "word" are connected with one another by the notion of "picking up." In order to understand this association, one has to inquire further into the terms which are descriptive of the most primitive agricultural process. The simplest way of getting food for man and animal alike was the picking up of edible seeds, fruits, possibly roots; some insects also were considered as delicacies. The way in which monkeys feed, by simply gathering edibles where they can be found, preceded any agricultural activity. This rudimentary technique of food acquisition corresponds to the infantile habit of picking up everything and putting it into the mouth.

The picking up of seeds and fruits is expressed in our languages by words which are used at the same time for denoting the elementary mental process, to speak and to understand what has been said. One cannot understand this strange coincidence if it did not refer to the primary identification of seed and word. The Greek verb *legō*, and also the corresponding Latin *legō*, refer, on the one hand, to "pick up something," or "to gather," "to take out, remove," "to pluck, strip, gather fruit from a tree," "to plunder." On the other hand, the Greek *legō* means "to speak, say," "to count, tell," the Latin *legō* means particularly, "to read." One can circumscribe well the realm of association centering around these words by considering the most usual compound forms: the Latin *col-ligō* means "to gather or collect together, to assemble, bring together"; it means that which has been picked up, and, one may elaborate, it refers to collecting fruits. The Latin *neg-legō* means "not pick up," or "not to care for," "neglect, disregard, not trouble one's self about." The early food-gatherers, much like monkeys, were more discriminative in taste and smell than modern man. The Latin *e-lect*, *se-lect* illustrate this discriminatory act, while the word *e-legans* shows the more abstract sublimation of taste implied in the primary acquiring of food. The Latin *leg-umen*, "vegetable," still reflects the original alimentary meaning implied in these words. The Latin *di-ligō*, "to like," from *dis-legō*, records the affection for the object singled out among others, "to esteem highly, to love, to be fond of"; the participle *di-ligens* shows the care invested in this picking up; it means "careful, diligent, attentive," all necessary qualities for food-gathering. (The prefix *dis-* generally carries a negative sense, but originally meant "twice," from *duis-*, thus the original implication was "to pick up twice.") The Latin *intel-ligō* (from the former *inter-legō*) properly means to pick up and collect "among others." It describes by this picture the thought process of perception which underlies the fruit collection as well as the speech process. An object picked up becomes identified and understood if it is placed "among" the other ones of its kind. The Gestalt psychologist would say: the singling out and picking up of the figure from the "ground" is the basic operation of perception. The Old Testament picturesque language said: "a word fitly spoken is like apples of gold in pictures of silver" (Proverbs 25:11). Singling out first the apple and placing it among the others in the category of "apple" and calling it by its proper name are the primary acts of intelligence.

The Germanic languages followed the same pattern. Old English *lesan* means "pick up, collect." This was the original meaning of the verb in the other Germanic languages. In German *auf-lesen* means "pick up," *aus-lesen*, "single out," *er-lesen*, "select," simply *lesen* means "to read." It is one of the favorite German word-thing explanations that the Germanic way of prophesying was throwing wooden sticks with inscriptions on the ground and then picking them up in order to decipher them. This is the origin of the German *lesen*. The trouble with this explanation is that it does not take into account the parallel Greek and Latin forms which connect "pick up" and "speak," "read" without prophecies.

The association of "word" and "seed," also of "speak" and "sow," is obviously deeply rooted in the language of unconscious fantasies. All the various verbal forms, to-

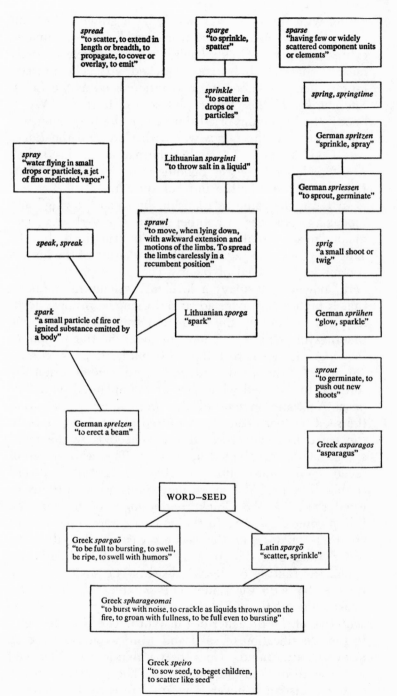

spread
"to scatter, to extend in length or breadth, to propagate, to cover or overlay, to emit"

sparge
"to sprinkle, spatter"

sparse
"having few or widely scattered component units or elements"

sprinkle
"to scatter in drops or particles"

spring, springtime

German spritzen
"sprinkle, spray"

spray
"water flying in small drops or particles, a jet of fine medicated vapor"

Lithuanian sparginti
"to throw salt in a liquid"

German spriessen
"to sprout, germinate"

speak, spreak

sprawl
"to move, when lying down, with awkward extension and motions of the limbs. To spread the limbs carelessly in a recumbent position"

sprig
"a small shoot or twig"

spark
"a small particle of fire or ignited substance emitted by a body"

Lithuanian sporga
"spark"

German sprühen
"glow, sparkle"

sprout
"to germinate, to push out new shoots"

German spreizen
"to erect a beam"

Greek asparagos
"asparagus"

WORD—SEED

Greek spargaō
"to be full to bursting, to swell, be ripe, to swell with humors"

Latin spargō
"scatter, sprinkle"

Greek spharageomai
"to burst with noise, to crackle as liquids thrown upon the fire, to groan with fullness, to be full even to bursting"

Greek speiro
"to sow seed, to beget children, to scatter like seed"

gether with *spring, sprout, spark,* have grown out of this primordial picture of the "word-seed." The sublimated expression is the Greek *logos,* "word," which properly means "that which has been picked up." The primary fantasy became elaborated and rationalized as the *Logos Spermatikos* of the Orphic philosophy. It is the "Word-Seed," the beginning of all things. "In the beginning was the *Logos,* and the *Logos* was with God, and the *Logos* was God" (John 1:1) is the affirmation of this belief. The Greek *spermo-logos* denotes also an "idle babbler." It refers to the infantile form of speech.

In Latin the same relationship between "sowing" and "speaking" emerges in another form. The verb *serō, -ere* means "to sow, to plant," as well as "to bring forth, beget." This supposes, once again, the basic identity of the human sperma and the seed of plants. The development of this verb, however, displays a level of agricultural thinking that is higher and more advanced than the primary technique of picking up the seeds and fruits. The purposive planting of seed is the new moment in the notion of "sowing." It developed the new implication as *in-serō,* "to insert"; the seed and the word *semen* originally referred to the seed which has been implanted with purpose. Another moment of this implanting reveals that the seed has not been just scattered about, but placed in the earth in some order; this is reflected by the word *sēr-ies* as being planted in a row. The association of "seed" and "word" brought about in Latin the word *sermō,* "sermon." This word may refer either to the scattered seed like the Greek *spermo-logos* or to the seed fitly planted in a row. In the first case *sermō* means just chatting, talking; in the second case it describes the orderly discourse. The primary source of this equation is, again, the fantasy of the word-seed. The sower and the speaker both do the same. The parables of Christ also evoked the picture of the sower as the symbolic representative of the preacher of the Word. The parables refer to the identification of seed and word as an idea rooted in everybody's mind. "Now the parable is this: The seed is the word of God" (Luke 8:11). The great experience of the Christian believer is worded thus by the apostle:

"Being born again, not of corruptible seed, but of incorruptible, by the word of God, which liveth and abideth for ever" (Peter 1:23). "The sower soweth the word," said Christ, and the word was "sown in their hearts" (Mark 4:14, 15).

THE ARCHAIC HERITAGE

Behavioral science can find no objective evidence for the existence of the "mind" or "consciousness," not to speak about the existence of an "unconscious." Watson formulated, in unequivocal terms, that: "There are then for us no instincts . . . we no longer need the term in psychology." If anything called instinct is "a result largely of training . . . belongs to man's learned behavior" . . . there can be no question of any "archaic inheritance." Linguistics, based upon behavioristic premises, also avoided any reference to the unconscious quality of language and classified unconscious processes as "mechanical operations." "Has the boomerang an instinct to return to the hand of the thrower?" Watson asked.[47] Linguists preferred, by the same token, to suppose that language is the manifestation of a speech machine built into the human nervous system, and it works like any other mechanism. Even Wundt's apperception psychology dealt with language as a perfect mechanism. This theory, like all similar ones, was based upon the laws of mechanics and, consequently, upon the general assumptions of the Newtonian physics.

This mechanistic concept of language which, seemingly, offered the most scientific approach is, however, nothing but a figure of speech. Even in physics, electric "power" or "laws" of gravitation are metaphors and anthropomorphic terms. One cannot speak about inner experiences other than in a symbolic way. But, even admitting the need for symbolic expression, one must realize that the mind is not a machine. One can take apart a machine, investigate separately each of its particles, and thus know the whole completely from inside and

94

outside. This is never the case with man. The "analysis" of the mind, psychoanalysis, is just another figurative expression.

In distinction to these mechanistic theories, psychology approached its field with the more realistic concept of the "dynamic" power of instincts. The difference between the unconscious forces and the mechanical concept is fundamental.[48] It can be well observed, however, that Freud still held the idea that psychic energy works like a mechanism: this "mechanism of the unconscious" remained the postulate of the dynamic interpretation. It was supposed that the more unconscious psychic processes are like the function of the glandular system, the more they approach the mechanism of mere physical-chemical changes; thus, psychology rests on biological foundations. By simply exchanging the idea of physical, thermal, electrical, or chemical energy for mental energy, or for drives and instincts, there remained an open question: What else, then, is this "unconscious energy" if not a mechanism?

The great turning point in philosophy was brought about by Kant. He pointed out the difference between the "pure reason" and the "impure" one depending on prior sense perception. The pure reason operates upon the *a priori* categories of thinking. A similar step in the interpretation of fantasies was made by C. G. Jung. He called attention to the "a prioris" of the unconscious. Beside or below the "individual" unconscious, Jung explained, there must be, so to say, a "pure unconscious" which does not depend upon individual experiences but contains the *a priori* elements called "archetypes."[49] This collective unconscious speaks to the conscious mind in symbols.* The archetypes are, according to Jung, "motives,"

---

* The classic exposition of the "Archaic Man" is Chapter 7 in C. G. Jung, *Modern Man in Search of a Soul* (New York: Harcourt, Brace & Co., Harvest Book, 1933). Jung's stimulating influence upon the scientific study of religion is apparent in the pioneering work of Mircea Eliade. The French school of sociology and anthropology developed the idea of "collective representations," the rational counterpart of the Jungian archetypes. Language is the primordial collective representation which holds the community together. See Émile Durkheim, *The Elementary Forms of Religious Life,* translated by Joseph Ward Swain (New York: Collier, 1961). Also Lucien Lévy-Bruhl, *How Natives Think,* translated by Lilia

"primordial images," fantasy products. Hence, they "do not refer to anything that is or has been conscious, but to something *essentially unconscious*.[50] In the last analysis, therefore, it is impossible to say what they refer to."[51]

It should be noted in all fairness that Jung never went as far as Freud did on the slippery way of radical Lamarckism.[52] Jung stated clearly and explicitly that, "I do not by any means assert the inheritance of ideas but only the possibility of such ideas, which is something very different."[53] He only stated the possibility of predisposing factors in human nature which precipitated the repetition of former experiences. Even though Freud stated in 1918, "I fully agree with Jung in recognizing the existence of phylogenetic inheritance,"[54] he went far beyond Jung in asserting the biological foundation of hereditary experiences. He said, with pronounced accent, that not simply instinctual dispositions and thought dispositions can be transmitted from one generation to the other, but also "ideational contents, memory traces of the experiences of former generations" can be inherited.

The basic issue with which Freud, Jung, and every psychologist is confronted when dealing with trans-individual phenomena such as language, myth, custom, and ritual,* boils down to two basic questions: Why should man be the only animal devoid of instincts which are obviously trans-individual qualities of the species? If instinctual behavior is a quality of the species, which man shares with animals, why do animals remain on the instinctual level of life and what made man transcend far beyond the animal instincts to create

---

A. Claire (London: George Allen and Unwin, Ltd., 1926). Also *The Soul of the Primitive,* authorized translation by Lilia A. Claire (New York: Frederick A. Praeger, Inc., 1966). Since language is the deposit of "everyday mythology," the scientific study of language cannot be divorced from the scientific study of mythology and religion.

* Bronislav Malinowski describes the difference between "individual ideas" and "social ideas" which are embodied in the institutions of the community, yet he is opposed to Durckheim's "collective consciousness": "The postulate of a collective consciousness is barren and absolutely useless for an ethnographical observer." *Magic, Science and Religion* (Garden City, N. Y.: Doubleday, Anchor Books, 1954), p. 274. He is even more opposed to the idea of a "collective unconscious."

culture, religion, art, and science? The difference between human and animal existence is raised by this question: Why was man capable of progress, while animals remained shut up in their instinctual nature? The answer to this fundamental question points, once again, to the symbol-creating capacity of man. He shares it with no animal. The symbolic languages hold the key for the understanding of human progress. Freud and Jung agreed on this point: the capacity of symbolic representation is an inherited characteristic of the human species. If only instincts would represent the trans-individual continuity of the species, animals also would build cultures, states, laws, religions, churches, arts, and sciences. It is obviously language, the vehicle of symbolic creativity, which lifted up the human mind beyond the stagnant animal repetition and opened up the road to progress. If memories of former generations are transmitted in the cultural process, it is obviously not a genetic-biological transmittance, like that of instincts, but the transmittance through language.

The biologist Julian Huxley pointed out the effect of "cumulative transmission" in human inheritance. This cumulative transmission of experience "constitutes a new accessory process of heredity in evolution, running side by side with the biological process, a heredity of experience to supplement the universal heredity of living substance."[55] Language is the primary carrier of this cumulative transmission of memory traces.

The philosophy of early ages tried to grasp the universe in the subjective experience of the mind. In the Greek cosmogonic fantasies, as well as in the Hebrew picture of the universe, two underworlds exist, one nearer to the earth, the other farther away. The Greek mythical fantasies distinguish the *Erebos* from the *Tartaros*; the Hebrew cosmological picture also differentiates between *Sheol* and *Techōm* as if depth under the earth had two stages, one deep below the other. The *Tartaros* is said to be as deep under the *Erebos* as the sky is high above the earth. These cosmogonic fantasies, which are a projection of self-experience, describe the unconscious mind in its double aspect—as a personal one nearer to the surface of the conscious mind and a deeper layer, the "bottomless pit."

The unique quality of language consists in this double

character of being rooted in the individual pre-conscious as well as in trans-individual or collective motives. C. G. Jung and his school concentrated on the study of myth because they were convinced that myth speaks the pre-verbal symbol-language of the collective unconscious. The myth was analyzed from this viewpoint as a collective dream of a whole community.[56] The archetypes constitute the focal points of such collective dream fantasies.

One may accept these basic assumptions by stating: myth cannot be fully explained or understood in terms of individual psychology. The picture language of mythologies appears to be nonsensical and absurd if considered in the daylight of physical realities because it springs from the trans-individual stratum of fantasies. However, the contention is maintained that language by its very nature is an even more genuine expression of these fantasies than myth. One could say that an "everyday mythology" is encased in language.*[57] This mythology is profane, often vulgar, as distinguished from the sphere of holiness which dominates the great mythology. However, just this everyday profanity causes the verbal expressions to reflect truthfully collective processes. The constant use of language reveals psychic processes more exactly than the solemnity of great mythologies.† Moreover, language has a greater continuity connecting prehistoric ages with our age than myth. The Greek, Latin, or Germanic languages, and

---

* Whereas one may learn to "know" a foreign idiom, one still can remain far from grasping its "everyday mythology." Knowing is not the same as believing. Mythology implies from the very outset acceptance; it is an act of trust and a confession of faith. An anthropologist may "know" the meaning of a "peacock" but not share the belief in it as an incarnation of the spirit of an ancestor. Mircea Eliade, *The Sacred and the Profane* (New York: Harper & Row Publishers, 1961).

† Franz Boas made the following statement on the "Unconscious Character of Linguistic Phenomena": "It would seem that the essential difference between linguistic phenomena and other ethnological phenomena is that the linguistic classifications never rose into consciousness while in other ethnological phenomena, although the same unconscious origin prevails, these often rise into consciousness and thus give rise to secondary reasoning and to reinterpretations." *Handbook of American Indian Languages* (Washington: Government Printing Office, 1911), p. 23.

the fantasies implied, are far more indicative of collective forces than the respective mythologies which died centuries ago and are not accessible any more to immediate experience. C. G. Jung stated, in explaining the "archetypes," that "what an archetypal content is always expressing, is first and foremost a figure of speech."[58] For this reason language is the most immediate recorder of unconscious fantasies.

As to the heredity of such fantasies, one must confess our ignorance. This raises highly controversial questions which are as unanswerable as is the issue of the origin of language. It is an inherent feature of man that he creates symbolic language. This capacity of creating and understanding symbolic representations distinguishes man from all other creatures. In this symbolism consists the essence of all language activities. There is no doubt that man learns languages, but the capacity of speaking and thinking in symbols is not a learned individual acquisition. It is the privilege of the human race. The philosopher E. Cassirer called man the *animal symbolicum*. This definition sounds paradoxical because just this capacity of symbol formation makes the difference between animal and man.

The linguistic process refers to the gradual permanent change of all verbal expressions. Language is, in one respect, repetitious and stagnant, otherwise it would not be understood. In another respect it is ever-changing. The Old English of *Beowulf* and the Middle English of Chaucer exhibit the radical change within the history of the English language. What has brought about this change of all verbal forms and meanings? Obviously, the change was brought about by the impact of the constant and permanent use of language by untold changing generations. Theoretically speaking, even the same person cannot utter exactly the same sentence twice because he is not the same twice. Much greater is the variance of language transmitted from generation to generation. Each generation reshapes the inherited lore according to its own tendencies. This change is brought about by projection. Each individual projects something out of his own, however small it may be upon the common verbal lore. However, such individual variances become obliterated in the course of history. They live no longer than the individual himself. If, however, this individual projection is congruent with the common tendency, if the individual projects the same content which others also do, in such cases it will result in an accumulation which has a lasting effect upon language.

In consequence of this process of cumulative linguistic change, the lasting motives of unconscious fantasies, which were operative since prehistoric ages, became incorporated in the present state of language. Once, Darwin described the variability of animal life during an almost infinite lapse of time. He came to the conclusion that each slight modification of structure which served the survival of the race survived through long-continued accumulation, while those which were injurious for the race became destroyed. The survival of linguistic forms is not a matter of survival of the race, nor is it a question of usefulness or harmfulness. The accumulation of unconscious projections necessarily moves in the direction of ever deeper, ever more constant layers of fantasies. One may suppose that the cumulative process will develop these motives which are trans-individual. Each speaker, by projecting (beside individual particulars) the common element upon language, makes a short step on the road of language development toward the common collective heritage.*

Even in admitting that language, by necessity, will arrive in its long, long history to the permanent elements of unconscious fantasies (besides the ever-fluctuating individual variants), it still remains an open question as to how such unconscious implications can be transmitted from one generation to another. Language once may have been embedded in everyday mythology during the prehistoric period of its formation, but it has lost its living symbolism in the course of development. How shall this long-forgotten symbolism become

---

* The study of comparative Indo-European mythology based upon comparative linguistics was long since abandoned and discredited when it emerged with new actuality within the French positivistic sociology. The whole scope of this "neo-comparativism" is still much contested, especially the influential work of Georges Dumézil, professor of "Indo-European civilization" in the College de France and director of these studies at the Sorbonne, Paris. See C. Scott Littleton, *The New Comparative Mythology: An Anthropological Assessment of the Theories of Georges Dumézil* (Berkeley and Los Angeles: University of California Press, 1966).

recrudescent in the mind of the modern speaker; how can such symbolism be passed on from one generation to another? Most interpreters make their points by raising such questions and referring to the seemingly insurmountable obstacle of any intensive analysis of verbal forms. They conclude: whatever may have been implied in language during its prehistoric growth, these implications do not exist anymore today. Language became a mechanism, a system of arbitrary signs, even if it was not that in its beginnings. Symbols are no longer symbols, but signs which are no longer loaded with all the heavy connotations which may have originally shaped the words. The etymological implications exist in linguistic papers, not in a "collective unconscious." There is no unconscious in the background of words. "The cultural anthropologist can make nothing of the hypothesis of the racial unconscious," Edward Sapir, the linguist-anthropologist, said.[59] The assumption that such an unconscious exists seems to be a disturbance for his thinking based upon the conviction that language is "a merely conventional system of sound symbols," a noninstinctive, acquired "cultural" function, as opposed to walking, which is an organic, instinctive function.[60] It seems to be rather paradoxical that scientists who stress the learned arbitrary sign character of language see no essential difference between human language and animal communication, as, for instance, the language of the bees which is obviously instinctive, inherited, and not learned. But, if this so-called animal language is instinctive, why should human language be considered as an arbitrary learned system?

These loaded questions and statements cannot be answered in this paragraph. In the following investigations many instances shall be presented which demonstrate beyond doubt that unconscious fantasies, which disappeared from the manifest surface of language for centuries, may reappear in a present-day speech situation, just as in dreams mythological themes never heard of in our culture may enter the conscious mind again. The same holds true with language. Fantasies which are termed as "collective unconscious" and which the individual never "learned" may appear in the individual speech. An association which was alive in the prehistory of the Greeks, but never was expressed in Germanic languages, suddenly may spring up on the lips of an English-speaking child today. Unconscious fantasies which were dormant for centuries may become alive under emotional stress. How can this be possible at all?*

One has to distinguish two moments in the process of transmitting psychological material: one is the learned material, the other is the readiness and receptiveness for learning. The material of language has to be learned. Not one syllable is inborn. The tremendous variety of languages is learned. However, man's capacity for learning language is universally the same. All learning supposes a predisposition for learning. One can learn only what one is ready to learn.† This capacity and predisposition for verbal communication are innate qualities of man; no animal has it. The human mind is ready for learning verbal communication. It is not a *tabula rasa*. Just as thinking is inseparable from its categories, fantasies also imply *a priori* elements. These permanent primary motives represent the grammar of fantasies. Since man has existed, there has always been a polarity of the I and the World, body and mind, birth and death, eating and voiding, mother and child, man and woman, sun and moon, day and night, earth

---

* I quote two contradictory statements: "If hypnosis can really be considered an archaic heritage of mankind and suggestion (or transference) a part of it, then we are justified in assuming that the tendency to establish identical perceptions—i.e., to revive old experiences, can also be inherited. In this case we have to agree with Freud's hypothesis that not only dispositions but also contents can be inherited." Herman Nunberg, "Transference and Reality," *International Journal of Psycho-Analysis* (1951), 32:8. "Again one must confess that how such symbolic representations are laid down is, up to the present time, a mystery. That it cannot rest to any very large extent upon the basis of racial imprints of old experience is proved by the fact that so often the objects used are shoes, automobiles, airplanes and the like whose racial history can hardly be said to be a lengthy one." Lawrence S. Kubie, "Body Symbolization and Development of Language," *Psychoanalytic Quarterly* (1934), 3:435.

† Birds do not inherit their songs either. This becomes evident when they are hatched in a soundproof room. But if such a handicapped bird is exposed in an aviary to the most confusing noise made by many different birds, it will invariably pick up out of the conglomerate of various sounds only the melody which is specific to its species. Thus it has an innate predisposition to learn the local characteristics of the species.

and water. The human body-self has been the most permanent and universal object of reference since man has existed on earth.[61] These are the permanent and recurrent motives of symbolic representation incorporated in language. The language the child learns is loaded with these elements. But there is an inside response to it, an involvement of the individual in the common lore, an addition which springs from the individual who has acquired language. This, plus that which comes from the individual, might be just the straw which breaks the camel's back. The common lore may open up. The acquired language supposes an underground which is eager to absorb this language. These permanent and common motives lie in this underground like extinguished volcanoes. They may erupt at any time and throw archaic material at the surface of verbal expression. Such an eruption is most probable in times when the conscious control is at a low ebb as in the case of dreams, neurosis, or schizophrenia.[62] One can find many instances when repressed, long-forgotten fantasies have shaped the verbal expressions of our present-day language.

It is common knowledge that the child "imitates" his parents. That is to say that the boy internalizes his father image and acts out this internalized image in walking, in gestures, in speaking, in handwriting. Children are good analysts. They respond with a wonderful sensitivity not only to the overt behavior of the parents, but also to the unconscious, repressed motivation which might be covered up for the outside observers. All projection tends to establish an "identity of perception," equating the new perception with familiar notions acquired previously. Each child is an example of the return of the past. It is a futile question of merely theoretical interest speculating whether the tendency of repeating past experiences and of establishing an identity of perception should be considered as an individual quality or an inherited disposition. If the child produces the same perceptions, ideas, associations which have been produced in the past by his ancestors, it makes little difference whether this phenomenon is called "identical perception" or is considered as transmitted from the common lore or the Id which is collective in its essence. The biological heredity is transmitted through the genes. The cumulative cultural "heredity of experience" the biologist Julian Huxley is speaking about is transmitted through language. Language is both, transmitter and transmittance, an archaic heritage. However, it is a cultural transmission which should not be confused with biological transmission through the genes. The so-called collective unconscious is no magic, no mystery. It is symbolic behavior, verbal and archaic by its very nature.

By way of illustration I insert a clinical example. Children in play therapy sometimes release their repressed hostility. A four-year-old girl, Linda, painted the play bathtub with red paint and wanted to bathe the dolls in this red paint. "I'll put some people in there and then they'll get all red."[63]

This little girl is acting out a fantasy. By using the analytical interpretation we shall come to a fuller understanding of her behavior than was possible for the child therapist. We know this fantasy, first of all, from the Greek myth of Agamemnon. When Agamemnon finally returned home from the Trojan War, he took a bath and was murdered in the bathtub by his wife Clytemnestra and her lover. Little Linda has surely nothing to do with Clytemnestra, yet her hostility produced a fantasy which is at least very similar to the Greek myth. Our language presents us with explanatory material. The word *massacre,* of French origin, is not very transparent. The older language used for this meaning the notion picture *bloodbath* which is also the general German term *Blut-bad* for "massacre." Linda could hardly have learned this not obvious association of "blood" and "bath." If she found it spontaneously, as in the Greek mythology, then she came to the idea that her brothers and sisters when in the bathtub, undressed, are defenseless. This is the best opportunity to kill them. The German language preserved this fantasy in another forgotten expression. In obsolete German *das Bad segnen,* properly "to bless the bath," means "to kill."[64] The Old English *blodi-sō-jan,* "to make bloody," is the original form of the verb *to bless.* The German speaker could not be aware of the fact that *das Bad segnen,* "to bless the bath," properly meant in English "to make the bath bloody." Linda surely does not understand Old English, nor obsolete German or Greek, yet we must accept it as a matter of fact that she produced in her murderous play the same fantasies which were implied in the pertinent verbal expressions. "Red" and "bloody" are also recurrent associations denoted sometimes with one and the same word.

In her exciting play the little girl was acting out what disturbed her, however repressed her feelings may have been. Her dramatic action cannot be fully understood, if it is considered only as overt behavior which can be observed and described, and if her intention, perhaps never verbalized feelings and fantasies with all their ramifications are not perceived as the background out of which the strange individual behavior emerged.

animal instincts in man, almost with the same severity as did all the great religious leaders. He explored the unconscious mental processes, but rejected them, associated them with dark refuse at the bottom of waters, and compared psychoanalysis with the draining of the Zuider Zee. He committed himself to the service of truth, to conscious scientific thinking. He trusted in the healing power of sound thinking. Making unconscious processes conscious meant to him to cure them, to defeat their poisonous effect, to tame them and make them harmless, as the castrated, domesticated animals were made harmless and useful tools in the cultural progress. His famous dictum says: "Where Id was, there Ego shall be." This means restraint and control of libidinous forces. Freud was a medical biologist, but also a moralist. His Darwinian biology was intertwined with moral principles of his age. The Superego personifies these moral principles and shows a great resemblance to Freud's personality. It is autocratic; it always says "Thou shalt not . . ." It is a prohibitive, negative agency. Yet, Freud realized that a negative power alone could not transsubstantiate animal instincts into those creative capacities which distinguish man from the animals. Thus, he introduced the new concept of sublimation. However, this concept transcends biology and has no foundation within the biotropic instinctual image of man. The sublime does not derive from the animal.

Freud committed himself to the objective observation of facts, to the search for truth and nothing else. This gave him the courage and the strength to defy authorities and doctrines, to face ostracism and academic contempt which branded his work as unscientific. This was a painful rejection for a man who identified his ultimate concern with science. Anything nonscientific, nonrational, such as religion, prejudice, superstition, fanaticism, magic and mysticism, appeared to him as a "black tide of mud." He observed the onslaught of this tide in war-torn Europe. The only saving power against these unpredictable forces, he was convinced, was inherent in the conscious part of the Ego, in sound, objective, scientific thinking. Psychoanalysis was first intended to be nothing other than a technique of psychotherapy, but it soon turned out to involve a new moral philosophy. The scientist, the explorer of unconscious mental processes, in Freud assumed, perhaps against his better intentions, the role of a moral reformer. Not by chance was he fascinated by the image of Moses. He discussed his ideas first within the small circle of friends and devoted disciples, a small, unrecognized sect, but he envisaged the great future. He turned the psychoanalytical theory into the "psychoanalytical movement." He could see how his ideas, during his lifetime, penetrated the closed doors of the medical practitioners and gave rise to a new "psychosomatic" medicine. The impact of the new "metapsychology" was felt far beyond the limits of clinical practice. It became the ferment which changed the mind of the twentieth century. At the end of his life, Freud protested and fought against the idea that psychoanalysis should be restricted to psychotherapy and remain a branch of medical sciences. It was more than that. It swept the whole field of intellectual life, education, art, literature, and philosophy like a new religion, and Freud hoped that his belief in the scientific truth one day would change the religions of the Western world. He could see how his teaching conflicted with the traditional image of man as created "in the image of God."

The transformation of a medical theory into a "movement," however, brought about all the dangers of a sectarian community. It developed its central dogmas such as the Oedipus complex or castration complex. It grew more scholastic, clerical, and intolerant than the competing academic psychology. It developed its own topological terminology which serves as passwords and reveals at once whether someone is properly initiated and accepted by the inner circle or is an outsider. The organization maintained the power to accept or reject those who wanted to be admitted to the profession, also to discipline the deviants. This transformation of a scientific doctrine into a social movement and professional organization developed rigidity and sterility and lost much of the esoteric meaning which pulsated in the writing and thinking of its beginnings.

The third answer to the riddle-question (what is man?) brought psychology into the realm of language, linguistics, and philosophy. Freud, the empiricist, rejected philosophy. He did not care much about Schopenhauer or Nietzsche, who anticipated many of his ideas. He wanted to build up a metapsychology that could replace metaphysics. A consequence of his limitation made him able to overlook the philosophical inadequacies of his theoretical system. It is inconsistent, contradictory, sometimes confusing, because Freud never hesitated to change his views if he found a better solution. The unresolved inconsistencies are confusing, especially to those who fail to see or are unable to follow the internal struggle of a great thinker. In retrospect, one can see that those who deviated were not heretics. They only opposed dogmatism and rigidity and developed the potentialities that were inherent in the original doctrine. Psychoanalysis, in the early years, was a fertile soil for new ideas. Those who changed the original design are often more sensitive for their innovations than for the indebtedness to the basic doctrine from which they departed. The germinal ideas reveal themselves in the contradictory positions that are inherent in Freud's thinking. He started as a biologist and became a moral philosopher. He rejected philosophy and laid the foundation of a new philosophical branch of psychology. He proclaimed causation, determinism, and introduced meaning, symbol, language, and many more nonmedical concepts. While searching for the "etiology" of neurotic symptoms, he discovered their "true meaning," their etymology, and thereby opened the door for ontological analysis. He had no real contact with the progress made in theoretical physics and mathematics, yet, led by his intuition, he undermined the classic physical concepts of determinism, certainty and prediction. Norbert Wiener,[2] one of the great pioneers of modern information theory, says that Freud, Gibbs, and the proponents of the modern theory of probability, "in their recognition of a fundamental element of chance in the texture of the universe itself, these men are close to one another, and close to the tradition of St. Augustine." Freud spoke as a medical biologist in terms of an abstract physical time, yet in practice he considered his patients as unique individuals in a concrete historical-social context which cannot be repeated. Instead of medical "case histories," he wrote individual biographies which cannot be generalized. He claimed professional aloofness on the part of the therapist, and at the same time discovered in transference and counter-transference the most effective healing factor.

The only disciple who "deviated" from his doctrine, yet remained a lifelong friend and follower, was Ludwig Binswanger, the pioneer on the new way of onto-analysis (*Daseins-analysis*).[3] He emphasized again and again his indebtedness to Freud's thinking. He defined his onto-analysis as a branch of psychoanalysis, developed upon the concepts of Heidegger's philosophy. Heidegger, to be sure, speaks the language of a philosopher which is very different from Freud's language, yet it could be demonstrated that in some essential points, such as in describing "being" and "nothingness," both say the same thing in different wordings.[4] Freud and Heidegger both searched for the "true meaning." The onto-analysis made this research its primary goal. It turned out that the analysis of the existence of things cannot avoid the analysis of symbols and words which disclose their existence.

> Suppose that as I sit on the bank of a river, I see a "flowing" "stream" of "water." What is the true essence of the "river"? I cannot perceive this "riverness" without projecting upon it various personal elements which refer to me, but have nothing to do with the objective essence of "river." I cannot even perceive "to flow," "to run," "stream" in itself; all are symbols. I do not perceive H_2O, but "water," which is something very different. When saying "river," my mind implies the horizontal direction; I know the flow is irreversible; it originates somewhere, will end somewhere, and thus, is goal-directed. I see not just the river, but a landscape, which brings up memories. I imply the "liquid" quality, the flowing, the pull of the stream, the temperature and freshness of water, and these are inseparable from memories of other waters, rivers, lakes, of swimming, rowing, sailing, skating, and many life situations, also pictures of floods and dangers of rampant torrents. Beyond all this, the "river" may appear as an image of "life," present, past, future time, of the eternal change and eternal identity. A whole personal world is implied in this one word "river." Without these and many more qualifications, I cannot grasp the essential "being" of the river.

Descartes, in the often-quoted passage of his *Meditations*, said: "I will close my eyes, my ears, and shut out all my senses, I will even wipe out from my thoughts all images of material things, or at least, because this hardly can be done,

I will consider them as false."[5] One can say: it cannot be done at all, or such a blank can be maintained only with great effort for a few seconds. Man cannot grasp with absolute objectivity physically existing things without implying his personal relatedness to them. Man cannot perceive the thing in itself, only its meaning. Man perceives the alloy of objective and subjective elements blended into an inseparable unity. Any objective definition or description implies, as Freud first recognized, an element of projection out of the totality of the subjective being.

This insight, basic for the understanding of perception, leads back to the starting point, to the understanding of verbal symbolism. The "things" disclose their "being there," but man grasps their mute, unrelated reality, not in an abstract vacuum, but by embedding them in his personal world of memories, emotions and fantasies. Man perceives this outside reality from his own standpoint. The term *river* originally did not refer to the "stream of water" at all. The word derives from the Latin *rīpāria, rīpa*, the "bank," "shore" of the water, as seen in the French-Italian *Riviera*. The word referred originally to the solid ground from which one could observe ·the stream. By *arriving*, from the Latin *ad-ripāre*, one reaches the solid ground.

The linguistic study of symbolism discloses the new concept of man as seen in his creative, reality-transcending capacity. This is the third, perhaps the best, answer to the riddle-question: "What is man?"

THE NORMAL AND THE ABNORMAL

The science of linguistics, just as the grammar of school days, relies upon the tacit supposition that the subject matter of its study is the "normal" language. It considers as normal language that which is spoken and understood by every sound and normal adult; consequently, it discards everything which does not belong to the accepted standard as, for instance, an occasional slip of the tongue, some personal accent or peculiarity in speaking in a given situation. In the same way "general psychology" was intended to be "normal psychology." Its subject matter is the behavior of the sound-minded, healthy individual. Thus, nothing could be more obvious than the axiom—which, however, can be the source of grave errors —that "normal" language has to be understood and interpreted in terms of "normal" behavior.

Relying upon this preconception, one finds oneself confronted with a paradoxical situation. Normal language is a system of symbols that is essentially unconscious. Language is supposed to be acquired in a "normal" way within the community in early childhood; hence, its structure never becomes conscious to the average speaker unless he is a linguist. The normal speaker never becomes aware of the complicated system of verbal forms by which he transforms conceptual and emotional contents into the reality of speech. He only uses language because it works. Moreover, language is the result of imperceptible changes within the language community; consequently, it came into existence by an unconscious process.

To these assumptions, the following interpretation considers verbal phenomena as the result of processes in terms of developmental psychology. This means that all the clear-cut polarities, described in the previous chapters, developed gradually by a slow differentiation, but in the early stages they were still one. At the early stages of development, also in regressed-autistic states, there exists no distinction between sign and symbol, no separation between speaking and thinking, between body and mind, between subject and object, between noncognitive sensation and cognitive perception; there is no distance between the I and the other, between the living organism and the material thing, or between the word and the thing to which it refers. The Ego and the World are still one.

Normality is a questionable concept in linguistics as well as in psychology.[6] One must bear in mind that grammatical concepts are inherited from the Latin Stoic philosophy. This school of thinking considered the imperturbability (*ataraxia*) of the wise man as the supreme good and tried, therefore, to shut out all troubles (*perturbationes animi*) originating from the agitated world with the iron wall of inner equanimity which alone could grant happiness. The Stoic ethics have shaped such words as *a-pathy* (properly "not suffering"), which denote an ideal emotionless state of mind protected against suffering. The word *passion* refers originally to "suffering." It originates from the Latin *passiō, patior, passus,* "to suffer." The same holds true for the German *Leidenschaft,* "passion," derived from the verb *leiden,* "to suffer." The troubles of the world affect the inside peace of mind by *affects* and *emotions.* Therefore, these disturbing forces have to be overcome, as does sickness or a harmful infection. This Stoic philosophy of emotionless apathy remained preserved in the linguistic concept of "normality," which sets, as a norm, the speaking of an imaginary emotionless man. Excluded from consideration remain all the irregularities or difficulties in speech which express some perturbation of the mind.[7] Linguistics relied upon the Stoic concepts with the paradoxical consequence that it considered as "normal" a state of mind which is, in fact, exceptional.[8] Apathy without emotions is an ethical ideal. It never occurs in reality, except in mental cases as a pathological symptom, as the outcome of general paresis. It results in stupor, silence, not in speech. Without the will to speak, there is no speaking, no language. The desire for communication is the basic condition of verbal expression. This primal motive of all verbal activity is not a rational force. It is permeated with irrational motivation, with emotions, with love and hatred of the fellowman to whom speech is addressed.

Language leads not to the normal, but to the abnormal psychology and psychiatry.

Behavioral phenomena generally considered as abnormal belong to man's normal life. Man is normal and abnormal at the same time. The schizophrenic personality displays these daily symptoms in excessive proportions, as if they were observed under a magnifying glass, while the normal one shows the same symptoms in an almost imperceptible degree. The psychology of the normal paid little attention to these symptoms until they were found in exaggerated proportions by psychiatry and psychopathology. Freud made the first positive step in the study of the psychopathology of language.[9] His point was to prove that little errors in pronunciation, a slip of the tongue, failure to recall names, the blending of phonemic patterns, the substitution of one word for another, even for one of opposite meaning—all these generally over-looked phenomena are not haphazard occurrences. They are *symptoms* and thus have meaning, just as the dream is mean-ingful, speaking its own language, which one must try to decipher. These blunders made in speaking cannot be ex-plained on the manifest surface of language, neither can they be understood by the overtly expressed conceptual context. They betray something repressed, a hidden motive which was not permitted by the speaker to be expressed, but which forced its way into speech nonetheless. It is characteristic of these abnormal symptoms which occur in normal speech that they are immediately recognized as blunders and corrected if they are brought to the speaker's attention. In the same way one recognizes dreams as such and separates their nonsensical content, with all their absurdities, from normal waking life. Because errors in speech are recognized and corrected, they do not affect the "inner language." They remain occasional and individual speech events. They do not enter into the field of the linguistic analysis of language.

There is, however, a large group of slips of the tongue

which did not remain individual and singular events, but passed through the needle's eye of social acceptance. Here, the abnormal became normal. The problem is this: why and how did the abnormal change into the normal? What made the pathological generally accepted? What made the difference between the countless cases of mispronunciation and those few cases which became accepted as correct by the whole language community? The following interpretation is interested in pathological phenomena as far as they have propelled their way into the ranks of normality. One may surmise that there are many normal phenomena in language which would be termed pathological if one could see into the privacy of their prehistoric background.

For such reasons it is maintained that the psychological understanding of language necessarily proceeds along the lines of developmental psychology and psychopathology.[10] The mental patient who says "I am mixed up," thus displaying the infusion of one perception into another, who perceives everyday things in a strange light, who translates material connections of cause and effect into retaliatory actions, "eye for eye, tooth for tooth," who behaves like Alexander the Great who, in his anger, scourged the sea because it destroyed his fleet—such mental patients, in their autistic-regressed fantasies, are like children. They are much nearer to the creative process, which shaped and changed our languages, than we are with our common-sense reasoning.[11]

One group of phenomena is almost "normal" in a psychopathological setting, but might become utterly disturbing for those who expect the reflection of proper social behavior in the development of language. These are the manifestations of biological-instinctual nature. Their uninhibited expression is characteristic of the infantile mind, they are common in regressive mental deterioration; by the same token they are prominent in the developmental process of language. Secretory, excretory and sexual functions appear as dominant topics in slang expressions, imprecations. One must be prepared to accept them as a recurrent theme of the early stages of language development, just as they are accepted as symptoms of mental disturbance. It would be an unscientific act to purge our verbal heritage of the improprieties, as some dictionaries do, because they conflict with our standard and proper language. One has to accept such fantasies implied in languages because the "things" perceived in early development appear to be loaded with humanlike vital powers and potentialities, among them with the anxiety arising from the creative and procreative capacity of man.

In order to demonstrate the technique of verbal interpretation, I refer to a recent outstanding piece of clinical work.[12] The case in question is that of a young hysterical woman who was seeking treatment because of her "spells." During these "spells" she "became rigid" and "talked wildly." It turned out, during the initial interview, that although working as a saleswoman, she liked to write and had written "many elaborate novels." (I suppose that she did not succeed in having them published.) Her able analyst did not encourage her writing, but commented with little sympathy that she "was obsessed with an intense ambition to become a famous writer." Here, one can observe a case clearly presented in which the therapist, otherwise an expert in hypnosis and even using hypnosis from time to time as an adjuvant, remained on the manifest surface of the patient's communication and did not grasp the key word *spell*, and did not use it as a leading symbol of his patient's unconscious fantasies. Consequently, he came to the final conclusion that the patient "was attempting to usurp the analyst's position." This interpretation obviously fits the unconscious of the analyst, but does not reflect the unconscious fantasies of the patient. It would be difficult to understand and connect the basic symptoms with one another: (a) "spells," (b) the obsession of creative writing, (c) the "rigidity," (d) "talking wildly." These symptoms somehow hang together on the unconscious level. They make sense, as fragments of a broken vase will become meaningful if one can see them as parts of the whole. I shall try such a reconstruction following the lead of verbal formulations.

1. The *spell*.* The patient emphatically called the onset of a hysterical attack "the spell." Her "spells" are related in her fantasies about "writing," also called *spell-*

---

* See p. 50.

124

ing. The expression *spell-bound* means "fascinated," properly "bewitched." There must be a common underlying fantasy, otherwise such different activities would not be called by the same word. One can see without much linguistics that "writing" is perceived on a regressed level as magic, that is to say that it is rooted in unconscious fantasies. The small child may look at the letters as magic signs. To *dispel* them is the privilege of the father. According to these fantasies, the magic of spelling became equated with the masculine behavior, and this seems to be significant for the understanding of the female patient in question.

2. "Rigidity." This symptom, which appeared during the "spells," confirms the inference of masculine fantasies. A typical fantasy structure is called "the body as phallus," as described in the classic paper by Bertram D. Lewin. The rigidity seems to infect the whole body with erection fantasies.* The blushing of the face may also indicate the presence of this symptom. Following the lead of verbal fantasies, one can add to the description by Lewin that the head was considered to be the seat of sexual power. The men of the early Stone Age and of Greek and Roman antiquity, like headhunters of more recent ages, share this conception. Aristotle believed that the region around the eyes is the "most seedy" (*spermatikō-tatos*). Such body fantasies are implied in the term *cerebrum,* archaic as they may be. They are significant in this case because they explain the following symptom.

3. "Talking wildly." This motive is deeply repressed and can hardly be brought to light without the lead of languages. This "talking wildly" means an outburst of words which occurs in the state of "rigidity" identified with "erection." I recall, in this connection, specifically the equation of "word" and "semen." Writing and speaking were perceived in terms of these body fantasies, *speaking* in particular is considered as *ejaculation.* The symptom of "talking wildly" means the ejaculation of the word-semen in the state of rigidity.†

* See p. 88.
† See pp. 86–93.

As a clinical illustration, I quote the following cases from the paper by Bertram D. Lewin; they shed some light upon the patient in question. "All three patients had a great ambition to write—two were stammerers, all three constantly produced dreams and associations in which they represented the body as a penis and words as a flow from the penis which possessed magical qualities." The "stammering" of the two patients appears in the form of "talking wildly" in the present case, magic in the form of "spells." The "word-seed" is a primordial image of verbal fantasies.

The ejaculation of speech in the state of rigidity, as experienced by the patient during her "spells," is best illustrated by the various terms which, in one way or another, are phonemically related to *to speak,* formerly *to spreak.* The patient is acting out the repressed fantasy about the word-semen, bursting out in "talking wildly." The Greek language is descriptive in this respect. It was mentioned before that the verb *spargaō* means "to be full to bursting, to swell, be ripe, to swell with humors";[*] *spargaomai,* "to burst with noise"; and *speirō,* "to sow seed, beget children, to scatter like seed." These terms, which are related to "speak," describe the masculine "spells," "rigidity" and "talking wildly" of the patient.

The patient also produced some dreams that could be interpreted properly in the light of these verbal fantasies. The dreams recorded seem to confirm this interpretation of the "spells" as the onset of masculine fantasies. The patient expressed in her dreams, through symbolic pictures, her great desire to be cured, to live on a higher plane in a beautiful, harmless society where the women are truly feminine. Thus, she dreams to be "way up high with a beautiful view" or "looking down upon a beautiful scenery." The relief from anxiety is depicted in her dream as a place sheltered and secure. She is in "a hospital bed . . . it's not an ordinary hospital, it seems rather to be a 'nursing home.'" It is a place of *hospitality.* Here she meets nurses: "I see the nurse's face or something . . . and it ought to startle me because her fingertips are

---

* See p. 86.

gone . . . on the first two fingers, down to the second joint . . . and I was going to interrupt and tell the nurse . . . if it is a nurse . . . that part of her fingers are gone . . ." The *nurses* should be understood in the original sense of the word, representing the "nourishing" mother. The nurses do not write; they have no fingers with which to hold the pencil, but they talk. She finishes her dream report by saying: ". . . but I hate to interrupt when they are talking . . . so I don't say anything . . . they are talking pleasantly and I'm comfortable." This "talking" is the opposite of writing, the feminine way of the nurses.

As an illustration of these subtle associations, I quote a few lines from Proust's writing: "a discipline of precision, elegance and applied intelligence controls with the *lightest of light finger touches* . . . the unheard and inner dialogue in the track of which *the pen* follows may fail to operate in conversation as happens inversely in the case of *great talkers* who lose their talent when it comes to writing."[13]

In order to make this verbal interpretation more transparent, I recall Sándor Ferenczi's analysis of the woman with a "masculinity complex."[14] This woman liked to use the pen and to write, as the present patient did, in order to express her masculine strivings. Ferenczi said: "The discoveries made during analysis enabled the patient to estimate her real penchant correctly: she is aware now that she usually seizes her pen when she fears that she cannot function fully as a woman. This analytic experience has assisted not a little in the return of the normal feminine capacity for gratification."

EXPRESSION AND REPRESSION

Every utterance is the summary and result of expressive and repressive forces. These forces work in opposite directions.

There is no speaking without the desire to speak, to express oneself. This desire is basic to human nature; it belongs to its very essence. Emotions are one with their corresponding bodily manifestations. These bodily changes are the physical expression of emotions, their primary symbols. The vocal utterances represent one type of bodily expression. As the reflex of the pupils of the eyes, or as any other facial expression displays an emotional state, so, too, does speaking. These bodily changes are primarily expressions not intended to communicate. The blushing of the face is the reflex expression of an emotional experience, not intended to communicate to others the feeling that one is embarrassed. On the contrary, it works as a vicious cycle. When one perceives that blushing is not merely an expression of embarrassment, but also a communication, this realization increases the disturbance which one would rather keep to oneself and hide from others. Thus, "blushing" has meaning. It speaks its own language and is understood by others against the subject's will. Expression is its primary function; communication is secondary to it. In applying this observation to language, one may state that not all expressions reveal a specific feeling beyond their conceptual content. The feelings of pain or of pleasure, of joy or of sorrow, of elation or of depression want to find expression, but not necessarily communicative expression. It is known that weeping and crying are only half as pleasurable to the child if they are merely an expression and not a communication appreciated by others.

"Expression" is a central concept of symbolic behavior. It refers primarily to the bodily changes of emotions, and thus means the outward visible-audible manifestation of internal events. Expression is an integral part of the emotion itself. Emotions tend to transcend the internal world and be transformed into physical processes. Pain wants to cry out, grief wants to shed tears. Language, however, reaches beyond this display of emotions by shaping the undefined, diffuse sensations, called pre-verbal, into symbols with conceptual content. This is the process by which one separates these feelings from the subjective pole of the self and translates them into an independent objective reality. If one says something, this saying goes out into the world and exists on its own account, independently of the speaker. This reaches to the very core of human existence. Man wants to transcend the subjective limitations of his Self and translate subjective experiences into objective realities. Only then can he grasp this part of his inner Self as any other part of the world. In the same way he will also strive to incorporate his futile sensations and thoughts into objective forms which are lasting and which will remain when the subjective experience has vanished. There is little need for further elaboration of this polarity which marks the very core of human existence. It is the polarity of the subject and the object, the Ego and the World.

In considering language from this point of view, one can understand the significance of Freud's contribution to linguistics. He discovered that bodily symptoms, especially those of hysteria, speak an expressive language, sometimes a peculiar jargon.[15] If emotions, for some reason, cannot find their bodily expression, if they cannot have their due share of the physical reality of speech, they renounce the speech organs altogether and start to use a substitute language. They manifest their presence in bodily changes called "symptom formation." The bodily symptoms have "meaning." They are symbolic expressions. Persons with functional disorders speak an organ language in place of the spoken language because they are prevented from using words. Freud brought psychoanalysis, through this discovery, into the realm of linguistics, although he was not aware of doing so. He called these emotions, which are cut off from physical expression, "strangulated affects," "imprisoned emotions." He discovered in them the very source of disturbance. His supposition was that these pent-up emotions would renounce the use of the jargon of bodily symptoms if they could find their natural symbolic expression through language. The verbalization of unexpressed emotions effects their release. The treatment which psychoanalysis offers to the patient is to make him speak. The name of this verbalization is not important: Breuer termed it "ab-reaction"; others used the terms "to unburden oneself of fantasies," "to let out the emotions," "to release," "to relieve," "to report," "to communicate," "to confess." The meaning is the same: to lead the emotions into verbal channels so that they will not "spill over" into bodily symptoms. The Greek term for this process is *katharsis*. This word properly means "purification, cleansing," and, especially, the discharge of bodily content, excretion or menstrual discharge. Plato and Aristotle used this term to denote the clearing of the mind, especially the clearing effect of the tragedy. Confession is a relief from the pangs of a burdened conscience; this is an age-old experience. One could quote, in this context, Nietzsche, who, long before Breuer and Freud, had a clear insight into the curative value of speech. He said, in one of his many concise formulations: "The man who 'conveys himself' gets rid of himself; who has 'confessed' will forget."

Even though the psychoanalytic verbal technique was called "free association," this term should not detract attention from the basic fact: this "free association" means the verbal expression of emotions. No matter how queer or absurd the conceptual content of this expression, what really counts is the release of never-before-verbalized feelings. These so-called free associations are never "free," are never without the steering will of the patient. This verbalization is never mere expression of emotions, but is conscious communication. Freud tried to diminish the communicative character of this verbalization. He took his seat behind the couch on which the patient lay, so that the patient would not see the analyst and would speak in a monologue, expressing himself. Yet the patient is well aware of the whole situation and knows that he is speaking in order to be understood. Although "free association" was aimed merely to achieve verbal expression, by necessity it became verbal communication. A communication is never "free," as is an expression, but is goal-directed and aimed at the addressed person.

Emotions are not satisfied by mere expression, but want to be communicated. Expression alone is senseless. Man does not speak unless he has an imaginary or real partner. The normal person speaks to someone; the abnormal speaks to no one or to himself. He speaks in monologue, and not in dialogue. His trouble is that he lost the interpersonal quality of verbal communication. Significant as this progress from expression to communication is for clinical practice, one must keep in mind that the interpersonal contact imposes restrictions upon language.[16] In communication one wears a social mask. Man will hide his personal secrets behind the mask. There are indications that even dreams are not simply expression, but are hidden communications addressed to the person who wants to understand them.[17]

That which is possible between the believer and his invisible Lord in the prayer situation is not possible between man and man, not in the clinical situation between the unseen analyst and his patient, despite the supposed transference. One never speaks as "a voice of one crying in the wilderness," nor does one babble like the small child, but one wants to say something to someone. If one sentence is said, a hundred may remain unsaid. Man steers his thinking, selects and rejects expressions in order to reach his goal which is to be understood through what he says. This process of selecting and rejecting, which makes the difference between spontaneous expression and intentional communication, makes "free" association on the couch almost impossible.

Repression, that force which is implied in the idea of a social mask, is a negative force present in all communication. Mere negative forces do not make language. However, behind repression, a positive force is at work, the language Superego built up by educational influences. The Superego, partly conscious, partly unconscious, is primarily an "inner voice," a verbal agency. The auditory sphere has its primacy. It has been demonstrated rather conclusively that the *mother tongue,* with its specific accent, is acquired by internalization, thus is qualitatively different from a foreign language learned during the later years of life. Stuttering and other speech disturbances primarily mar the mother tongue and may not disturb the second language.[18] The reason for this conspicuous symptom is the difference between acquiring the mother tongue, which is involved in all emotional conflicts, and the rational learning of the grammar and vocabulary of foreign languages, which is thus founded upon the conflict-free sphere of the Ego. The classic example which made history in psychology is Breuer's patient, Anna O

> "At first, it was noticed that she 'missed' words (in her German mother tongue); gradually, when this increased, her language was devoid of all grammar, all syntax, to the extent that the whole conjugation of verbs was wrong. Most of the time she utilized an infinitive formed out of a weak past participle, and she never used any articles. In the further course of this development, she missed words almost continuously, and searched for them laboriously in four or five languages, so that one hardly understood her. In March, 1881, the paraphrasia disappeared, but she now spoke only English, seemingly without knowing it, and quarreled with her nurse, who naturally did not understand her. And not until a few months later could I convince her that she spoke English. Yet, she understood her German-speaking environment. In periods of great anxiety she stopped speaking altogether, or she mixed together many idioms. During her best and most lucid hours she spoke either French or Italian. Between those periods and those during which she spoke English, there was a complete amnesia."[19]

The language Superego of Anna O. spoke and understood German, but did not understand English, French, or Italian. The aggressive impulses of the patient were embedded in the German mother tongue. There was an unconscious fight going on in the patient in the German mother tongue, but the Superego could not control the outflow of her impulses in the foreign languages.[20] The Superego wants to be heard. Obedience comes from hearing. The Latin *audīre*, "to hear," has, as a derivative, *ob-oedīre*, "obey," the verb of "obedience." The German *horchen*, "listen," has, as a derivative, *ge-horchen*, "obey." The same relationship exists between the

Greek *akouō*, "to hear," and *hypakouō*, "to obey." Obedience supposes this submissive acceptance of the voice of authority. It permits, only in a restricted way, the free outlet of impulses driving toward expression and communication. Some people who crave love, affection, or appreciation are talkative and communicative almost to the limits of exhibitionism. They want to show themselves, expose their inner secrets. They speak as if in a confessional. On the other side, there are persons who observe restraint in revealing their internal affairs. They are taciturn and impose upon themselves a code that results in silence, rather than in talking. They follow this code with respect to the given external situation, but also with special regard to their own critical conscience shaped by educational influences. If there did not exist a controlling Superego within a speaker, and if the external reality did not impose its curb upon every spoken word, the "Id-language" would come to a free outflow. However, everyone socially educated keeps his "Id-language" under control. He observes taboo avoidances with respect to obscenities, vulgarities, and verbal formulas evoking magical power, such as cursing and swearing. The surprising fact is that this vulgar language kept under control is nevertheless present in the mind of the speaker; although he would never speak this language under normal conditions, he understands it fairly well. Thus he learned it once, probably in early childhood. This layer of language, which normally is not used by the adult, can be termed pre-conscious.

Beyond this layer, however, there exists another layer of a long-forgotten language which is not accessible to the normal speaker. This language may be partly repressed; it is partly an archaic heritage, unconscious by origin; it can be disclosed only by intensive interpretation.[21] This is the "Id-language" proper. I refer to the words of Plato's *Republic*: "When the reasoning, gentle ruling part of the soul is sleeping, a beast-like violent part, full of meat and drink, gets up on its legs . . . and looks for an outlet . . . freed from all control and shame and reason. It does not stop short of attempting in its dreams sex relation with a mother, or with any man, beast or god whatever, it will go for the worst of crimes and eat any sort of unholy food." This gives a fairly complete description of the repressed instinctual forces. It exhibits the resurgence of infantile impulses and fantasies which regularly disappear from the manifest surface of language. This does not mean, however, that they do not exist. They are striving for expression, but are counteracted by the social-educational influences of one's better conscience, the internalized agency of the Superego. In analyzing language, one will be reminded, time and again, that our most sublime tools of thinking and communication are derived from prehistoric sources through an unbroken tradition. The Stone Age man surely did not impose upon himself the same restrictions we are used to. The repressive tendencies emerged gradually in the course of history. They shape and modify only the cultural surface, the social mask, but do not reach to the very core of the language heritage itself. Verbal phenomena on the manifest surface of expression are the outcome of the interaction of antagonistic forces striving to say something and not to say it, to reveal something and to conceal it. While one's better Self observes prohibitions and taboo rules, drives and instincts resort to verbal symptom formation in the search for a permissible outlet. Every utterance represents the final compromise between forces striving for expression and repressive forces. The sound mind acts in obedience to the facts of reality and the claims of morality.

Repression achieves its best results when it succeeds in channeling unrestrained psychic forces into positive cultural values. Negative repression is but a secondary consequence of the positive power working in the human mind. This is man's inborn striving to higher and ever higher values.

Repression, however, would fall short without acknowledging the positive force of sublimation. There is power present —the imperative of the Superego. This power, which permeates thinking as well as language, is the repressive force proper. Veneration, awe, and fear are inseparable from one another. Man's most sublime achievements are motivated not only by fear and anxiety, but also by the desire to transcend his own being.

The effect of repression can be demonstrated best by approaching the topics which are tabooed most in our present society. Life, love, and sex become charged with anxiety and feelings of guilt, especially if they assume an incestuous coloring, yet they refer after all to the positive human strivings which draw people together. They represent the uniting forces which deliver man from the evil of loneliness. For such reasons they were not so strictly tabooed in our cultural setting as those other topics which reveal the negative aspect of life: the separation from the mother, the separation from the body, and the final separation from life which is death. I chose as illustration of the repressive separation anxiety a few examples which refer to the bodily separation through the digestive system. Patients often feel free in talking about their sexual sensations but grow embarrassed while talking about their digestive functions. The final separation from life is still a more embarrassing topic.

Obscene and disgusting fantasies, which became vehemently rejected and repressed by our standards, may still linger in the unconscious reservoir of language. Such fantasies may become attached either to the genital level or they may regress even more frequently to the anal stage of infantile development.

Repressed genital fantasies emerge on the manifest surface of language in such accepted terms as *cock-tail*, *bloody Mary*, *hot dog*. Such genital fantasies, though repressed, might be utilized on the manifest surface of language by trade names of *perfumes* (from *fumus*, "smoke") such as *My Sin* and others. Taste and smell are intimately interrelated.

I chose for interpretation the repressed genital fantasies implied in the preparation of food: the words *bread* and *leaven*. Why was the "leaven," Hebrew *sēor*, strictly forbidden in Old Testament sacrifices? The concept of "leaven" seems to have been equated with corruption and decay, one may surmise, with digestion itself, turning the "good" food into "bad" excrements. "Seven days shall there be no leaven found in your houses: for whosoever eateth that which is leavened, even that soul shall be cut off from the congregation of Israel, whether he be a stranger, or born in the land. Ye shall eat nothing leavened; in all your habitations shall ye eat unleavened bread" (Exodus 12:19-20). One may interpret these prohibitions: the leaven in itself was not so dangerous and defiling, but the repressed fantasies connected with it were.

The "leavening" obviously refers to some internal bodily process. The Hebrew *sēor*, "yeast-cake," is a derivative from the primary root *shā'ar*, "to swell"; by the same token the Latin *fermentum*, from the verb *fermeō, -ēre* meaning "to cause to rise, to swell," also "to sour, to spoil"; *fermentum* can also mean in this sense "corruption." The original implication can be found in the related verb *fervō, -ere*, and *ferveō, -ēre*, "to be boiling hot, ferment, glow"; it can apply also to emotions, "to be violent, furious." The noun *fervor* denotes this "boiling heat, vehemence, ardor, passion." One will not be far from the truth in supposing that the bodily process implied in the fermentation is not simply the digestion of food but impregnation and gestation, the more so because the kneading of the dough in the trough evoked similar fantasies. The "swelling" of the dough in the trough became equated with the bodily process; thus the "yeast" became symbolic of the "semen." The unleavened bread is the virgin bread. It is desexualized and thus fit for religious purposes just as the victim animal of sacrifice became desexualized by castration. This understanding of the "leaven" is supported by the teaching of Christ. He made use of the symbolism of the bread. The "leaven" may mean in His language the "leaven of Pharisees"; this is the "old leaven" Paul was speaking about, but Christ implied a new symbolic meaning in the fertility of the leaven: "Whereunto shall I liken the kingdom of God? It is like leaven, which a woman took and hid in three measures of meal, till the whole was leavened" (Luke 13:20-21). Christ spiritualized the meaning of fermentation. The Greek term *dzumē* for "leaven" is derivative from the verb *dzeō*, "to be hot, to boil of liquids, to glow of solids, be fervid." His teaching was the spiritual fermentation of men. The Germanic languages reflect the same associations. The "old" bread was unleavened. Its name remained preserved in the Old English *hlāf*, English *loaf*, and in such terms as *lord* and *lady*. These terms seem to be symbolic denotations of the marital relationship, much like the Slavic terms which call the man "owner of the fireplace," or to elaborate, where the *loaf* is being prepared: *ogni* means "fire"; *ogniste,* "hearth," and *ogniscaninu,* properly "owner of the fireplace." It became the generic term for "man." The English *lord,* "master, ruler," is beyond doubt a compound form. The Old English *hlāf-ord* seems to derive from a former *hlāf-weard,* "loaf-ward," meaning properly the "guardian of the loaf." This Old English compound has a parallel word in *hord-weard,* "treasure-keeper, guardian." The meaning implied in this case is a question open for discussion. Such question is the more justified since the corresponding *lady* derives from the Old English *hlaef-dige.* The first part of this compound is again *hlāf,* "loaf"; the second part possibly hangs together with *dough* which means to "knead." The realistic interpretation which states that the lord is the provider of bread perhaps fits the concept of the master, but the kneading of the dough does not fit the lady. What kind of marital relationship might be associated with the preparation of the bread, making the man acting as guardian, the woman as kneader? One will surmise, in contradiction to all our best reference dictionaries, that this whole picture language about bread is of the same order as "plowing" is symbolic for the *hus-band* or the fireplace is the property of the owner of the wife.

When fermentation was introduced, the name of the *loaf* changed to *bread,* a noun related to *brew* and *brewing* of beers and ales on the one hand, to *breed, breeding, brood,* Old English *brōd,* on the other. The concepts of *gestation* and *di-gestion* are related in the Latin language as in many other languages.

REPETITION

Repetition is of special interest for the understanding of symbolic behavior. While the interpretations of dreams have to deal with the more or less imperfect verbal report of the dreamer, the repetitive actions appear within the overt behavior during the normal waking life; thus they are accessible for observation and description. They belong to the "normal" behavior, but are also prominent among neurotic symptoms.[22] Every organism tends to settle down after inordinate random performances to an average routine because it is economical, it requires the least effort to do the same thing over and over again. Conditioned behavior is based upon repetition. The neurotic symptoms, however, differ from the daily average rituals. There is a "must" behind them which is not otherwise implied in daily routine actions.

A generally known literary example is the following:

> Lady Macbeth developed the habit of rubbing her hands as if she would wash them. "It is an accustomed action with her," the attendant gentlewoman says, "to seem thus washing her hands: I have known her continue in this a quarter of an hour." On the stage, of course, one can observe Lady Macbeth doing so in a trance of sleepwalking, but one may surmise she makes the same strange movements with her hands several times a day. Shakespeare made it very plain that this frequent rubbing of hands has meaning. Lady Macbeth says, still in her somnambulic delusion: "Yet here's a spot." She still sees, in her delusion, a spot on her hands. "Out! damned spot!

137

out I say! . . . Here's the smell of the blood still: all the perfumes of Arabia will not sweeten this little hand." She helped Macbeth to kill King Duncan. "Yet who would have thought the old man to have had so much blood in him," she says. Thus, the origin of the rubbing of her hands was the shocking experience of having her "little hands" soiled with the blood of the murdered king. She surely washed her "little hands" carefully after the deed, for she wanted to get rid of those painful memories; repression, however, resulted in her case in an obsessive action carried out repetitiously. Her hands are not any longer stained with blood. She does not even wash her hands frequently, but only makes an imitative gesture of handwashing. The gesture is senseless in itself, but in doing so she seeks relief from a tension which remained with her.

Upon investigating further into this imaginary handwashing, according to languages, two associations may have helped to develop this individual gesture. One is the fantasy that sin or guilt is a "stain." The other is the horror implied in the British speaker by the word *bloody*. A "bloody stain" must have been charged with anxiety, indeed. In the Greek language *miasma* means "stain, defilement, especially by murder or any foul crime; the taint of guilt." The relative adjective is *miaros*, "stained with blood," "defiled with blood." The relative verb *miainō* means "to stain, to dye," as well as "to pollute, especially by great crimes as murder." The Greek language made the abstract idea of sin or guilt concrete by visualizing the blood upon the hands of the murderer. In Latin, *macula* means a "mark" on the skin, a birthmark which cannot be removed, but it means also, in the moral sense, "blemish"; the corresponding verb *maculāre* means "to soil." All the expiatory and piacularly actions performed for the undoing of the committed crime come under the notion of *lustrum*, from the verb *lustrāre* which means "cleansing." The idea of the "cleansing of sin" suggests that sin is a stain which can or cannot be washed away. Lady Macbeth's obsession is not just an individual case. Her fantasies speak the same unconscious language which has been elaborated by spoken languages.

"I wash my hands" carries a moral implication. "When Pilate saw that he could prevail nothing, but that rather a tumult was made, he took water, and washed his hands before the multitude, saying: I am innocent of the blood of this just person" (Matthew 27:24). In this case the handwashing is an expressive symbolic gesture, yet its source is the same as that of Lady Macbeth's obsession.

Handwashing is in itself a normal performance. It is not easy to draw the proper borderline between the normal act and the obsessive one. The reason for obsessive repetition is, as a rule, not so overt and plain as in Shakespeare's literary example. In clinical cases the reason is usually unknown to the subject. The individual himself realizes, for the most part, that the whole performance is senseless, yet he feels some compulsion, foreign to his Ego, to repeat it over and over again. The obsessive character of repetition is marked by its rigidity. It must be carried out in exactly the same way each time, for otherwise the anxiety which is implied in it would increase rather than diminish.

The word *bloody* illustrates the same mental operation on the verbal level.* The blood was tabooed for many reasons. It became an object of sacral ritual. Contact with it was carefully avoided in normal daily life. The word became a tabooed word, especially difficult for the educated British speaker to utter. Repression of the repudiated meaning resulted, however, in its obsessive repetition. A word which should never be used "in vain" became used most frequently in low colloquial cant. It has lost its meaning in such expressions as *bloody hungry, bloody tired, bloody expensive, bloody far.* It is practically void of meaning, just as is the obsessive handwashing gesture of Lady Macbeth, but in using this word, the speaker seeks some relief from a tension. When the original meaning became repressed, the word remained without conceptual content, but kept something of its original emotional intensity. By being added to another word, it acts as an intensifier, one that is a bit stronger than *very.* It imparts, by virtue of its emotional force, an expressiveness to

---

* See pp. 181, 218.

the word to which it is attached. The same applies to the word *lot*.

Originally, *lot* denoted a sacral cultic object, feared and venerated at the same time, subject to vigorous repression.* However, it was not obliterated from language, but the sacral meaning was forgotten. As a consequence of this repression, the word came to be used most frequently in such expressions as a *lot of work, a lot better, a lot more*. It intensifies the word to which it is attached. The intensifying words often display the same phenomenon: some nouns, formerly feared and carefully avoided, reappear after repression on the surface of language with the function of making a weak expression "strong." The word *awful* is typical in this respect. *Awe* originally denoted the ambivalent mixture of fear and veneration that lies at the root of "taboo."[23] It describes man's feelings toward the numen. Instead of being avoided and excluded from everyday language because it pertained to the sacral sphere, it became used frequently in profane language as an intensifier. The same holds true for *terrific*.

This preliminary consideration of verbal examples will explain the impact of obsessive repetition upon language. It has been pointed out that "psychiatrists, neurologists, endocrinologists, neurosurgeons, and psychoanalysts have all been groping toward a realization of the fact that the nucleus in the neurosis is the repetitiveness of its phenomena, and that the protean manifestations of the central neurotic process are relatively of secondary importance."[24]

Repetitiveness is the nuclear phenomenon in language, too. This idea will help to draw a clear dividing line between the psychological interpretation, on the one hand, and, on the other hand, the statistical-mechanical approach. The frequency of some words or of parts of them has been observed and described—the more so since this "distribution" can be exactly measured and counted. However, mere counting does not explain the reason of repetition. While, in the descriptive sense, the frequent occurrence of a verbal phenomenon is considered to be the cause, it seems to me that it is the consequence of an energy which drives the speaker to repetition. That the word *bloody* lost its original conceptual content and

---

* See pp. 193–195.

became a meaningless intensifier is not the consequence of being used frequently, but, on the contrary, the result of the repression of its original and anxiety-filled meaning. This is the way with most taboo prohibitions. The complementary phenomenon of *taboo* avoidance is the *noa* (properly *noa-noa*), which denotes a most common and general occurrence. One may state that there is no taboo without the repetitive and meaningless use of the repressed. The prohibition came first; the repetition is secondary to it. Swearing and cursing were once magic religious rituals, thus tabooed and prohibited. They became repetitive actions on account of the repressive anxiety invested in their meaning. The worst imprecations in the Old Testament and those in vulgar use in all languages reveal the basic topics of anxiety hidden in unconscious fantasies since prehistoric ages.

In descriptive linguistics two elements can be distinguished in every utterance. On the one hand, there are independent words, nouns, proper names, called *autosemantica*. On the other hand, one can find verbal elements, *synsemantica*, which cannot be used independently. Once, the Latin grammar made a similar distinction, erroneously classifying "vowels" and "con-sonants." This distinction was first introduced by the inaugurator of descriptive linguistics, Anton Marty.[25] This is a logical separation of two categories of verbal expression, which does not take into account the psychological implications. The synsemantic elements are more frequently used than the nouns, but one may ask why some words are used independently, while others make sense only in dependent positions in connection with other words. In the former examples it was observed that *blood* and *lot* were independent nouns; after repression took place both lost their autosemantic character and were declassified into synsemantica, transferred from the vocabulary proper to the grammar. These words have no meaning any longer, only a function. The process of repression produced functional elements of grammar in these cases.

Besides the verbs proper, there exists the grammatical category of the so-called auxiliary verbs used in connection with other autosemantic verbs as synsemantica; consequently, they are used frequently. It seems obvious that in such instances as *I have written, I have been writing*, the auxiliaries *have* and *been* are used more frequently than the verb proper. Let

us first consider in this group, as an example, the verb *to get*.
It is used in a synsemantic position, ranks high in frequency,
especially in vulgar language. One must notice, however, that
at one time this vulgar language was the only one. This verb
has reached the state of being void of any meaning; it functions only as a grammatical auxiliary intensifying another
verb. In such formulas as *he has got to write*, instead of *he
has to write*, the verb *got* does not carry any express meaning;
it is inserted, however, in order to release some tension in the
speaker by making the whole expression more intensive. One
may ask what is the driving power behind the repetition in
vulgar language of just this one verb, as in the formula *he has
got to get*. The frequency of usage is not the reason for the
loss of the original lexical meaning, but its consequence. The
driving motive of repetition cannot be found in the manifest
content, but in the latent meaning. The original meaning was
"to procreate," as still preserved in *be-get; get* as a noun
means, in obsolete language, "child." The original concept was
charged with anxiety, therefore it became repressed and
obliterated from the manifest surface of speech. The word
lost, however, only its notional concept, not the emotional
intensity invested in it. It still can release some of its energy
and impart it to another weaker verb with which it is
connected.

The most common synsemantic verbs among all verbs are
to be and *to have,* in German *sein* and *haben,* in French *être*
and *avoir.*

The verb *to be* holds a unique position in the whole
vocabulary. While words denote various things which
exist or are, the verb *to be* denotes existence itself. It
denotes something primordial and universal which is
underlying all other partial existences. It is not just one
of the many concepts, but the most fundamental of all
concepts. How does language approach this presupposi-
tion of all existing things?

At first glance one perceives that this most important
of all verbs is called "irregular" in grammar because three
different verbs became united into one paradigm: (a)
am, are, is; (b) *was, were;* (c) *be, being, been.* Similar
combinations of different verbs for denoting "existence"

are found in all related languages. This proves that "being" was once experienced so much in its specific concrete immediacy that its different modalities were denoted by different verbs. Man has lost his original relationship with "being" which was still alive in pristine ages and sees now only a whimsical irregularity of grammar.

Things which man watched closely and felt to be important were always perceived in their singularity; consequently, they could not be classified into a common category. For instance, "brother" and "sister" had no common name in English. They were felt to be two disparate concepts which could not be grouped together as has been recently done, calling them "siblings" like the German *Geschwister*. Many languages have no word for "parents" because "father" and "mother" were too different to be united by one word. While we say "camel," the Arabs use a quantity of words to denote the varieties of the "camel." In our culture the domesticated animals were closely watched and specified as "bull," "ox," "cow," "heifer," "calf," "cattle," and so on. The same holds true for the most immediate experience of "being." One may say, with some gross simplification, that "to be" in the present, in the past, and in the future were felt as qualitatively incongruous modalities of existence, therefore, they could not be brought under the same verbal denominator. We have no difficulty with "write," "wrote," "written," "writing," using one verbal form, but this was not the case with "I am," "I was," and "I shall be."

Beyond this implication of present, past and future, the own existence, subjectively experienced, was also qualitatively different from the objectively perceived existence of others. For this reason the *I am* is separated from the *he, she, it is*. Similarly, the Latin *sum* and *est*, French *je suis* and *il est*, or Old English *beō*, "I am," and *is*, German *ich bin* and *er ist* are clearly differentiated forms. *I am* denotes an essentially different experience of being than "he is." One can also observe that all these verbs are "defective," which is a characteristic symptom of repression. The verbs are used frequently; their numerical distribution index is high. Yet despite the repetitious usage, the verbs became empty vehicles. They carry no meaning. If they had one in the past, this meaning became obliterated to such an extent that these verbal forms now serve only in the grammatical function of a "copula" connecting subject and predicate. What does the verb "is" actually mean in a sentence "the house *is* new"? Many languages, for instance the Semitic or the Hungarian, can do without it. They simply state: "the house new." This "is" made world history in religious disputes. Anxiety eroded the essential meaning. The repressive anxiety was the primary anxiety underlying all other anxieties; this was the ultimate concern about "to be or not to be." The idea of "being" is inseparable from its opposite. Man can think of it only in contrast to the abyss of "non-being," the Nothing. But man did not think in the abstract at early ages. He thought in symbols. He could not conceive of the primary idea of "being" other than in symbolic terms of already existing beings. "To be" is, in his thinking, inseparable from "to be alive," to live with all the concrete manifestations and modalities of live, to be born, to grow, to proliferate, and to die. Repressive anxiety blocked out not only the meaning and the basic forms of these verbs, but asserted its power through the repetitious usage.

The positive and clear assertion of "being" is *I am*. The present being is complete in itself. It has no room for past or future. It is timeless. In this ideal sense Parmenides understood *ōn*, "being," but one may state that such ideal "being" which is not affected by that which has been or by that which will become never happens in psychological reality. The "I am" in its perfection is stated in the Old Testament when the Lord "said unto Moses: I Am That I Am" (Exodus 3:14). This is not the exact translation of the Hebrew original, which implies futurity, "I shall be,"* or perhaps causation, but it nevertheless points to the fact that the "I am" cannot be

---

* The proper interpretation of the enigmatic "I Am That I Am" is perhaps "He causes to be what comes into existence." The Creator personifies all becoming. See William Foxwell Albright, *From the Stone Age to Christianity: Monotheism and the Historical Process* (Garden City, N. Y.: Doubleday, Anchor Books, 1957), p. 261.

translated into "he is." The Israelite God, as I Am, is complete in himself, has no father and no son. This *I am* is, as Descartes said, the rock-bottom, *fundamentum inconcussum,* the primary proposition, *propositio prima,* of all further propositions. This most important verb of all verbs became a defective, almost meaningless functional element of grammar.

Different from the present being *I am, it is* is the past *I was, it was.* It is another verb and another concept. It refers not to being, but to that which has been, that which does not exist anymore, thus, it refers to non-being. If we say there is no presence without a past implied, there is no *I am* without *I was,* which means, in other words, there is no "being" without the implication of "non-being." The verbal symbols which describe this *I am* with the implication of the past point, in Germanic languages, to "dwelling, abiding," to something that remains. The "house" became the symbol of being with the implication of "has been." In English, one can observe, even in present-day language, the tendency to make an equation between "to dwell" and "to live." One says "he lives in New York," not "he dwells in New York." What might be the reason that living and dwelling mean the same thing? Common-sense realism is always at hand; however, such explanations do not reach to the point where to be alive means to dwell in the house. This is the case, however, if these words are understood as symbols, if the "house" is perceived as the symbol of "mother." In pre-natal states, "to dwell" and "to live" are indeed inseparable from one another. The "house of being" (Heidegger) unites past, present, and future. One can still trace, in the distant related languages, the original meaning of English *was* and *were,* German *war,* "was," and *gewesen,* "been," with the noun *Wesen,* "essence, being." The corresponding Sanskrit verb is *vasati,* "he dwells"; the Sanskrit noun *vastu* means "house," much like the English *to abide* and *abode.* This "being," as "housing," "dwelling," "abiding" and "be alive," must once have been felt in its actual reality. For instance, it is said: "And Enoch walked with God: and he *was not*; for God took him"

146

(Genesis 5:24). In this case the *was not* clearly means disappearance. He did not exist anymore.

In English, a term for "abiding," "dwelling," is *to stay*. It is the symbolic term for the opposite of "moving" or "changing." It describes a modality of "being" in reference to past and future in spatial terms. It means to *withstand* against the rush of time. It points to the lasting moment in all changes as petrified in the presence, *existing*, from *ex-sistere*, properly "to make to stand out," at the same time *re-sisting*, properly "make to stand back," also *per-sisting*, "make to stand through" all motions and changes. The Latin *stāre*, "to stand," developed as a past tense into the French *été*, Spanish *estado*.

The third verb, *to be, been*, denotes in English the generic concept of *being*. The verb also survived in Old English in *beom*, "I am," in German as *ich bin*, "I am," *du bist*, "thou art." The lost implication of "becoming" can be traced in the related forms in Greek, Latin, and other languages. The Greek *phuō* means "to bring forth, produce, put forth; to beget, engender, generate"; in the passive "to grow, spring up, arise, come into being." The Greek *phusis* denotes "nature" conceived as the generating, moving power, as in *physics*. The word *phuton* means that which has grown in a natural way, "plant, descendant, child." It denotes everything "swelling" like an ulcer, "growing" and increasing. The whole word complex, with many related forms in other languages, refers to the natural process of fertility, proliferation, procreation, tumescence, swelling, to come into existence. All these notions are symbolic representations of the primary process as to be alive. "Being" is understood in this aspect in the image of the own body.

It is probable, though not provable, that the Greek *phuō* was interconnected in the earliest ages with *phainō*, "to bring to light, make to appear; to make known, reveal, disclose"; in the passive "to come to light, appear, to be seen." If this relationship of the two verbs is a genuine one, the concept of "to be" was originally equivalent with "to appear." In the early ages no differentiation was made between true being and outside appearance. The Greek thinking was conceived in the world of light, in

discloses its meaning in the world of light.[28] This interpretation, however, does not account for the fact that the verb *to exist* did not follow the way of *re-sist, per-sist, con-sist,* which are characteristic of the "being as essence," but joined the words for "becoming," "growing," "fertility" and "procreating." To exist, in its original meaning as "made to be standing out," fits the biological aspect of "being." The present reality of this being is pointed out by the French term for the present: *main-tenant* "now," properly "to be held in the hand." The "outstanding" reality of being as becoming can be grasped with the hand. The Greek term for "to become," *gignomai,* later *ginomai,* originally meant "to be born." In German *entstehen,* "to rise into erect position," assumed the meaning of "arise, become."

The other auxiliary verb most frequently used is *to have,* German *haben,* French *avoir.* This verb does not denote being in general, but indicates a specific mode of it as "being in possession" of something.[29] The old forms denoted this modality of being simply in spatial terms as "being with" or "being to," like the biblical "peace *be unto* thee" or "peace be *with thee*" (Judges 6:23, 19:20). These forms became replaced later by "have peace." In Greek *moi esti* and in Latin *mihi est* simply mean "I have."

The nearest and most perfect "being with" or "to have" is the possession of the own body-self. This is called in English *to be-have.* Thus, *be-havior,* a hybrid form of "behave," and the French *avoir* mean, in this understanding, not simply "to have" something, but emphatically to "be-have" it thoroughly, to be in full possession of the own self. The primary possession among all things man has is the possession of his own body alive. The English language expressed by this one word that which otherwise has been described in philosophical circumlocution, for instance, in the German language as "to be-in-itself-for-itself." A rock or a tree exists in itself, but man alone exists also for himself. He knows about his own existence. Knowledge is a kind of acquisition. Man *has* himself because he knows that he exists. "Behavior," in its original sense, is a specific human characteristic. It supposes the awareness of the own existence. The word lost much of its full meaning when it became applied to animals which do exist, but do not truly "behave" because they are not in the full possession of their own existence.

Possession, as "having" something, appears in two different relationships between the owner and the owned. One relationship supposes creation; the other acquisition. Creation establishes the primary possession. Man owns, first of all, his own creation. Acquisition does not supersede it. An artist, for instance, is the owner of his work, whosoever may acquire it. In early ages the father owned his children because they were considered to be his creation. He also owned women and slaves by acquisition. He bought them. Acquisition implies the aggressive act, "to grasp," "take hold," "to know" someone or something. The aggressive component of "to have" is brought out clearly by the corresponding forms of the related languages. The English *to have* does not derive directly from the Latin *habeō, -ēre*, "to hold," also "to dwell," as in *habitō, -āre*. The tenant, from the Latin *tenō, -ere*, "to hold," is a "habitant." The primary "holding" is, once more, the own self. Thus, *habitus, ūs* and *habitudō, -inis* denote how one "holds" his own body, thus "appearance," which, however, is expressive of moral qualities. The German equivalent term is *Haltung*, "comfort"; *Körperhaltung*, properly "body-holding," refers to the body posture and appearance. The French *avoir* derives from this Latin verb "to hold" which is symbolic of possession.

The English *to have* and the German *haben* perceive this "holding" of the possession in the dynamic aspect "to take hold," "to grasp," "seize," which is denoted in Latin by *capiō, -ere, cēpi, captum*. What made this verb into a synsemantic grammatical function used frequently as in "I *have* written," "I *had* written," "I *have to* write"? One will not be far from the truth by pointing at the aggressive component as the same power which destroyed most forms of *to be*. The verbs *to be* and *to have*, also *to get*, indicate that the notion "to have, to possess" primarily referred to human relationships. It implied "to make, create, generate" which underlies the idea of "being as becoming." The creative act makes the creator the sovereign owner and master of his creation. It denotes, at the same time, to bring and rise into "existence," to become. "To be" and "to have" are, for this reason, interconnected with one another.

"Being," for the reflective mind, seldom appears as in "it is," stating the here and now of a present essence. The positive modality says "it must be," "it is by necessity." On the negative side, the "it is" can be restricted by the "perhaps," "it is probable," in a lesser degree "it is possible," still lesser "it is improbable," and the final negative statement, the opposite of "necessity," says: "it is impossible, it cannot be." These objective modes of existence, with various admixtures of nonexistence, are experienced in the subjective sphere as "I will," "I may," "I must," "I can," "I should," with all their negative forms.

It is a conspicuous quality of these verbs that they are termed by the descriptive grammar as irregular. With regard to the frequency of these irregular verbs which denote various modalities of existence, one can observe, once more, the work of a repressive power. Some strong unconscious motivation cut out all the present tenses of these verbs. The present "essent," the *it is,* shows the meaning of "being" in its clearest form; it arose from the basic anxiety of being and not being. This process of the obliteration of all present tenses began in pre-Germanic ages. A verb deprived of the present tense of its actual meaning is defective indeed. It is only the shadow of its full meaning. Through this decapitation the verbs lost their one-time independence; they became auxiliaries, synsemantica. They attach themselves to other verbs which have a substantial independent meaning. They modify the meaning of other verbs describing various positive forms of existence, of doing or suffering, of various activities, but have no concrete meaning of their own. This loss, however, is compensated by the frequency of usage.

Repression resulting in repetition can be observed in many formative elements of languages. The English -*ing,* a most frequent formative element, was originally the name of *Yng,* the German Dionysus, a most holy taboo

word.[30]* The English *thing* was also a numinous taboo.
It occurs on a Roman-Germanic altar inscription: the
altar has been dedicated to *Mars Thingsus,* to the god
Mars with a "thing."[31] The Roman god Mars was a god
of war; in peacetime he was the god of agriculture and
fertility. Now we say *some-thing, every-thing, any-thing,
no-thing.* The word simply became a form void of meaning. Suffixes such as *-ship* (friendship), *-hood* (man-hood,
child-hood), *-head* (god-head), and so on, present plenty
of opportunities for intensive analysis of the repressed
meanings. I do not suppose, however, that all these words
came about in such a way that, to a basic nominal concept, a modifying ending was added. Sound associations
and rhyme words which form together a coherent verbal
complex point toward another interpretation. It is to the
credit of the great linguist A. Ludwig that he first discovered the principle of "adaptation" in the formative
processes of languages.† Instead of an agglutinative

---

* The Gothic tribe shows no evidence of Yngvi-Frey cult. It is
also a conspicuous fact that the suffix *-inga* is also absent in the
Gothic language while it is the most productive suffix in the other
Germanic languages. See Friedrich Kluge, *Nominale Stammbildungslehre der altgermanischen Dialekte* (Halle: Niemeyer, 1926),
p. 3. Also *The Subconscious Language,* p. 214.

† The theory of linguistic adaptation was first developed by the
great linguist K. Ludwig, 1867, but it remained unnoticed until
the leading American linguist Maurice Bloomfield pointed out
its fundamental importance for the understanding of languages.[32]
Ludwig illustrated his theory on Sanskrit material; Maurice Bloomfield, then Hanns Oertel and Edward P. Morris applied it to the
Greek and Latin languages.[33] Maurice Bloomfield said: "Every
word, insofar as it is semantically expressive, may establish by
haphazard favoritism, a union between its meaning and of its
sounds, and then send forth this sound, or sounds, upon predatory
expeditions into domains where the sound is at first a stranger and
parasite." He clearly realized that "the question as to how much
plasticity may have been imparted to the lexical value of words
with meanings not too far removed which hover over them would
form one of the most fruitful and profound investigations in linguistic history" (p. 409). This eminent empirical linguist wrote
these words years before Freud published his *Interpretation of
Dreams.* He came very near to the basic ideas of understanding
unconscious processes.

process, one word or another carried, so to say, a magnetic power and attracted many other words into their sound-meaning association. This attracting power in some words derived from the repressed desire invested in their meanings. These were "charged" words; they emanated their emotional stress and forced other words to adapt themselves into the same sound-meaning complex. The new words which have thus been attracted are not formed by individual agglutination but are brought into a "congeneric" association with the whole complex in sound and meaning.*

A typical case is the concept of *body*. It goes without saying that the human body as a whole is taboo. Moreover, "strictly speaking the body as a whole is an erotogenic zone." The word "body" also came under taboo restriction because it denoted a dead body, a corpse, and thus was associated with "death." This avoidance may be the reason that the biblical Hebrew has no word for "body." One cannot suppose that such a highly developed language community had no notion of the human body as a whole, and yet the Hebrew language avoided calling it by name. In Greek, *sōma*, "body," and *ptōma*, "corpse," form a conspicuous verbal complex. The equivalent Germanic term is the Old English *līc*, "body" (a living as well as a dead one), and the Germanic term is *Leich-nam*,

---

* The basic ideas of K. Ludwig, Maurice Bloomfield, Hanns Oertel and Edward Morris were later elaborated on by the linguist F. A. Woods.[34] He stated: "Equally active with the rime-element in the formation of words is the rime-idea. The rime-element fixes the outward form, the rime-idea the inward meaning. The one gives the word the body, the other the soul. And as words may be cognate in form and yet unrelated in meaning, so they may be kindred in meaning though alien in form. In one case they rime to the ear, in the other to the mind . . . if, however, words fall together in meaning, they will have the tendency to be assimilated in form if they are somewhat alike."

A specific study along these lines was made by Edmund D. Cressmann.[35] He said that he wanted "to examine certain word-building suffixes for the purpose of finding out if possible what the force of the suffixes themselves is and how the nouns formed with them get their meaning" (p. 52). In 1914 Hermann Güntert gave a comprehensive presentation of this problem.[36]

"corpse, carcass" (English *lich*). Repression wiped out the primary concrete meaning and developed, instead, more pleasant meanings, such as the adjective *like*, "similar," the verb *to like*, "to be fond of," *to liken, like-ness, likely*. It is another question as to how these meanings are related to one another and, especially, why one *likes* that which is *a-like*. This highly tabooed word is used most frequently with, so to say, cleansed meanings, not only in independent words, but also as the suffix *-like*, as *home-like, child-like*. This still transparent suffix carried a strong stimulus for repetition, for in the form *-ly* it became the most frequently used formative, repeating again and again the once tabooed concept of "body" in adjectives, adverbs and pronouns. The German *-lich* developed in a similar way. The almost infinite class of words ending with *-ly*, however, did not come about by individual agglutinations with the repressed meaning of "body," but by the adaptation of new words to an established complex of words which all had the same ending. The tendency to bring into a rhyming sound association the grammatical congruence or the coherence of meaning resulted in this adaptation of "weaker" words to those with stronger emotional intensity. Repetition was, in this case, the formative principle of language.

Repetition results in the formation of verbal patterns and formulas, just as the obsessive repetition of a performance may result in "ritual" in the sphere of religion.[37] Language as a whole is much like a ritualistic religion. It is a system of patterns and formulas, all charged with emotions. The gradual shaping and re-shaping of verbal formulas, an unconscious process, is the very essence of the primary language process. Repression is the dynamic power driving toward and creating ever new stereotypes in language. These formal elements can be, just as in any ritual or other social performance, classified into two categories. The formulas are either structural or empirical. They are structural if the sequence of element is constant; they are empirical if, beyond the sequence, the content also became definitely fixed. A structural formula is a pattern of word order, in Latin the accusative with infinitive. While the structural formulas permit more or less free choice for individual elaboration within the frame of a bound sequence, the empirical formula, for instance, this sentence structure, *How do you do?*, can only be repeated verbatim. The vulgar and common language is formalistic, repeating the same vocabulary, the same speech patterns over and over again. It is, in this respect, much like the epic style of Homer. Language, in its primitive manifestation, is not at all "free prose" as it is understood in our age, but appears to be bound by formulas, stereotypes, and fixed colloquialisms. The most primitive ritual texts display rigid formalism. The formulas have often become devoid of meaning to the speaker, yet not a syllable can be changed, for otherwise the whole ritual would lose its sacral and spiritual power.

Speaking in direct quotations of recurrent formulas is characteristic of the low, the primitive, and the ritualistic way of expression. Messages in the Old Testament, just as in Homer, are conveyed not in their essence as indirect speech, but as direct quotation, verbatim, however long they may be. A dialogue is reported not in its outcome, but in its full length as "I told him . . ." and "He told me . . ." always quoting the speaker verbatim. Repetition is not avoided; on the contrary, it makes the oral text stick in the memory. This concrete adherence to words, resulting in repetition, is also characteristic of the neurotic estrangement from one's own mother tongue. Unconscious fantasies, notion pictures, are pre-verbal by their very nature, so one may expect that they will drive the speaker to unprecedented innovations in expressing sensations never before named. In fact, schizophrenics are often neologists. They seem to create a language of their own; they speak so-called word salad. But there is no expression without repression, without repetition. The lowest layer of language (one may call it the language of the Id), this immediate outflow of the unconscious, is built upon stereotypes and formulas. The unconscious is, in this respect, extremely conservative and it adheres to firmly established patterns. Nature manifests itself in patterns. The so-called collective unconscious consists of just such repetitious formulas. The Greek Tartarus, the Netherworld, which gives a dramatic picture of the unconscious, looks much like a mental asylum. There is Tantalus, who stands in water which always dries up when he wants to drink. He tries to pluck fruit from the tree, but the branch always snatches the fruit away at the last moment. He must repeat the same action again and again forever. In another record he is doomed to stay under a rock which is about to fall upon him at any moment, but never does; thus he suffers eternal anxiety. There is Gknos, the man who eternally twines one end of a rope, while a she-ass continually eats up the other end of the same rope. Sisyphus forever rolls a heavy stone uphill, but when he reaches the top, the stone rolls down again. The endless repetition of the same act is the distinctive feature of all those doomed to the Netherworld. All psychic activity and cultural progress are based upon repetition. However, there still remains a distinction between the obsessive and the normal repetition. The most immediate outlet of the unconscious language, such as exclamatory interjections, vocatives, imperatives, demonstratives, *this* and *that*, *yes* and *no*, questions, answers, cursing, blessing, greeting, counting—all run along strictly fixed stereotypes which can be repeated, never created.

This primary layer of verbal formulas is learned first and will remain longest with the patient even in serious mental deterioration.

The neurotic escape into formulas can be observed best if a beginner in a foreign language is exposed to a frustrating speech situation which he cannot master. He will then resort to ready-made sentence patterns which he remembers and will try to avoid the dangers and difficulties arising from individual sentence construction. He will renounce personal communication and hide behind depersonalized formulas. In the same way neurotics avoid dangerous speech situations. *Idiotism* denotes the individual speech in both senses—as constant formula and as mental deficiency. The empirical formula is necessarily a depersonalized expression. It corresponds best to the depersonalization of the neurotic individual.

Idiomatic and proverbial formulas—empirical sentence structures—display the same symptoms found previously in isolated words. Repetition is, in this case, also correlative with repression. After repression has taken place, there remains an almost senseless truism, a declarative statement about a platitude which means nothing. The repetition of such proverbs can be as senseless as the hand-washing of Lady Macbeth. *How do you do?* no longer means what is actually being asked. In quoting such sentence formulas, one is speaking without saying anything. It may be useful for hiding, as behind a mask, one's true personality.

PROJECTION

Since Freud introduced the concept of "projection," this idea has grown into the discipline of projective psychology.[38] It is a concept basic for the understanding of language.

"Projection" modifies perception through memories of previous experiences. Through the projection of a memory image upon a new sensation, this sensation becomes meaningful. It becomes perception. The lack of perception despite sensation is pointed out by these biblical words: "that seeing they may see, and not perceive; and hearing they may hear, and not understand" (Mark 4:12). The picture of the world a person carries in his Self is never an objective recording, but the assimilation and integration of this recording into his personal world. This makes the essential difference between man and man. It is the kind of world man carries in his mind and into which he assimilates new impressions.

It should be noticed in this connection that the words *conscience*, *conscious*, and *consciousness* suppose this basic understanding of man. The underlying idea is "knowing together," from the Latin *con*, "together," and *sciens*, "knowing." One may readily ask, "Together with whom?" The answer might be the inside image together with the outside perception. All experienced knowledge is shaped, colored, selected, and modified by each individual in his own way. This means the personality as a whole is present in the picture of the world. If one prefers to call this out-reaching of the Ego upon the world "transcendence," one may state that the great mission of psychology is to find out just what makes the crucial difference between the normal transcendence and the abnormal one.

There is always implicated in this differentiation the basic dichotomy between the Ego and the World. This polarity is involved in all analytic understanding of language.

The fusion of object perception with unconscious fantasies was an active force in shaping the system of symbols developed as language. One can demonstrate best the operation of projection in language in the assimilation of foreign words into English. The foreign words undergo a change when they become assimilated into the English system. This change may affect the phonemic pattern as well as the meaning.

As an example, the word *orange* may serve the purpose. This fruit was once something unknown, nameless, for the Old English language community. Its Persian original is *narang*, in Arabic *naranj*. In Spanish and in many other languages *naranja* has been accepted as the proper form of the name. In other Romance languages, however, *auranja, orenge,* is the form. Those who prefer a formal explanation may state that this is a mere change of word borderlines because *un (n)auranja* became assimilated as *un auranja*. But, if one supposes that even such a slight misperception of the foreign word has some psychological reason, one will find that the Latin *aurum*, "gold," continued in late Latin in *aur* and the French *or*, interfered with the new concept. The color of the fruit may have actualized this association with the "golden apples," an old and widespread mythological fantasy, elaborated in the Greek myth about the golden apples which grew in the garden of the Hesperides. Such motives made Goethe speak in German about *die Gold-Orangen*, "the golden oranges," or suggested the trade name *Sunkist*, "sun kissed," for the oranges of the Gold Coast.

In such cases as the above examples, it seems that not simply an individual is speaking the language, but an archaic heritage is speaking through the individual. Being confronted with a resurgence of age-old mythical fantasies within the process of perception, one no longer feels sure that simply the memories of previous experiences modify objective perceptions. These "previous experiences" might have been modified by motives which reach beyond the individual.

The assimilative process in language was formerly called "folk etymology." This term, however, rather rationalized than explained the underlying process. This amalgamation of an old concept with a new one into an alloy is a continuous ever-recurring phenomenon in changing meanings. Through the endless chain of oral transmission which connects the pre-historic past with the present, language has been transmitted from man to man, from generation to generation, from mother to child. Each new speaker translates the newly acquired language into his own world, adding a slight change to the accepted common lore. Language is the collective work of millennia. It shows the results of a cumulative process of projection within the succession of countless generations.

The slight changes which each individual introduces in his speech do not change the language as a whole. However, language is always in a state of slow and gradual change. This change is imperceptible to the individual concerned. We speak our language as if it had always been the same and would always remain the same as spoken by the present generation. Stability is an imperative for all communication. Grammar, teaching, tradition, language authorities, literacy, all work together to promote unity and stability in language. Language changes, nevertheless. The Superego in language is the conservative power. Changes in language are brought about in defiance of this Superego by unconscious forces. A look into the King James version of the Bible, into Shakespeare, into Chaucer's Middle English, and then into an Old English text will make everyone aware of how thoroughly the English language has changed in the course of a few centuries. This total transformation came about as the cumulative result of subtle individual variations. It worked much like erosion in nature. One drop of water does not change anything as far as man can see, but a dripping and trickling through the ages may alter the course of a river. There can be little doubt that the force which brought about such essential changes in English, through imperceptible, minute alterations, originates in the unconscious. It resulted from individual projections, adding up and magnifying that in which individuals agree with one another and obliterating that which is at variance.

E. Sapir, the anthropologist-linguist, once said that all

verbal forms drift as if they were moving on a slope.* One may clarify this statement by adding that the "slope" Sapir is speaking about is the unconscious quality of language. The process of projection implicit in all perception makes it self-evident that the shift in language exhibits those motives which are the most powerful, the most constant within the language community. The unconscious quality of these forces reveals itself in a slip of the tongue, in the whole dynamic of speaking, in dreams; it is present in the individual. There exists no other mind but the mind of the individual. Language, however, is the work of projection adding up individual qualities. It exhibits the collective nature of man.

This invokes no magic, no mystery existing apart from the individual. It means, simply, to denote those qualities which have grown through projection into general human qualities in the course of countless ages of prehistory, as distinct from those individual qualities which vanished with the individual. If, however, it is evident that the body is being built, is growing and decaying according to an inherited structure, if the physiological, biophysical, and biochemical processes follow strictly inherited patterns, it is difficult to think that the mind should not follow some structural elements which are *a priori* given with the very existence of the human race. Such collective unconscious structural elements make the unique character of language. Language offers the most immediate approach to the collective qualities of man. It is the most deeply ingrained part of the unconscious in which ancestors continue to live in the present generation, and the thoughts and dreams of today's generation will continue to exist in ages to come. Language materializes the collective quality of man which is operative in every individual. This growth of language through projection permits speaking about the "wisdom of language." This wisdom, the deposit of common experiences through the millennia, is the knowledge of the "collective" and unconscious motives of man.

---

* Edward Sapir, *Language: An Introduction to the Study of Speech* (New York: Harcourt, Brace & Co., Harvest Book, 1949). He says: "The drift of a language is constituted by the unconscious selection on the part of its speakers of those individual variations that are cumulative in some special direction" (p. 155). He does not discuss what this "special direction" might be.

THE INTERPRETATION
OF DREAMS AND WORDS

The Analysis of Etymologies

The dream is an intrusion of the "abnormal" into normal life. Freud demonstrated in his classic work that the interpretation of dreams "is the Royal Road to a knowledge of the unconscious element in our psychic life."[39] The contention of the following pages is to show that the intensive analysis of verbal expressions, traditionally called etymology, offers another method of exploring unconscious fantasies. While the dream is a projection relevant primarily for the individual, language is like a collective dream, the projection of the whole community.*

The history of dream interpretation has much in common with the history of etymology. Both were held in high esteem in ages past, were considered as sublime wisdom, philosophy or knowledge of vital importance, were considered everyone's business, as public affairs upon which the wealth and happiness of the state and individuals depended. They were not what they are today, merely a field of scientific interest. The "reading" of dreams, the understanding of the "language of

---

* Erich Fromm, *The Forgotten Language: An Introduction to the Understanding of Dreams, Fairy Tales and Myths* (New York: Rinehart and Co., Inc., 1951). This "forgotten language" is not a verbal language, thus it has nothing to do with linguistics. For a comprehensive scientific presentation of dream interpretations, see W. V. Siebenthal, *Die Wissenschaft vom Traum: Ergebnisse und Probleme—Eine Einführung in die Allgemeinen Grundlagen* (Berlin-Göttingen: Springer Verlag, 1953).

dreams" as practiced through the ages makes it evident that language and dreams have something in common. The interpretation of words was a matter of mental health, and so was the skillful reading of dreams. It goes without saying that neither etymology nor dream reading developed objective criteria before psychology laid the foundation of their understanding. Voltaire once said that in etymology consonants count for little and vowels for nothing. The interpretation of dreams had no better credentials. The "understanding psychology" brought about the change.

The era of the great discoveries and of the foundation of scientific thinking began in the field of etymology a few decades before Freud started on the exploration of unconscious fantasies. The question of scientific evidence and control, however, despite the positive achievement in both fields, remained a precarious one. Freud was willing to set a question mark or a restrictive "perhaps" after each step of his dream interpretations. He also admitted that many dreams are ambiguous and permit at least two different interpretations. He also admitted that some dreams have no interpretation at all. The same situation prevails in etymology. The discovery of remarkable consistencies in phonemics did not change the fact, obvious to anyone familiar with the intricacies of word studies, that question marks have to be set after the most plausible interpretations, that opposite explanations are equally possible or impossible, that even the most familiar terms of everyday language (such words as *cut, put, pull, fit, fun*) have remained unexplained in phonemics, to say nothing of their meaning. The claim that linguistics has achieved scientific exactness is based upon one-sided phonemic considerations, while the interpretation of meanings remained on the level of naïve common-sense reasoning, just as dream reading was in the age of the Pharaohs, or etymology in Greek and Roman antiquity. "One man's guess is just as good as another's," said one of the wisest of all modern linguists, Otto Jespersen.[40] The more reliable an etymological dictionary is, the more question marks, "perhapses," and "doubtfuls" one will find inserted. A. Meillet, one of the best experts, estimated that for *one* fairly reliable etymology in a good dictionary, one must count at least *ten* doubtful or false interpretations. Such an eminent expert in etymology as the American Carl Darling Buck finally came to set the following test for the reliability of etymologies: "Only those that are reasonably obvious and certain give genuine satisfaction. The specialist can recognize these and at the same time is aware of how large a proportion of current etymologies, even in most of the best etymological dictionaries, are uncertain, with varying degrees of probability or plausibility."[41] Thus, this great scientist refers, as the final authority, to the subjective criterion of insight as giving genuine satisfaction. This is exactly the same criterion that was used by Freud to verify the reliability of the interpretation of dreams. The patient's reaction to the interpretation of his dream is still considered to be the best criterion for the truth of the interpretation. The trouble in this respect, however, is that a vehement denial often means the same as a confession; the "no" of the patient means the same as his "yes." The emphatic refusal on the part of the linguists is often the indication of a correct etymological interpretation.

There is another common point in the general attitude toward dream interpretation and etymology. Both fields are the favorite playgrounds of hobbyists and dilettantes. They lost their prestige in this modern age of sciences. One makes a sharp separation between the stuff of the night-dream and the reality one perceives in waking life. The only thing one is supposed to do with dreams, according to the rules of common sense, is to forget about them as soon as possible. Dreams have nothing to do with reality, and to ruminate about them is contradictory to the realistic approach to life. It is not proper to comment on one's dreams in society. The same situation prevails in respect to etymology. Who cares about the forgotten meaning of words, about meanings that were valid once upon a time, but are not valid any longer? Otto Jespersen expressed this opinion in stating that etymology, at best, "tells us not what is true, but what has been true."[42] In other words, it is a matter of mere historical curiosity with no bearing upon the present. It amounts to the same thing when the eminent linguist Hanns Oertel said: "A word does not really become a symbol for an idea until it ceases to describe, and the link between sound and idea, phonetic form and psychical content, has become purely external and mechanical, in brief, until all etymology of the word is forgotten while the word is being used."[43] If this is true, then etymology is not just a harmless hobby of looking for curiosities in language, but a rather harmful impediment of speech. One hears the same "forget about it" which reflects the general attitude in respect to dreams. Etymology and dreams, one is told, have first to be forgotten in order that one should be able to make the proper adjustment to reality. No wonder that descriptive linguistics, concentrating on the present status of languages, is disinterested in etymology, since etymology is disturbing to the observation of the present data, just as behavioral science has nothing to offer in respect to dreams.

From the very outset one must be aware of the fact that all interpretations are subjective. The interpretation of projective data involves the personality of the interpreters, too. The interpretation of dreams should grow out of the whole situation, out of the insight into unconscious fantasies as revealed by free associations; thus, it is intimately connected with, if not completely dependent upon, verbal expression. However, in relying on verbal communication, one must take into account two of its inherent limitations.

The first and foremost difficulty will be found in describing the dream. The dream is in its very essence ineffable. It can be related in a few propositional statements as well as in a description luxuriating over hundreds of pages. It is not destined for communication, for it lacks the decisive motive of any verbal communication: the desire to convey something and the intention to be understood. It reflects the narcissistic attitude, which by its very nature is pre-verbal and does not filter through the sieve of the conceptual language. The essence of the dream content may be just that which has not yet been verbalized, which has not yet reached the level of conceptual symbolization, or which may be expressed in many different ways. Reporting the dream by translating its diffuse, emotionally charged content into plain declarative sentences may result in complete misunderstanding. In doing so, one introduces verbal-conceptual categories of the English mother tongue which are not necessarily present in the dream, but which are surely unknown, for instance, to the Eskimo. The logical thinking of the waking state is bound to such categories as space, time, numbers, and causation. These categories do not apply to the dreaming mind.

Words are used in their plain lexical meaning in the dream report, but they may stand for complex ideas and unknown sensations never before named. One destroys the symbolic meaning of a religious ritual by reporting its details in matter-of-fact behavioral terms. One destroys the essence of a poem or of a picture by depriving it of its genuine artistic symbolism. One does so to a much greater degree when one attempts to transliterate the dream into the terms of a clinical dream report. Shakespeare was right in saying: " 'Tis still a dream, or else such stuff as madmen tongue and brain, either both or nothing, or senseless speaking, or speaking such as sense cannot unravel."

The other difficulty is connected with the verbal level upon which the dream operates. This is not necessarily identical with the normal level used in propositional language. It may be referred, rather, to abnormal language as it appears in speech disturbances, aphasia, or schizophrenia. Derealization, depersonalization, alienation, these great motifs of neurosis, drive the patient out of reality, out of his familiar setting, out of his social personality, out of his mother tongue. They result in the disintegration of language. In such cases man uses his mother tongue as if it were a poorly acquired foreign language. So does the dreamer. The general disturbance of the whole language structure dissolves the connection between phonemic patterns and meanings which are strongly fixed in normality. The sound-figures become loose and shaky, become blended with one another, and with similar forms. The distinctive features of meanings vanish and become diffuse and ambiguous. It was the contention of dream interpretation to prove that this confused dream material makes sense and has meaning if deciphered properly. It seems rather strange that Freud, despite having raised the problem of the "dream language," gave no priority to the linguistic consideration of this strange language through which the dream speaks. He referred to mythological and ethnological parallels, but paid little attention to the linguistic analysis of verbal expressions. If one does not understand the hieroglyphics of the Rosetta stone, this does not mean that the inscription does not make sense. It simply proves the lack of understanding. Freud supposed that the dream speaks an unknown, forgotten language which seems to be senseless for our understanding. He tried to decipher this unknown language.*

In the following pages four observations of the dream work shall be investigated with special regard to their linguistic significance. I shall deal first with the verbal phenomenon of association by sound; second, with the phenomenon of "condensation"; third, with the question of symbolization, with special regard to the concept of "secondary elaboration" as found in etymological dreams; finally, an objective linguistic control test on Freud's well-known interpretation of the "Three Casket Story" will demonstrate the interdependence of dream and verbal expression.

Sound Association and Rhyme

The phonemic affinity of words is a phenomenon that has long aroused the interest of psychologists. Freud dealt with it in interpreting slips of the tongue, puns, and mispronunciations; he came across it again as a recurrent motif in the interpretation of dreams. A German-speaking patient reported that she felt a longing "toward Italy" (in German, *gen Italien*). Freud supposed that the sound similarity with "genitalia" (German *Genitalien*) brought about, in the dream, the strange wish to travel "toward Italy."[44] Such examples occur in many stereotyped verbal formulas. An Italian proverb says: "Matrimony and macaroni are good only if they are hot."[45] The two nouns bring together two disparate concepts by sound affinity, but they indicate another connecting link, the idea "hot," which is associated with "fire" and "marriage" in many other respects. When an Italian patient reports that he dreamed about "cold macaroni," this appears to be just a pun of the dreaming mind, a veiled expression of a repressed derogatory opinion about marriage. It must be asked, however, if the witty effect of the pun arises in the dreaming mind or if this is only the reaction of the waking mind. Did the dreamer intend to

---

* Freud realized that the picture language of dreams is closely connected with language. "The dream indeed is so intimately connected with verbal expression that Ferenczi justly remarks that "every tongue has its own dream-language. A dream is, as a rule, not to be translated into other languages." *The Interpretation of Dreams*, Standard Edition, 4:99, footnote.

play with ambiguous words at all? The answer to this question must be in the negative. Some sayings of schizophrenics can be understood as extremely funny by the bystander, but to call them so would reveal a complete misunderstanding of the whole situation. A similar effect may occur if someone is exposed to an alien environment and has to speak and understand a poorly acquired foreign language. He may happen to say "foolish things" which are utterly ridiculous or objectionable to the normal bystander, but which are not intended to be so on the part of the speaker. He may misunderstand sentences by guessing and projecting out of his own resources. Beginners in foreign language are guilty of mispronunciations and misperceptions in hearing. The dreamer may have been stimulated by a phonemic impression during the daytime, then at night the dreaming mind re-echoes it with mistakes in hearing and speaking just as if it were said in an unknown language.

Freud pointed out that this kind of association is brought about by "assonance, verbal ambiguity, and temporal coincidence without inner relationship of meaning."[46] These so-called superficial associations are only the outward substitutes which cover up the latent repressed meanings. "Whenever one psychical element is linked with another by an objectionable and superficial association, there is also a legitimate and deeper link between them, which is subjected to the resistance of the censorship." The sound affinity is thus much like a detour or side track used only when the main road of communication has been blocked for some reason. This interpretation has been substantiated by word association experiments.

The great interest in sound association on the part of psychology found little response in linguistic literature. There prevails instead a skeptical discarding of the whole problem. This was due partly to the supposition that rhyming words are only an adornment of poetry and, as such, are not relevant to linguistics, which deals with everyday prosaic language. This aversion to rhymes has, however, another source of primary importance. The basic assumption still is the axiom that the phonemic form is an arbitrary sign for the respective meaning. If this is not so, they say, one and the same meaning could not be called forth by the most various sound forms. The eminent linguist Hanns Oertel has put this axiom into the following formulation: "A name is not in any way felt to be descriptive of the object any more than a wardrobe check is descriptive of the coat for which it calls."[47] This is so obvious that it needs no further discussion. But (staying within this simile), what shall one think if similar wardrobe checks call for similar coats? The interpretation of sound association has put the finger on a very sensitive spot in linguistic thinking. In grammar and in vocabulary many rhyming words occur. They are generally laid aside with the comment, "just chance." This is a delicate expediency because scientific thinking tries to eliminate references to chance happenings. Such a reference does not explain anything in terms of cause and effect. But what should one think of this "chance" if not one instance or another is found, but many, an abundance of words, not in one language, but in all languages from the prehistoric Indo-European ages to our present time? The phenomena of rhyming words with affiliated structural meanings are very disturbing facts to the whole system of linguistic thinking. Freud called attention to the association by sound, a problem which strikes at the heart of the philosophy of language.

This interest in sound association, however, should not be considered as another essay in support of the assumption that sounds are, by necessity, connected with meaning.* This idea has attracted many dilettantes. Sound symbolism is a topic for the Gestalt theory of language.[48] I am not dealing with the question of whether or not some sound patterns are felt to be *a priori* expressive of the idea denoted, whether or not *trap, split,* or *monotonous* are phonemically descriptive of the respective meaning; whether or not, for instance, the name *Lumumba* is suggestive of a bending, curved, rounded line, while the name *Tshombe* suggests rather a chopped one. Such assumptions can be investigated experimentally and formulated statistically if one wants to do so. The case in point is, however, another more significant phenomenon. There are always some words which seem to emanate their sound-meaning context and impose it upon other words. If the meaning of a "fellow word" is, in some respect, similar, but the sound form different, they force the sound form to rhyme.

---

* See p. 335.

On the other hand, if the sound form is consonant, but the meaning different, they make the meaning rhyme; that is, they bring it into some context with their own meaning. There are such words as *spot–blot–clod–clot–dot,* or *botch–blotch–patch–splash–clash,* or *crush–squash–smash–mash–dash,* or *quench–squelch–squench,* or *sniff–snuff–snub–snob.* These words are definitely separated from one another by their etymological origin; they are also distinct in their meaning by definition, yet it is difficult to maintain that they do not hang together in some hidden way. It means little to attempt to derive one of these words from the blending of two other words. It is safer to confine the observation to the given matter-of-fact data and call such a conspicuous interdependence in sound and meaning of different words a "cluster."

Such structural coherence can be found in German, for instance, *Fleck,* "spot"–*Kleck,* "blot"–*Dreck,* "dirt, clod"; or *Latz-plotz* (as in *plötz-lich,* "suddenly") –*potz* (as in *potz-blitz*), or *Batzen–Butzen–platzen.* One will find in the Greek language such structures as *surinx,* "pipe"–*salpinx,* "trumpet," *larunx,* "throat"–*pharunx,* "windpipe"–*spelunx,* "cave."[49] In Latin such a structure appears in *flectere,* "flex, bend"–*plectere,* "to twine, braid" –*nectere,* "to tie, connect," and so on.[50] A German mental patient replied to the word *Bett,* "bed," "*bett, bett, bett, dett, dett, dett, ditt, dutt, dant, dint, dutt, dett, datt*—if I started I continue till the end."[51] In view of the infinite variations of such clusters in every known language, one will come to the conclusion that no word can stay alone for very long. It soon becomes entangled in some structural context. One seldom knows which individual word is actually accountable for forming a cluster.

One only can describe the fact that a cluster has been brought about by a similarity of sound and meaning. Every cluster posits a psychological problem; for instance, the two words *womb* and *tomb* are surely distinct in etymological background as well as in lexical meaning, yet they attract one another and do so not merely by phonemic similarity. "The babe is at peace within the womb . . . The corpse is at rest within the tomb . . . We end wherein we begin," Shelley said. These verses show that the thrill of a good rhyme consists in this analytical experience of bringing into consciousness the unconscious latent content of a rhyme structure. The rhyme word calls forth the silent partner which is virtually attached to it by sound and latent meaning.* For this reason the picture of the latent dream may call forth the corresponding rhyme word in the dream.[52]

Upon inquiring further into the underlying motivation of rhyme association, one will find once more an instance of the remarkable fact that mythical traditions, like verbal forms, have stored up a better understanding of unconscious motivation than the rational interpretation of later ages. I refer to the mythical figure of Echo, the nymph who died in her vain love for Narcissus. Reproaches have been voiced against Ovid for supposedly not having understood the Greek myth of Narcissus, for otherwise he would not have introduced Echo in this story.[53] We are told by these critics that Narcissus fell in love, according to the old tradition, with his own body by seeing its image in a pool of water; then Echo is as inseparable from this sensation as seeing is from hearing. The echo is complemental to the mirror by its psychological implications, and the legendary Echo must be understood, then, as Narcissus projected into the acoustical field. Common-sense psychology has well observed that if someone likes to hear his own voice, this is a symptom of an infantile interest in his own self. The tape recorder has become an acoustical mirror involving all the implications of narcissistic interests in the own body-self.[54] The infantile source of this acoustic self-reflection can easily be detected. It is a well-observed sensation of early childhood. When the child starts to babble in endless repetitive syllables, he enjoys hearing his own voice. This "echolalia," as it has been termed, appears to be a primordial experience of the self-identity. Hearing one's own voice while babbling is basic to the early development of consciousness. This integration of articulatory and acoustical sensations into one whole corresponds well with the early egocentric pleasure. It represents the narcissistic, reflexive layer of speech which is prior and fundamental to the development

---

*It is a worthwhile projective test to specify the word association by calling for a rhyme word. The rhyme word given spontaneously in measured time is often surprisingly revealing of personal traits and complexes.

of language proper. Deaf children miss this pleasure; therefore they are "mute" in the sense of retarded speech. The development of language begins when the child has learned to distinguish between babbling on the one hand and the knowledge, on the other hand, of when to keep silent and when to speak, or when to express and when to repress.

The impact of echolalia upon language is characteristic especially of infantile and vulgar language. One may suppose that in the Stone Age there was only one language: the vulgar one. By studying this primitive feature of language one will perhaps approach one of the constructive principles of language development. The infantile character is present in the infinite quantity of echo-words in all languages, in regressive colloquialisms such as *hugger-mugger, hurly-burly, hocus-pocus.* The point in question is that all these words show the positive tendency to form a cluster. If resistance enters this process, the aggressive component becomes manifest, as in the German formula *Reim dich oder friss dich* ("either rhyme or devour yourself"). Narcissus may have said thus to his acoustic alter ego, Echo. An empirical formula becomes more expressive as such if it is fixed by a phonemic accordance, as *near and dear, high and dry, health and wealth,* or by alliteration, as *safe and sound, thick and thin, kith and kin, watch and ward.* The rhyme, therefore, makes the proverbial formula more obvious by suggesting that the phonemic accordance is but the outward sign of the intrinsic coherence of truth. Such suggestive truisms in English are: *a little pot is soon hot;* or, *no gains without pains;* or, *haste makes waste;* or, *fast bind, fast find.* The German *es reimt sich* ("it rhymes") means "it makes sense," just as the English *rhyme and reason* supposes that the rhyme has some unconscious connection with reason.

The more the speaker's mind regressed to the babbling level the more pleasure he will find in the phonemic accordance. For this reason the rhyme and phonemic accordance held a specific significance in primitive ritual. It was the phonemic formula which could work as a spell or as magic, and which made these powers more effective.

When there is an association of sounds, there will also be an association of meanings. This basic assumption found full support in the sound-meaning cogency described as clusters.

The opposite view considers the rhyme as a meaningless acoustic occurrence (*homotheleuton,* as Aristotle called it in his *Rhetorics*). It was repeated over and over again since Augustine's definition: *"idem in sono, in significatione aliud"* ("the same in sound, different in meaning"). If one inspects, however, one or another treatise on rhyme, one will find again and again an unwitting affirmation of the psychological interpretation through philological data.

Medieval poetry preferred the stereotyped rhyme formulas. These formulas were scrutinized by countless speech experiences till they reached the general acceptance of a stereotype; consequently they display with special distinctiveness the very characteristics of the rhyme. In German medieval poetry the most general rhyme stereotype is the connection *lîp : wîp* (the modern German *Leib : Weib,* "body" : "woman"). The German *Leib,* however, means not only "body" and "body-self" in the obsolete language, but also "womb"; *Mutter-leib,* properly "mother-body," means simply "womb." This rhyme was repeated with obsessive obstinacy over and over again in all German medieval poetry. In Wolfram's "Parzival" it is found one hundred and twenty-three times, and similarly in other poems. What is the reason for the repetitive use of this rhyme formula? One knows from pathological instances that such repetitiveness is the outflow of repression and anxiety. The "womb"–"woman" association is the great source of repressive fear and anxiety. There are many other similar examples.

In the centuries of increasing individualism such stereotyped rhyme formulas were worn out so completely that they became the stigma of the poorest poetry. Every poet of respect avoided them carefully like taboos, but from the psychological viewpoint these taboo-rhymes which were avoided in the poetry of the eighteenth century are as revealing as the stereotypes of the Middle Ages.* I select just one of these trite rhymes as a control test for the above interpretation. In medieval times the German *muot–guot–tuot–bluot* (the modern German *Mut*, "boldness"–*gut*, "good"–*tut*, "does"–*Blut*, "blood") was a frequent formula; it seems to say simply that braveness (of the heart) does good things. This formula resulted in the trite taboo-rhyme *Blut–Mut*, "blood–boldness, bravery." I chose German rhyme words because the equivalent English words, *blood, boldness*, do not rhyme. If, however, these two concepts stick together in English too, then this association came about through the unconscious connection of the meanings.† In this case, however, the German rhyme formula cannot be a mere sound association either. Looking into Shakespeare's language one will find that *blood* and *boldness*, though not forming a rhyme association, appear as attracting one another. Shakespeare says: "The world will say, he is not Talbot's *blood*/That basely fled when noble Talbot *stood*." The rhyme is different but the association of the respective meanings is present nevertheless. Another instance in Shakespeare's language: "Be *bloody, bold* and resolute"; or "He is *bold* and *blushes* not at death"; or "O the *blood* more stirs to rouse *a lion* than to start a hare." Such instances could be multiplied and collected in a whole vocabulary proving the finding that phonemic associations are indicative of the meanings.

---

* Shakespeare had some conceptions about the unconscious qualities of rhymes when he said: "I can find out no rhyme to *lady* but *baby*, an innocent rhyme; for *scorn horn*, a hard rhyme; for *school fool*, a babbling rhyme; very ominous endings." In *Much Ado About Nothing.* In his "An Essay on Criticism," Alexander Pope said: "While they ring round the same unvaried chimes, With sure returns of still expected rhymes. Where'er you find 'the cooling western breeze,' In the next line it 'whispers through the trees'; If crystal streams 'with pleasing murmurs creep,' The reader's threatened, not in vain, with 'sleep'" and so on. The point, however, is that such trite rhyme-words are associated not only by sound but by their meaning, too.

† The missing link between "blood" and "boldness" is supplied by the word *courage*, from French *coeur*, "heart," which refers to the blood.

In summing up, one may say that these instances prove that the meanings in question are associated in English without rhyme; consequently, if they are connected by the rhyme, as in German, this rhyming supposes the "rhyming of meanings," too. This thesis has been vehemently denied by laboratory psychology,[55] but became confirmed through the interpretation of dreams.

Sound associations elicit some pleasure from the store of narcissistic echolalia as experienced by the small child. It springs up from the earliest unconscious layer of language. It is genuine with the forgotten language of unconscious fantasies. The analytical interpretation tries to translate the language of unconscious fantasies into the common spoken language. The rhyme is one of the characteristics of this almost forgotten and unknown language of fantasies.

Condensation

To begin with, Freud introduced the idea of translation in the interpretation of dreams. The Greeks had the concept of *hypo-noia*. It means properly an "under-thought," a "hidden thought, suspicion, conjecture, guess, supposition," but at the same time it denotes "the real meaning," a "covert meaning, insinuation." The word derives from the verb *hypo-noeō*, "to think secretly, to *su-spect*." Such hidden thoughts appear in dreams. They invite interpretation and translation from the secret language into the overt language. Freud said: "The dream-content appears to us as the translation of the dream-thoughts into another mode of expression whose symbols and syntactic laws we must learn by comparing the original with the translation."[56] One may even specify this concept of translation by stating that it sounds as if it were carried out in a poorly acquired foreign language. The latent content of the dream appears in the manifest dream like a poor translation of a beginner—it can hardly be compared with the colorful and rich content of the original text. Everyone familiar with the intricacies of translation will realize that the transfusing of a symbolic and emotionally charged text of poetry from one language into another is, in the strict sense of the word, impossible. Often the best of the original content becomes lost even in a good translation. It seems to be significant that the Latin *tra-ducere* (from *trans-ducere*), "to lead across, to lead over," has continued in the French *traduire*, "translate," and in the English *traduce*, "to defame, slander, vilify." This applies in some respect to all translations, even to the careful translations of the Bible. One deprives oneself of the very best of understanding if one does not proceed from the translated text to the original, from the manifest expression to the latent content. In accepting a verbal communication at its face value one often does not perceive whether it is a translated text or the original one. It is, however, a shortcoming in clinical or literary understanding if one takes the translation for the original.

Freud defined the translation of the latent dream into the manifest dream as "dream work," and found that the changes brought about by this process can be classified in three groups: total omission, partial omission, and the blending of two concepts into one (this last is the condensation proper). The recasting of the whole dream content is all the more necessary because the dream proceeds on the pre-verbal level. The verbalization may in some cases be opposed to the picture writing which the dreaming mind applies, and the content may be such that it fits only the visual diagrams and remains ineffable in vocal language. The verbal element of the dream content is apparent if one speaks in the dream, if one dreams in language (generally in the most familiar one), if one experiences in the dream dramatized situations in which one speaks, answers, questions, disputes, and argues. This can result in the motor discharge of the speech organs; then it can be heard by others. But the kinetic reaction may fail. This is the case in anxiety dreams when the dreamer wants to scream but feels his speech organ paralyzed: "their tongue cleaved to the roof of their mouth" (Job 29:10) as says the recurrent formula of the biblical language describing the symptom of motor aphasia in dreams.

The "condensation" of the dream work is operative also in language. It was termed so as "condensation of meanings" (*Bedeutungsverdichtung*) by Wilhelm Wundt. The dreamer displays in this respect no other phenomena than those known through linguistic evidences. The process of blending different phonemes, morphemes, meanings, and sentences into a composite is such a general tendency in all sections of the structure of language that it seems obvious that this process is also going on in dreams. The neurotic disintegration of the whole language structure in dreams results in the vanishing of the distinctive features of sound or meaning figures and brings about blendings, fusions, and confusions. The words blended may preserve their phonemic pattern unchanged. Thus A and B become C; for instance, *sweetheart* does not state that the "heart" is "sweet" but says the same thing that is meant by "my sweet" and "my heart." In the same way *mother tongue* is neither "mother" nor "tongue," and *honeymoon* is neither "honey" nor "moon" (following the Latin *mellis luna*). It makes no sense to construct a logical relationship between the component words if such a relationship does not occur in the mind of the speaker. Each of such compound words could be subjected to an intensive analysis and it will turn out in each case that a repressed latent content is translated into the express language of lexical meanings by the constitutive part of the compound. In other words A does not explain B, or vice versa, on the manifest surface because both hang together with the repressed latent C. The composite words condense at least two sentences into one formula, but it would need many more sentences to explain in propositional terms all that which is condensed and understood by "sweetheart," "mother tongue," "honeymoon," "hot dog" or "cocktail." Freud pointed out this capacity of the dreaming mind to bring large diffuse matters into one concise picture. One may even state that the dream sums up the whole existence of man—past, present and future—in one picture or event which stands for the whole experience of life. In other cases the words blended do not preserve their phonemic form intact but combine them as well as the meaning. Such blending may occur in all "clusters," as *black, spot, blot, clod, clot, dot.* Cluster words may be related to one another in many ways, and it is probable that some are blended forms. Such blendings may be elicited by repressed aggressiveness in the form of pun or witticism. From such witty playing with words originated for instance the American *gerrymander,* a blending of the name of Governor Gerry and *salamander.* The projection of one word upon another in the so-called folk etymologies resulted also in condensed blendings. The point in question, however, is not the mere descriptive observation that two different words begot a third one, but the reason for this fusion. In most cases it can be demonstrated that underneath there is a repressed energy at work seeking outlet by creating new forms of speech. The greater the repressive anxiety is, the more conspicuous are the changes brought about on the manifest surface of language.

Etymological Dreams

The interpretation of dreams holds some involuntary though genuine affinity with linguistic etymology. Freud wanted to decipher the "true original" meaning of the dream just as he was eager to find out the etymology of meaning in neurotic symptoms. The great linguist Karl Vossler, quoted before, said that all good etymologists are interpreters of dreams. There is a common ground in method and principles upon which the dream as well as verbal forms can be understood. This common ground becomes evident in cases when the dreamer dreams etymologies. The etymological dream, a frequent occurrence, is a remarkable fact for the interpretation of language. It is the more so because it is known that schizophrenics show a special capacity of understanding dreams. They seem to stay closer to the forgotten language of the unconscious which the interpretation of dreams and the etymology of verbal forms attempt to decipher. Analysts found many instances when subjects in a regressed state, in hypnotic age regression, or in free associations, produced "archaic" material as if they were coached by a linguist. They grasped a latent meaning which once had shaped a verbal expression but does not exist anymore on the manifest surface of language.

A clinical dream report may serve as illustration.

> Bertram D. Lewin reported a dream of his patient; the dream was related to a dental irritation. "The dreamer found himself in the House of Lords. The Lords were seated not in rows but in a semicircle. Suddenly a very large rubber axe blade chopped down between two of the Lords on the right, and the dreamer awoke to find an irritating fragment of food between the teeth of his jaw in an exactly corresponding position."[57]

I do not think that the irritating fragment of food is the full explanation of the dream content.[58] Why did the dreamer dream about the House of Lords? In the English language one can find no clue for such association. But in Latin the *genuini* denote the teeth "of or belonging to the cheek, jaw-teeth, back teeth," and this word refers to *genus* which means "birth, descent, origin, a race, a stock," "in particular birth, for high and noble birth." Thus an old symbolic association between teeth and noble birth became reactivated in the dream by a dental irritation. We have lost completely this association which once was alive and became incorporated in our languages, yet the dreamer has rediscovered it and understood it. He did not have to learn it through a dictionary. The teeth are indeed a conservative body in the whole bone structure.*

Another clinical example of etymological dreaming follows.

A girl college student reported the following dream: she went with her boyfriend to the junior prom. The boyfriend brought her a *carnation*. She was very pleased and in high spirits. She wore a beautiful white evening dress. They entered the ballroom exuberantly. They went in together. They attracted everyone's attention but to her great embarrassment she first perceived some bloodstains on her white evening gown and soon found out the blood dripped from her carnation. The flowers were bleeding. She left the ballroom in great embarrassment. She awoke with palpitations.

The dream is not an unusual one, it might even be termed a recurrent dream. (Freud also referred to a flower dream with reference to *carnation*.[59]) The first idea which may come to the mind seems to suggest that the dream expresses menstruation anxiety. The dreamer visualized a hypothetical danger situation. But why did the blood drip from the carnation? This motive still remains unexplained. Another association though more repressed is also at hand. It is suggested by the verbal form *de-flower* which might be connected in the mind of the dreamer with "bleeding." The presence of the boyfriend, the white evening gown, almost a wedding dress,

---

* See p. 284.

the whole solemnity of the moment, to be the focal point of attention, the prom as a kind of *initiation*, the "going in together"—all this may point to the *de-floration* association. The Latin *in-īre*, "go in," means more than just entering a room, therefore "initiation" means some introduction into mysteries. The Latin *in-īre* seems to be associated with *co-īre*. The Romance languages made this latent association manifest by uniting these two concepts: the French *commencement* developed from *con-in-itiation* meaning "going-in-together." Reporting the dream, the dreamer stressed this point in verbal expression: "we went in together," though the symbolic meaning of this "going in together" was unconscious to her mind. Thus, one may interpret, the dream does not speak of menstruation anxiety but rather of a penetration anxiety which might be an attribute of self-conscious virginity.

The bleeding of the carnation remains still to be explained. Analysis cannot be satisfied by the simple verbal reference *de-flower* or *de-floration*. One would like to know what lies behind this verbal formulation; especially, why does the carnation start bleeding? The girl knew nothing of Latin, she was unaware of the fact that in Latin *carnis* means "flesh." She did not think even of *in-carnation*, "becoming flesh," and had no idea how this word *in-carnation* could have anything to do with her "carnation." One may say in this case, not the carnation started to bleed but *vulnera recrudescunt,* an old scar started bleeding, an old forgotten meaning which did not exist in the conscious mind of the dreamer received some vitalizing energy from her unconscious, and became alive again in her dream. It is the case of the return of the repressed.

While withdrawing from the perceptual daytime world and regressing to the state of dream, this girl found an association which once was an actual idea in the mind of our prehistoric ancestry but has been long forgotten by the present generations. She associated *blood* and *flower* and said in the picture language of her dream: flowers are bleeding. This was once a natural association in an age which knew nothing about the categorical separation of man, animals, and plants but perceived all organic life, in whatever form it may appear, as essentially one. The flowers are the procreative organs of the plant, they are bleeding like the women. In Greek, *haima* means "blood" on the one hand and "sap" of the tree on the other; both are basically the same.

The word *blood,* the Old English *blod,* has no other relative forms than the Old English verb *blowan, blew, blown,* "to bloom, blossom."* There must exist a hidden underground contact between the notion of "blood" and that of "bloom, flower," but this contact has been completely obliterated on the manifest surface of language. It must have existed, however; otherwise the phonemic forms would not hang together. The authoritative *Oxford New English Dictionary* says at this point: "*blood* is doubtfully referred to the verbal root *blō,* 'blow, bloom,' which suits the form but is less certain as to the meaning." In other words: the phonemic connection is so obvious that it cannot be denied, but the writers of the dictionary simply cannot subscribe to the nonsense that "blood" and "bloom" mean the same. They have tried, perhaps, to find out some logical link between the two notions and have come to the conclusion that there is none for sound-minded thinking.

Our languages, however, show in many instances that there exists a hidden association between these two conceptually distinct notions. For instance, the Authorized (King James) Version of the Bible translates the Hebrew taboo laws concerning the woman who is "sick of her flowers" (Leviticus 15:24, 33). The Revised Version dropped this poetic expression and replaced it by "uncleanness." Our dreamer never heard of it. The German and the French Bible kept the reference to "flower." In French this euphemism was especially well motivated because the Latin *menstrui fluores* (Augustine) became assimilated first as *flueur,* "flow," then as *fleurs,* "flowers." One would perhaps accept such a linguistic-phonemic explanation and accordingly suppose that the whole "blood-bloom-flower" complex came about through the confusion of *fluor,* "issue, flow," and *fleur,* "flower."

---

* *New English Dictionary,* s.v. *blood.*

This is, however, not the whole truth. It can be demonstrated by other languages which have nothing in common with the Latin *fluor* that a genuine relationship exists between the notion of "blood" and that of "bloom, flower." In German "blood" and "flower" are related to one another as singular and plural, thus as grammatical categories of one and the same word: *Blut*, "blood," is the singular, *Blüte*, "flower," is the plural. In non-Indo-European languages, too, one can find a similar relationship between the two concepts. In Hungarian, a Finno-Ugrian language, *vér* means "blood," *véres*, "bloody," *veres*, "red," and *ver-ág*, *virág*, "bloom, flower." The blood, the flower and the fountain, they all "spring" in Hungarian (*fakad*); they keep the same sphere of association which is an indication of an old, genuine relationship.*

The idea "blood" is heavily charged with meaning and affect. As long as it is invisible, inside the body, it carries high emotional values, but when this *se-cret* fluid is *ex-creted*, turned into a visible reality, discharged from inside, it becomes an object of fear, disgust, and loathing, hence the menstruation complex which is so deeply rooted in Western civilization. Outside the body the blood is *cruor*, "gore," which also means "filth, dirt, dung." Its emotional value is indicated by such words as *crude* or *cruel* which are its derivatives.

The difference between the emotional qualities of the inside and the outside blood can be demonstrated best in respect to the female organism. According to primitive fantasies the conception of a new life in the female organ occurs as the coagulation of the blood which otherwise appears as discharge. They surmise that the cessation of regular periodicity must be caused by the clotting of the blood. Thus conception means clotted blood, the carrier of a new life, the incorporation of a new soul, *in-carnation*. The clotting of the blood is considered to be the act of supernatural power, it is the fruit of the womb, the "blessing" of the spirit. If however, the blood is dis-

---

* Shakespeare said: "Well, I'll find friends to wear my bleeding roses" (Henry IV). A classic illustration is Baudelaire's "Fontaine de Sang" (Fountain of Blood) in *Les Fleurs du Mal*.

charged, it changes into "flowers," translated as "uncleanness." It becomes an object of fear, avoidance and taboo.

This interpretation of the dream was foreign, incomprehensible, rather nonsensical to the dreamer in question, yet she dreamed this dream. The meaning implied is completely lost for the normal speaker of English. If, however, this interpretation is correct, then the dreamer has resorted to the original meaning of the word which exists only in etymological dictionaries. One may even say in this case that the original meaning with reference to "blood" and "flesh" first had to be forgotten, repressed, in order that the secondary meaning, "flower," could be established. The etymological meanings of many words exist only as hypotheses in linguistic literature (sometimes as very questionable hypotheses), and have completely vanished from the spoken language. How is it possible that such meanings emerge in dreams? Do only linguists dream etymologies, or is this a general feature of the dream work?

Some cases can be explained in terms of projection by the so-called folk etymology. It is then just a chance happening that the dreamer is not led astray by some sound associations, but has arrived on the right track to the proper linguistic interpretation. It is generally assumed that folk etymologies are false, rather funny etymologies. Such erroneous folk etymology appears in cases when Freud's dreamer analyzed *liability* as *lie ability,* or when a patient with the name William asserted, "Will I am." But sound associations do not lead necessarily onto a false track; it may happen that they are correct as to the origin of a word. This is the case with "carnation." However, there are cases when it is impossible to find the etymological meaning by sound association, yet it emerges in a dream. Freud assumed in such cases that in a dream on the verbal level one may sometimes restore words to their original meaning or follow the change of meanings "a little way back." The German writer Jean Paul once said that language is the cemetery of dead metaphors. In the dream these metaphors seem to rise from the dead and become living symbols again, "flesh and blood." The language of the Bible, Shakespeare's language, Goethe's German—all these have a special power to revitalize dead symbols. In

connection with the former key words "carnation" and "de-
flower," Shakespeare makes these symbols alive in such formulas as "before milk white, now purple with love's wound";
or "the pale and maiden blossom became bleeding." He said
about his power of revitalizing old forms: "So all my best is
dressing old words new/Spending again what is already
spent/For as the sun is daily new and old/So is my love, still
telling what is told" (Sonnet 76).

How can one explain the fact that words that have been
dead metaphors for a long time recover their emotional content in dreams? The dreaming mind discovers in such cases a
track of associations which was once used but had been
abandoned by the normal language a long time ago. The forgotten original meaning is unknown to the normal speaker,
yet it has been restored and reactivated in the dream. The
dreamer went the "little way back" as Freud called it, even
though this way may have been a very long way in the history
of language. The dreamer reached, in such cases, almost blindfolded, the goal which is to be approached by the scientific
procedures of etymology. This phenomenon has been observed and described as a symptom of the language of
schizophrenia. As the facts stand now they can hardly be
interpreted otherwise than by supposing that the normal language is more compatible with the psychopathology of dream
and schizophrenic behavior than with the psychology of the
normal waking mind. The mental activities characteristic of
the development of language do not work in accordance with
the criteria of reality. They display absurd, unreal elements,
as does the dreaming mind. Illusions, hallucinatory and vision-
ary experiences, and hysterical obsessions are as much instruments of the verbal expressions as is their conscious elaboration into understood communication. It is interesting to notice
that Wilhelm Wundt once realized correctly: "In the dream
we can live through almost all the phenomena met with in an
asylum." It is all the more surprising that this great psychologist of language did not carry over this insight into his
interpretation of language but was satisfied with the logically
formalistic classification of changing meanings. It is of little
value for the better understanding of language if one is told
that the distinctive feature of a word has changed or not
changed, or that the association between "blood" and "flower"

came about either by contiguity, or by distant association. One may readily say that "blood" and "flower" show a very distant association, indeed, but such classificatory labels give no insight into the processes which have brought about the verbal expression. These formalistic descriptions of the changing meanings necessarily degenerate into platitudes. They do not take into account the fact which applies also to dream pictures and mythical presentations; namely, that symbolic complexes are pregnant with many potential meanings. One can observe in the early Greek philosophy the unique process by which such primary symbols as "Fire," "Water," "Sun," "Blood," "Flower," "Seed," were in the course of history reinterpreted and transformed into reality concepts, how the divine "Fire" became the utility household fire, how the myth of reality has been turned into the physics of reality.* The original symbols implanted life and personality into things. These living symbols, "living waters," "live fires," "the life is in the blood," became simple reality concepts. Our languages are deeply involved in this great process of transformation, and language can be called indeed the cemetery of dead symbols. The "little way back" Freud spoke about refers to this resurgence of symbols in the dream. Language was primarily figurative, symbolic, descriptive, and concrete, like picture writing; it developed later on into a conceptual communication. The development of language is the classic illustration of the translation of a latent symbolic content into the rationalized manifest expression which is the characteristic of the dream work. The dreamer transforms repressed complexes into plastic representations. In doing so, he recapitulates the same work which once took place in language, but he proceeds in the opposite direction. He performs the task which etymologists often fail to do. He restores the original full content to a conceptual verbal expression. In the verbal form he rediscovers the living myth which has been lost from everyday language. The evocative language works in the same way as the dreaming mind. If one considers this resurgence of long-forgotten meanings in poetic diction and in the language of the dream as some

---

* Francis M. Cornford, *From Religion to Philosophy: A Study in the Origin of Western Speculation* (New York: Longmans, Green, 1912).

kind of "recollection," one must accept that the dreamer calls back in such a case something which was never within the scope of his personal experiences but which occurred perhaps many centuries ago in the language community.

Recurrent Dreams

Emotionally charged word complexes show an affinity with a special kind of dreams, the so-called recurrent dreams or typical dreams, such as falling and flying dreams, missing the train, funeral dreams, examination dreams, nakedness dreams. Freud admitted "with great reluctance" that his technique of dream interpretation proved to be disappointing in interpreting these dreams.[60] The so-called *vagina dentata* dreams occur in male homosexual fantasies at the present time just as they did on Greek and Roman vase paintings. The individual free-associations in such cases are almost beside the point because a collective fantasy entered the dreamer's mind, or to put it in other words: the dreamer is not original but is translating a long-forgotten message coming from the unconscious. Word complexes and their associations emerge in the same way as do the "recurrent dreams." The association of "head" and "cup," or "vessel" and "female organ," or "blood" and "bath," "blood" and "flower," or "smug" and "creeping-in smuggler," or "carnation" and "bleeding," emerge like the typical dreams today as well as in the language of the Bible or in the Greek tragedies or in prehistoric ages. The study of word complexes enlarges the scope of the recurrent dreams. They are the typical dreams of the whole language community.

Freud used the free-association method in order to go the "little way back" from the manifest dream to the latent content. The free associations were supposed to recall long-forgotten images from the cemetery of dead metaphors, and to lead to the true original meaning of the dream. This method applies to the individual and interprets the dream as a unique event which makes sense only for the dreamer in question.

In the following, the course of another method will be demonstrated. The problem is this: does the dreamer really create his own personal picture language or does his mind go along pathways that have been established by the whole language community? In place of the individual free associations the free associations of our languages will be consulted. Besides the individual associations one has to be aware of the associations that have been developed by countless generations since prehistoric ages, not in one, but in many language communities. One will try to find an objective background for the highly subjective free associations. I use for this purpose a story that has been analyzed in an ingenious way by Freud.[61] It is not a dream report but an equivalent verbalized in literature and poetry. Shakespeare used it as the story of the "three caskets" in *The Merchant of Venice*. His words are far more descriptive and communicative than the report which a patient on the couch can give about his dream.

Shakespeare found the story in the *Gesta Romanorum*. Here we are told that Portia has promised to marry the suitor who makes the right choice among the golden, the silver and the lead caskets by choosing the one that contains her picture (it is in the lead casket). Freud also pointed out correctly that the old King Lear in distributing his kingdom had to make a similar choice among his three daughters. He made the wrong one by excluding Cordelia, his third daughter, from the inheritance. He did so because Cordelia remained speechless while the other two sisters attested eloquently to their love for their old father. It should be noticed at this point that the parallel between the three caskets story and the story of Lear's three daughters did not occur first in Freud's mind. It also went through Shakespeare's mind. Regan, the second daughter, speaks as if she were the silver casket. She says: "Sir, I am made of the same metal as my sister and prize me at her worth." Freud has shown by analyzing both stories that the third possibility, the lead casket and the silent Cordelia, is symbolic of "death." It is the wishful thinking of the dreaming mind to suppose that there is a possibility of choosing when there is in reality no choice whatsoever but an imperative necessity saying, our life has to come to an end. The necessity of the inevitable end is transformed and substituted by a reference to Chance. Freud's interpretation started from the common element which is present in the meaning of "lead

casket" and in Cordelia who "loves and is silent." Gold
and silver are "loud"; lead is "silent" as Cordelia is. "Thy
paleness moves me more than eloquence," Bassanio says
in choosing the lead casket. Analyses of dreams have
shown, Freud says, that speechless silence is a familiar
representation of death.

I shall consider one by one the key words upon which
the story hinges, and describe the aura of associations
that is characteristic of them. The procedure is the same
as that which is generally applied in free association. In
doing so one can reach the verbal structures which absorbed the unconscious fantasies. One may surmise that
the latent content can be found in an unconscious verbal
complex, while the manifest content as told in the story
represents its secondary elaboration.[62] The elaboration of
these fantasies exposes the different modalities of existence and nonexistence. They deal with life and death.[63]
They describe the "must" of necessity and the great "perhaps" of chance which makes probability, possibility, improbability an ingredient of existence. The choosing of a
casket by chance evokes a mode of existence that is
neither necessary nor impossible.

NECESSITY.   The latent content of the Lear story is the
eternal rebellion against the acceptance of death as necessity.* Languages display almost the same negative attitude
toward death as the old Lear does. The unconscious fantasies cannot accept the fact that man exists with the idea
of nonexistence. The acceptance of this idea, as Hegel
stated, is the beginning of all philosophy. It is the privilege
of conscious self-reflection which man shares with no
animal. Our languages, however, interpret the fact of
death as if it were not the necessary implication of life.
Some languages denote "man" with the name "mortal,"
but this is rather a philosophical or religious term, not
compatible with unconscious fantasies. It is well known,
and has been often described, that some people have no
word for "to die." They can only say "to kill." In their
understanding man never dies of necessity by arriving at

---

* See *The Subconscious Language*, pp. 269–270.

the end of his life, but is always killed by some hostile agency. The categories of natural death and violent death are not separated in their understanding. Even sickness was inflicted upon man by some evil will; if fatal, it must be avenged according to the laws of retaliation. This seems to prove that the idea of death as necessity was perceived as so frightening an event that it became blocked out from consciousness and was replaced by death as contingency. If verbal expressions refer to the so-called natural death, they do so by the formula "to die the own death," in Latin *morte suimet mortuus est,* or *suam mortem habens.* The accidental killing resulted simply in "death," but the necessity of death was called "to die the death of death." To die was more frightening than to be killed.*

What are the primary fantasies of "necessity" which appear to the conscious mind in the form of death? In other words, if death is not necessary what is then necessary at all? One approaches through this question the realm of infantile fantasies. The child does not know about death. He perceives necessity in the image of the father whose sovereign will is compulsory. The religious formulation of the cause of death as "the Father has called," expresses the basic psychological truth about death. The child perceives "necessity" either as a superior force operating from the outside, or as an instinctive urge originating from within. Elimination in particular appears as such superior force pressing from within. The pertinent words display the full illustration of the general picture of a severe authority and its commands, as found in child

---

* The formula "to die the own death" was found in the Old Persian inscription in which King Darius immortalized Cambyses. This formula was misunderstood as meaning Cambyses committed suicide, until Wilhelm Schulze demonstrated in a classic linguistic paper that not suicide but "natural" death was so defined. See Wilhelm Schulze, *Der Tod des Kambyses,* Sitzungsberichte der königl, Preussischen Akademie der Wissenschaften (Berlin, 1912), 32–34, pp. 685–703. The oldest Hungarian text, the so-called Funeral Sermon, also says: *halalnak halalaval halsz* ("you will die the death of death"). This means: "you have to die by necessity."

analysis. "In no period of life is the opposition between the Ego and Superego so strong as in early childhood."[64]

The verbal instances demonstrate in their own way the psychoanalytical insight into the interrelationship which exists in unconscious fantasies between elimination and death. Both are modalities of necessity.

The German term for "necessary" is *not-wendig*. The first part of the compound word refers to violence as can be seen in *Not-wehr*, "self-defense," or *Not-zucht* "rape," properly "violent pulling"; the phonemic equivalent is the English *need*. The second part of the compound, *wendig*, refers to something "winding." The German equivalent of the English "need" is *Not-durft*. In this word again the idea of "violence" is compounded with the verbal complex *dürfen, darf*, "be permitted," but the original meaning is "to be in need of." The word also developed the meaning of "defecation." The same holds true for the German *Be-dürf-nis* which also means "need" and need for "evacuation." From whatever angle one approaches these words they show the close association of the ideas "violence"–"need"–"elimination." The pressing bodily urge appears as the primary representation of "necessity." The idea of "death" enters the picture in the Gothic word *nauths* which denotes on the one hand the "corpse," and on the other "necessity." It is the phonemic relative of the English *need* and German *Neid*, "envy," which formerly denoted aggressive "hatred." That fear and anxiety were implied in this notion is indicated by the fact that the verbs referring to it have become defective. They lost their present tense which is a symptom of repression. Thus the above-mentioned German *dürfen, darf*, "it is permitted," is a defective auxiliary; it lost its original present tense. The same holds true for the other verbs representing the demands of consciousness. These are *should* and *must*, in German *soll* and *muss*; they also have lost their present tense. It seems significant that *must* associates the idea of coercion with "idleness" as can be seen in the German *Musse* and *müssig*, "idle." It is also associated with the idea of "to find room" in the Gothic *gamotan*, or with the idea of "to be disposed" or "to be in condition to do something." The other verb *should* (German *soll*) is connected with the idea of "repayment," "debt," and "guilt," as in the German *Schuld* and the adjective *schuldig*. The infantile fantasies connected with elimination are elaborated in various other European languages. "Necessity" means "misery," "distress," "terror," "danger"; in Celtic it means "that which comes," it is met with "disgust, dislike" in the Bohemian *ne-vole* (properly, "un-will"). One distinctive feature of "necessity" is that one cannot get around it, therefore it has frequent association with *in-evitable*—the German *un-um-gänglich*, "unavoidable," properly, "not possible to go around." This is also the implication of the Latin *ne-cesse* in distinction to *pro-cesse* and *re-cesse*. This "unavoidable" character should not be confused with the opposite idea that "necessity" is something "winding around." This meaning is present in the German *not-wendig* and the Gothic *bisunjanē*, "round about." It is continued in the Italian *bisogno* and the French *besoin*, meaning "need, necessity," but also used for elimination. The aggressive impulse implied in this pressing "must" comes out most distinctly in French *il faut*, "he must."

The French *il faut* is used only in the third person denoting the compelling necessity. This verb is a derivative of the Latin *fallit*, from *fallō, -ere, falsum* meaning "deceive, trick, dupe, cheat, disappoint"; it also means "to conceal from, to escape the notice, elude the observation, be unseen, remain undiscovered," thus *fallit* means also: "I do not know," "it is concealed from me, unknown to me." Why did the Latin idea of deception become used in French for denoting the idea of necessity? How did the form "it is deceiving" come to mean "it is compelling me," "it is a must"? These psychological questions never were asked. I see the answer in accordance with the psychology of the earliest childhood. The small child experiences the conflict of two kinds of pressures: one from within, this is the "need" for elimination, the other from without, this is the authority of the parents opposing the internal pressure. This first and basic conflict of internal need and external authority occurs in the development of the small child at the age of toilet training.

The internal pressure says: "You must do it," "You have to do it," while the internalized voice of the parents says: "No, you are not permitted to do it!" The internal physiological pressure is felt as alien to the Ego, therefore it is properly termed by the impersonal *It*. The external command, even if internalized as Superego, is also felt as opposed to the *It* and alien to the Ego. There is no way out of this conflicting situation. For this reason the weak Ego resorts to deception. It has often been observed that the small child starts lying just at the age when his privacy is still controlled by the parental authority, when the parental voice or look strikes the child just in the moment he wants to hide and his secrets are found out at once by the "omniscient" parents. When the child feels "*I* am cheating because the *It* forces me . . . to do it," he wants to relieve his guilt feelings by shifting first the blame of cheating to the impersonal *It*. Then by a second step he also shifts the compulsion to this *It*. So he changes the "I am cheating" because the *It* forced me to do it into the "*It* is *cheating* that I do it," as said in French "*il faut que je le fasse.*"

In summing up the various evidence one may say that coercion and elimination, together with aggressive tendencies, are associated with one another in verbal expressions. According to these early fantasies death has been brought about by the superior will of the Father. His will is absolute necessity. As this superior will stands in the way of life, so it stands also in the way of pressing bodily needs.

The aged King Lear acts childish. He revolts against necessity and resorts to infantile fantasies. He raises the question in front of his three daughters: "Which of you does love me most?" This is the narcissistic formulation of the age-old frustrating question, whom do you love more, your father or your mother? Lear's question arises from the same source as the aggressive fantasies of necessity, and the anxiety connected with them. The child escapes from the inexorable necessity by making an appeal to a higher power—"chance." This "chance" we love most.

CHANCE AND LOT.   Chance is not as inexorable as is necessity. It is in some respects its opposite. Rational thinking has accepted the supreme rule of "Necessity" and tends to eliminate Chance completely. It will state that man appeals to chance only when he does not understand the inexorable sequence of cause and effect. The unconscious does not accept this logic. Wishful thinking considers Chance a higher instance than Necessity. So does the small child when one of his parents, his father, rejects his will. He will try to move the mother to overrule the father. This is the kernel of Lear's story. He appeals to contingency as a supreme power which can overrule the necessity of death. In the Greek religion *Anangkē* represented "Necessity," *Tuchē* was "Chance." In Latin this Chance is called *Fors Fortuna*. The name is a derivative of *ferrō*, "to bring." Fors Fortuna is the "Bringer," she brings something—sometimes good things, other times bad things. She displays an utter indifference toward her children. The psychology of this whimsical Chance is also the core of the three caskets story. The suiter seemingly has a free choice among the caskets; however, his decision is not free, but subject to the blind ruling of Chance. The unconscious fantasies crystallize around this idea of Chance in the Latin verbal cluster *Sors–Fors–Mors*; in the English *dead–lead–lot,* in the German *Tot–Lot–Los*. These are, of course, mere sound associations, but rhymes sometimes reveal an underground communication between disparate meanings.

The Germanic word for "chance" is continued in the English *lot* and the German *Los*. This word came to be used in a more specific sense, just as did Greek *kleros*, which denotes "that which is assigned by lot to a person as his share or portion in an inheritance"; *to lot* means "to divide land into lots." This meaning remained preserved in such words as *al-lot* and *al-lotment*. One may say that Lear's story gives the secondary elaboration of the meaning condensed in the word *al-lotment*, illustrating the distribution of his land by an appeal to Chance. If dream and language can make alive dead metaphors, such is here the case. The daydreaming mind of the poet went "the little way back" and visualized the concrete situation which is implied in the abstract meaning of "allotment." Unconscious fantasies followed the verbal passageway of "death"–"necessity"–"chance"–"lot"–"allotment." Lear's distribution of his land is made not in preparation for his death, in acceptance of the necessary end of life, but in protest against it.

It can well be observed that the original meaning of the word *lot* has been repressed. Anxiety was implied in it. We lost in our rationalized world the respect for "Chance" which was a living element in former ages. The "lots," originally pieces of wood covered with carved sacred signs, were in Germanic antiquity sacred objects. They have been described as such in Tacitus' *Germania* (Chapter 10). The word denoted also the due share of the divinities in the sacrifice, especially their share in blood sacrifices. In Latin one may observe similar veneration of the numinous *sortes*. The original *sortes* of Fors Fortuna were venerated in the temple of Praeneste, described in detail by Cicero in *On Divination* (II, Chapter 41). Similar religious implications account for the change of meaning in the Greek *kleros* which originally denoted the wooden lots, just as did the Latin and the Germanic terms. From this concept developed the Greek adjective *klerikos* and the Latin *clericus*, continued in our *clerk, clergy, clerical*. The lots were means in the hands of the higher powers; they were handled by the "clergy" representing these higher powers. It seems obvious that they were approached, or rather avoided, with awe, veneration and anxiety. The sacred objects were tabooed as well as the words referring to them. Once they had been tabooed, the meanings became repressed, forgotten, obliterated from the surface of language. The psychological effect of repression was in this case obsessive repetition. After the original meaning was repressed, the word became used most frequently to mean simply "a considerable quantity" or as a mere adverb meaning "a great deal." We say *a lot of fun, a lot better*. The numinous word lost all its religious and awesome content, and lost its independent existence as well, becoming a functional element of grammar.

TO FALL.   The lots which were originally cast became intimately associated with the idea "to fall," thus we say that *the lots fall,* or that *it falls to him as his lot.* This means that the Supreme Power—Chance—manifested her will through the falling lots. The other form of *allotment* by blindfolded choosing, as in the three casket story, seems to be of secondary origin. The idea of "falling" is implemental in such words as the Latin *casus,* from which are derived the English *case, casual, casualty.* The same is true of *chance,* from the Latin *cadencia,* "falling," and also of *accident, accidental,* from the Latin *ad-cadere,* "fall to." Similar associations are implied in the German *Fall,* "fall," *Zu-fall,* "chance," properly "fall-to," *Un-fall,* "accident." Fors Fortuna seems to be only in exceptional cases *fortunate* for the Latin and for most Germanic peoples. For the Nordic peoples, Chance always is gracious: *hap,* "chance," is affiliated with *happy, happiness, happening.*

The underlying idea of the falling lots is associated through unconscious fantasies with the verbal cluster in English of "lead" and "dead," in German of "Los" and "Tod."

The idea of falling is present in the Latin name of the metal *plumbicum.* It is of no account that some authorities want to derive this word from an unknown loan word of an unknown language rather than accept the principle of sound symbolism. Even in case the word happens to be such a mysterious loan word, such foreign phonemic patterns are easily understood or misunderstood by the native speaker through sound symbolic associations. They are susceptible of the misperception, sound substitution, and projection described in connection with folk etymologies and which are frequent occurrences in dreams. The word *plumbum,* however, evokes symbolically the falling of a heavy object; even though it might be originally a loan word, it became absorbed by this symbolism. In English *plump* means "to drop, fall," *plump,* "heavy, clumsy," *plumb* (from the French *plomb*) meaning *plummet*; and also *plunge,* from the French *plonge,* which comes, in turn, from the Latin *plumb-icāre.* One can find similar echo words referring to the falling of a heavy object in the German language as *plump, plumpsen,* "to fall," *Plum-sack*—and so on in all the other languages.

The further question is that if "lot" is associated with "lead," why should the name of the metal also be associated with "death," as we supposed is the case also in the German cluster "Lot"–"Los"–"Tod"?

The idea of the "Fall" holds not only in biblical language a close association with "death," it is implied also in the season when leaves fall from trees. It is the primordial distinction between the "living" and the "dead," in that the living being stands erect while the dead one falls. The perception of "dead" as "falling" is present in the Greek *ptōma,* meaning both "corpse" and "a fall," and as a noun derived from the verb *piptō,* "to fall." The same is true for the Latin *cadaver,* derived from the verb *cadō, -ere,* "to fall." The English *plumb* shows a repression which results in repetition. We use the word without meaning as a mere intensifier with the adverbial function of "directly, exactly, bluntly," for instance, *to say it plumb out, plumb crazy, plumb in the same direction.* The repetition of the word indicates repression; but why should repression have obliterated the meaning of the metal *plumbum,* if not for the reason that it was connected with "death"? The source of avoidance must be in the coherence of the cluster *lot–lead–dead.* This is also indicated by formulas which use interchangeable "plumb" and "dead" as *plumb sure* or *dead sure;* the German *tot sicher; or to run plumb away, to run dead away.*

SPEECHLESS. The speechlessness of Cordelia is still a problem. This speechlessness in the symbolic language of dreams is a figurative indication of death. The dead do not speak. The Latin *Tacita* or *Muta* is the goddess of death. But the question is, why should the "lead" casket denote "speechlessness"?

The words in the cluster *plumb–plump–numb–dumb–blunt–dull* have nothing in common according to lexical meaning. Even though one knows nothing about the etymological origin of these words, it is supposed that they are completely independent of one another in etymological extraction. For the speaker of English, however, these words were, and still are, associated by their sound affinity which resulted in a diffuse meaning denoting something which is heavy, immobile, insensible, dull and speechless, in one word—dead. The implication is in the last analysis the same as in "fall." One may notice the following lexical meanings listed in dictionaries: *dump*, "a thick ill-shaped piece of a lead counter used by boys' games"; *to dump*, "to let fall in a mass"; *in the dumps*, "a gloomy state of mind"; *dumb*, "mute, silent," but originally "dull, stupid" (like the German *dumm*, originally *tumb*, "dull, stupid"), also *numb*, "destitute of power of motion." Every heavy object is in some respect immobile—plumb is numb. Fors Fortuna is represented in the visual realm as blindfolded. In the oral aspect this means dumbness. It has been expressed in proverbs. In German it is said that *der Dumme hat Glück*, "the stupid has luck"—that the "dull" and stupid child is Fortuna's favorite. "This third, *dull lead*, with warning all as *blunt*," says the suitor who happened to choose the golden casket. In Shakespeare's fantasy "lead" is not only a metal but a symbol with distinctive personal characteristics. So he says: "heavy and pale as lead," "base lead," "dull and heavy lead," "is not lead a metal heavy, dull, and slow?" One will understand why the lead casket is the favorite of Mother Chance. The suitor who chose the lead casket had the best grasp of unconscious fantasies.

PALENESS. "Pale as lead," Shakespeare says, though this attribute seems to be more appropriate to Cordelia than to the metal. This association shows the cluster "lead–dead" from the aspect of color perception. "Lead" and "tin" are denoted as the same in many languages. In Latin *plumbum album*, "white lead," is the general term for "tin"; so also is the German *Blei-weiss*, "lead–white." The idea of something which is "white, shining" is implied in the German term *Blech*, "tin," or in the French term for "tin," *fer-blanc*, properly "white iron." The German *Blech*, "tin," is related to *bleich*, "pale," while *Blei*, "lead," and *blau*, "blue," also have some relationship to this group. The colors of death, which sometimes include "violet," are associated with "lead." "Thy paleness moves me . . . ," Bassanio says to the lead casket. On the other hand, the German *er-bleichen* or *ver-bleichen*, properly, "to grow pale," is the appropriate term for "to die." Life is red, death is white. A German proverb says *heute rot, morgen tot*, "today red, tomorrow dead." The unconscious implication of "white, pale" has come in this case into open expression.

CASKET–BASKET; TOMB–WOMB. The verbal cluster *lot–lead–dead* absorbed fantasies which are pre-verbal by their very nature. It will be no surprise to find that the same complex which can be found in the meaning of "death" can also mean the reverse, by which "death" is just another aspect of life. In religious fantasies death is interpreted as the consequence of sin and guilt, of the Fall; the Fall in turn is the consequence of the forbidden gratification of an instinctual desire. The same verbal complex which appears in the projection of the old Lear as "death" can mean "love" for Portia and her suitors.

In the *Gesta Romanorum*, the girl (Portia) originally was bound to choose by chance among three possibilities. Her choice is also a blind one, depending on chance. She chooses the lead casket for the sake of morale, so the medieval storyteller says, but this permits her to express freely that which she really would like to do. She wants to have the silver casket with this inscription: "Whoso chooseth me shall find what his nature desireth." She responds to this inscription with the words: "My nature craves for fleshly delights."* The lots fall in her case in favor of life and her story must be interpreted accordingly.

---

* These are her words as translated by an obsolete English version; the original Latin text, however, is more explicit at this point. It reads: *"nunquam natura debit quod patris filia deberat copulari filio Imperatori."* Hermann Oesterley, *Gesta Romanorum* (Berlin: Weidmann, 1872), No. 251, p. 655.

The sound associations *casket–basket* and *womb–tomb* indicate again a word complex that is accessible to intensive psychological analysis. The notions of "treasure box" and "coffin" are in close association with one another, as is best indicated by the changing meanings of *casket*.

Freud read Shakespeare in German translation, so the double meaning implied in the English *casket* meaning "treasure box" and "coffin" which is in fact the connecting link between the Lear story and the three caskets story escaped his attention. The word *casket* is indeed "the plastic word representation" of the latent dream content. The English *casket* is the equivalent of the French *casette*.

In the Latin text the three caskets are called *cophinos* (*"statim fecit fieri tres cophinos . . . tertium cophinum erat de plumbo"*). The Latin *cophinus* is a derivative of the Greek *kophinos*, meaning "container, basket"; the Latin word is continued also in the German *Koffer*, the English *coffer*. Freud found plenty of evidences while interpreting dreams that the notion of "coffer, treasure box" is symbolic for "womb." The *casket–basket, womb–tomb* word complexes are not mere haphazard and individual sound associations.* They are very definite meaning complexes implying the notions of birth and death. They are not individual associations but firmly established connections of the forgotten language of unconscious fantasies.

---

* The Egyptian *khā-t* also means "body, house," and "womb, tomb." H. S. Darlington, "Ceremonial Behavior Respecting Houses and House Burials," *Psychoanalytic Review* (1931), 18:181–200.

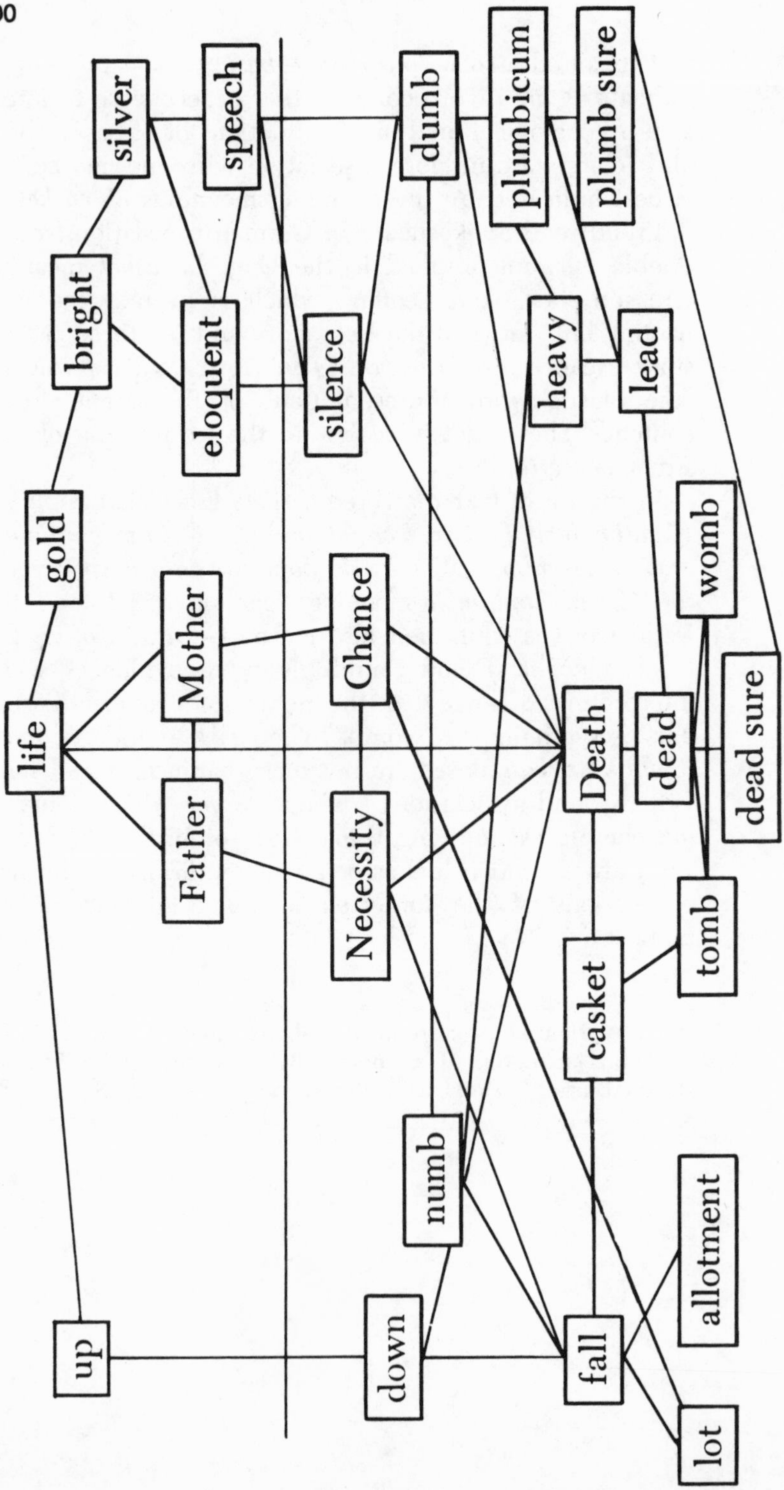
up
life
gold
bright
silver
speech
eloquent
Mother
Father
down
Necessity
Chance
silence
dumb
numb
fall
casket
Death
heavy
plumbicum
plumb sure
lead
dead
womb
tomb
dead sure
allotment
lot

PART THREE

THE SYMBOLISM OF THE BODY

INTRODUCTION

All analysis of the normal mind will arrive at the primary grammatical fact which cannot be explained or reduced any further: this is the basic polarity of the subject and the object. The dichotomy of the "I" and the "World" is implicit in all experience, in all verbal expression. This means that the meaning of "I" stands on one side, while on the other stands a whole vocabulary and grammar which refer to the "World."

The discovery of the own body and its functions is the great event of earliest childhood. The discovered Self is primarily the body-self, the skin making the distinctive line between the Ego and the World. The polarity of the subject and the object makes the basic structure of consciousness, but does not apply to the nonconscious experience. This is still beyond the primary partition of the Ego and the World. No philosopher ever described in more impressive language the emergence of the conscious Ego out of the ocean of the unconscious than did Hegel in his "Phenomenology of the Spirit" (*Phenomenologie des Geistes*). He described the difference between plants and animals, and between the animal which exists, but does not know about its existence, and man who exists not only in the world but also for himself. We cannot experience the primordial state of the newborn infant in which the Ego and the World were still fused in an undifferentiated unity. It belongs to human destiny that man wants to reestablish this primary one-ness which existed before the splitting into subject and object occurred. The Ego feels incomplete as a mere subject and wants to recover the lost object, be it the breast of the mother or even his own body, with which it once was one. In this earliest self-experience subject and object, child and mother, lover and beloved, Ego and World are united. Man likes his own self, therefore he projects his likeness into the world. One cannot repeat the unique process of the rise of consciousness. One can only proceed in the opposite direction toward the gradual loss of consciousness as brought about by sleep, anesthesia, hypnosis or intoxication. The unconscious is paradoxically accessible only insofar as it is not unconscious, but limited to the floating state of transition from one pole to the other. Such floating toward the loss of consciousness is denoted in languages by references to "swimming," "submerging," "swimming head," to "whirling," "reeling," so the French *la tête qui tourne,* and *vertigo,* from the Latin *vertere,* "to turn." Our terms *dizzy* and *giddy* developed their meaning from the original notion of "insane," "foolish"; *drowse* from the notion of "to sink," "to submerge."

In "losing oneself" and approaching the unconscious state one loses the fixed point of orientation. There will soon be no "before" and "behind," no "over" and "under," no "right" and "left," and even no "right" and "wrong." The partition of consciousness was symbolically depicted as the great separation of light and darkness, of day and night, or in religious wording "to know good and evil." This is the great schism dividing the "I" from the "World."

In this partition is implied the primary difference between the inside and the outside experience. Man knows only himself in the true sense from inside; he is observed by others as an object, just as he observes them—from outside. This indestructible barrier is implied also in all verbal communications. By approaching the interpretation of verbal phenomena we are confronted with the same duplicity. Verbal forms can be considered as objects which have to be explained through external observation. In contradistinction to this approach it will be attempted in the following chapters to understand language in the same way in which one can understand others through identification with their inside selves.

The normal conscious mind is a continuous unity, that is, man has a primary experience of his self-identity. "I know" that despite all changes "I am" and will always remain one and the same. In pointing out this unity implicit in ego-consciousness, one must, however, realize that this "I" exists only because of the polarity of the subject and object. There is no empty consciousness without a world, and the world as a meaningful unity would not exist if it were not perceived as such by the conscious mind. The I and the world are categorically different, yet inseparable from one another. Consciousness is necessarily the consciousness of something; knowledge, love, hatred, fear, desire, suppose an object and an intention. The existence of consciousness implies transcendence. "I am" insofar as I am conscious of that which "I am not," of the world which exists outside myself. The unique personal character of the Ego arises out of this individual world which it contains. Every individual carries in his mind an individual picture of the world. Language reflects the common picture of the world as it has been accepted by the whole language community. The consciousness can maintain the ego-identity only through an uninterrupted intake of sense perceptions. Sensory deprivation, as experienced during a sleepless night, solitary confinement, or in hypnotic trance, may result in an altered state of ego-consciousness. Without an object there is no subject. In transcending the objective world man can grasp his own existence as being in the world. Man is the only self-reflective being on earth. He considers himself as to what he is and what he is not. He is planning, hoping, growing, reaching out toward a future which does not yet exist as reality but appears in fantasy as a possibility. Man transcends in this way his own being. He is more than what he is in fact. By shaping his own future he makes decisions, and by this very act he has already changed his present existence. In this respect one again finds that man is a unique existence. Animals are "in themselves"; man exists "in himself and for himself," as Hegel said.[1]

The world also means people. Consciousness is the consciousness of others. We know ourselves primarily from the reflection of our existence upon another person. No lonely human being lives on earth. Life is always life in a given setting. Consciousness supposes the contact and communication with other individuals. It supposes language. It is the result of an interpersonal process, of a mutual mirroring of one mind in the other and their mutual reflection till the infinite.

THE INSIDE AND THE OUTSIDE

Among all those words which refer to some object reality, the words relative to the human body are the most accurate in naming. Nothing is more real than one's own body.[2] Its reality is the most intensively felt existence because it is felt by the congruent and simultaneous experience of being outside like other objects and being inside of the skin. The hands, feet, are all object realities like other physical things, but are at the same time subjectively experienced. They belong to a reality which is of a subjective order. The meanings of the words *hand, thumb, foot, knee, tongue, tooth, skin,* can be defined as objects one perceives on others, and they are so described by definition in dictionaries with clear-cut limitations. However, they can be felt to exist just as the subjective sensation of the own *hand, thumb.* Such sensation from within which is implied in their meaning eludes clear-cut definition. It can at best be expressed by a metaphor. A molar tooth can be exactly depicted and described, but the subjective experience of toothache defies verbal expression. The internal sensation of "foot" is felt distinctly in the case of the "phantom limb" after amputation.[3]

The separation of the objective perception from the subjective sensation may account for the striking phenomenon that *eye* and *seeing, ear* and *hearing*—the sense organs and their functions—are usually denoted by two different words. The "eye" and the "ear" can be perceived but "seeing" and "hearing" are subjective experiences which cannot be explained to the blind or the deaf.

This subjective component which is implied in the meaning

of the body must be the reason for the extreme variance, and inconsistent vacillation in the naming of body parts, whereas one would expect great exactness. It can be understood that "finger" and "toe" are denoted by one and the same word, as in the Greek *daktulos,* although Greek *cheir* "hand" and *pous* "foot" are strictly distinguished from one another. The common-sense interpretation supposes in this case that this word *daktulos* was primarily applied to animals and consequently no difference was made between "hand" and "foot." This interpretation may fit the object realities but fails in supposing that man named the body parts of animals first and transferred these terms to his own body-self.

It appears rather strange to our understanding that such confusion in naming the body parts prevails in languages. There seems to be an insecurity in distinguishing "jaw–cheek–chin–beard," or "neck–throat," or "shoulder–arm–hand," or "bosom–womb–lap–breast," or "thigh–loin–leg–knee," or "eye–face." Especially conspicuous in this respect are the words referring to the *back* part of the body. Some authorities even question whether the word *back,* in German *Backe,* is the same as the word in the German *Hinter-backe,* "buttock," in *Kinn-backe,* "cheek," *Backenbart,* "whiskers," and in *Backen-zahn,* "molar tooth." This fusion of the front and back sides of the body has always been conspicuous. It underscored the mythological illustration of the primeval androgynous unity which became subsequently divided. Such diffuse vacillation in the naming of body parts becomes more perplexing if one considers the shifting meanings of some phonemic patterns in related languages. For example, the same phonemic form assumed in German the meaning "limb" (*Hachse*), in Old High German "knee," in Sanskrit "armpit," in Latin "hip" (*coxa*), in Irish "foot, thigh." As far as reality is concerned these meanings are strictly separated from one another, but they are not separate in subjective experience. For instance, "neck" can mean "throat" in the subjective experience, so the German *Halsweh,* properly "neck-sore," means "throat-sore." In the same way the subjective sensation of tickling, an experience of early infancy, may identify separate erogenous zones in one diffuse "limb–knee–armpit–hip–foot–thigh" sensation.

The fusion of the objective perception of one's own body parts with their internal sensation can be traced in another layer of verbal expressions. Though sense perceptions are obviously internal events, because *I feel, I hear, I see,* yet one thinks of them as belonging to external objects,* and so one says *it feels, it sounds, it appears* or *seems to me.* This projection onto the objective reality originated from cases in which the object referred to meant the same in "I see" as in "it appears to me," when the *I* and the *it* were indeed identical. This holds true only in reference to one's own body-self. If applied to one's own body-self, the meanings of "I feel cold" and "it feels cold" are identical. Only one's own voice "sounds" as "I hear it," and it is again one's own body image which "appears to me" as "I see it." The Ego and the World, strictly separated from one another in the normal state of consciousness, are not so distinct on the level on which language operates. The more one approaches the unconscious, the more this separation vanishes. The borderline where the inside world comes to an end and the outside one begins, becomes increasingly indistinct. The more the objective part of the word meaning approaches the subjective grasp of this meaning, the more it will lose its distinctive limitations and merge with the inside experience, a sensation which is in its essence ineffable. Freud called the merging of the subject and object the "oceanic feeling." The child and the mother once were subject and object in one. In state of regression the individual may experience this characteristic feeling of earliest infancy.

Two opposite tendencies can be discerned in the process of naming the parts and functions of the body. Their outside appearance tends to be named by more specific terms because the nearest objects are known best, observed most keenly, and consequently named most distinctly, and nothing is nearer to us than our own body. The grasp from within operates in the opposite direction. It shows the definite tendency to correlate this variety of object perceptions with the inseparable unity of the inside experience.

---

* Wolfgang Köhler stated that the noun *body* is "dangerously ambiguous . . . a distinguished psychiatrist formulated this as the most difficult problem to be found in all the relations of the mind and body, that things appear as being outside of us whereas we should expect them to be in our interior." *Gestalt Psychology* (New York: Mentor Books, 1959), p. 127.

The perception of a given external reality and the name attached to it, seemingly an arbitrary label, have some affinity with one another. The primitive perception, just as the perception of the small child or the perception in regressed states, is not the same as we experience it and consequently label the notion of our highly differentiated perception with a name. Primitive perception is diffuse, syncretic. It does not imply the differentiation between subject and object, between the cognitive act and the internal noncognitive feeling, between the idea of the thing and the pertinent action, even not between seeing and hearing or between person and thing in a given situation. The Rorschach inkblot test is characteristic of the perceptual organization as reflected in the naming of things. The naming would correspond to a "poor whole" response. The thing is perceived as any signal, as a cue for action, as a challenge or temptation inviting the perceiver to do something with it. A match invites the making of a fire, a glass of water calls for drinking. An excellent lady involved in political action said: "I don't have the slightest idea doing what. Things come. You don't have to go out and look for them."[4] The things call for action, thing and action are perceived in one act. The diffuse syncretic perception is on the level of the pre-verbal organization. When this hazy pre-verbal material becomes verbalized by this process it is analyzed and broken down into distinct concepts.

The syncretic characteristics of pre-verbal perceptions incorporated in languages can still be illustrated by the verbal instances of synesthesia. A voice may have a specific "color," so one speaks of *chromatic scale*, the Greek *chrōma* means "color." A color may be "loud" or "cold" or "warm." The inside experience integrates color, temperature, and sound perception into a diffuse meaningful whole.

The encroachment of the subjective feeling upon the objective content may explain why words referring to the body and its functions are often blended with one another in their phonemic form—an indication which shows that there must be some pervasive element in their meaning, too. Some of these words belong, along with numerals, to the most archaic stock of our languages; consequently, the development of their meaning can be traced back into the remote past. It can, for example, be observed that the words denoting "eye," as the Latin *oculus,* are supposed to have an initial *o* or Germanic *a,* but the Germanic words for "eye" begin with an initial diphthong, as in the Old English *eage* or the German *Auge.* It seems very probable that these words derive their initial diphthong from the words denoting *ear,* such as the Gothic *auso,* "ear." Eye and ear are strictly separated from one another in the world of outside realities, but "seeing" and "hearing" are not so distinct in the realm of inside experience.

The subjective experience may even contradict the perception of the objective reality. We "see" in *one* act, yet we have *two* "eyes," we hear *one* sound yet have *two* ears (Cyclops effect). Some languages, like the Hungarian, accordingly denote the two eyes by the singular "eye," the two ears by the singular "ear" (*füll*), two hands, feet, shoes by the singular of hand, foot, shoe, and consequently denote "one eye," "one ear," as "half eye" (*fél-szem*), "half ear" (*fél-füll*), "half hand" (*fél-kéz*). "Half" thus means practically "one of a pair." These verbal fantasies, which are distinct from self-perception, may appear under pathological conditions. The *migraine* is notably a malaise of women. It is embedded in verbal fantasies. The Greek *hemi-kephalon* or *hemi-krania* means properly "half-skull." The same with the Latin *hemi-cranium* which is continued in *migraine.* It seems to be a folk-etymological rationalization that it refers to a pain on one side of the head or face. The body fantasy can grow into a delusion.

A schizophrenic patient called by the Greek name Doria Mykonos is described thus: "Doria's most prominent symptom was her delusion that she had only half a head." To this she clung "tenaciously and nothing had heretofore budged it." She was "schizophrenic" in the true sense of this word.[5]

Such instances can be multiplied, but the result will remain the same. Though it is assumed that these terms relative to the human body reveal most distinctively the reality of objects, even these words referring to the most intensively felt reality cannot be taken at their face value. They refer to something else or something more than they factually denote. They are infested with elements which belong to the inside experience.

The body-self has set the primary patterns for all subsequent understanding of the world. It is still said: "the chair stands" or "the wind is blowing," implying that objects do something even though one knows they have no active will and cannot do anything. One speaks as if an internal power would manifest itself in these objects as well as in man. The outside and the inside grasp of the Self has found its deepest and most universal expression in the insight that man exists as body and mind. The idea that an invisible mind is dwelling in the body is a figurative expression. It is the translation of self-experience into the objectivity of the body. There is no Self beside or outside the Body, it is ever the Body-Self. If one's body is sick, one is sick, because one is the own body.

However, this does not mean that an estrangement or separation is not possible. In such a case as "I have a sick body," the "I" may withdraw from its body. The "I" may even experience its freedom most acutely in the case of physical collapse. In such a case man feels strange to his own body.

> The body was called in Hebrew *bāsār*, "flesh." "I myself" was expressed as "my flesh." "All flesh" meant like verbatim English *every-body*. While in the Old Testament Hebrew the body-self is primarily the body, the flesh, in the New Testament Greek the body-self is primarily the self. Thus the Greek *sōma*, "body," does not mean the flesh but the Ego, the inside experience of the body.

Words referring to the body describe internal sensations. They have to answer the supposed question: "How do you feel?" The answer to this question is necessarily vague because internal sensations defy verbal interpretations. The parts and organs of the body are used as similes in order to indicate in the figurative language of bodily symptoms the unspeakable sensations of the Self. They may describe anatomical or biological absurdities. On the level of anatomy, "my heart goes out" or "I have a sinking feeling in the pit of my stomach" do not make sense, yet such words describe true inside sensations.

As an example of "dissociation" of the Ego from the body I refer to the colloquial "I went to pieces." This obviously refers to an absurdity if understood as physical reality. Yet, it expresses a true subjective experience. A clinical report says:

"In another case the patient felt that her head was flying away so that she was in danger of stepping on it. Her body is dispersed in space, her arms are flying around and she has to go into a hallway in order to collect her limbs again . . . I am completely in pieces . . . There is no ground under the feet when you are not on earth."[6] Such sensations are frequent in hypnotic depersonalization.

The depersonalization is conspicuous in the ancient Hebrew and Greek perception of the own self. The *psychē* was thought to be a foreign element indwelling in the own self. References to language and speaking are replete with such instances. "My little finger told me" is just one example.

THE SKIN

The skin is the boundary separating the Self from the external world; thus it participates both in the subjective and the objective reality. The lexical meaning of the word *skin* is consequently charged with fantasies emerging from internal sensations. These fantasies refer to something hidden by the skin, to the secrecy of the Self. This implication is conspicuous in the word *hide* which means "skin," "pelt," and as a verb "to keep out of sight." This is also the case of *fell* which is the phonemic equivalent of the Latin *pellis*, "skin." The repressed meaning implied is still manifest in the Gothic *filhan*, "to hide, bury." Some languages consider the whole body as a "cover" and call it "body-cover." Old English *līc-hama* and the Dutch *lichaam* kept this old concept of "body" while the German developed it in *Leich-nam* in the specific sense of "cadaver." The implication of the idea of covering up simply indicates that the body is *hiding* the privacy of the Self.

The skin is the mask behind which the true Self is hidden. In Latin *trahere pellem*, properly "to pull off the skin," means to take off the mask which conceals a person's faults. "I know you thoroughly" is expressed in Latin by *ego tu intus et in cute novi* ("I know you inside and in your skin"). The skin being such a protection of the Self against the outside world, to say "you get under my skin" is the expression of utmost irritation. That the skin might be flayed off and the skinless body might be exposed, is one of the deeply repressed anxieties of man. This might be the reason for denoting the skin, not as a covering mask, but by a reference to the uncovering or flaying of the protective hide. The Greek *derma*, "skin,"

213

refers to the verb *derō*, "to flay." The English *skin* implies the same meaning by the verb *to skin*; the parallel German verb is *schinden*, "to flay."

The skin is for these reasons like a screen upon which repressed fantasies become projected. The skin speaks an expressive language of its own. The blushing of the cheeks, though it seems to be merely a reflex, is in the language of the skin expressive of shame, modesty, or embarrassment. In the same way paling is expressive of an "appalling" effect; "goose flesh" is also an automatic reaction independent of conscious control, yet expressive of special qualities of fear. All these skin reactions are understood by others. They prove that the skin is not simply an outside object but an integral part of the Self. The reference to the skin has a great role in colloquial and slang expressions, as "save one's skin" means to save one's total personalty.*

The extensive psychosomatic literature on dermatology yields an endless series of case studies demonstrating that the skin is an organ of expression much like the symbolic language of gestures. It can reveal repressed unconscious fantasies.[7] Such skin conditions as neurodermatitis (atropic eczema), psoriasis, local pruritus (itching) or sudden development of bald areas on the skin might be produced by unconscious fantasies. Psychogenic effects on the skin are best demonstrated by blisters produced by hypnotic suggestion.[8] While the various skin conditions can be defined in dermatological terms, the underlying emotional reasons are not so well understood.† Causative agents were described in nonspecific terms as a "variety of neurotic symptoms and character traits," "widespread impairment of ego functions," "emotional stress and strain," "repressed hostility, anger, and

---

* Such colloquialisms as to "jump out of the skin" as a symptom of irritation can easily be understood, but other formulas as "by the skin of one's teeth" are not understood anymore without intensive interpretation. The Latin language also knows the *dentes pruriunt* (the teeth are itching).

† It is not explained why fear and anxiety produce just the same skin reactions that appear as a consequence of cold (for example, shiver, "goose skin," "make one's hair stand on end"). Shakespeare's Juliet says while taking the cup: "I have a faint cold fear thrills through my veins that almost freezes up the heat of life."

remorse," guilt feelings. Erythema and blushing in general have specifically been referred to infantile conflicts around exhibitionism.[9] The emotional factors involved in urticaria have been carefully specified as "repressed aggressiveness," "masochism," "repressed exhibitionism," "infantile skin eroticism," also with frustrated sexual desires pleading for love and dependency.[10] In an experimental verbal test, it has been demonstrated that emotionally loaded stimulus words bring about a positive change in skin temperature.[11] Verbally expressed fantasies generally show that "sin" and "guilt" are often associated with "stain," "uncleanness," while white and clean are symbolic for the sinless state of innocence. "Cleansing" is equated with washing away the marks of sin. Such fantasies may have contributed to the process of expressing guilt feelings through skin conditions. The skin is supposed to be a smooth surface. Skin irritations might be expressive of emotional irritations.

The strange interrelationship between urticaria (hives) and weeping deserves special attention.[12] It has been observed clinically that urticaria subsided when an outburst of weeping occurred. How do these two symptoms hang together? From the verbal viewpoint, it is a remarkable fact that *tear* as a noun refers to weeping, *to tear off* as a verb is synonymous with *to skin, to flay*, as to *tear off the skin*. This relationship appears to be a superficial homophony, yet this homophony is conspicuously old: the noun is in Old English *taer*, in Middle English *tere*, the verb is in Old English *teran*, past *taer*, in Middle English *teren*. The same parallelism is found in Old High German: the verb *riozan* means "to weep," and *rīzan* means "to tear apart, separate." The same relationship exists between the German *Träne*, "tear," and the verb *trennen*, "to separate"; also between *Zähre*, "tear," and the verb *zerren*, "to tear off," and *zehren*, "to destroy," the old meaning behind which is "to flay," thus the separation referred specifically to the skin. In English the skin and the tears are *shed*, which properly means "separated," from the Old English *sceadan*, "to separate." The same association is implied, though unrecognizable, in the German *die Tränen ent-rinnen*, this from *trennen*, "to separate." In obsolete English, separation means also "menstrum." This strange old association is clinically illustrated by the weeping patient who said: "No tears, no menstruation, no

going to the bathroom, I am like the Dead Sea with no outlet."[13] The urticaria seems to be the only expression left. One
does not really understand the coherence of "weeping,"
"urticaria," "urination," and "separation," so one does not understand the coherence of the pertinent verbal expressions
either but this does not mean that such coherence does not
exist. The English weeping, just like *crying*, originally referred to the vocal outburst, to cry out, as in *burst in tears*.
The skin is "breaking out" in similar way.

The outbreaking skin demonstrates that the silent language
of the skin can be very expressive, it can speak without the
awareness of the speaker, it can even contradict the conscious
verbalization. This makes the terms *hide* and *skin* meaningful.
The skin reveals in such cases what the speaker wanted to
"hide." This is obvious in cases of embarrassment when the
speaker wants to hide his feelings, but the blushing or sweat-
ing face expresses his anguish contrary to his will. The private
language of the skin has been most thoroughly investigated
in respect to the galvanic skin response (GSR). The central
nervous system has no command over the reflexes of the sweat
glands which regulate the electrical conductivity of the skin.
The GSR, like the electroencephalograph or the electrocardio-
graph and other "bio-sensors" called in popular parlance "lie-
detectors," combined with word-association tests do not prove
that the tested person is lying but indicate that he is hiding
behind his skin; thus they explore the full meaning of *hide*
and *skin*.

Another telling illustration of the unconscious fantasies
speaking through the skin can be observed by tickling. The
stimulation of the skin by light touching or gentle rubbing
elicits characteristic reactions. Why is titillation characterized
by a feeling of pleasure, resistance, excitement, giggling,
laughter which may turn into crying, and spasmodic contraction of the whole body? These typical responses cannot be
explained simply in terms of skin sensitivity (tickling of the
sole?), because they show by their interrelatedness that the
response as a whole corresponds to repressed fantasies. Not
the skin as such but the meaning attached to it is primarily
reflected in this blended composite of reactions. The point in
question is: Who is tickling? One does not generally tickle
one's self. It is consistent with the repressed meaning that

girls at the age of puberty are most sensitive to it, while the symptom disappears later on in the course of normal marital life. English *tickle*, originally *kittle* (like the German *kitzel*), can mean, after repression has obliterated its sexual connotation, to be excited by a pleasant tingling or thrilling sensation, to please, to amuse, and *tickler* appears as a slender steel rod used for "stirring the fire." (As a slang expression it means the "clitoris" of the female, the "moustache" of the male.)

By the same association with the skin the Latin *pruritus* means "an itching" and "sensual desire," from the verb *pruriō, -īre,* "to itch or long for a thing," "to make a wanton display." Even the English *itch* preserved this double reference to the irritating skin condition and the constant desire to scratch it on the one hand, and a craving as an "itching palm" on the other. Skin irritation was interpreted either as an indication of an internal repressed desire or by unconscious projection as a message coming from a higher power, thus coming from outside. The "itching palm" can be understood in the first interpretation as the bodily symptom of the repressed desire to hit someone, according to the second interpretation it is a message of an impersonal power notifying one that one soon will receive money.

A specific frequent gesture is the scratching of the scalp. This once was a significant gesture to the Greeks and Romans because the head, in opposition to modern thinking, was considered to be the seat of sex.[14] The itching (Greek *psōra*) of the scalp was accepted as an involuntary manifestation of this desire. The expressive language of the skin was met without embarrassment as the message of a trans-individual will. Socrates had a *psōra*, "itch," for young boys and this is discussed freely by Plato. The scratching of the head with the middle finger was generally understood in ancient time as an overt symptom of homosexuality. In any event, the middle finger was called in Latin *impudicus*, the "impudent" one.

THE CIRCULATORY SYSTEM

The body fluids and all material discharged from the body are loaded with repressed meanings. They are not simply what they appear to be. Their meaning is charged with fantasies. It is not by chance that *secret* is the same word as secretion, the material *secreted* from inside the body. That fantasies are implicated in this meaning becomes apparent by the special loathing that appears in our cultural setting whenever internal body substances enter the outside world or any part of the body becomes separated from it. Nails and hair appear as adornments, yet if they are separated from the body, nail parings can become an object of disgust. The inside substances, as long as they belong to the total Self, are considered with awe and respect; if excreted, with disgust. They became taboo objects, except milk, but it should be noted that animal milk is an object of loathing, like any other excretion, in some parts of the Far East.

The *blood*, the word and the thing both are charged with emotions and fantasies. As long as the blood is inside the body it is regarded with awe and reverence but outside the body it is disgusting. The blood holds such an important part in rituals, covenants, and sacrifices, also in the food restriction of the Old Testament, that its magic significance seems to be evident. This means in other words that *blood* is not simply a biological substance but also a psychological reality. The belief in the psychological reality of the blood is not based upon any specific knowledge of the cardiovascular system. On the contrary, the various terms and references rather conclusively prove that no physiological knowledge of the blood was anticipated either by Homer or by the Old Testament. There prevailed a confused overall fantasy about the equation of blood and life. Homer had the simple observation of the life blood at hand showing that the loss of blood is followed by death; therefore the blood flowing out of the wound meant to him that "life" is leaving the body. The Greek *haima*, "blood," came to denote, according to these fantasies, "life" and also the *thumos*, "life-soul." The same idea found expression in the Old Testament: "For the life of the flesh is in the blood" (Leviticus 17:11). The blood has kept this equation with "life" in popular belief till the present day.

The various terms show that the blood appears in the language of fantasies as the body fluid concentrated in the chest, warm and fuming, its vapor becomes the *thumos* within man. This word, the basic Greek concept of the psychological essence of man, cannot be properly translated by any of our terms. It means something vaporous inside the body but blended with the outside air. It was grasped rather correctly as the interaction of the cardiovascular and the respiratory systems. These primitive fantasies perceive man, plant, fruit, as a biological unity: the plant or fruit is alive as long as there is juice in it, when dry it is dead. This symbolic equation of "blood" and "juice, sap" is present in the Greek *haima* which means "blood" and "sap" in plants or fruits. This "sap" is present in the raw meat.

In Latin it is called *cruor*, "blood," also "dirt, filth, dung"; its Germanic phonemic equivalent is *raw*, related words are *crude* and *cruel*. Our *juice* and *juicy* also refer to all the fluids of the body, for instance a *juicy steak*; specifically the red grape juice is called "the blood of the grapes," a recurrent biblical expression (Genesis 49:11, Deuteronomy 32:14). The previously discussed dream of the "bleeding *carnation*" illustrated that in a regressed state the mind still can fathom the lost idea of the liquid of life.* The equation of "blood" and "flower," as the instances show, is very old and general. So also are the withering of the plant and the "drying" of man; both were considered to lose freshness, vigor, to shrink, wrinkle or decay. The blood separated from the body is drying, thus dying, and as an aspect of death it becomes loath-

---

* See p. 179.

some. The Greek term *brotos* means on the one hand "blood" that has run from a wound, gore; on the other hand, with a difference in accent, it denotes "the mortal man." It is the human destiny that man is mortal, for his blood becomes *brotos*, while the gods are immortal because they have *ambroton*, "immortal" life substance. So the verb *brotoomai* means to be "stained with gore," also "to become man" as said of Christ, "incarnation."

Not so transparent is the equation of "blood" as the essence of life which is inherited by the children from the parents. It means "race," "blood relationship" on account of fantasies which have no support in physiological reality. Referring to his great ancestors a Homeric hero says: "Of this generation and blood do I claim to be." And Odysseus says to his son: "If you are really mine and of our blood . . ."[15] Shakespeare uses "blood" in the same sense. This meaning is still alive in such expressions as *half blood* or *blue blood*. It is once more the subjective experience of "blood" and not the physiological body fluid and metabolism which is felt to be "hot" or "cold," which is referred to as "burning shame." All those words which describe emotional excitation, lust, love, or hatred in terms of "burning" or "irate fire" translate into figurative language, the unspeakable subjective experience which means on the physiological plane a higher pulse rate and blood pressure.[16]

The belief in the inheritance of this "blood" is not based upon any knowledge of blood types or groups but upon primitive fantasies. These fantasies can be explored by looking into the background of the religious term *blessing* used so frequently in the Bible.*

According to primitive fantasies the conception of a new life in the female organ occurs as the coagulation of the blood which otherwise appears as menstrual discharge. They surmise that the cessation of regular periodicity must be caused by the clotting of blood. Thus the fetus is considered as a lump of clotted blood within the mother. Inside the mother, this blood is the carrier of a new life, an incorporation of a new soul. The clotting of

* See *The Subconscious Language*, pp. 245–247.

the blood is an act of the supernatural Spirit, it is the "fruit of the womb." When discharged, it is "flower," translated as "uncleanness." It is filthy, dirty, loathsome, an object of disgust, fear, avoidance, and taboo.

At this point one may gain an insight into the word *blessing* which is misunderstood by our best dictionaries. This word cannot be interpreted properly when the reality concepts alone are taken into consideration without the implication of unconscious fantasies. The word *blessing*, from former *blōd-sung*, is a derivative of *blōdisō-jan*, (from *blood, bleed*) and thus means properly "to make bloody."

Blood is for all reasons tabooed and so is the word. Word and thing are inseparable for primitive fantasies. One can observe in this case the effect of taboo avoidance upon language. In British English, to use the word *bloody* is almost impossible (not so in American English). It has to be avoided like other four-letter words. Such a sentence as the biblical "Surely a bloody husband art thou to me" (Exodus 4:25) is disturbing to the British speaker. The tabooed meaning has to be repressed. As a consequence of repression, the word lost the conceptual meaning "blood" but kept its original emotional intensity. Repression of the meaning "blood" resulted in the obsessive repetition of the word *bloody*. "In foul language a vague epithet expressing anger or resentment or detestation, but often merely intensive as 'not a bloody one,' is used in place of 'not one' or 'none'" (NED, s.v. *blood*). This usage, the Oxford linguists say, "in modern low English is a deeper corruption"; however, the psychological fact is that the word, after its original meaning was repressed, became transferred from the vocabulary to the grammar. Having lost its independence, it became a functional element of language. Its function is to intensify by adding its original emotional power to other words to make them more expressive.

THE RESPIRATORY SYSTEM

The respiratory exchange between the organism and the external world[17] reveals very distinctly that the material aspect covers but half of the meaning; the other half, if not the greater part, refers to something immaterial emerging from inside experience. Primitive fantasies sensed the interdependence of respiration and pulse rate, of breath and blood, as both are affected by the slightest emotional change, thus both are conceived as primary symbols of emotions, expressive and communicative at the same time. The "sigh" as in the "sobbing" child, "catch the breath," "breathe more freely," "hold the breath," is understood immediately just as blushing or paling of the skin are such elementary manifestations.

In the Old Testament Hebrew *ruach* and *nephesh* cover the material as well as the nonmaterial aspect; both words denote "breath" and "soul." One must, however, keep in mind that such translations remain but poor approximations and never cover the meaning of the original Hebrew terms. The Hebrew *nephesh*, translated either as "life" or "soul," seems to be represented in the physical reality by the blood, but the origin of the word points to "breath" and "respiration" which are felt to be in close connection with "blood" and "heart." This identification of the *nephesh* of man with his blood explains the blood taboo, also such expressions as "the voice of thy brother's blood crieth unto me from the ground" (Genesis 4:10). Not the blood as such but the *nephesh* present in the blood is still speaking after death.

The Hebrew *ruach* is translated sometimes as "wind," "blast," sometimes as "soul" or "spirit." In distinction to the

222

nephesh, the *ruach* is never identified with the human blood. It seems to be located rather in the brain and spinal liquor. The visions of the prophets came about when the *ruach* of Yahweh entered man and possessed him. The *ruach* is speaking to man through "thy dream, and the visions of thy head upon thy bed" (Daniel 2:28). The references to the head, brain and spinal liquor refer to the procreative powers, in a more general sense to the creative capacity of man.

The same interrelationship between "breath" and "soul" can be found in various Indo-European languages. It obviously represents a very old and very general fantasy. The Sanskrit *atma* means "breath" and "soul." In Greek the closest approximation of the Hebrew *nephesh* is the noun *thumos,* a term which is said to be "untranslatable" in our languages. This word is phonemically related to the Latin *fumus,* "smoke," "vapor"; it denotes "breath" and "soul," the living quality of man which can be perceived by his respiration. This *thumos* appeared in the vaporous exhalation; the Greek mind connected it primarily with the evaporation of the warm blood. The English *to fume* still denotes "to give off gas, smoke or vapor" and "to show or give way to anger, annoyance, in *fumes.*" The Greek *thumos* refers to no anatomically defined part of the body. It may point to the chest, lungs, heart as the seat of emotions, but it also may refer to the limbs if these are felt paralyzed by a shocking experience. The word defies translation because it denotes an unspeakable inside experience which affects the respiratory system as well as the circulatory system.

The Greek *psychē* is in some respects different from *thumos.* This word derives from *psychō,* "to breathe, to blow, to make cool," and in the passive "to be frigid," thus it refers also to respiration. While *thumos* suggests the conscious part of the person, *psychē* renders the unconscious part which may persist after death. While the *thumos* is destroyed through death, the *psychē* goes to Hades and persists as a "shadow" or a "phantom" (*eidolon*) of the person, by which one recalls the person in dreams.

Similar associations are present in the Greek *pneuma,* "wind, air, breathed air, respiration and spirit." The same relationship is present in the Latin *animus* and *anima,* meaning "breath" as well as "soul"; the equivalent Greek word *anemos* means "stream of air, wind." The Latin words once more are without equivalents in our languages. The *animus* denotes the consciousness within the chest, or respiration, and the *anima* refers to a kind of "vapor, air, breeze, wind." The Greek *thumos* approximates the Latin *animus* while *psychē* shows the qualities of *anima*. The same holds true for the Latin *spiritus* which is a derivative of *spirō, -āre*, "to breathe."

Within the realm of Germanic languages, the English *soul* (from Old English *sawol*), the German *Seele* and the Gothic *saiwala* are in phonemic correspondence with the Greek *aiolos*, from a former *aiwolos*, meaning "quick-moving, nimble, rapid." The substantiation of these qualities is *Aiolos, Aiolus*, the mythical personification of the breeze. The same identification of "breath," "breeze" and "soul" prevails in the Slavic languages (*dusha*) and in many non-Indo-European languages, e. g., in Hungarian (*lélek*). Respiration appears in this very archaic conception as the distinctive feature between the living organism and the dead one, and consequently it is also considered as "life" or "vital force." The Greek *aiolos* is related to *aiōn*, meaning "life time," "spinal marrow," which is the seat of the generative power. However, it would result in misunderstanding to suppose that "breath" is the primary meaning and "soul" is its secondary figurative extension. Such interpretation does not fit the primitive fantasies which shaped the pertinent verbal expressions. One's own breathing is a primary experience of life. "Wind," "breeze," and "breath" are denoted by the same word because they mean for primitive fantasies virtually the same thing. All these terms refer to a unitary internal sensation located in the central chest area with a vague awareness of the interdependence of the circulatory and the respiratory systems. For instance, our verb *to pant* refers to respiration: to breathe quickly as from exertion, but it refers also to the pulsation of the heart; both meanings are fused by a unitary emotional sensation: "to long eagerly, to yearn." Even though both systems record the slightest emotional changes and reveal something about the intensity of the excitement, they reveal relatively little as to the cause and the quality of the internal experience. Our languages indicate in some general way that anxiety is accompanied by difficulties in breathing. The insufficient pulmonary ventilation is indicated by the terms *anxiety* and *anguish*, the equivalent German *Angst* and the French *angoisse*.* All these words derive from a basic form, the meaning of which can be seen in the Latin verb *angō, anxum,* which means in reference to an outside pressure "to bind, draw or press together, to throttle, to strangle"; in reference to a pressure arising from within it denotes "to cause pain, to distress, torment, torture, vex, trouble, to feel distressed, to suffer." The throat and chest area is still often recorded as the phenomenological experience of anxiety.

The *sigh* is a deep and shallow respiration, generally interpreted as a symptom of fatigue, depression, or grief, therefore the verb *to sigh* means also "to lament, mourn over."

Yawning, another respiratory symptom, is generally understood as an approach to sleep, drowsiness, dullness, and boredom, brought about by any monotony, as by inducing hypnosis. It is thus a symptom of regression, perhaps to the post-natal breathing difficulties and gasping of the neonate.

Breathing takes place through both the oral and nasal cavities. The nose became in this way the vehicle of inside experiences, also an organ of communication.[18] "The glory of his nostrils is terrible," Job says (39:20). The inside experience is odor perception, to the outside the nostrils communicate in the biblical language the anger of the Lord. Because the Lord formed man of the dust of the ground and "breathed into his nostrils the breath of life" (Genesis 2:7), Job says: "All the while my breath is in me, and the spirit of God is in my nostrils" (Job 27:3). So the Latin *flātus* means "breeze, breath," but with the connotation of "odor." The same holds true for the Greek *pneō* which means "to breathe" and also "to send forth odor." Even the Greek *anemos* covers both meanings: "a stream of air, wind" and also "wind of the body." It is probable that the physical phenomenon "wind" received its name from the bodily experience. The Latin *animus,* also the congeneric words in the Slavic languages, denotes both "breath" and "odor." The English *breath* developed from the Old English *braeth,* "odor." The German *Backe* means both the cheeks and the buttocks. The confusion of the oral and anal polarity is a frequent symptom of schizophrenics who require while eating the privacy of the toilet.[19]

---

* See *The Subconscious Language,* pp. 236–241.

226

The confusion of the oral and anal aspect of the body-self can be illustrated by the clinical case of a girl, ten, who refused to speak during the session but wrote notes, usually on lavatory papers, although on leaving she repeatedly shouted, "Good-bye, Stinker!" She began to talk suddenly when the fear "that the breath that came out of her mouth when she spoke would stink like the gas, which came out of her bottom" was interpreted to her.[20] The Latin *animus*, the Old English *braeth*, proves how old this identification is.

These words show that the idea of "soul" has been conceived as respiration, observed from the outside and experienced from inside. When observed in others it is called "respiration," "breath," and when experienced from inside it is called "soul, psyche, spirit, animus." Respiration appears by these verbal interpretations primarily as the manifestation of the nonmaterial agency of life, beginning with the first intake of air and ending with the last exhalation.

Considering such words as *psychē*, *pneuma*, and *spiritus* phonemically, it is difficult to deny, even though it cannot be substantiated by scientific evidence, that some sound symbolism is also operative in their meanings.* The combined explosive and sibilant consonant cluster in the initial *psy-*, *pneu-*, *spi-*, suggests the explosive exit of air (*pneumatic*). The implication of the odor perception of the outflowing air may explain how this sound cluster became expressive of anal fantasies connected with disgust, loathing and contempt. Such are some interjections in English as *pooh, pshaw, pish, fie*. The same sound complex is present in the German *pfui* or the French *fi*, or the Greek *phu* and *psy*, and in the Latin *fu* and *fufae*. These words make use of this sound symbolism which is expiratory in character, in defiance of all phonemic rules.

The phonemic equivalent of the Greek *pneuma*, "spirit," is the Old English *fneo-san*, Dutch *fniezen*, and Old Nordic *fnysa*, all meaning "sneeze." Other terms for the same concept developed from an initial *pster-* or *kseu-* cluster. Sound symbolism is again probable although not provable.

---

* See p. 338.

This equation of "spirit" and "sneeze" calls for an explanation. One will understand this strange connection by taking into account the special reverence which Greeks and Romans, and also Hindus and other people, felt for sneezing. It was considered as an involuntary action which was an intrusion of a higher power into consciousness. Being independent from the personal will just as other automatic bodily functions, it was understood to be a message of the *psyché*, anima, located in the head. It was not the manifestations of the unconscious, but rather of a super-conscious part of the soul. An illustrative case is told by Homer (*Odyssey* 17:539-547).

> Penelope said to Eumaeus: "Oh, if Odysseus might come and reach his fatherland, soon would he with his son avenge the violence of these men." So she spoke and Telemachus sneezed loudly and it resounded around the roof terribly. And Penelope laughed and said to Eumaeus: "Go I pray; call the stranger even so before me. Dost thou not see that my son has sneezed at all my words? Wherefore not unfilled should be death for the suitors . . ."[21] Sneezing and sexual excitement were the two conspicuous manifestations of the indwelling *psyché*, both being independent of the individual will.

It should be remembered in this context that the Greek *psyché* represents a trans-individual element in the individual life, thus "psychology" in reference to respiration and in the original meaning of the word deals with this element which reaches beyond the life of the body.

THE INTERNALS

The internals belong to the "hidden" elements of the body. They are not accessible to inspection. The words referring to them demonstrate that they denote not mere objects but fantasies about these unseen objects. They refer to the internal parts in the same sense as found previously in connection with the *secreta*. One does not see one's own internals, therefore one may expect that the pertinent words denote simply things which were observed by dissecting animals, and thus belong to the physical reality and have no subjective implications. It has been supposed in the pertinent literature that the naming of internal parts derived from autopsies of corpses and of animals. However, the verbal instances show that besides the object perception there exists also an imaginary anatomy referring to the invisible and immaterial attributes of the Self. The correlation of these two aspects may seem fictitious in many of these terms, yet there are instances anticipating an insight into organic processes which are unconscious and have a definite emotional significance. This has been brought to light by advanced biochemical procedures. The subjective meaning implied in the internals, for instance in the heart, could not be derived from the observation of the animal heart. It was one's own living, throbbing heart, the experienced invisible imaginary Heart, to which the word referred.

The internals are felt as constituting parts of the Ego; thus they mean much more than they appear to in anatomy, outside the body. Their meaning is derived from the unconscious perception of their function within one's own organism. This becomes evident also through their specific significance in the rituals of sacrifice. It is not simply the heart, the blood, or the liver which is offered in sacrifice to the divinity, but primarily the immaterial spiritual power, the soul, which was thought to be alive within these internals. The internals are the materialization of the potentialities which are present inside the Self. In Latin, *haru-spex* is the common denotation of the "bowel-gazer" who foretells the future. The inspection of the internal parts of the victim in order to gain knowledge of things to come is a striking instance of fantasies which suppose that the intestines have something to do with the fate of nations. The autopsy supposedly makes visible that which is usually invisible. The internal parts of the body supposedly reveal the mystery of the hidden, immaterial, or supra-natural forces which entered the body at birth and which leave it at death. Man is not simply, according to these fantasies, an individual as he appears to be. A principle transcending the individual is operative in him. The presence of such power, be it called "life" or "soul," necessarily results in the identification of the Ego and the World. The human organism and its biological functions are thought to be essentially phenomena of a universal order. In this respect there exists no strict borderline between the I and the non-I, between man, animal, and plant. The cosmic nature can be understood as personified in the human body and mind. Man can be understood in terms of the universe. This is the approach of the physical sciences to human "nature." Man is the microcosmos, the universe the macrocosmos; both are essentially one. They follow the same laws; they depend upon one another in all their manifestations. The "bowel-gazer" wants to read in the internals the intrinsic laws of the cosmic order, and hence to predict the future. He is the forerunner of the "predictive psychology."

VISCERA. Greek mythological fantasies reveal the most awful horror of horrors in the visions of Cassandra (Aeschylus, *Agamemnon*, 1232). She sees the shadows of children who carry their own intestines in their hands.[22] These intestines represent, of course, the hidden inside Self; the "innermost," we would say. They carry in their hands the infantile complexes of their personality. Yet even by opening the body and inspecting its content the invisible "soul" has not been made visible.

There are various words in all languages which refer to the internals in the same pervasive way, just as an unspecified pain may be felt vaguely without distinct localization in the abdomen. The Greek *splangchnon* (plural *splangchna*) denotes the "inward parts, especially the nobler pieces, the heart, lungs, liver, kidneys which were reserved to be eaten in sacrifices; they were distinguished from the *entera* and *koilia*, which referred primarily to the intestines and the genitals." The pertinent verb, *splangchneuō*, assumed on the one hand the meaning "to eat the *splangchna* of the victim after the sacrifice," and on the other hand "to prophesy from the innards" in the same sense as expressed in the Latin *haru-spex*. The Latin *viscus* (plural *viscera*) refers in an even more general sense to the "inner parts," "the innards" or "innermost parts." It is said to denote "the nobler parts: the heart, lungs, liver, as well as the ignobler, the stomach, the entrails." It means also "uterus, testicles, flesh lying under the skin." These examples show that our dictionaries still insinuate moral values into the internals by distinguishing between "nobler" and "ignobler" parts, obviously because these internal parts and their functions are fraught with emotions. Most instances show that the alimentary canal and the genitourinary systems are perceived as being identical; thus they are denoted by the same name. Such identification is, of course, an anatomical absurdity, but it is in accordance with infantile fantasies. The ideas of "fetus" and "excrements" may also appear in this connection as identified with one another. The Greek *splangchnon* denotes, besides the internals, the female genitals as well as the babe. In the same way the Latin *viscus* denotes, besides the internal parts, "uterus" and the "fruit of the womb." The Greek plural *entera* means as a generic term "guts, bowels, intestines," but also "womb," identifying again the gastrointestinal system with the female genitals. The word is from a grammatical viewpoint the comparative of *entos*, "inside," just as the Latin *interior* is the comparative of *intus*, "inside." The grammatical form reveals in this case that not simply the "inside" but the "more inside, the innermost," is referred to. The Greek *koilia* denotes "belly, any cavity of the body, stomach, intestines," and also "excrements"; it refers to the digestive system as well as to the female genitals. In the same way the Greek *gastēr* means "paunch, belly" as well as "womb." The Latin *venter* also applies primarily to the alimentary canal, "bowels, entrails," but also means "womb" and "fruit of the womb." Infantile as these fantasies are in connecting the "womb" with the "intestines," they may derive from the observation of egg-laying and the projection of it upon the mother. In French, *entrailles* can mean "children." Shakespeare says: "thine own bowels which do call thee sire." The Old Testament is replete with examples of this fusion of the alimentary system with the generative system. The "belly" (Hebrew *me'im*) is such a vague overall concept including the generative organs of the woman as well as of the man. It is said of Abraham: "He that shall come forth out of thine own *me'im* (bowels) shall be thine heir" (Genesis 15:4). Another Hebrew term for "belly, abdomen," is *beten*; that is also used indiscriminately of men and women. "The fruit of the *beten* (body)" is a recurrent formula used for men as well as for women (Psalm 132:11, Micah 6:7).

It can be demonstrated clearly that this general denotation of the "internals" refers not simply to the human anatomy but to the subjective experience of the "wisdom of the body." The indwelling *ruach, psychē, animus* may have their own way or own power different from ours. The abdomen is according to these fantasies the seat not only of the generative power but also the center of wisdom which reaches beyond our mental capacities.* When Elihu, after a long silence, finally starts to argue with Job, he says: "For I am full of matter, the *ruach* (spirit) within me constraineth me. Behold, my *beten* (belly) is as wine which hath no vent; it is ready to burst like new bottles" (Job 32:18, 19). The higher wisdom is in this example definitely located in the abdomen. There are many instances proving that the abdomen was considered by these primitive fantasies as the source of the highest spiritual as well as creative capacities of man. The outstanding example which can be understood on this supposition is the saying of Christ: "He

---

* In the Chinese picture writing, *speech–stomach* means "to express in speech what is in one's interior, stomach." H. G. Creel, Chang Tsung-Ch'ien, and R. C. Rudolph, *Literary Chinese by the Inductive Method* (Chicago, Ill.: University of Chicago Press, 1948), p. 142. In Hungarian, "to speak from the belly," *hasból beszél*, does not mean *ventriloqui* but speaking "unprepared, to extemporize."

that believeth on me, as the scripture hath said, out of his belly shall flow rivers of living water" (John 7:38). Because the abdomen is considered as the seat of generative power, one will understand that all manifestations of love and tender emotions are also thought to originate primarily from the "bowels." "My beloved put in his hand by the hole and my *me'im* (bowels) were moved for him" (Song of Solomon 5:4). Joseph saw Benjamin and "his bowels did yearn upon his brother" (Genesis 43:30). The words "my bowels were moved for him" may appear in modern understanding as a metaphorical expression but, even so, behind the surface stands the fact that bowel movement is felt as expression of love. Defecation is according to these primitive fantasies a giving act and the lover wants to give to the beloved, perhaps an anal child. I quote as explanation from an abundance of clinical material concerning this position:

"It is known, too, from other sources, from fantasies of neurotics and from their dreams, that defecation often has to the unconscious the meaning of giving birth. We hear often enough from our patients that their stool is not a dead thing, but something alive, a part of their body."[23]

A clinical example of this receiving and giving relationship projected upon the alimentary canal is the following:

"I refer to the egocentric, neglectful artist's wife who during her marriage of two years suffered from an obstinate form of constipation. This was spontaneously relieved on the day on which her husband brought her a bouquet of flowers, the first gift since their marriage. To this gift she reacted with the first spontaneous evacuation in two years. This present from the husband destroyed her dynamic formula, "Inasmuch I do not receive, therefore I do not have to give."[24]

It is rather difficult, if possible at all, to relate noncognitive internal sensations to specific disturbances of the alimentary process. Our whole vocabulary is aimed at the perception of outside realities and one is not prepared to perceive, differentiate, and describe internal sensations. "Tension," "stress," "frustration," "emotional upset," "breakdown," "insecurity," "resentment," even "anxiety," "fear," and "anger" are general terms approximating individual feelings and do not serve well the purpose of differential diagnosis. An example is epigastric pain. Conclusive empirical studies have been made in order to describe the type of personality that is most prone to duodenal peptic ulcer or to colitis or to chronic constipation. Such personality studies suppose, however, an intensive analysis which goes far beyond the individual self-perception. "Fear" produces almost the same gastric symptoms as "anger." If "hostility" is found to be the emotional state corresponding to symptoms of gastric disturbance, it depends upon what kind of hostility is present. It has been demonstrated that the acting out of anger or its overt expression in verbal invectives may produce the so-called psychic secretion (Alvarez);[25] it may result in hyperacidity, the gastric mucosa may become as engorged with blood and as reddened as the face. However, in case the anger is not expressed but remains repressed behind a friendly smile, its effect upon the alimentary canal might be just the opposite: the gastric secretion might become inhibited and a decrease in the flow of saliva and other symptoms of nervous anorexia may appear.[26]

For such reason the testimony of our verbal legacy is significant because it resulted much like folk-medicines from the empirical experiences of untold generations. For instance "anger" is called in Hungarian "poison" (*méreg*), to "be angry" means to "become poisoned, to eat poison or to be eaten by poison." These expressions describe the empirical experience of "anger" in relationship to the alimentary process. One may interpret "poison" as referring to the repressed hostility because "to take out the anger" is denoted as "to throw up, expectorate poison." Clinical experience has shown that the typical peptic ulcer pain produced by hyperacidity also might be relieved by vomiting which is on the emotional level the expression of intense disgust and resentment. In English, *nausea* denotes the stomach upset producing the impulse to vomit. It is also expressive of a strong *dis-gust*, loathing. The word derives from the Latin and Greek *nautia*, "seasickness," properly "ship-sickness," from *naus* "ship." The German call "nausea" *Übelkeit* with reference to "evil," the French call it *mal au coeur*, properly "sickness of the heart," *écoeurer* means "to nauseate." The English *to throw*, properly to twist, hangs together with the German verb *drehen*, "to twist." To *throw up* as a bodily manifestation of *dis-gust* refers to the impulse of twisting up from the stomach against someone. The idea of "re-proach" also illustrates the same impulse. The word *re-proach*, from the late Latin *re-propriāre*, properly says to bring something back and near, *re-* means "back" and *prope* "near." The German picture is somewhat clearer: *vor-werfen*, "to reproach," means "to throw before," *aus-werfen* "to throw out or up." The Hungarian is even more outspoken: *szemre-hány*, "to reproach," properly means "to throw in the face, to throw into the eyes" of the other person. The French colloquial language says *jeter à la figure de quelqu'un*, "to throw at the face of someone," meaning "to make a reproach."

The Greek *splangchna* denotes, besides the internals, such emotions as "anger," "anxiety," and "pity." The New Testament translates the *splangchna* as "bowels of mercy": "How greatly I long after you all in the bowels of Jesus Christ," Paul says (Philippians 1:8). It is difficult to explain why the "bowels" have in the Old Testament language assumed the meaning of "mercy" because we know no such specific bodily reaction expressive for mercy and sympathy. The usual explanation that the "bowels" were considered to be "the seat" of these emotions seems to be suggested by modern theories of cerebral localization; the pertinent expressions, however, could not have developed out of such considerations. These were originally not metaphorical expressions, as the heart is said to be "the seat of the feelings and affections" (Liddell-Scott, s.v.), but these emotions were in fact subjectively perceived in the abdomen by the alimentary or by the genital system. If the "word-thing" explanation were the right one and the inward parts of the body were named with reference to autopsies and the anatomical parts as they can be defined as physical realities, the meaning of "anger," "anxiety" and "mercy" would never have emerged, however carefully these objects were dissected. On the level of object realities one never found in the "bowels" the idea of "mercy" implied. In Hebrew the singular *rebem* means "womb," the plural "tender mercy." One must suppose that the emotions in question were primarily experienced by the autonomous sensations in these organs, just as "love" or "affection" was experienced by the higher heart-rate. The *splangchna* may serve the oral-aggressive strivings; in this case they suggest the meaning of "anger." They may be instrumental in generous giving and "forgiving"; then they suggest the meaning of "pity" or "mercy." But they also may serve for expressing the conflict between the infantile oral cravings and their rejection by the adult conscience; in such cases the *splangchna* will express "anxiety" and "guilt." The American English colloquialism "What is eating you?" also refers to this digestive function stimulated by the repressed desire for dependence. Such a person consumes himself instead of food.*

There can be little doubt of the origin of this inside gnawing of guilt. The English *re-morse* is the derivative of the Latin verb *re-mordere, re-morsum*, meaning properly "to bite again" and in an expanded sense "to vex, torment, disturb." The German is more expressive by calling this "remorse" *Gewissens-biss*, properly "the bite of the conscience." The Superego may in such situation be biting, eating, consuming again and again the Ego which seeks relief at the early happiness of oral dependency.

The alimentary process is related to the idea of the "soul" just as is respiration. Hesiod called the departed souls of those who once lived in the Golden Age *daimōnes*. This word is a derivative of the verbs *daiomai* and *daidzō* which mean "to slay, rend, divide or tear asunder," in reference to alimentary mastication.[27] The word for digestion also carries such implication; it is derived from *di-* "apart" and the verb *gerō, -ere* "to carry." The idea of the *stomach* refers to these fantasies. In Latin *stoma* means "mouth," *stoma-chos* means properly "little mouth." The diminutive may indicate not simply that this "mouth" is small but that it is an inside, fantasy "mouth" which one feels but never sees. As illustration of this inside "digestive bite" of an imaginary mouth, I refer to its description by an ulcer patient.

"The emptiness is like having nothing in the stomach; like the need for food. It is like a claw crushing me inside,

---

* Sándor Ferenczi and Franz Alexander in analyzing the "gastric" type of conflicts, I suppose, followed the lead of their Hungarian mother tongue, which says about personal frustrations *emészti magát*, "he consumes or digests himself."

tearing my stomach and dragging it downwards. The painful hunger of ulcer patients must be like that—like an electric shock. It is as if there were nothing except the stomach and the sensations of the whole of the body converging in the stomach; as if I were to bite my own stomach. To bite and to pinch must be the same thing. It is as if someone were scratching and tearing my stomach although the sensation is in the epigastrium; I picture the stomach . . . I was thinking of a Walt Disney film where Pluto is punched in the face and swallows his teeth which then bite his stomach. The film shows something like an X-ray of the stomach with the teeth inside biting it while the poor dog is yelping."[28]

The indwelling *demon* is thought of as a slaying, flaying, rendering agency. This is obviously a very archaic fantasy which fits the preying animal and the carnivorous man. The underlying idea seems to be as cannibalistic as implied in the word *sarko-phagos* which properly means "flesh-eater." What happens to the food which enters the mouth in its way through the alimentary canal? Digestion is but the bodily aspect of this process of transmutation. The subjective experience of this process became projected into the idea of the *daimonion*. Socrates called this the spirit which dwelt within him. The intake and the output of the alimentary system, just like the similar exchange in respiration, appear to be a way of expression and of communication between the Ego and the World. The Greeks were aware in their fantasies that digestion and respiration are not merely bodily processes, but also functions which participate in the immaterial aspect of the Self. The more organic and biophysical these processes are, the more unconscious is the layer of the Self which they represent. They speak a language of their own and reveal secrets which the spoken language never could grasp. We still speak in reference to the alimentary system of "mouth-watering," "to swallow, to digest, to stomach something"; we assert by such statements that the bodily function covers but one part of the experience, the other part emerges from unconscious fantasies. The autonomic nervous system does not react to the conceptual word-language, it responds to the picture language of fantasies. It is well known that a mere fantasy may produce disgust and even vomit. Even Pavlov's salivating dog, if responding to a red light, salivates not to the red light as such, but to the fantasy or expectation of food which is associated with the red light.* The language of unconscious fantasies is for this reason of primary importance for understanding the alimentary system. The demon is the projection of such fantasies.

The inside demon may be one of either a good or an evil nature. The Greek *eu-daimon* means "blessed with a good daimon, fortunate," but refers primarily to "outward prosperity, well off, wealthy," the pertinent verb *eu-daimoneō* more expressively states that the good *daimonion* provides man with material blessings; even *eu-daimonia*, Plato's and Aristotle's perfect happiness, primarily referred to material prosperity. Translating these fantasies into verbal expression they would say: the spirit implied in digestion, however aggressive the flesh-eating and rendering demon may be, is essentially a good one and personalizes the drive for material prosperity. One may insert at this point a reference to a condition which is termed in this country as "Wall Street Stomach." Careful analyses have shown that those patients who suffer from a permanent overactivity of gastric secretion resulting in ulcer drive themselves very hard for material prosperity, permit themselves and others no leisure, no relaxation, while in their repressed fantasies they hide the opposite tendency: they yearn for peace and dependence, they want to return to the "Golden Age" of earliest infancy, to enjoy the carefree life protected by a good spirit. The Greek fantasy for this is the *eudaimonion*. For the small child food and love are fused into the one concept of the mother. The craving for love is translated into the craving for food which keeps the gastric secretion flowing, but on the conscious level these fantasies are rejected and substituted by the relentless drive for material success. The intake of food and drink equals "happiness," "wealth," "abundance." Alcoholics, craving the "bottle," sometimes seek this escape from reality. The German verb *schwelgen*, "to abound," is the phonemically akin form of the English

---

* For reason of this anticipation, conditioning does not work if reality precedes the fantasy, that is, if the unconditioned stimulus of meat or food precedes the conditioned stimulus of the red light.

verb "to swallow." Many instances prove the assumption that the content of the alimentary canal is expressive of "gold," "wealth" and "generosity." The "bowels of mercy" still exist in our world, still project unconscious fantasies of goodness, forgiveness, and mercy upon the alimentary canal in protest against the world dominated by merciless competition, but the result of such projection might be a stomach ulcer.

The intake of food thus became associated with the fantasy of a good demon, a benevolent protective spirit which bestows wealth and happiness upon man in our present age, just as in Socrates' time. Elimination and evacuation, on the contrary, became associated with the idea of an "evil" spirit (*kako-daimon*). It is a popular belief that the presence of an evil spirit is indicated by an evil sulfuric odor. *Demon* became synonymous with "evil spirit" in New Testament Greek and so English *demon* evokes the idea of a harmful and aggressive agency. The "demon" could "possess" man and it was a general belief in early ages that mental sickness was the result of "demon possession." To translate these fantasies into our present language, man is "possessed" by an evil spirit if compulsory sadistic fantasies emerge from the unconscious and are felt as being foreign to his Ego. The hostility implied in elimination may result in a permanent peristalsis and desire for evacuation, but this hostility if rejected can also be turned inward, against the own Self, resulting in "remorse," "anxiety" and "guilt." Christ had such an idea in mind saying: "There is nothing from without a man, that entering into him can defile him: but the things which come out of him, those are they that defile the man" (Mark 7:15).

The digestive process is expressed in Latin by the verb *macerō, -āre*, "to make soft or tender," "to soak, steep, macerate." On the emotional plane it means "to weaken in body or mind," "to waste away," "enervate," "to fret, vex, torment one's self." The same implication is present in the Latin verb *mordeō, -ēre*, "to bite," which also can mean "to vex, mortify," "to be attacked, tormented," "to squander," or even "to feel the sting of conscience," the same psychical implication as *re-morse*. The Gothic *idreiga* means both "bowels" and "repentance." The Latin *stomachus* refers like the Greek *stomachos* to the alimentary canal, but as good digestion it can also mean "peace, rest, quiet." If not indicated as such, however, it denotes "distaste, dislike, irritation, vexation, chagrin." The verb *stomachor, -āri* means "to be irritated, peevish, pettish, vexed, angry, out of humor." All these words describe a psychological condition which often results in diarrhea.

The opposite condition is that of the person suffering from chronic constipation. This state is described by the Greek *gemos* which means "intestines," the verb *gemō*, "to be full, to be filled," and the corresponding Latin *gemō, -ere* meaning "to sigh, groan." Such a relationship exists also between the Greek verb *steinō*, "to confine, to be narrowed," "to become full, be thronged" and "to be distressed." Our verb *cramp* carries also these double references: it can denote "to compress," and also "to have a painful contraction." Even *stomachy* means in the obsolete language "spirited, obstinate, irritable," "having a paunch." The verb *to stomach* means like the Latin *stomachari* "to be resentful, to resent, to take offense at." All these meanings together give a fairly adequate description of the unconscious motivation of chronic constipation.

THE GENITOURINARY SYSTEM. The genitourinary system is often termed the "ignobler" part of the internals; however, the Greek and Latin languages prove that this internal system is as significant and expressive of well-being and health as is respiration or the alimentary process. The Roman equivalents of the Greek *daimōnes* are the Latin *genii*, the guardian spirits which decide man's destiny. The word is a derivative of the verb *gignō, -ere*, "beget," and thus one may surmise that the *genius* denoted primarily the genital potency of man, his semen. The outflowing semen is another excretion, and consequently another appearance of the internal spiritual Self in the world.

In order to understand the associations which cluster around this idea of the *genius* one must change some ideas about the body-self. We are accustomed to consider the sex organs as the seat of the generative power, while the intellectual capacities, and all that which is specifically human, are centered in the head. The Greeks and Romans and other people of early ages considered the generative power and the vital force of man to be located primarily in the marrow of the bones. The marrow was the daintiest food of prehistoric cannibals. The semen was produced, according to these fantasies, by the spinal marrow and the brain, which was also considered to be marrow. These are the reasons why the Greek *psychē* and the Latin *genius* were located primarily in the head of man. The primacy of the head in the fantasies about the Self developed not because the brain represented the conscious personality. On the contrary, it was venerated for being the source of fertility, of a vital power which reaches beyond the individual life. The phonemic pattern which is expressive of "I can, I am able to," the Latin *possum* from *pot-sum*, also *pot-ency*, is used in some languages to denote just the Self; even in the ancient Hittite language the "Self" is denoted by this same old root *pat*. In the Hungarian, for instance, "my seed" is the same word as "myself" (*magam*). This is another instance proving that the semen is considered the true realization of the personality. The Latin *genius* came to denote not only "semen" but also "birthday," which is in this interpretation the feast of the ideal seminal unity of father and son. However, it goes without saying that to say "the son inherited the genius of his father" originally meant exactly what it says. The fantasies which have grown out of the repressed genital meaning of *genius* display once more the dynamic process of sublimation. The meaning shifted from the body to the soul, from the procreation to the spiritual creation. In Latin the guardian spirit *genius* was first of all in charge of the protection of man's instinctual demands, of the satisfaction of his sexual desire: *genius indulgere* denoted this indulgence in "lechery." In a further development this meaning became repressed and the word developed instead the idea of the exalted type of man who is creative in the sublime spiritual sense. Productivity and creativity are the highest values which spring up out of the Self. Through these values man may even transcend the limitations of his nature and continue his existence on a level higher than biological procreation by incarnating his *genius* in his work.

A similar change from the genital meaning to the spiritual one can also be observed in the pertinent Greek words. The English word *soul* (Gothic *saiwala*) corresponds phonemically to the Greek adjective *aiolos* (from *aiwolos*). This belongs to the noun *aiōn* (from *aiwōn*), denoting "one's lifetime, life"; the same phonemic pattern in Sanskrit means "vital force, vigor, strength." In interpreting this relationship it was found that the inside experience of "life, vigor, strength" has been substantiated in the idea of the "soul." A more specific and concrete meaning of the Greek *aiōn* refers to the "spinal liquor." In Greek thinking this "spinal marrow" is the very essence of the vital forces. This word points again to the same idea found in connection with *potis* and *genius*. The vital force of man, his semen, was supposed to flow from his "spinal marrow." As observed previously, *soul, aiolos,* associate the spiritual Self with the gas exchange. This respiratory concept of the soul became blended in the early fantasies with this new idea of the materialization of the soul which is in the generative potency of man. "Soul," "breath" and "semen" are associated with one another in these words.

The Greek mythology shows a generally known re-interpretation of this etymological complex by the joint connection of *Eros* (the Roman *Cupido, Amor*) and *Psyche*. One is inseparable from the other. Both are repre-sented with wings, attributes of their aiolial-aerial nature. There are Greek vase paintings which make this connec-tion between Psyche and the implication of "spinal liquor," *aiōn*, more explicit. They picture a divinity whose outflowing semen is transformed into butterflies flying away. What is the meaning of this strange picture? The Greek *psychē* denotes both the "soul" and the "butterfly." The underlying associations evidently suppose that *psychē*, this invisible double of the Self, is not to be con-sidered an immaterial personal complement of the body-self, as in most modern psychologies, but as a "departed soul" which has made its transient seat within the body. It has entered the body at birth and will leave the body at death. It will fly away and survive in Hades. The night-fluttering butterflies, the moths, are called in Greek *phallaina;* this form is grammatically the feminine of *phallos*. This supposes again the same association which exists between Amor and Psyche. Greek vase paintings also depict the "winged phallos" through this same asso-ciation which connects the idea of the soul with the genitourinary system.[29]

THE LIVER.   The liver is another incarnation of the invisible "soul," according to primitive fantasies. Liver models with magic inscriptions were found on Etruscan, Babylonian and Hittite (Bogaskeuy) territory. These relics attest the religious significance attributed to the liver. In the search for the "soul" man studied the liver. However, the tangible liver models do not prove that the anatomical study of the liver was the source of religious fantasies. On the contrary, the subjective phenomenological experience of the secretion of the bile was the primary motive which led to religious fantasies and to the anatomical study of the liver. Neither anatomy nor the dissecting of animals revealed the remarkable fact that there exists a relationship between emotions and metabolic changes.

The Germanic word *liver* is not generic in other Indo-European languages. It must originate from a word complex familiar with the Germanic languages. It seems to be a derivative of the verb *to live*. The German *Leber*, "liver," is in the same way derived from *leben*, "to live." In the Old Nordic poetic language the "brother" is called *lifri*, meaning "of the same liver." The liver is considered in these terms as the very center of life. The liver was characterized as the source of aggressive impulses in the Greek *cholos* or *cholē*, which means both "bile" and "anger." Its derivative is *cholera*, denoting the disease, although this should not be understood as "liver sickness," but rather as a reference to the association of "anger" and "diarrhea" which was observed in the case of the Greek *splangchna*. In Latin the word, like the English *choler* and *bile*, also denotes "irascibility" and "anger."

The liver as the source of violent emotions, love and hatred, was in Shakespeare's mind when he said: "to quench the coal which in his liver glows." The words *to glow, gall, gold* and *yellow*, Old English *geolo*, German *gelb*, are interrelated and developed out of one basic phonemic pattern. The secretion of the liver, the *bile*, is found in the *gall*. This word, Old English *gealla*, originally meant "shining yellow," which is also the quality of gold. This golden-yellow shine explains the *glow* attributed to the liver. It made the liver the seat of "ardent" passions.

The bile is secreted into the duodenum, it helps digestion. Thus it became the carrier of the aggressive intention implied in all digestion. Its overflow is a sign of irritation, vexation or anger. If someone becomes irritated, it is said in German: "something runs over his liver" (*ihm ist etwas über die Leber gelaufen*). If someone freely expresses his irritation, it is said in German, "he speaks out of his liver" (*er spricht von der Leber weg*). To be "vicious" means in Hungarian *rossz máju*—"having a bad liver." Envy is often characterized as "yellow" or "green," hostility as "bitter." Yet it is not the hatred that is yellow or bitter but rather the bile secreted by the stimulation of this hatred. Such expressions suggest that anger may manifest itself in a concomitant increase in the secretion of bile, a biological observation which the early Greeks could hardly have made through experimentation. The bile is normally yellow-green in color: it may turn dark green in case of accumulation as a result of high emotional irritation. The Greek *melan-cholia*, properly "black-bile," denoted the despondent state as a disease of the bile. In this case depression has been correlated with the secretion of the bile.[30]

THE SPLEEN. Relatively little is known about the psychology of the spleen. The spleen releases reserve blood supplies by contraction. The term *spleen* also means in English "bad temper." This seems to be the internal perception of the contraction of the spleen in tense situations. The original Greek term denotes besides the vascular organ the "affections of the spleen as one dying with anxiety." The word is a phonemic variant of *splanchnon*, "internals"; thus the person afflicted with a sickness of the spleen becomes a "hypochondriac." In English *spleen* came to denote "melancholy," "low spirits," "bad temper."

Early physiology attached great significance to the *humors*, body fluids thought to be decisive for health and sickness of body and mind. The *temper*, from the Latin *temperāre*, "to mix," just refers to a specific state of mind as a result of mixing the body fluids.[*] The ideal mixture keeps the mind in balance, thus *temper* means also "equanimity," "composure," and to lose one's temper means a disturbance in the supposed balance of internal metabolism. The term *phlegm*, derived from the Greek *phlegma*, denotes a "clammy humor of the body," *phlegnon* denotes "a burning heat, specifically an inflammation beneath the skin." These words raise some paradoxical questions because four disparate meanings were united by them.

---

[*] See p. 379.

First: the Greek term *phlegma* properly means "flame, fire, heat," the noun belongs to the verb *phlegō*, "to burn, become hot, take fire." Second: the noun denotes one of the four body fluids of early physiology. This body fluid was supposed to be, not hot as one would expect, but "cold and moist"; it is the "clammy" one. Third: this body fluid seems to be dominant in the *phlegmatic* personality. Fourth: *phlegm* means also mucus secreted, especially by the respiratory passages and discharged through the mouth. How can these four denotations be united in a meaningful whole? It has been clinically observed that the discharge greatly increases in case of the inflammation of the mucus.[31] This might be the reason why the idea of "inflammation" became associated with the mucous discharge. The relationship between mucous discharge and the "phlegmatic" personality is not always well understood. Such personality is described as sluggish, not easily aroused or moved; apathetic, calm, composed. This interpretation of the pleasant, "calm and composed" personality covers up the basic meaning which refers to the viscous, moist discharge of respiratory passages. This discharge, called also *slime*, is generally identified with the viscous secretion of the skin of slugs, snails, catfishes; these are "cold-blooded" animals, the body temperature of which is not internally regulated. This word, *cold-blooded*, is also a characteristic of human behavior. It refers to a lack of the expected excitement or feeling. The *phlegmatic* person is thus "sluggish" like a *slug*, is calm as any "cold-blooded" being can be, not simply "composed," but rather "slimy," implying the disgust with which the discharge of the "phlegm" is perceived. The phlegmatic person must be full of slime, thus he might suffer from an "inflammation beneath the skin."

The theories of early physiology are misconceptions if taken at their face value as physiology; if understood as psychology they anticipate an insight in the psychosomatic interdependence of metabolism and emotions.

THE HEART. The heart still remains in present-day fantasies the bodily seat of tender emotions, obviously because the cardiovascular changes in excitement are felt most distinctly. "My heart knocks at my ribs," Shakespeare says. The heart formerly represented another part of the Self as understood in the present-day popular language.[32] The Greek term *phrēn* is characteristic of the general and diffuse insecurity shown in the naming of the internals. It means properly the diaphragm, midriff, or muscle which separates the heart and the lungs from the lower viscera; then it may mean everything about the heart and the liver. It is used for denoting the "heart" in particular; in the plural it may denote the intestines. As inside experience it stands for "soul, spirit," and is the objectivization of "anger," of bodily appetites such as "hunger," also of "courage" as in modern English, but in clear distinction to bodily fantasies it is the center of "mind" and "wit." The identification of the "heart" with conscious mental activity can also be seen in such related words as *phroneō*, "I think"; *phrontis*, "worry"; *sō-phrōn*, "wise"; *eu-phrōn*, "hilarious," "benevolent." The Greek physiology did not divide the Self by the polarity of "brain" and "heart" as popular fantasies distinguish these organs of rational thinking and sympathetic feelings. In the Greek concept of the Self the brain was not valued as highly as by primitive headhunters and modern neurologists. The brain was considered to be simply "marrow": "for many think the brain is really marrow," Aristotle says (PA 652). The Greek language denotes the "brain" by *enkephalos*, meaning simply "in the head," as the content of the skull. The intellectual capacity of man was thought to be located in the heart. The internals, and especially the heart, were considered as the undivided incarnation of man's intellectual and emotional qualities. This may be the expression of a most primitive concept of the Self. It is noteworthy that the Egyptian deities are represented with animal heads and human bodies, while in the Greek fantasies the personifications of instinctual drives appear as human above the diaphragm, as animal below it. Language fantasies seem in this respect more archaic than mythology. They still combine "intestines," "heart," and "spirit" into one undifferentiated unity, the location of which are the internals. The Greek *chondros* denotes the "cartilage of the breastbone"; *hypochondria* denoted the soft part of the body above the navel and "below the cartilage." In Latin the word *hypo-chondria* assumed, besides the anatomical meaning, the emotional meaning of a "morbid anxiety as to one's health."

The same associations prevail in the Latin *prae-cordia* which denotes the "diaphragm" and the "intestines" and also the "heart." The Latin *cor, cordis* means the "heart" in particular. The related word *re-cordor, recordatus* means "I remember" (English *record*) and thus implies a conscious intellectual activity in the heart. Such biblical expressions as "let thine heart retain my words" (Proverbs 4:4) or "write them upon the table of thine heart" (Proverbs 3:3) prove how generally retention and learning were attributed to the heart. The English *to learn by heart* refers to these ideas. It is still a folk way to comment on a hiccup as "someone is thinking of me," associating in this way the diaphragm (the spasmodic contraction of which makes the hiccup) and "remembrance." The changing of the mind also has, according to the Latin language, something to do with the diaphragm. The Latin says in this sense *mūtare praecordia*, "to change the diaphragm." The words for "heart" are in Latin as well as in Greek used for "intestines, belly, stomach," and also for "spirit." The Greek *kardia* and *kēr* mean "heart, stomach, spirit"; *ētor* means "heart" and "belly"; the Latin *cor* denotes besides the "heart" also the "stomach"; and the Latin *cordatus*, properly "hearty," means "wise." The heart still has an intellectual function according to these terms. It still holds the position which is occupied by the brain in later thinking. In the New Testament Greek *kardia*, "heart," refers to the true inner Self of man, to the Ego, and it is used almost in the sense of a personal pronoun.

THE TONGUE

The tongue is an external part of the body as well as an internal one. This word may serve as a transition from the internal to the external perception of the body-self. It refers to an anatomical and to a psychological reality. In Latin the word for "tongue" should have an initial *d-* like *dingua*, yet the word became *lingua*. For what reason may the *l-* have replaced the original *d-?* It is more than probable that this change came about through the influence of *lingō, -ere*, "to lick," as a blending which fused the objective anatomical reality of the tongue with the subjective experience of "licking." The Hebrew *lāshōn*, "tongue," also derives from *lāshan*, "to lick."

Another association connects the "tongue" with the idea of "fire." The stars were perceived as "little tongues" of fire in Germanic languages, so in the English *tungol*, "star." This strange connection between "star" and "little tongue" has been questioned on the semantic side; however, the spheres of associations of both words indicate that they were once connected with one another. The "astrology" was denoted in Old English *tungol-spraece*, properly "little tongue-speech." The stars are fire and the flames have licking tongues. In German the flames "lick," *züngeln*, properly they lick with "little tongues," whereas it is said in English "the flames leap." This idea of the fire-tongue became dramatized in the Greek myth when the woman becomes pregnant by the "tongues" of fire. The same idea of the fire as symbolic for "heat" is expressed in other languages, as in German *brennen*, "burn," *Brunst*, "fire, sexual drive," and *brunzen*, "urinate," are denoted by the same word. In the Old Hungarian the "star" is termed by the same word as "urine" (*hugy*). The Hindu god of fire, *Agni*, is the inventor of speech. "The tongue is a fire," the biblical language says (James 3:6), or "his tongue is as devouring fire" (Isaiah 30:27). The implication of these figurative expressions is the same: the creative power of the spirit is concentrated in the tongue.[33]

> The religious meaning of "tongue," "language," and "fire" is found in close association in the biblical record about the Pentecostal outpouring of the Holy Ghost upon the apostles (Acts 2:3, 4). "And there appeared unto them cloven tongues like as of fire and it sat upon each of them. And they were all filled with the Holy Ghost, and began to speak with other tongues, as the Spirit gave them utterance." This is an illustrative instance which may elucidate the proper meaning of "tongue." The tongue in question is not simply the anatomical tongue but the tongue of fantasies, the part of the invisible Self. This is the tongue in the spiritual, religious, and mythical understanding. This "tongue" refers to a subjective experience. The "babbling" (Greek *glosso-lalia,* translated as "speaking in tongue") of the apostles is an internal language and cannot be construed as speech for communication to be understood by others. It is like the stammering of the small child when it learns to speak and first experiences the subjective meaning of "language." The "cloven tongues" of fire are an appearance of this inside tongue projected into the outside world.[34]

No other parts of the body, not even the eyes, are infested with so many meanings as the tongue. It is a general feature of our languages that they denote themselves by *tongue,* but again this is not simply the anatomical reality in question. It is rather the subjective kinesthetic feeling of the motion of the tongue while speaking. The tongue is, of course, only one part of the whole vocal apparatus. Other organs, for instance the vocal cords, remain mostly unconscious to the speaker. The motion of the tongue is experienced by the speaker while the motion of the mouth and lips can be observed on others.

Through this equation of "tongue" and "language" which

is present in the Greek *glossa,* the Latin *lingua,* the German *Zunge* or obsolete English *tongue,* this meaning complex absorbed the attributes which belonged originally to the creative and generative spirit. The "Tongue" as the incarnation of the Spirit does not belong to the individual self but represents a supra-personal agency acting within the self, sometimes intruding into the self against the individual's will.

I quote from a clinical report:

> A twenty-eight-year-old schizophrenic male patient says: "I have a subconscious feeling when I see a woman that I am entering that woman. It is a mental state only. When a man speaks it feels at times as if the organ of the man was in my mouth . . . When a man talks and his organ flies in my mouth it makes me feel I am a woman."[35]

These words refer to an inner experience. One should not suppose that the anatomical tongue is the real one, the other "tongues" represent the figurative use of the word. The subjective experience is as real as the outside reality. This subjective experience associates the tongue with the generative spirit. The creative word appears as a primary act of the generative spirit. "Creation" means according to these fantasies "to call a thing by its name." The Egyptian god who is the creator of all things, created first himself by going up to the top of a mountain and shouting his own name, thus he became real. We still say "to call into existence," German *ins Leben rufen,* "to call into life."

The creative word precedes existence according to early thinking. "In the beginning was the word" (*logos*). The biblical record of the Creation is an outstanding illustration of the creative word. "And God said, Let there be light: and there was light" (Genesis 1:3). The psychological truth of such words consists in the fact that "things" become real if one perceives them as organized wholes, thus they can be named. By calling them by name they can be singled out as figures from the ground. It is also in accordance with infantile fantasies that the small child may attribute unlimited power to the word of the father. The tongue of the father is omnipotent, filled with supernatural power. Therefore it may be said:

"their tongue is as an arrow shot out" (Jeremiah 9:8), "soft tongue breaketh the bone" (Proverbs 25:15), or "A wholesome tongue is a tree of life: but perverseness therein is a breach in the spirit" (Proverbs 15:4). This omnipotence of the tongue is a recurrent fantasy in Shakespeare's language: "O that my tongue were in the thunder's mouth, then with passion would I shake the world." The generative power of the creative spirit may be felt to be in the tongue. Its most concise religious expression is: "the Word was made flesh" (John 1:14). The "gift of the tongue" belonged originally to the creative spirit and was imparted to man. The religious experience refers to this spiritual generation through the creative word as second birth. It is said: "Being born again, not of corruptible seed, but of incorruptible, by the word of God, which liveth and abideth for ever" (I Peter 1:23). The "gift of the tongue" is the human participation in the spiritual creative power of the "Word of God."

The primitive penalty of cutting out the tongue should be understood, like blinding or castration, as a spiritual act depriving man of his generative power. This barbarous penalty is still present in Shakespeare's fantasies: "I shall cut out your tongue." Like the fear of castration, the fear of losing the tongue is present in such references as to become "tongueless" or the "pain of losing tongue." However, it would be an arbitrary interpretation to suppose that the cutting out of the tongue is simply a symbolic substitute for castration. The tongue is a primary organ of the spiritual capacity of man; to be deprived of it is as primary a frustration as castration. In the final instance the "losing of the tongue," just as castration, is still a living element in verbal fantasies. Formulas found in the biblical language as well as in Shakespeare's say: "their tongue cleaved to the roof of their mouth" (Job 29:10), "my tongue cleaveth to my jaws" (Psalms 22:15), "the tongue of the sucking child cleaveth to the roof of his mouth for thirst" (Lamentations 4:4). Jesus cured the deaf who had also an "impediment in his speech": "his ears were opened, and the string of his tongue was loosed, and he spake plain" (Mark 7:35). The same inner experience of the tongue is used by Shakespeare: "tongue-tied sorrow" or "tongue-tied patience," "Be not tongue-tied!" Such words obviously refer not to some anatomical absurdity of a "tied tongue," nor of an especially "heavy tongue," nor to a physiological phenomenon, by saying: "my tongue cleaves to the roof within my mouth," or "my very lips might freeze to my teeth, the tongue to the roof of my mouth." Such words of Shakespeare grasp from within and describe phenomenologically a subjective experience (such formulas are found also in Chinese); this is the paralysis of speech in the agony of fear, a general symptom of nightmares when one wants to shout, cry, and cannot do so. It is obviously the subjective experience of the "inside tongue" which elicited such fantasies.

One can observe time and again that this imaginary "tongue-tied" or "frozen to the roof of the mouth" condition has been misunderstood not only in linguistic literature but also on the level of everyday reality. Until recently, a surgical operation, called "clipping of the tongue," was performed under such tyranny of words. Mothers, misled by the spell of verbal symbolism, always found physicians willing to perform such surgery on their children—cutting the frenulum, the adhesion of the tongue to the floor of the mouth. Such routine operations were carried out in good faith on the newborn infant as a prophylactic measure, an age-old practice that can be understood as a ritual just like circumcision rather than as a sanitary performance. However, this "clipping of the tongue" may show once more, for all the other similar instances, that taking verbal expressions at their face value and referring them to the anatomical reality may result in complete misinterpretation in linguistics and psychology as well as in surgery.

THE EYES

Subverbal communications implied in the eye reflexes, facial expressions, skin reactions, postural gestures, are generally understood.[36] Such words as *in-spect, ex-pect, su-spect, prospect, re-spect, intro-spect, in-sight, fore-sight, over-look, regard, behold, watch out* refer to the language of the eyes. One understands this body language even when it may contradict the verbal expression. This is remarkable because the speaker might be unaware of a blink or an askance look. He may communicate something and not know it. The interpretation of meanings expressed by the eye reflexes will help one understand the verbal language. Sometimes one may say something one does not want to say because it is not admitted, or is repudiated, by the verbal Ego or Superego.[37]

The interpretation of the look might also be a symptom of paranoid tendencies. These tendencies reinforce the semantic sensibility. The interpreters of dreams and languages somehow share the semantic sensitivity with their patients. While the normal speaker can happily skate on the thin ice of the verbal surface, the one with scientific understanding will know how deep the lake is, how thin the ice, and how easily it may break down altogether. This manifest surface of language shall be interpreted and understood in light of the subverbal strata of communication. In the following, the symbolism of eye movements shall be investigated.

EYE AND WINDOW. The identification of eye and window is but a small segment of a more general equation identifying the house with the body, the fireplace with the genitals, the door with the mouth, and the windows with the eyes. These equations are found in various languages. They are very old, dating back into prehistoric ages. In Greek, *phaos* or *phōs* means the "light of the eye," the plural *phōta* means "eyes" and "window." The same holds true for the Latin *lūmen*, "light," "light of the eye," plural *lūmina*, "window." In English, the word *window* originates from the former compound *wind-auga*, "wall-eye." Another Old English term for "window" is *eag-duru*, like the Old High German *auga-tora*, "eye-door." A third Old English term for "window" is *eag-thyrel*, properly "eye-hole."

Restricting the linguistic material to these few words, the following observations can be made:

First: the human body and its functions are the primary frame of reference in naming objects of the perceived world. Man speaks a body language even if he refers to objects. Second: this reference to the human body is seemingly absent, totally unconscious to the modern speaker, so much so that even Webster does not understand it and rationalizes the Old English *wind-auga* as "wind-eye." The identification of "eye" and "window" is, of course, an absurdity which has escaped the control of common sense; it might be the delusion of a paranoiac mind. To say "the walls have eyes" is as nonsensical as to say "the walls have ears." The door is in the same way identified with the mouth. A schizophrenic patient said: "The (open) doors eat me up." The connection between "eye" and "window" became completely obliterated on the manifest surface of language, yet it may reappear at any moment. I quote a few instances from Shakespeare's language. Shakespeare says: "eye's window," "windows of thine eye," "her two blue windows faintly she upheaveth," "crystall window, open, look out." Let us suppose as some critics do that the original reference to the human body does not exist in the mind of the modern speaker, and, consequently, the word *window* carries this reference to the eye only by a mechanism of functional autonomy completely independent of the long-forgotten past. If this would be true, Shakespeare never could have found these just quoted verbal expressions. People did not dig out the original meaning from an Old English dictionary when they called the "window shade" *Venetian blind*. The window totally covered by a shade is *blind* indeed. In dreams this seemingly nonexistent symbolic implication may spring up to the manifest expression. I quote as a clinical illustration from Freud's analysis of the wolf-dream:

> "One day the patient began to proceed with the interpretation of the dream. He thought that the part of the dream which said that suddenly the window opened of its own accord, was not completely explained by its connection with the window at which the tailor was sitting and the wolf came into the room. It must mean: my eyes suddenly open. I am asleep, therefore; and suddenly wake up . . . "[38]
> Freud made no reference to the linguistic equation between "window" and "wall-eye" nor to the implication of "into the room" as a self-perception of the body-Ego.

The identification of "eye" and "window," however repressed for the normal speaker, especially if his mother tongue is not English, may spring up in the language of the schizophrenic.

> Renée, the French-speaking schizophrenic patient of M. A. Sechehaye, told her psychoanalyst: "When you let me go for three weeks at the beginning of the analysis (vacation), I felt that I was starting to *close the blinds* and only analysis could help me in keeping them open."[39]

A third consideration forces upon us the question: Why did the "window" come to be called "wall-eye" at all? Rudolf Meringer, the great advocate of Word-Thing linguistics, demonstrated in this case, as in many other similar instances, that the object "window" was originally, when primitive blockhouses were first built, an opening cut into the timber in the shape of an eye. The windows of the primitive blockhouses of our ancestors looked, indeed, as if they were "eyes" of the wall. A certain round window is called *bull's-eye* in modern English. It is also called so in Sanskrit; it must represent a very old and general association. If this Word-Thing interpretation is right, the eye-shaped windows of blockhouses existed first without name and then were named for their shape afterward. This would suppose the reversal of the body-language projected upon the outside world, which can be demonstrated by innumerable verbal examples and clinical evidences. The basic question is still in this case: Why did the ancestors cut out the openings of their houses in the shape of eyes? I do not insist on the primacy of the verbal expression, nor believe that in the beginning was the thing, but assume that in the beginning was the body and the fantasies about the body-Ego. These fantasies became expressed in both—in words and in things. In other words, verbal expressions do not refer to the physical reality of the environment, but to ideas, fantasies, to the myth of the Eye and Window. Speaking of the "wall-eye" is symbolic, just as saying, for instance, "the table stands on four legs." The table does not "stand." It is a piece of wood which does not do anything. It is placed by man in this position. It has no "legs" even if some tables have their legs artistically elaborated in the forms of animal legs, thus acting out fantasies of ossified verbal expressions. If Victorian prudery dressed up the legs of the piano with stockings, it was acting out repressed bodily fantasies. So does one act out bodily fantasies in shaping the windows and handling the window shades.

THE DOWNCAST LOOK. One can observe a custom which has achieved, in some parts of the country, the compelling force of law. It is customary to cover the windows with Venetian *blinds*. The pulled-down Venetian blinds are acting out fantasies implied in the downcast eyelids. The window shades became identified with the eyelids. The downcast look is expressive of decency, of aggressiveness, or of guilt feelings.

The pulled-down shades follow an unwritten law of modesty and decency, just as the downcast eyelids do. They express the reversal of the looking impulse, skoptophilia, its repression resulting in symptom formation. It is significant that the "window-eye" is not perceived, as the word-thing interpretation supposes, as being seen from the outside as any object reality, but as an inside entity. It belongs to the inner house, the Ego. Thus the downcast look does not mean protection against *intro-spection* or *in-sight*, but serves primarily the aggressive looking impulse, the *ex-pectation* into the outside world. The closed Venetian blinds pretend that they serve the purpose of warding off the intruding onlookers. In fact, their primary purpose is the looking out from the privacy of the house as through a mask, without being discovered by others. To see but not to be seen is the basic technique of animal aggressiveness, camouflage, mimicry, and adjustment. The preying animals use this tactic of nature. It is human, too.

Shakespeare, commenting on the "Venetian" blinds in the *Merchant of Venice*, said that Shylock sees a thousand lurking eyes full of lust and aggressive intention behind the shut-down shades. "You would have thought the very window spoke, so many greedy looks of young and old through casement darted their desiring eyes." This aggressive force has been turned from the positive to the negative and became, in the course of cultural development, the attribute of decency, modesty and virginity. I quote a clinical instance of this reversal:

> A seven-year-old boy with denial symptoms developed a fear of death, and a tic which bore the imprint of his particular mechanism of denial. It consisted in his "first closing his eyelids and then casting his eyes back until only the whites showed." With these movements, he was symbolically saying, "I see no danger. Therefore, no danger is present." The danger referred to his awareness of the sex difference.[40]

The original aggressive intention behind the downcast window shades as described by Shakespeare is also present in the Old Testament term for "window." This is the Hebrew *arubhah*, which properly means "lurking," the participle of the verb *arab*, "to lurk, lie in ambush," obviously behind the shades of the window. The Romance languages are more specific concerning this aggressive looking impulse. The French *jalousie*, the Spanish *celosia*, and the Portuguese *gelosia* all denote "window shade." The ultimate source of the word which comes from the Latin *zelosus* is the Greek *dzēlos*, "ardor, rivalry, hatred, jealousy"; the verb *zēloō* means "seek with ardor"; *zētros* means "executioner, hangman." In the Old Chinese picture writing, the notion of "jealousy" is expressed by "woman at the window."[41] The association of "jealousy" and "window" must be a very old and general one; otherwise it would not be expressed in the same way by so large and so distant language communities.

The English verb *to watch,* from the Old English *waeccian,* originally meant "to be awake, to keep vigil" on the one hand, and "to be on the lookout" on the other. One may interpret: sleepless nights were spent looking out of the window, waiting and watching.

Dante, fountainhead of medieval symbolism, also knows about the "Lady of the Window." After the death of Beatrice he became attracted to this lady though she did not hide behind the shades. Dante felt he became unfaithful to the memory-image of Beatrice by his sympathy for the other woman. He felt guilty. He said:

> "Wherefore I taking heed of the trouble I was in, lifted my eyes to see if any beheld me. Therewith I saw a noble lady, young and very fair, who was looking at me from a window . . . Through the sight of this lady, I came to such a pass that my eyes began to take too great delight in seeing her. Wherefore I was often angry with myself and held myself for very vile . . ."[42]

The little hunchback tailor "Peeping Tom" was struck blind when peeping out at Lady Godiva behind the closed window shades. (I enclose the drawing of a twelve-year-old girl with paranoid tendencies. The mother is the house, her Ego a growing tree. The shadow of the tree points to the "mouth-door" of her mother, commanding "obedience.") The Latin *ob-oedire,* from *ob-audire,* just as the German *ge-horchen,* "obey," from *hören,* "to hear," point to the auditory character of the Superego, while the "windows" suggest the "evil eye."

The aggressive component of the half-closed eyes and window shades can be clarified further through the symbolic eye language described in the Bible.[43] The "evil eye" of the Bible does not denote the magic eye of folklore,[44] but refers to a more specific gesture of the eye which sheds some light upon the infantile origin of aggressiveness.[45] The term *de-spise,* from the Latin *de-spicere,* in English the expressive colloquial "looking down the nose," may point in a similar direction toward the origin of this aggressive disdain. The "evil eye" of the Bible is associated with anal characteristics. It is equated with the

stinginess of the miser, with "niggardliness." The following instances do not leave any doubt of the kind of eye
movement which is called "evil" and equated with stinginess: "Eat thou not the bread of him that hath an evil
eye, neither desire thou his dainty meats" (Proverbs
23:6); "He that hasteth to be rich hath an evil eye, and
considereth not that poverty shall come upon him"
(Proverbs 28:22). What kind of look does this evil eye
of the rich actually mean? It means a look with almost
shut eyelids. It seems to me that the word *stingy*, always
misunderstood in vocabularies, can be properly interpreted in this context: the new meaning did not develop
from the basic sense "sharp-tongued in bargaining," not
that the words were stinging, but as the Old Testament
eye symbolism implied, the piercing, penetrating look
through the almost closed eyelids may be felt as a sting.
There exists a parallel between the eyes and the hands.
"Stingy" can also be called "tightfisted." ". . . and thine
eye be evil against thy poor brother, and thou givest
him nought; and he cry unto the Lord against thee, and
it be sin unto thee . . . For the poor shall never cease
out of the land; therefore I command thee, saying, Thou
shalt open thine hand wide unto thy brother, to thy poor,
and to thy needy, in thy land" (Deuteronomy 15:9, 11).
This *closeness* means, on the anal level, constipation. Anal
fantasies are implied in these terms: *stingy* implies a

grudging reluctance to part with anything belonging to one; *close* suggests the keeping of a tight hold on what one has accumulated; *niggardly* implies such closefisted-ness that one grudgingly spends or gives the least amount possible.

The evil eye can also express the aggressive intention by an askance look, or a glance with one eye while the other eye is shut. The look is *askance* if one glances side-wise, obliquely, with suspicion, disdain, disapproval or distrust. The slanting look conveys a twist of mind when the speaker wants to indicate that what he just said should be understood by the hidden meaning implied in his words. To *connive* derives from the Latin *conivere*, "to shut the eyes," "to blink," "to shut to half close when heavy with sleep." It also means "to leave unnoticed, to overlook," obviously as if one were half asleep.

In English, *connive* means "to feign ignorance, to pre-tend not to look at something distasteful or irregular, to cooperate with secretly, or to have a secret understand-ing." The *wink* of one or both eyes implies, according to the Old Testament's interpretation, a twisted mind, not just benevolent tolerance as we understand it in our English. "He winketh with his eyes, he speaketh with his feet, he teacheth with his fingers. Frowardness is in his heart, he deviseth mischief continually; he soweth dis-cord" (Proverbs 6:13–14). "Let not them that are mine enemies wrongfully rejoice over me: *neither* let them wink with the eye that hate me without a cause. . . . For . . . they devise deceitful matters against *them that are* quiet in the land" (Psalms 35:19–20). In these cases the closing of the eyelids expresses not stinginess, but the aggressive deceitfulness of the speaker.

How does this biblical eye language apply to the window shades? As an answer to this question, one may refer to the often-misunderstood passage of Christ's Ser-mon on the Mount. Christ knows the Old Testament's polarity of the downcast, stingy or twisted look, on the one hand, and the straight, simple, childlike look of the wide-open eyes on the other. Projecting this body symbolism upon the windows, he said, "The light (win-dow) of the body (house) is the eye; therefore when

thine eye is single (Greek *haplous*, simple, wide-open),
thy whole body (house) also is full of light; but when
thine eye is evil (Greek *ponēros*, almost-shut window
shades), thy body (house) also is full of darkness"
(Luke 11:34).

In distinction to the aggressive *ex-pectation,* the verbs *in-
spect* and *intro-spect* refer to the guilty conscience. In these
cases, they want to shut out the light so that no one should
have an *in-sight* or should *look into* the Ego, represented by
the house. The window shades serve as defense now. The verb
suspect is an adequate expression of this defense. The Latin
verb *suspiciō, -ere* originally meant "to look up or upwards at
a thing," from *sub-spiciō*; thus its primary meaning is "to look
up with admiration, to respect, regard, esteem, honor." Yet it
also developed into "looking secretly or askance, to mistrust,
suspect"; *in suspecto loco* refers to an "uncertain, critical, dangerous" place. The light coming from outside is coming from
above and is met with ambivalent feelings.

The words *respect, regard,* reflect the reaction of the good
conscience. The Latin *re-spiciō* originally meant "to look back
upon" and, by the extension of this meaning, "to have a care
for, to regard, be mindful of, consider, respect." Thus, it can
meet the look coming from above with open eyes and open
windows. The guilty conscience, on the contrary, is casting
down the eyelids and pulling down the shades. Not the eyes
are "evil," but the conscience is evil, and, as Christ said, the
body is full of darkness. The downcast look may amount to a
confession of guilt and shame. Man would like to escape from
this painful situation by making himself invisible, but if hiding
becomes impossible in front of the all-seeing light, he closes
his eyes, and thus suggests that the Superego should do the
same, at least connive.

Freud came across the association of the closed shutters
and masturbation. He referred in *The Interpretation of
Dreams* to the old German student song, "When the
queen of Sweden by closed window-shades with Apollo
candles . . . " Freud interpreted the candles, but not the
shut-down window shades.[46] Apollo is, however, the all-
seeing god.

The story of the ostrich putting its head into the sand never happened in nature; it is a human fantasy. The small child does so if he cannot face the searching look from above. "Adam, where art thou?" is the expressive formula commanding that man must make himself visible just when he wants nothing more than to hide.

The eagle is a father symbol because "he is said to have such wonderful eyesight that, when he is poised above the seas—not even visible to the human gaze—yet from such a height he can see the little fishes, and coming down like a thunderbolt, he can carry off his captured prey to the shore, on the wing." So the medieval Bestiary describes the all-seeing eyes of the eagle, the genuine representative of the sun. It is said that "he flies up to the height of heaven, even unto the circle of the sun." This Father-eagle tests his sons as to whether or not they can face the sunlight with open eyes.

"It is claimed that an eagle presents his young to the sunbeams, and holds the children up to them in mid air with his talon. If one of them, when stricken with the sun's light, uses a fearless gaze of his eyes, with an uninjured power of staring at it, that one is made much of, because it has proven the truth of its nature. But the one which turns away its eyes from the sunbeam is thrown out as being degenerate and not deserving of such reward." This is the proper illustration of re-spect.[47]

THE SUN EYE. The Sun-god, the most universal divinity in prehistoric ages, is the "seeing god" of the old Egyptian religion.[48] He is denoted by the emblem of an eye. He appears in the form of the watchful Helios in the Greek religion. *Hēlios* means "sun." He became identified with Phoebus Apollo. He is the shining god, he brings the hidden things into the open daylight. King Oedipus, when blinding himself, says: "Apollo, Apollo! Dear children, the god was Apollo who brought the curse upon me, but the blinding hand was my own." The light of the sun and the light of the eyes are the same.

Homer describes the following situation (*Iliad* 14:344): "The all-seeing Father Zeus wants to make love to his wife Hera. She says, 'You want to make love on the top of the mountain where anyone can see . . . ' She invites him to her bedroom. Zeus answers, 'My dear, you need not be afraid that god or man will see. I will gather about us such a golden cloud that Helios himself could not see through and his sunlight is the strongest light there is.' "

"The sun will detect it" (*die Sonne bringt es an den Tag*), the German proverb says. The sun sees everything. The biblical language says:

"I will take thy wives before thine eyes, and give them unto thy neighbour, and he shall lie with thy wives in the sight of this sun. For thou didst it secretly; but I will do this thing before all Israel, and before the sun" (II Samuel 12:11, 12).

The Irish language is most revealing for the New England custom of pulling down the shades. It calls both the "sun" and the "eye" by one and the same word: *suil*. The sun represents the omniscient Superego. It should be noted in this connection that the "sunlight" is, in primitive thinking, a very material substance, etheric, fluid, not heavy; *light* is *light*.* To shut it out means to protect oneself from it.

Early Christianity brought about many changes, also the new evaluation of the symbolism of light.[49] It introduced the change from the daylight to candlelight as a symbol of the "inner light" shining in the darkness. It is consistent with these fantasies that man feels more secure with the self-made internal light, be it a flickering candle or an electric bulb, than in the full sunlight. The internal light is the true representation of the Ego surrounded by the deep and infinite darkness. This light is the favorite of the mystagogues because it remains always a "light in darkness," sheltered by the cover of darkness, a "light put under the bushel" (Matthew 5:15, Mark 4:21). The artificial light is complemental to the pulled-down shades. It deprives the wall-eye-window of its primary function, the separation of inside darkness and outside light.

The "photophobia" became understood as a typical symp-

---

* See pp. 320–324.

tom of paranoid reference.[50] Freud analyzed the Schreber case and demonstrated that in the delusional system of Schreber, the sun is a father symbol, and Schreber projected his relationship to his father upon the sun. Schreber claimed that after his "recovery," he was able to look into the glaring sun; he never could do so when he was sick.

> "Schreber has a peculiar relation to the sun. It speaks to him in human language, and thus reveals itself to him as a living being, or as the organ of a yet higher being lying behind it. We learn from a medical report that at one time he 'used to shout threats and abuse at it and positively bellow at it,' and used to call out to it that it must crawl away from him and hide. He himself tells us that the sun turns pale before him."[51]

The sun-eye becomes thus to the disturbed conscience the symbol of omniscient God. The pressure of the conscience is somewhat relieved by the following hallucination of a small boy:

> ". . . he replaced his fantasy of an omniscient God by an imaginary television apparatus which belonged exclusively to his fantasy and thus was completely at the disposal of his wishes and plans. 'God sees everything but the television apparatus sees only if *I* turn it on.'"[52]

The eye in the sky, seeing everything, penetrating into all the secrets of man, is feared because it supposes an omniscient mind. If man is confronted with such superior power, he becomes aware of the limitations of his existence, and the meaning of the "tremendum" becomes revealed to him. If man cannot see, hear, feel or perceive the Invisible by his senses, yet he nevertheless perceives its presence, he will react with anxiety. He can meet the challenges of the physical reality by some action. He can consent or resist, can fight or escape, but when confronted with the absolute "beyond" of all sense experiences, he can but fear and tremble. "Therefore am I troubled at his presence: when I consider, I am afraid of him," Job says (23:15).

THE EXTERNAL PARTS

Among all reality objects the external parts of one's own body are observed best and known most intimately. Their outside-inside apperception constitutes the essential elements of the conscious Self. They are also the never-changing objects of reference since man exists on earth.[53] The symbolization of the body is the central motive of unconscious fantasies. In the final analysis the whole world is perceived in the image of one's own body. The parts of the body and their interrelated functions make the wholeness of the Self. However, the loss of external body parts does not destroy this Self.

It is consistent with this preeminence of the body-self that such words as *eye, ear, arm, foot, knee, nail, tooth, liver, rib,* belong to the most archaic stock of Indo-European languages. The *thumb, finger, hand, toe,* originate in the younger layer of the Germanic language community.

Two different aspects can be distinguished in the conception of the body parts in general. The body-self, being the most concrete reality, came to be the realization of the concept of *concrete* which properly means "grown together," from the Latin *con,* "together," and the participle of the verb *crēsco, -ere, crētum,* "to grow." One may ask: what has grown together? In the unconscious fantasies each member was first an independent entity which afterward grew into one body. There still remained a strife and competition between the former independent members. The word *part,* from the Latin *pars, partis,* means "part of the body," especially "the genitals." The word *part* is a derivative of the Latin verb *pariō, -ere, partum,* "to give birth." This means that the members of the body were born either out of the trunk or out of one another.

The altered state of consciousness in regression may result in the disintegration of this unity. In hypnotic regression, for instance in the levitation of the hands, the subject may experience the sensation that the hands are moving on their own accord without the action of the "self."

> Greek philosophy and biblical thinking constantly demonstrate that the various parts of the body, despite their different functions, are integrated with one another in the unity of the Self. Paul explained the meaning of the many members of the *one* body (I Corinthians 12:12–27): "For the body is not one member but many . . . And the eye cannot say unto the hand, I have no need of thee: nor again the head to the feet, I have no need of you. Nay, much more those members of the body, which seem to be more feeble, are necessary: And those members of the body which we think to be less honourable, upon these we bestow more abundant honour; and our uncomely parts have more abundant comeliness . . . that there should be no schism in the body; but that the members should have the same care one for another." These words indicate how unconscious fantasies and emotions were implied on the meanings of various body parts. Body parts are neither honorable nor dishonorable, neither comely nor uncomely, but the fantasies about them are so. Otto Fenichel once reported a case of a man who suffered from anxiety while walking on the street. His fears were accompanied by the feeling that his legs were being pulled or that they were running away of their own accord . . . This was the basis of his agoraphobia.[54]

The analysis of body symbolism is in itself a large field of study. It almost covers the essential core of the total vocabulary. I shall restrict this inquiry to three examples but refer in all subsequent illustrations, as in the previous ones, to the body and its functions. This is the constant element and common denominator of our vocabulary. The imaginary anatomy and physiology serve as it were as the grammar of the forgotten language of unconscious fantasies.

THREE EXAMPLES

Hands and Fingers

The words relative to "hand" and "finger" are not as old and genuine in the Germanic languages as the terms for "arm" and "foot"; however, the fantasies implied in these words are ageless.[55] The hands are the most familiar tools of man. They participate in all creative activity. Properly, all tools, machines, and weapons are an extension of magnified or multiplied hands. The primitive tools and machines did the work man once produced by his hands alone. The hand is the symbol of man's creative power. "Thy hands have made me and fashioned me," says the Psalmist as he praises his Maker (Psalm 119:73). It can be understood that the meaning of arms, hands, and fingers has been carried over in the terminology of techniques. *To grasp, to perceive* (from the Latin *per* and *capere*, "to take") or *to conceive* (from the Latin *con* and *capere*, "to take") project the work of the hands upon the work of the intellect.

Besides this functional significance in cultural development the hand in itself is particularly expressive of the personality as a whole. Palmistry is an age-old practice which tries "to read" from the hand and to interpret the lines and forms of the hand in terms of human destiny. If this chiromantic practice has no foundation in the empirical reality, it contains some germs of truth in the figurative or symbolic sense as far as the human race as a whole is concerned. The hands are in any case very important parts of the Self. They are perceived as tools and weapons since earliest infancy. It goes without saying that the hands are charged with emotional meanings and fantasies.

266

The polarization of "right" and "left" refers primarily to the hands, and permits an insight into the fantasies which became ossified and preserved in languages as prehistoric relics.[56] The opposition of *right* versus *left* appears to be equated with *right* versus *wrong* in almost all our languages. The sphere of associations of "right" is indicated by "straight," "correct," "righteous," "fair," "good," "just"; in Hebrew by "the stronger"; in Old High German as "the better" (*diu bezzer hant*), so also in Hungarian. On the other side all disgrace and moral infamy were cast upon the "left" hand. The left hand appears to be the scapegoat upon which man could project his aggressive impulses. It is called "crooked," "bad," "illicit," "useless"; it is the *awk-ward* one (this meaning properly "turned the wrong way," as the sinful one); it is also called in opposition to the "stronger" the "weaker" one.

The right hand is denoted by an old genuine term which can be seen in the Greek *dexios*, Latin *dexter*, and so in many other languages. The left hand, on the contrary, came to be denoted by a variety of terms, which are all of secondary character. Many evasive terms were used for denoting it because its real name was ignominious. One can hardly find an idea more repudiated or more repressed than that of the left hand. It is reflected in verbal fantasies as a feared taboo, much like sex. In Paul's saying that there are honorable and dishonorable parts of the body, the right hand is surely honorable, the left hand dishonorable.[57]

One can observe in this case how the repercussion of the strongest instinctual demand results not in repression but in the reversal of the meaning into the affirmative opposite. This is usually the case when the repudiated impulse is too strong to be repressed. Such reversal of meaning is operative in most cases of the so-called euphemisms. Verbal examples show that the ape made a frightening impression upon the Greek mind. The ape must have appeared as a terrible distortion and negation of the ideal form of beauty which is reflected in the human being. Yet they called the ape *kallias*, meaning "beauty," from *kallos, kalos*, "beautiful." Nothing could be more frightening to the Greek mind than the obsessive idea of the persecuting Erinnyes, yet they called these furies *Eumenides*, "the gracious, loving ones." Similar reversal of meaning has been used in the denotation of the left hand. It has been called "the better one" in the Greek *aristeros*; "of good repute" in the Greek *eu-onumos*; "the more useful one" in the Latin *sinister*; "the more desirable one" in the Old English *winestra;* "the dear one," "the pleasant one," "the desirable one," "the good one" in other related languages. However, all these complimentary terms are used with mental reservation. They stand as opposites of the right hand which is "right" and "righteous"; consequently they are all cover words masking an idea which is better left unmentioned by its proper name. This original name must have referred to the idea of "bent" or "crooked." This was also the original implication of *left,* meaning "bent"; the same is true of the French *gauche,* "left," from *gauchir,* "turn aside," or of *awk-ward.* The meaning "curved" is also inherent in *wrong* and in the verb *to wring.* The noun *wrong* denotes in obsolete English the curved "rib" of the ship's frame. This may suggest an answer to the question why Eve was made from Adam's rib. The rib is the curved bone. The woman as sexual object elicits the "wrong" of man, and the curved rib is her symbol. Out of the curved bone came evil into the world, much like out of the *pythos* of Pandora in Greek mythology.

Why has the straight line assumed the meaning of "right," "correct," "just," whereas the curved line is the crooked one, symbolic of bad conscience? The answer to this question seems to lie in the realm of elementary symbolism; however, it is more difficult to explain just why the right hand is the "straight" one, while the left hand became identified with the curved line. It is a bad auspicium for Homer if the birds fly left (*Odysseus* 20:242). The left hand is the false and crooked one. It tries to spoil the good done by the right. For such reasons it is said in Christ's teaching: "But when thou doest alms, let not thy left hand know what they right hand doeth" (Matthew 6:3). The right hand is in the biblical language virtually synonymous with "might," "power" and "the will of the Father." "Thy right hand is full of righteousness," the Psalmist says (Psalm 48:10). In this sense the Latin says *in manu sua est,* and in German *es liegt in seiner Hand,* properly "it lies in his hand," meaning "it is in his power." The Old English *mund* denotes "hand" and "protection." With both meanings goes the feminine; in the masculine concept the word means "man," "a man of power and strength," "a protector."

One must turn to the opposite in order to find out what is wrong with the left hand. It seems significant that "arm" and "finger" are in most of our languages masculine concepts, whereas the "fist" and the "hand" are feminine. Even the Latin *manus, -us,* "hand," which one would expect on formal ground to belong to the masculine category, is in fact feminine just as the Old English *mund* is in the masculine "man" and in the feminine "hand." The hand is a feminine concept, according to our languages. This concept does not fit the right hand which represents the creative power and the will of the Father, as symbolized by Rodin's wonderful "hand," or the creative finger of the right hand as Michelangelo depicted it as the Creator awakens Adam to existence. The right hand of the Father contradicts this feminine concept. It must be the left hand, like the curved rib, which implies the feminine idea. It has been demonstrated that the left hand represented the power of the mother in matriarchy as the right hand shows the will of the father in patriarchy. Isis, the Egyptian "Great Mother," was venerated by processions in which the imitation of the left hand as her symbol was carried by the priests. "The fourth (priest) carried the model of the left hand with the fingers stretched out," said Apuleius, who described such a procession. Greek philosophy tried to come to an understanding of the origin of sexes. According to their philosophy, the male children come from the semen of the right testicle, whereas the female ones came from the left testicle.[58] Similar thoughts are present in Chinese philosophy. It has long preserved and elaborated as basic principle the dualism of *Yang* and *Yin,* classifying all things, either as male and good or as female and bad. The left hand, ever since body symbolism developed, came to be equated with the female principle and with motherhood which is opposed to, or in open revolt against, the father, and in this instance helped by the loyalty of the children.

Left-handedness is not necessarily connected with left-footedness or left-eyedness. In order to prove how deep-rooted is the unconscious meaning-complex of "right" and "left," I refer to a clinical example. The patient in question knew nothing about the "right-masculine" and "left-feminine" association.

The patient (in his early thirties, a science teacher, predominantly hysterical in character), examining stained specimens through a microscope, noted that he perceived things differently with each eye. He claimed to see better at times with one eye than the other. When his left eye was better, he led a vivid fantasy life which was concerned in the main with clothing, cooking, jewelry, designing, and other manifestations of feminine identifications with the mother. The periods when his *right* eye predominated coincided with self-critical, depressive periods, and the development of painful insights concerning his shortcomings as a man.[59]

The right hand represents in patriarchy the law, the right of the father. The word *right*, and the German *recht*, "right," derive from the Latin *rectus*, which is a participial form of the verb *regō, -ere, rectus*, meaning "erect," and then "set straight," "straighten out," "stretch out," "to lead," and "to govern." In German the law is called *Recht*, as it is in the English *right*. Thus, law, right, righteousness, are conceived in our languages in the concepts of patriarchy. In patriarchal thinking the left hand represents the illicit way. A marriage "with the left hand" means an illegitimate marriage. Similar associations are revealed by such uses of the word as "most men inclined to the left-hand way are precipitated into all uncleanness." Some preachers warned their flocks against "moral left-handedness." The left hand is of ill-repute in all our languages.

The various terms which stand opposed to "right" reveal on closer inspection the typical character traits that are attached in fantasies to the effeminate or castrated man. Some languages say about such a person that "he has two left hands."

The Oedipus situation is also tied up with the concept of the "left." King Laius, the father in the story, is named, accordingly, the Greek *laios*, the Latin *laevus*, meaning "left-handed." He was a homosexual, an effeminate man.*

Freud in describing the mother fixation and the homosexual trends of Leonardo da Vinci made only a short reference to the left-handedness of Leonardo without

---

* See *The Subconscious Language*, pp. 85–86.

comment. It is, however, a symptom which fits into the total picture. In the anatomical drawing of heterosexual intercourse (if the reconstruction of the picture is correct), Leonardo drew the right foot of the man with the big toe on the right side, and the left foot of the woman with the big toe on the left side, contradicting any reality perception.[60]

One can demonstrate the whole naming complex in connection with the English verb *to woo*. The Old English term for the curved line, *wo, woh*, "bent," says more about the left-handed person: as an adjective it describes such qualities as "bent," "crooked," "deceitful," "unjust," "wrong," "depraved"; as a noun it denotes the body's curved lines as "joint," "fold," "bending"; it also means "perversity," "error," "wickedness," and as a verb it is continued in our *to woo*, "to court, to make love, usually with the intention to propose marriage," and *wooer*, "suitor." One may ask what kind of wooer is this man who is identified by this sphere of meaning? The usual explanation that the curved line indicated in this case simply "to incline another toward oneself," does not sound very convincing. Other associations of the word are: *woh-handede*, "crooked-handed, lame," *woh-fotede*, "crooked-footed," *woh-ful*, "full of wickedness," *woh-nys*, "crookedness, perverseness, error, wickedness, sin," *woh-haemed*, "unlawful marriage, adultery," *woh-haemere*, "adulterer, fornicator," and many more. The Latin *tortus* means "bent, curved," as does French *tort*, "something unjust, wrong." The derivative Spanish *tuerto* means "squint," the Portuguese *torto*, "goggle-eyed," and the Italian *tortire*, "lead astray," in the "wrong" way, "awkward." The left-handed person may develop, according to this primitive characterology, a squinting look or a limping gait and, one may add, stuttering.*

Words denoting *thumb, finger, toe*, are of Germanic origin just as is *hand*. The origin of these words is not very clear.

---

* Arabian proverbs: "Let us rather be thrown with stone than to meet a goggle-eyed in the morning." "Do not permit to your father to enter your house if he is one-eyed." "God beware that the squinting man should obtain power," etc. O. Rescher, "Psychologisches im Arabischen Sprichwort," *Beiträge zur Kenntnis des Orients*, edited by Hugo Grote (1911), 9:55–61.

Hand seems to preserve an old word for "ten," while *finger* may be related to "five." The fingers are highly individualized parts of the body. They are all masculine. However, only the *thumb* is termed by a special genuine name; the other fingers were named according to their function (index finger), position (middle finger), specific quality (ring finger) or size (little finger). One of these names is a euphemism. The reference to the position is of secondary nature. Our present name *middle finger* translates the Latin *mēdius* (*digitus*) and Greek *mesos daktulos,* but these are cover words which stand for the repudiated and repressed colloquial terms. In German dialects this finger is called *der namenlose Finger,* "the nameless finger." Its name has been obliterated because of the meaning connected with it. In Greek antiquity this finger is charged with the most opprobrious crimes. The Latin language called this finger *impudicus, infamis, famosus.* The same ignominy can be observed in all our languages. Even among the fingers there is a difference, as Paul said, between the honorable and dishonorable, comely and uncomely qualities which are, of course, not in the finger but in the meaning attached to it.

The thumb definitely holds a distinct and superior position among the fingers.* It assumes this special emotional role in thumb sucking in early infancy. It is the thumb alone which is named not by a compound of "finger" but with a special name. If called "finger," as in Greek, it is distinguished as "big finger," *megas daktulos,* Polish *wielki palec,* and Russian *bolshoi paletz.* It may be conceived as "anti-hand" as in the Greek *anti-cheir,* in reference to the separation of the thumb from the fingers, a unique anatomical characteristic of man and apes. The thumb and the big toe also hold a specifically distinguished role in rituals, a role which one would like to understand better: so, in the Old Testament sin offerings, the law says: "And the priest shall take some of the blood of the trespass offering, and the priest shall put it upon the tip of the right ear of him that is to be cleansed, and upon the thumb of his right hand, and upon the great toe of his right foot" (Leviticus 14:14, 17, 25, 28, etc.). The thumb of the right hand and the big toe of the right foot must hold a special

---

* See *The Subconscious Language,* pp. 46–50.

reference to the sin from which the individual should be cleansed by the ritual.

The origin of the word *thumb,* and of the Latin *pollex* and *pollicaris,* "thumb," is not very clear. The Latin word must be related in some way to *polleō, -ēre,* meaning "to grow strong." In Irish the underlying idea is "hammer." The English *thumb* and the German *Daumen* are phonemically related to the Latin *tum-ere,* "to swell," *tum-or,* "swelling," displaying again the capacity of swelling and growing stout and strong. The corresponding Hebrew word for the thumb also implies the idea of "thick" (*bōhen*). This is, of course, an imaginary implication because as a matter of fact the thumb is not a swollen finger. Inquiring further into the individual characters of the fingers one may consult the myths and fairy tales in order to learn more about the "swelling" and the religious significance of the thumb. In Greek myth the *daktiloi,* in German fairy tales the *Däumlinge,* "thumb-lings," are personifications, significantly, not of the fingers, but of the thumb. From the descriptions of the common characteristics of these fantasies one can observe that these mythical beings appear as little boys or dwarfs like *Tom Thumb* who are seemingly very small but can accomplish great things. The "swelling," "growing stout and strong" implicated in their names is consistent with their character. They are "smaller than small, bigger than big." They appear in the plural. A special quality attributed to them is that they are supposed to dwell and work under the surface of the earth, secretly and invisibly; they are inside fantasies which cannot be found in the daylight of reality. They have something to do with mining, metals, forging, and the work of the blacksmith. These are references to the inside of the earth. They work with a characteristic tool, the hammer. They also have a very specific dress: their head is covered by a hood which is one piece together with the rest of the clothing. Such a hood is called in Latin *capucium,* "capuche, cowl," like the Capuchin (Franciscan) monks wear. This word displays a conspicuous sound association with *praeputium,* "prepuce," which association one would consider mere chance if there were no association of the meanings. The phallic nature of these "thumblings," however, is too conspicuous to be simply brushed aside. The whole sphere of association suggests the fact that at some early age

274

the boy's fantasies identify the thumb with genitals. The thumb displays its phallic nature also in the age-old gesture language. "To show the fig" is an insult. In Greek *suko-phantes* means "fig shower," in Italian *far le fiche*, in French *faire la figue*, in English *fig*, "insult with *fico*." Colloquial and obsolete usages also attribute special qualities to the thumb. The thumb is symbolic of complete subservience, as *under the thumb of*, meaning "entirely at the disposal of"; *to turn over the thumb* means "to get under one's control." The thumb seems to be identified in these formulas with the Self. It is also indicative of secret pleasures: *under the thumb* means "secretly." It is also very sensitive: *to hit one over the thumb* means "to punish or reprove sharply." *To bite the thumb at* is an insult much like the *fico*. It denotes great intimacy to say *the finger next one's thumb* (one's closest friend) or *to be finger and thumb* (to be on intimate terms). Dictionaries try to explain such formulas as *there is my thumb*, or *as easy as kissing my thumb*, or *to bite one's thumb* (which is an expression of anger); however, as long as these inter-pretations stick to common-sense reality they have little chance to reach a real understanding. The "thumblings" (the German *Däumlinge*) are called *wights* in English. They are character-ized in Germanic mythology as are the *Daktuloi* in the Greek myth. The thumb is a significant part of the Self in the fan-tasies of early infancy.

The Foot and the Knee

The *knee* belongs to a cluster of words dating back to Indo-European prehistory. This cluster is also represented by the verb *know*. There exists an obvious coincidence in the phonemic forms of these two words, yet the great divergence of the meanings presents a perplexing problem. What could be the common denominator of *knee* and *know*? The mean-ings of "angle" and "generation" also seem to be included in this word cluster: "angle" goes with the meaning of "knee" and "generation" with the meaning of "know." How the mean-ings of "know" and "generation" hang together was discussed in another context.* The following words are interrelated with

---

* See *The Subconscious Language*, pp. 72–82.

one another through their phonemic forms: in Greek "beget, generate" (*gi-gno-mai,* perfect *ge-gon-a*); "angle, corner" (*gonia*); "knee" (*gonu*); "lap" (*gonata*). In Latin the basic words of this cluster are: "beget, generate" (*gignō, genō*); "knee, node of plants, herbs, joint of the water pipeline" (*genu*). In Old English the pertinent words are *cneow, cneo* for "generation," for "knee," and for "know, knew." If there exists a conspicuous coherence of the phonemic patterns, one can suppose that some hidden connection exists between the meanings also. It is this interdependence of meanings that might be the cause of the phonemic coherence.

It is interesting to observe how various authorities in the field of linguistics react when confronted with this perplexing discrepancy of meanings. Some linguists try to solve the problem in a radical way by stating that there is no problem at all. The *knee* has nothing to do with *to know,* the two words have developed independently from each other, and the seeming similarity in the phonemic patterns is just a chance happening with no other significance. However, the reference to a chance homophony is again the last emergency escape for scientific thinking when all other ways are blocked. Now, if there is nothing but a mocking contingency of coincidence in the phonemic patterns, one will readily assume that the meanings of these words have indeed nothing in common. However, if there exists some conspicuous connection between the meanings, there is little probability left that the coincidence in phonemics is mere chance.

Another group of linguists admitted that a coherence of the two words is possible though not probable; therefore they try to find out some pathways between them and to explain by logical arguments how one meaning has developed out of the other.[61] Ingenious as such constructions of lexical meanings are, they represent modern thinking and have no foundation in the prehistory of languages.

A third way of interpretation followed the lines of "Word and Thing" theory. Many data have been collected in anthropological literature proving that in early ages, and in the Old Testament age, the "kneeling birth" was the most general one. The Egyptian hieroglyph for "birth" depicts a kneeling woman. Many references in Greek literature also corroborate that kneeling was the natural posture at birth. Thus it can be assumed on the basis of those facts that an objective relationship exists between the word "knee" and "beget, give birth to." The relationship of the words is based upon the relationship of things to which these words refer.

Many examples of the "kneeling birth" can be given, yet the primary question still remains unanswered: What does the connection of these things mean to the connection of words? According to the word-thing theory the line of development has been in this case: "knee"–"kneeling"–"kneeling birth"– "birth." The kneeling parturition was the connecting link between "knee" and "beget." This connection is not figured out by mere common-sense reasoning but is proven by an abundance of historical and anthropological evidence. Convincing as this argument seems to be, it does not solve the linguistic problem, which is of a psychological nature. According to this interpretation the primary meaning of "beget" would be "to kneel," in the sense in which now used, as *lie in,* or as the German uses *nieder-kommen,* "come down"; in obsolete German *eines Kindes liegen* is the common expression of parturition. The "thing" explanation seems to be very plausible in this case, but language does not refer to things but to fantasies about things. These fantasies, repressed unconscious elements, may refer to an absurd, nonsensical idea which has no model in the world of realities. Moreover, the cluster of words to which *knee* and *to know* belong was an exceedingly productive one. The English *knave, can, king, kin, kind,* the German *Kind,* "child," also belong to it. This productivity of the "root meaning" is an indication that a strong impulse became repressed and was seeking an outlet. It is futile to attempt to bridge the gap between "knee" and "birth" when all the other forms remain unexplained thereby.

The "knee" has to be understood in the light of fantasies about the body-self. These fantasies were objectively represented in myth and depicted in mythical art with all their anatomical absurdities. Such are the blending of human and animal anatomy as monstrosities having many heads like Brahma, a hundred arms like Briareus, many legs or breasts, and, one may suppose, many genitals. Fantasies compensate by wishful thinking. The delusion of having many legs might be the dream of someone who is inhibited in walking. The

reduplication of body parts shows that there is an organ inferiority present. It might be a symptom of a cerebral disturbance.[62]

> A fourteen-year-old boy who developed difficulties in urinating and had to be catheterized reported that he had more than once had a dream about several penises. "There were four alongside each other in a horizontal plane, each about the same size. When urine failed to come out of one, he tried another."[63]

Such an anatomical absurdity is the Greek *tri-skelion,* a figure composed of three curved legs radiating from a center. Such representation may be the outgrow of pathological fantasies such as found with schizophrenics. This figure shows the primary meaning which was also implicated in the four-legged figure, the model of which became famous as the "swastika."

In Greek *skelos* means "leg above the knee," relative to *skolios,* "curved." The corresponding Latin word *scelus* means "crookedness, wickedness." The two legs above the knee form a curved line, and the curve itself appears to be the seat of wickedness. This will help to explain the observation made concerning the *left* hand that the curved line became identified with the morally "wrong."

The imaginary conception of the body-self is a primary element of the infantile Self. Its reference to the anatomical reality is still diffuse. The parts of the body which are anatomically different (thus denoted by words completely separated in their lexical meanings) can mean the same idea in infantile fantasies. The words *breast, lap, bosom, womb,* display this characteristic fusion and shifting from one concept to another. The two legs above the knee form a part of the "lap" or "bosom." The early fantasies concerning the body-self thought of the two legs as forming a curve, a corner or angle which is the very location of impulses considered "bad." Some formulas, however, think otherwise. They refer to the opposite aspect (as the German *Glück im Winkel,* "happiness in the corner"). In clinical practice there occur various references to the primary "angle." For instance:

In a dream report of the "feminine Moses" is said: "There is a green house with a very pitched roof—the pitched roof reminded her of the angle between her legs. The green house was 'where things grow,' a greenhouse. When she finally uttered the word 'niche' she experienced another attack of panic and faintness because, for her, to say it aloud was to give up the fantasy of having a penis and to accept the inferior feminine role."[64]

The two lines forming an angle are called in Greek skelos, in Latin femur, in German Schenkel (related to Schinken, "ham")—all denoting at the same time the segment of the leg which is between the trunk and the knee. For this reason the angle became charged with a repressed sexual meaning. The Latin femur also means the genital parts.

The English leg was tabooed in Victorian language and limb was used instead of it; limb is used "now only, especially in the United States, in mock-modest or prudish use," the Oxford English Dictionary says. The thighs have assumed the meaning of the generative parts in Hebrew as well as in the language of biblical translation, which even changes the Hebrew "thigh" to "loin" in order to make the original meaning more veiled and repressed. Thus the standard practice was to call the child "the fruit of his loins" or to say the child "came out of his loins" (Hebrews 7:5, 10, etc.). It should be noticed that this formula refers to the father, while the child's relationship to the mother is denoted by calling the child the "fruit of her womb." From a physiological viewpoint it is, of course, nonsense to say that the child is the fruit of the loins of the father, but this formula shows once more that two lines forming an angle were charged with a genital meaning.

In similar way the repressed genital meaning came to ʰ attributed to other "parts" of the body, especially to the knˀ The Greek skelos means "thigh"; the word is phonemˀ related to kullos, "curved," kolē, kolēn, "the upper parˀ leg," and kolon, "part of the body, member," uˀ euphemism. The curve formed by the two legs, thⁱ the legs," also "between the knees" (Genesis 48ˀ primary pattern for "member" and "part of tʰ sceptre shall not depart from Judah, nor ˀ between his feet" (Genesis 49:10). The C

denotes the upper part of the leg. The corresponding Latin word, *membrum*, refers in general to "part of the body." *Membrosus* is the attribute of Priapus, meaning "with the big member." The feminine *membrana* denotes "the fine skin covering the member." Considering these words, one can hardly avoid the impression that the "parts" of the body were charged with sexual fantasies. As observed previously, this word *part* is in the final instance related with *pareō, -ere*, "give birth to." All the "members" are in this imaginary anatomy organs of generation or are born out of one another.

Investigating further into the anatomy of the "knee," one will find that it is not only a "member" or "part" forming an angle or a curved line but also a "joint" connecting two members together. The meaning of "two members fitting aptly together" is denoted in Latin by *co-pulāre*, from *co-apulāre*. The related verb *apiscor* means "to grasp mentally," but the original meaning of this grasping was repudiated; therefore it became obscene in early ages. This is shown by the fact that its present tense came to be blocked out completely. They used the past tense of the verb with the meaning of the present tense: *co-ēpi* came to mean "I begin."

This "fitting together" of two members does not mean simply a "being united" but implies also the flexibility of this connection. The implication of "flexible joint" has become identical with "angle" and "curve," and also with "member" and "generation." The connection of the two legs has again set the primary pattern of the "joint," as can still be seen in the German *Ge-lenk*, "joint," which is related to the English *link*. It originally denoted the flexible part of the body between the upper part of the thighs in Greek and was afterward shifted from the genital zone to the other joints, such as the knee. According to these fantasies the "joint" was not the connecting link between two members, but the member itself was identical with the joint. The "joint" is called "member" for this reason, as in the Greek *ar-thron*, meaning "member" and "joint," and in the Latin *artus, -tus*, meaning "member" and "joint"; the German *Glied*, from *ge-lid*, covers both meanings.

The English *joint* is a derivative of the Latin *jungere, junctum*, meaning "yoked together," and refers to the yoke as symbol of *con-jugium*, "marriage." This reference may appear doubtful at first glance, but it will become more convincing by the sphere of its associations. The *joints play* together; *die Gelenke spielen,* is the proper German expression. What does the word *play* mean in this strange connection? This question is the more appropriate because in the Romance languages, too, the "joint" is named by words derived from the late Latin *jōcare,* "to play." What is this "joints playing together"? Play means in this connection that two objects are fitted in, in a way of having space enough for free motion; this space is called in German *Spiel-raum,* "play-space." The English *play* is in some respects even more explicit.* It means, besides "to move freely within limits," primarily "to move swiftly, erratically to and fro"; it also means "to discharge, eject or fire something." If there remains any doubt concerning this "playing" of the joints the biblical reference to it will make the repressed fantasies clear. How the function of the joints was considered as the criterion of the sound body is vividly expressed by these words of Paul: "From whom the whole body fitly joined together and compacted by that which every joint supplieth, according to the effectual working in the measure of every part, maketh increase of the body unto the edifying of itself in love" (Ephesians 4:16). The Greek term *sum-bibadzō,* used in the New Testament language for the "playing together" of the joints, means "walk together"; it is the parallel of the Latin word *co-īre.*

Since the joints are primarily the "joints of the thighs," they are expressive of the state of health.

> In clinical description of a twenty-eight-year-old schizophrenic these fantasies read as follows:
> "Ira arrived very elated, stating that he had made a marvelous discovery. 'It is wonderful to have an arm or a leg. It can do all sorts of things and it is a part of me.' He then tried to explain but became very confused concerning to whom the arm belonged before, with the feeling that arms and legs had an autonomous existence and joined up with the body in and of themselves."[65]

This will explain how the "loosening of the joints" came, in this forgotten language of fantasies, to express the loss of

---

* See *The Subconscious Language,* pp. 341–346.

health, and the loss of the generative power of the male. The decaying health of Belshazzar is described by these words: "Then the king's countenance was changed, and his thoughts troubled him, so that the joints of his loins were loosed, and his knees smote one against another" (Daniel 5:6). The loosening of the "joints of the loins" (which occurs in women during parturition) as a physiological symptom characterizing man's physical impotency should be understood in the light of fantasies, because such a symptom does not exist in reality.

The deciphering of unconscious fantasies may enable one to understand some biblical passages which cannot be understood on the level of lexical meanings. The story of Jacob at Peniel may serve as an example: "And Jacob was left alone; and there wrestled a man with him until the breaking of the day. And when he saw that he prevailed not against him, *he touched the hollow of his thigh; and the hollow of Jacob's thigh was out of joint*, as he wrestled with him. And he said, Let me go, for the day breaketh. And he said, I will not let thee go, *except thou bless me. . . . And he blessed him there*. And Jacob called the name of the place Peniel: for I have seen God face to face, and *my life is preserved* . . . the sun rose upon him, and he *halted upon his thigh*" (Genesis 32:24-32).

The meaning of "to bless" was analyzed before. If this analysis was correct, the implication was "fruitfulness." In the Old Testament barrenness was evidently the great disgrace of the woman, while in later centuries the incapacity of the man was felt more heavily as a reproach. In this case, however, the aging Jacob, obviously in his dream, was praying for "blessing." His prayer was answered by the words: "And God said unto him, I am God Almighty: *be fruitful and multiply; a nation and a company of nations shall be of thee, and kings shall come out of thy loins*" (Genesis 35:11). This blessing appears in its full meaning: the origin of the people was a miracle because Jacob, the ancestor, lost his generative power: his thigh was out of joint. The Lord took this power from him during the night (this is the meaning of the hopeless wrestling before the breaking of day), and when the sun rose the Lord restored it again by blessing him. Thus Jacob says: "My life is preserved." But the after-effect, the "halting in his thigh," the bodily symbol of impotency, remained with him.[66]

This biblical example will clarify the contention that the association of "knee" and "generation" has not been brought about by the reference to "kneeling birth." The concept of "generation" refers primarily in our culture to the father, not to the mother. The association in question became established by the identification of the "knee" with the primary curve formed by the thighs. There are indications showing that the knees have indeed absorbed unconscious fantasies about the generative parts. The "knee" stands for the "womb" in Hebrew: "Why died I not from the womb? . . . why did the knees prevent me?" (Job 3:11-12). This refers not to "kneeling parturition" but to "generation" in general. In the Hittite language the "knee" and the female organ, and in the Akkadian language the "knee" and the male organ, are denoted by one and the same word (*birku*).

The Homeric formula "on the knees of the gods" is not an exact translation; the literal translation is "*in* the knees of the gods" (*theon en gounasi kettai*); the German translations (*in dem Schoss der Götter*, "in the lap of the gods") obscure in another form the original meaning which is not understood any longer by the modern speaker.[67] The Old Testament curse, "the Lord shall smite thee *in* the knees" (Deuteronomy 28:35) is the polar opposite of "blessing." The dying Hector says to Achilles: "I beseech you by your *psychē* and your knees and your parents let not the dogs devour my body" (*Iliad* 22:338f.). The knees were important by implication as were the *psychē* and the parents. The pertinent verbal forms reflect the expansion of the primary meaning of generation (male as well as female), to the "knees," to "angle," "joint," "copulation" (referring to the father or to the mother), and in the passive to the common notion of "to be born" and "offspring." This interdependence of meanings must have been the reason for using the common phonemic pattern. In German *Glied* denotes "member, genital organ, joint" and "generation." The biblical usage of "generation" is again indicative of fantasies. In such formulas as "*the third* (generation)" (Genesis 50:23), or "*from* (generation) *to* (generation)" (Exodus 17:16), or "*the third and the fourth* (generation)" (Exodus 20:5, etc.), the word *generation* is omitted in the Old Testament language. It was taboo. *Generation* refers to the generative act. But in German (*bis in das dritte Glied*) the word "member, joint" is used in this context. One can find the same equation of "joint" and "generation" in the Sanskrit language, and in all Slavic languages; moreover, it is a common phenomenon in all Finno-Ugrian languages, in Finnish, Estonian, Lapp, Hungarian (*iz*). To declare all these instances as chance happenings does not explain the facts. Those linguists who give preference to the phonemic form in relation to the meaning must accept the evidence that the Latin *genu-inus,* "proceeding from, belonging to, authentic," and also the synonymous *in-genu-us* (the English *in-genu-ous*), refer by their phonemic form to *genu,* "knee," and not to *geni-,* the basal form for "birth," from which the English *in-geni-ous* derives.

These words do not refer to an anatomical reality but to a reality of a psychical order. This is the fictitious body image emerging in the fantasies of earliest childhood when the infant discovers his body simultaneously through outside observation and inside experience. In this early development of ego-consciousness the joints appear as many erogenic zones. This is the reason why the armpits and the hollows of the knees are so sensitive to tickling, which is an indication that they became identified with the genital zone. The members of the body are in permanent copulation with one another, or they are "parts" born out of one another like the child "out of the thighs." The primary angle between the thighs is thus the birthplace of the first "generation," the knees are the "joints" of the second generation, and the ankles of the feet represent in this imaginary anatomy the third generation. Again, it may be a chance homophony, and it is considered as such, that the old German equivalent of *thigh* covers both meanings: *diech, diech-schenkel* means "thigh," and *diech-ter,* "grandchild." In the same way the German *Enkel* means "ankle, joint of the foot," and also "grandchild," properly "little grandfather." This is in fact a homophony; however, one never knows where fantasies come to an end and playful conscious imagery begins. It should be recalled in this connection that these generations of joints "play" together. R. Meringer, the great realistic-minded linguist prominent in the exploration of the word-thing relationship, came through his investigation of the word *knee* to the remarkable insight that this and related words have developed from an imaginary idea of the body-self.

He said: "in a fantastic conception: as the child comes out of the womb, so seem the members to develop from one another . . . That psychological significance has been attributed to the knee may appear strange only for the first moment. The people, the primitive men, are poets, and the etymologist should not forget about it. Merely from a rational—so to speak logical—aspect the changing meaning cannot be explained; completely different forces are at work here."[68]

The Teeth

The unconscious fantasies which may be present in the concept of "tooth" can be illustrated by a clinical example:

> A patient dreamed after sexual intercourse that one of his teeth was pulled out. The patient's association to this dream revealed his idea that good teeth were necessary implements of masculinity. Good teeth made sex more powerful and he had his teeth fixed for this reason.[69]

Quoting a biblical instance: "Confidence in an unfaithful man in time of trouble is like *a broken tooth, and a foot out of joint*" (Proverbs 25:19). The reference to the "foot out of joint" has been discussed, so one may suppose that the "broken tooth" covers fantasies similar to those that are present in "foot out of joint." The meaning of the whole proverb can be clearly understood on this basis and needs no further elaboration. The point in this case is not the meaning but the wording. How did these two similes referring to two such different things as "tooth" and "foot" come into the speaker's mind? The words *tooth* and *foot* are in sound and meaning different; why are they brought here in a strange way under a common denominator?

The investigation of patients led to the conclusion that tooth and leg are mutually replaceable symbols in dreams. Their loss expresses the infantile desire to be carried and nursed by the mother.[70] This interpretation was made without any reference to languages. The question in this case will be: Will this interpretation stand the test of linguistic analysis? Can this intuitive interpretation be verified by objective verbal instances?

Looking into the verbal expression one will first of all observe the rather strange fact that *foot* and *tooth*, in distinction to other nouns, form their plural as *feet* and *teeth*. This is a rare grammatical category by which both nouns have preserved an old form of the plural. There must be some reason that these two nouns have deviated from the common rule. There must also be some common element present in these two words which made them resist the pressure of such a general rule as the formation of the plural by *-s*. However, there is a third word which resisted in the same way: *goose–geese*. I see no connection between *goose* and *foot*, yet even in this case one becomes suspicious of a hidden association considering the wholly irrational word *goose-step*, a marching step with stiff legs. (I never saw a goose walking with such steps.)

> This seeming unrelatedness of "tooth" and "foot" becomes more suspicious if one considers the pertinent Greek words *pous*, "foot," and *odous*, "tooth." The Greek nominative *pous* is an irregular form. The genitive is *pod-os*, so the expected nominative should be like *pōs*, from *pod-s*, in place of *pous*. The *ou* in this case originates from a contraction of an *on*. From whence came this *n* to be planted in the word for "foot"? There is no other *n*-stem among the words for the body parts except *odous* (genitive *odont-os*), "tooth." This nominative *odous* seems to have influenced the word *pōs* so that it has changed into *pous*. Thus there must be operative some hidden association between the two concepts. But the whole assimilation might be once more nothing but chance.*
>
> In Latin the word *genu-inus* is a derivative of *genu*, "knee." But this word *genuinus* also carries the meaning of "molar tooth." This coincidence makes the whole chance theory improbable. If this is not a chance happening, what is then the hidden connection between the words and the notions of "tooth" and "foot"?

Linguistic evidences show that the words for "chin," "cheek" and "jaw" are taken from the genital complex which

---

* The word for "foot" is masculine in all Indo-European languages.

denoted the "knee." Thus in Greek *genus* means "jaw" and "chin," and *geneion,* "cheek"; in Latin *gena* means "cheek." These words are in one way or another derivatives of the *gene-, geno-* phonemic pattern which was used to denote the "generation" of life. The teeth are, of course, a sensitive part of the body and an irritation of the teeth might be translated by the language of the dream into various symbols. There exists some linguistic relationship, difficult to understand, between the Greek *gonu,* the Latin *genu,* "knee," on the one hand, and the Greek *genus,* "jaw," "chin," *geneion,* "cheek," on the other. One cannot grasp this relationship by considering the relationship of objects, because these terms refer to the esoteric "tooth" and "knee." First of all one will observe the fusion of the concepts of "jaw," "chin," "cheek," and even "beard." Aristotle said in his anatomical teaching: "Furthermore, there are two jaws: the front part is the chin, the hinder part the cheek." We still use *jaw-bone* and *cheek-bone* with the same meaning. The jaw is in German a "box"—*Kinn-lade,* "chin-box." This holds true also for the Latin *capsa, capsus,* "box," which developed in Spanish as *guijada,* "jaw" and "cheek." What does this "jaw-chin-box" contain? Obviously the teeth. The teeth encased in this "box" are significant because they have proven to be that part of the body which outlasts even the skeleton. It can be observed in another connection that strings of teeth are used as jewels and money. This is again an indication that the teeth were not appreciated for their exchange value, nor for their use value, but for the invisible charm power which was thought to exist within them. This is reflected in popular handbooks which say that a dream about the loss of a tooth means "death." According to the popular belief someone has to die before a new life can be conceived ("conceived in the box" which is in many languages identified with the "womb"). The teeth became associated in these fantasies with the *gene-, geno-* generative complex. They were considered as representing the principle of the continuity of life, just as the notion of "semen" for the father and "navel" for the mother are similar symbols of continuity. The teeth encased in the jawbone appeared to symbolize the seat of potential lives. In about the same sense it is said in biblical language: "As arrows are in the hands of a mighty man; so are children of the youth. Happy is the man that hath his quiver full of them" (Psalms 127:4, 5). So it is said: "Thy teeth are as a flock of sheep which go up from the washing, whereof every one beareth twins, and there is not one barren among them" (Song of Solomon 6:6). In this picture the washed-clean teeth appear as the safeguards of fertility. They are symbolic of the generative power. Freud came, without linguistic lead, by analyzing dreams, to the conclusion that "a particularly remarkable dream-symbol is the falling out or extraction of teeth; the primary significance of this is certainly castration." Such a meaning was suggested by the analogy of the "broken tooth" and the "foot out of joint."

> The Greek myth knows about armed soldiers which came to life from the dragon's teeth sown by Jason: this seems to be again an absurdity but can be understood by the fantasies implicated in "tooth." Through the analysis of these fantasies one comes nearer to understanding these difficult words of Samson: "And Samson said, With the jawbone of an ass, heaps upon heaps, with the jaw of an ass have I slain a thousand men" (Judges 15:16). It is pointed out that the "jawbone of an ass" which Samson found was "new." The ass was symbolic in the Orient of the sexuality of the male (as developed in Apuleius' novel *The Golden Ass*).

There are many historic and anthropologic parallels which illustrate the veneration of teeth but they do not add much to the facts which can be disclosed through the analysis of language. The "tooth" and the "knee" derived their names from fantasies about the generative power of the body-self.

ADDENDA

COLOR SYMBOLISM

Color words function mostly as adjectives, as distinguishing qualities of specific objects.[1] Objects were perceived as colored in connection with many other qualities, long before "colors" were perceived in themselves. Such an abstraction as "redness" is a rather late result of the perception of the red blood, red rose, and other red things.

The human body and its functions, the skin, the hair, the eyes, hold the primacy in color perception as in many other respects.[2] Beyond one's own body, the color display of animals, then of plants and minerals, may serve for naming color qualities. With this in mind, one will understand that the abstract concept of "color" is missing in many pre-literate languages. It is also missing in the conceptual world of the small child. If the concept of distinct "color" ever enters his mind, it is the pigment, the material paint of a specific object, which carries emotional significance.

Thus, "color" is, first of all, the color of the human complexion. Beyond doubt, the fresh, fair skin of youthful cheeks was accepted as pleasant and normal in the Western world. On a more sophisticated level the complexion became tinted with a tinge of rouge in order to appear more youthful 'and beautiful. The color of the complexion has been an important personality factor since prehistoric ages. The color of the skin served as a racial characteristic, as one speaks about the "yellow race." It could also be the distinctive quality of people, as we speak of *redskin* Indians. The *Ethiopians* were called so by the Greeks, *aithein* meaning "to burn" and *ōps*, "face," thus "burnt-faced." The color of the face may also serve as a social class distinction. In Sanskrit *varna* denotes "skin, color," and "social caste." The color of the skin might be perceived as indicating health or sickness, as in the case of *jaundice,* from the Latin *galbinus,* "yellowish." It can be a symptom of an emotional condition, as indicated by *paling* or *blushing.* The psychology of colors is more an aspect of emotional skin reactions than optometry or chromatometry.

The identification of "color" and "skin" is best represented by the Greek term *chrōma* or *chrōs,* which denotes both "skin" and "color." One may state: color was perceived primarily as the color of the skin. In a shift of meaning it came to mean the pigment, the "make-up" applied to the face, then paint and dye in general. Even the word *al-cohol* derives from an Arabic term which denoted the powder which women used for coloring their eyelids. "Color," in the thinking of pre-literate people, means a powder, dye, paint, a very substantial pigment; not an abstract concept. The reddish rouge was the most important paint. In Spanish *colorado* does not mean "colored," but "red." In Baltic languages, "color" and "beauty" are termed by the same words. The corresponding terms in Russian are *krasna,* "beauty," *kraska,* "paint," and *krasnyj,* "red." I suppose that the popular distinction of cold and warm colors should also be understood in terms of skin reactions. The cold colors are bluish, or near to green, while the warm colors are near to red. The skin feels cold or warm, not the color.

The English term *color,* from the Latin *color,* points to a more sophisticated perception of the complexion. It might refer to the natural color, and also to the artificial make-up; but this cosmetic tainting is perceived as something "superficial," hiding or concealing the truth. The noun *color* is derived from the verb *celāre,* "to hide," as implied in *occulere,* from *ob-culere,* "to conceal." The color of the skin may "hide," as in English the *hide,* "skin," and *to hide,* "conceal," perceive the skin as a cover-up. This was in the mind of Shakespeare when he said: "truth needs no colors" or "truth fears no colors." It is a generally known psychological fact that colors elicit rather emotional responses, while the perception of the matter-of-fact reality prefers the gray or the black and white outlines of form and shape.

While the physical-optical qualities of colors can be described in objective terms, the corresponding subjective experiences, the psychological colors, are best recorded by their verbal expression. Man perceives not only the hue, but also the brightness and the saturation, thus, physically, an almost infinite variety, a much greater variety than words can express. How specific color terms refer to specific hues and shades selected from the color solid, how words single out figures distinguished from the background, differ widely with individuals and cultures. The naming of violet, blue, green, yellow, orange, red, brown, and the achromatic gray, black, and white resulted from a rather late, highly developed classification. Color names can be understood only within the "field," as distinguished from, or contrasted with, one another within a language community.[3]

The Old Testament Hebrew used about twenty different terms for colors, yet besides the white-black contrast, only the red and the yellow-green are distinctly named by generic terms. The Russian language, for instance, has not one, but six different "browns." One brown refers exclusively to dark brown eyes, another only to dark brown horses with black streaks, another to light brown horses, still another to light brown horses with yellow streaks, and a different "brown" is the coloring of the human sunburned complexion. The hide of a horse, the color of eyes and of the skin were obviously primary important realities which could not be termed by the one comprehensive term "brown."

Perception implies the "constancy" of color also, the expected color which might often be different from the real color. The conspicuous fluctuation between black, gray, and white may reflect the gradual change in the colors of the hair. Green-yellow-red are often termed by one word because the ripening of fruits and seeds was perceived as one unitary process. We speak of "deep," dark colors, for instance, of the "deep blue" of the ocean. The ocean is deep, not its color.[*]

The classification of colors is not, as sometimes stated, a

---

[*] "Yellow" and "green" were denoted by *one* word in Hebrew, *jereq,* or in Sanskrit, *harita.* The iron was called by Homer *polios,* "gray," or *ioneis,* "violet," from the flower *ion,* "violet," sometimes *aithon,* "bright." Hesiod called the iron *melas,* "black." The Latin *caeruleus* means "blue" and "green." The Latin *flāvus,* "yellow, blond," corresponds to the Old German *blaō,* "blue," but in Medieval German *blā* means "yellow"; now *blau* is again "blue."

question of quantitative mechanical "codability."[4] People pre-
occupied with cattle-raising or fur-trading will develop many
terms for the colors of hides and furs, but may have no generic
terms for colors, however "codable" such terms might be.
They may have no generic term for "cattle" or "mink" either.
The development of their color terminology is rather a question of cattle-raising or horse-trading than of quantitative
"codability." The specification of domesticated animals is
indicated by the word *peculiar*, from *pecus*, "cattle."

The differentiation of colors results from the emotional significance of colored objects within the language community.
The German term *Farbe*, "color," from the former *fara-wa*,
once referred to the total "look," "figure," "pigment," especially to the "speckled" animals. The English *hue*, which now
serves as denotation of the specific color quality, is related
to the Swedish *hy*, "skin, complexion," and the Gothic *hiui*,
"form, shape." These words prove once more that color was
perceived in its substantial concreteness, still undifferentiated
from shape and other qualities.

If color names were simply a question of "codability," the
power of color magic and color symbolism never could be
explained. Yet, the "color language" is a reality in pre-literate
cultures as well as in modern merchandising techniques. The
symbolism of the red rose cannot be understood by counting
the syllables because it is rooted in unconscious fantasies.[5]
Linguistics cannot avoid psychology. Optic measurements are
not substitutes for the psychology of colors.

In the following, specific color terms shall be considered in
order to illustrate this thesis and prove that the human body,
especially the skin, then hair and eyes, are the primary realities
to which color symbolism refers.

1. Gray

"Gray" holds a central position, not only in the color solid
but also in psychological reality. Absolute black and absolute

---

The corresponding Old Irish word *blár* means "green." The Hebrew
ādhom means "red" and "brown," and so on. The fluctuation in
color names shows that the objects to which these adjectives referred changed their color. It was not the meaning that changed
but the object of perception.

white exist only in optics. In reality one sees something in between black and white, depending on the background, shading into some blue, green, or yellow. *Brown* especially is such an indefinite, mixed color. Its Latin term *fuscus* means "dark, swarthy, dusky, tawny." This color, however, was an important characteristic of various animals. The *bear*, Old English *bera*, is identical in its origin with Old English *bernu*, "brown." The bear was a feared animal; its old name was avoided and, as a substitute, it was called "Mister Brown" in children's fairy tales. The American term, *Smoky*, for "bear" perceives the dark ash-gray color in the animal.

Our languages distinguish two kinds of gray: one is bluish, the other has a green or yellow tint. The pure ash-gray is often perceived with a shade of color because hairs and plants may rapidly lose their pigment, or the dark, blue sky may suddenly turn into colorless darkness. The syncretic perception of withering objects may suggest calling various fading colors gray.

Bluish gray mostly overlaps with the terms for "blue." Therefore, the bright bluish gray is termed *kuaneos* in Greek. It describes well the iridescent light playing on the waves of the deep, dark blue sea. Bodily references are at hand in this case. Poseidon, the god of the sea, is called *Kuano-chaitēs*, "dark haired," by Homer. The eyebrows of Zeus, the hair of Hector, the beard of Odysseus are also described by Homer as *kuaneos*. This applies also to the eyes and to the look of the eyes. These eyes are not dark. Dark eyes are called *melas*, "black," in Greek. This kind of blackness is often associated with evil; its linguistic background brings up the notion of filth and dirt. The somewhat brighter color of dark eyes is termed *charopos* in Greek. It means a blue shading into light gray, but the emphasis is not on the hue, but on the brightness. There is a "bright glare" in these eyes, therefore, they are described as the "eyes of youth, sparkling with joy." Even less blue and more gray are the eyes called *glaukos*; the glaring is their characteristic, not the color. *Glaucoma* describes exactly this kind of perception of gray—a blinding glare of light with low saturation either of blue, yellow, or green mixed with gray. Homer called the sea so sometimes when its surface appeared "gleaming silvery" with no specific color.

The Latin language developed similar terms for gray. The

bluish gray is called *caeruleus;* also *caesius* is said about eyes if they are eyes like the eyes of cats. Minerva had such catty eyes shining at night. The noun *caerula* denoted the azure, deep, dark sea, reflecting the blue sky. It can also mean dark green or "steel color," which is, in English, *iron-gray,* and also "gloomy," dark gray with all the evil connotations of black. One may observe that in Shakespeare's language the gray mostly shades into blue. When he says, "It struck upon him as the sun in the gray vault of heaven," one wonders whether the "vault of heaven" is blue or gray. He says, "the morn is bright and gray." The same perception of the morning prevails in the German term *Morgen-grauen,* properly "the graying of the morning." When Shakespeare says, "Mine eyes are gray and bright," he surely refers to a gleaming bluish gray in which brilliance is more conspicuous than hue.

The English *gray* and German *grau* referred not to the bluish, but rather to the greenish-yellowish gray. One may surmise that the decoloration of the skin and the withering of plants gave to this shade of "gray" its symbolic meaning. The phonemic equivalent of the English *gray* is the Latin *rāvus,* former *grā-vus,* which denoted specifically the strange, yellowish gray of eyes.

A term for "gray" reserved for the skin is *pale.* It is specific with the English language that one is *growing* pale, greenish yellow, just as fruits and plants "grow." The according Latin term, *pallidus,* means yellowish gray with no brilliance. As an emotional reaction, it means fear, fright, but also might be a symptom of anemia, as in "pale with love." The original concrete meaning is best exposed by the according Greek *pelios,* also *pelos* or *pellos.* It is said "properly of parts of the body discolored by extravasated blood," "black and blue," "livid." It means a dark, ash-colored spot on the skin. The related *polios* refers primarily to the grayness of the hair with an accent of venerability. The sky also can be *polios* with serene brightness.

Phonemically related is the English *fallow.* It means to grow "pale," coloring the skin yellow-green-gray. Shakespeare says the "ashy pale showed the fear." The *appalling* skin reaction to a shocking experience is generally known. The skin reaction to fear and anxiety is used symbolically as "pale-hearted." Shakespeare says: "I am pale in mine heart to see thine eyes so red." In his observation, even the eyes can turn pale: "Look, how thy eye turns pale."

The Hungarian language is less repressive than the Western languages. It calls "pale," *halovány*, from a word which means "death," *halál*. The paleness of skin, the withering decoloration of plants are forebodings of death. This opens up the emotional significance of "gray." It is the color of despair and depression. In mourning and melancholia the world loses its brilliance, everything appears drab, gray, just as all food may taste like sand or sawdust. Gray is the color of de-realization of all hues. The de-realization of the visual world corresponds to the parallel de-personalization of the inside world, the void and emptiness which are its characteristics.

2. White

"White," "bright," "light," "shining" were once inseparable, overlapping concepts. It made no difference whether the radiant energy was emitted or reflected. The meaning of "white" depended primarily on the emotional significance of light-emitting or reflecting objects. Because light discloses the visual world, it became symbolic of life and man's mental capacities. Thus, the attribute of "light" and of luminous qualities became mental attributes. Man can also be *bright, enlightened, splendid,* properly meaning "shining." He can be *brilliant,* which means "sparkling, bright," as resplendent or lustrous objects radiate light in darkness. His face can be *radiant, beaming,* in the state of elation. Similar expressions in all languages suggest the symbolic equation of radiant light with man's mental capacities.

The skin, the hair, and the eyes were the primary objects to which the symbolic meaning of "bright" and "white" referred. *Bright* originally did not describe intellectual excellence, as it is mostly understood in our intellectual age, but denoted "radiant health," happiness, superior vitality, and for that matter, "holiness," *healthy, holy,* and *wholesome* being interrelated concepts.

The "brightness" and "brilliance" of the outstanding personality was symbolically expressed by applying various ointments which made the face, and especially the hair, "brilliant." While all colors appear, on a primitive level, first as material pigments, the cosmetic dying and coloring substances held the priority among pigments. The oldest and most general substances applied to the skin were, however, not colors, but animal fats and vegetable oils. They gave men the appearance of brightness. It would be misleading, in the application of fatty substances, to search for dermatological reasons like those which resulted in the modern use of oily cosmetics. The symbolism of "brilliance" is rooted not in sanitary considerations, but in unconscious religious fantasies about the divine nature of man. When Moses came down from the mount, "the skin of his face shone," so much so that his people were afraid of him (Exodus 34:29–35). The shining face was the true symptom of the fact that he had had immediate contact with the Lord.

If sanitary considerations were implied in oiling as in the oiling of the head, emotionally important objects were not made shining by oil. The shields were oiled before battle but not for sanitary reasons. "Arise, ye princes, and anoint the shield," the prophet says (Isaiah 21:5); or, "there the shield of the mighty is vilely cast away, the shield of Saul, as though he had not been anointed with oil" (II Samuel 1:21). The shield, made from animal skin, served as a protection and projection of the personality behind it. The shining shield represented the "bright" personality.

Long before the fine Oriental scents, oils, balsam, and myrrh became known in Germanic antiquity, people smeared their faces and hair with animal fats and butter. The old terms for butter do not denote a food to eat, but an unguent with which to smear the body, especially the hair. This Germanic custom can hardly be interpreted as a cosmetic or sanitary device. If it were a medicament, the word *bright*, Old English *beorht*, German *-brecht*, would not appear so often since the earliest ages in personal names. *Bertha*, the former *berahta*, properly means the "bright, shining one," and the name *Al-bright*, German *Al-brecht*, former *adal-berht*, properly means "bright through nobility," etc.

Ointments were also used for daily toilet purposes, but this custom appears as a rather secondary development, different from the original sacral-religious use. "Anoint thine head, and wash thy face," Christ said (Matthew 6:17). The anointing oil, which consecrated the high priest, should never be used for profane purposes, according to the Old Testament law: "This shall be an holy anointing oil unto me throughout your generations. Upon man's flesh shall it not be poured, neither shall ye make any other like it . . . it is holy, and it shall be holy unto you" (Exodus 30:31, 32). The "brightness" belonged primarily to the king, the high priests, then to the priest. It became the symbol of consecration. The glittering oil was applied liberally during the consecration of the high priest: "The precious ointment upon the head, that ran down upon the beard . . . that went down to the skirts of his garments" (Psalms 133:2). The priest was thus consecrated: "Then shalt thou take the anointing oil and pour it upon his head and anoint him" (Exodus 29:7).

The Greek language used different words for the perfumed oil used for anointment and for the unscented oils with which, for instance, the wrestlers smeared their bodies. The verb *chriō* meant "to touch the surface of the human body, to rub, anoint with scented oil"; the noun *chrisma* means "anything smeared on," and also "whitewash." The full meaning of "bright," in the concrete sense, thus remained enshrined in the name of *Christos*, the Anointed One, which is the translation of the Hebrew *Messiah*. Christ appeared to His disciples: "His face did shine as the sun and His raiment was white as the light" (Matthew 17:2), or "His head and His hairs were white like wool, as white as snow, and His eyes were as a flame of fire" (Revelation 1:14).

The consecration ceremonial of the king and the high priest gradually became expanded to the anointing of the dead, which surely cannot be explained as a sanitary practice, even though it became an important motive of embalming. The extreme unction of the dying is one of the seven sacraments of the Roman Catholic Church. The association of "holiness" and "healing" made the anointment of the sick not a medication, but a religious healing agent. Sanitary considerations are also excluded in the use of ointment as an expression of reverence, hospitability, and respect. Jesus said to Simon the Pharisee: "My head with oil thou didst not anoint, but this woman hath anointed my feet with ointment" (Luke 7:46).

Bright is still used with the meaning of cheerful gladness, as in "bright future." Its primary expression was the *radiant* face and the *beaming* look. In the same way the anointing was used as an expression of happiness and elation. "Go thy way, eat thy bread with joy, and drink thy wine with a merry heart . . . let thy garments be always white; and let thy head lack no ointment" (Ecclesiastes 9:7, 8). Contrariwise, the anointing of the head had to be discontinued in times of mourning. Dust and ashes took all brightness away. The oiled, brilliant hair is in harmony with the white-rosy complexion. The white skin was highly esteemed in the Near East in males as an attribute of beauty, even when the hairs were not blond at all: "My beloveth is white and ruddy . . . his locks are bushy, and black as a raven" (Song of Solomon 5:10, 11).

While "bright" and "radiant" are expressive of vitality, the "pale-white" might be the symptomatic skin reaction of sickness, old age, and even death. The primary reference to the skin and hair is, once again, obvious. Shakespeare pronounces the curse: "Let the white death sit on thy cheek for ever."

The rapid change in the coloring of the complexion is well observed in our languages. "How white and red each other did destroy," Shakespeare said. The skin reaction to age and sickness is expressed in the picture language of the Bible. The "Nazarites" were once "purer than snow, they were whiter than milk, they were more ruddy in body than rubies," but now "their visage is blacker than a coal . . . their skin cleaveth to their bones; it is withered, it is become like a stick" (Lamentations 4:7–8).

An unusual white coloring of the skin, especially white spots, was observed as the symptom of sickness. In Greek *leukē* is "a cutaneous disease, so called, from its color," *leukos* means "light, bright, brilliant," but, like most Greek color terms, denotes object qualities which are between white and gray. Thus, *leukē* denotes "a kind of leprosy or of elephantiasis," a skin condition which reminded one of the hide of an elephant. The Latin term *albus* denotes "dead white," not shining hair, complexion; it corresponds to "pale." The according Greek term is *alphos*, "a dull-white leprosy, especially on the face." The most feared "white" of the skin was the symptom of a leper. "The hair in the plague is turned white" (Leviticus 13:3). "Miriam became leprous, white as snow" (Numbers 12:10).

It is rather difficult to understand why white, as an attribute of heart or liver, is symbolic of cowardice. Shakespeare says: "I shame to wear a heart so white" or "livers white as milk." Such a reference to internal organs sounds rather paradoxical because their coloring cannot be observed, as can the skin's reaction to emotions. It does not seem probable that the early physiology observed the differences between the red hemoglobin corpuscles and the colorless "white" cells (leuko-cytes) in the circulatory system. The verbal expressions rather suggest that the bile, the secretion of the liver, was held responsible for the anemic skin. In Greek *leukainō* means to "grow white," *leuko-phlegmatōs*, "suffering from white phlegm," *leuko-phlegmatōdēs*, "affected with chlorosis" (which is called, in popular parlance, "green-sickness," a kind of anemia mainly affecting girls at the onset of puberty), *leuka*, "white menstrual alba" of young girls, different from the *eruthra*, the red discharge. The pale, light yellow or greenish complexion was interpreted as a symptom of timidity and attributed to the "white heart" or "white liver."

The sacral "bright" and "white" also suggested the symbolism of cleanness and virginity. White animals were preferably chosen for sacrifice, to be made "holy." Cleanliness suggests the contrast of bright against dark, of white against black or brown. Innocence and virginity suggest the contrast of white against red. One may interpret the red spot as red blood. "Many shall be purified, and made white" (Daniel 12:10).

3. Black

"Black" is inseparable from "dark" and "deep" as is "white" from "bright" and "light." The absence of light was perceived either in spatial terms, referring to "depth," or as some substantial thing, especially clouds, covering the source of light. The abyss without light was in Shakespeare's mind when he said: "my black and deep desire." The other black, which results from the covering or contrasting of the light, is never absolute; it always shades into gray and twilight: "In the twilight, in the evening, in the black and dark night" (Proverbs 7:9). When it is said: "The heaven was black with clouds" (I Kings 18:45), the source of light is covered. The term *nuance,* as a delicate difference in shade or meaning, is derived from the Latin *nubes,* "cloud." Light and shining go together in sensory experience with "fire," "flame." In contrast, darkness evokes the ideas of coal, soot and ashes. Cheerful happiness was indicated by brightness and anointing of the head; by the same token, in mourning not only anointing had to be discontinued, but dust and ashes were heaped upon the head, thus taking away the brilliance. The prophet shall "comfort all that mourn . . . to give unto them beauty for ashes, the oil of joy for mourning" (Isaiah 61:2, 3). The brilliance of oil and the colorless ashes are expressive of the contrast of elation and depression.

The Latin language distinguishes two kinds of "black," as it also distinguishes two kinds of "white." The difference is in the brilliance. One black is *ater,* the other *niger.* The term *ater* refers to the nonshining "coal-black." The corresponding "white" is *albus,* "dead-white," without brilliance or luster, rather pale or ash-gray, the white of sickness or old age. The attribute *ater* definitely denoted the blackness as the consequence of fire; it meant "blackened, burnt by fire." The entrance hall of the house was called the *atrium.* It has something in common symbolically with the fireplace. The other term for "black," *niger,* also refers to fire, but denotes a brilliant, shining black, reflecting light. This glistening blackness is opposed on the white side by *candidus,* "shining, dazzling, clear, white," from the verb *candeō,* "to be brilliant, glittering, thus glowing hot and radiating."

The perception of fire—one moment shining, glowing black, the next moment coal-black and sooty—might be the reason that, in some languages, "black" and "white" are termed with almost identical words. Perhaps the change in the color of hair or the black and white coloration of domesticated animals may also have contributed to the syncretic perception of black and white. Even the English *black* and the relative *bleak* show this strange phonemic relationship with *blank, bleach* and *blink,* which originally referred to "shining." Milton still says, "the blank moon," instead of the "shining moon." In the Dutch language *blaken* means "burn, glow"; the word is related to the Latin *flagrāre,*" to flame, burn," or to the Greek *phlegō, phlōx,* "to burn, blaze." The German *blaken* is said about the smoky sooting of candle lights, but *blecken,* former *blak-jan,* means "to show the white of the teeth."

The symbolism of "black" developed in diametrical opposition to the meaning of "white." The reference to the skin is still of primary importance. "My skin is black upon me and my bones are burned with heat" (Job 30:30). The white, fair skin means beauty in the Western world; black spots are equated with *ugly* in the original sense of the word, which was "dreadful." White skin, however, could be covered by black hairs. If the skin was shaggy, covered with thickly grown wooly hair, it was a sign of strength in the Greek heroic age, and is called *lasios* in Greek. Achilles was *lasios.* Hercules, the paragon of masculine strength, was even called *melanpugos,* "black-bottomed." Later on, however, the hairy skin lost its appeal and came to be considered as a mark of man's coarse, animal nature. It also implied the propensity for intrigue and cunning. Such skin characteristics still survive in various verbal expressions. For instance, in Hungarian, a "shaggy, hairy heart" (*szörös-szivü*) describes an insensitive, callous, "thick-skinned" personality. The French called their soldiers *poilu,* "hairy."

In the Near East the darker skin is normal, yet it still has to be excused. "I am black but comely," says the bride, "look not upon me, because I am black, because the sun hath looked upon me" (Song of Solomon 1:5, 6). Shakespeare had a similar idea in mind when he said: "The air has starved the roses in her cheeks and pinched the lily tincture of her face that now she is become black as I."

While "white" became symbolic of "cleanness," black became equated with "dirt" and "filth." The obsolete English *swart* and the German *schwarz,* "black," developed from the same phonemic form which also appears in Latin as *sordēs,* "filth," or *sordidus,* "filthy, dirty." Also, the Greek *melas,* "black," has parallel forms in Sanskrit meaning "filth, dirt." Blackness was perceived in substance contrasted with the "clean" or "white" background. While "white" represents sinless innocence, the black color became translated into the moral sphere; it became the attribute of anything considered evil, wicked, or perverted—"black as hell." "That black name Edward, black prince of Wales," Shakespeare said.

4. Red

Red holds some prominence among all colors. It is the oldest genuine and most widely spread among the Indo-European color terms. It developed in many specific denotations from scarlet to bright crimson, to orange and brown. In all these variations one can distinguish three layers. One refers to the skin and to blood, another to the "red-hot" flame of fire. A third layer refers to plants, minerals, and various dying substances. Such material designations are *orange, violet, purple, scarlet,* or minerals such as *ruby,* from the Latin *rubeus,* "red," red *carnelian,* red *coral.* These objects describe exactly a specific kind of red. Slavic languages denote the *purple*-red in referring to "little worm." The same holds true for the French *vermeil,* "vermilion," from the Latin *vermiculus,* "little worm." Similar animal reference is implied in *purple,* from the Latin *purpura,* Greek *porphyra,* "purple fish." Intense red dyes were obtained from these animals.

The human skin, its coloring by blood, and in some cases, the color of the hair, define specific kinds of "red." One can question whether or not the outside fire, which can be observed objectively, or the inside fire, the subjective experience, brought about the close association of "hot" and "red." There exists in English a conspicuous cluster of words which obviously influenced one another to such an extent that their clear separation is a question for lexicographers rather than for speakers of English. *Flush, rush, flash, rash, blush*—each can be defined in lexical terms, but in sound and meaning these terms are somehow connected with one another. They suppose that a *rush* of blood causes a *blush* of the face. This is an outside symptom of the *flush* of blood experienced subjectively as a *flash* of heat. It might bring about a *rash* of the skin, but is generally perceived as a blooming, like a "flushing meadow." Shakespeare speaks about the "flush of May," "flush of youth"; "now the time is flush" means the time is ripe. The flash-flush, hot-blood, and heat-red association may reflect the primary experience of a skin reaction.

The word *red* preserved the old, genuine term, which also remained in the Greek *e-ruth-ros,* "red," the Latin *russus,* "red," from *rud-sus,* also *ruber,* and the German *rot,* "red."

This group of words originally referred to the blood. The corresponding words in Sanskrit also mean "bloody" or "blood"; in Slavic languages they refer to the flushing or blushing of the face.

The symbolism of the red rose is rooted in the meaning of the red blood, just as the red wine is called "the blood of grapes" (Genesis 49:11). "Blood" and "flower" are equated with one another.* In German the singular noun *Blut* means "blood"; its old plural is *bluete, Blüte,* "flower," with the meaning of blooming. In Hungarian *vér* means "blood," *véres,* "bloody," *veres,* "red," and *ver-ág,* "flower." The blooming of the flower is perceived as bleeding, or, the other way around, bleeding is equated with blooming. The authorized version of the Bible translates the difficult Hebrew terms as "a woman sick of her flowers." The flower symbolism of the "red rose" refers to blood symbolism. Shakespeare speaks of "bleeding roses." Hamlet called Ophelia the "rose of May." This is in accordance with the above-quoted "flush of May" or "flush of youth," meaning the prime of life. The flower "rose" can be red, white or yellow, but as a color name, *rose* characteristically means *pink*, not red. It describes the blood reactions of the skin: as color, it means a red with low saturation, mixed with white. It has a variety of "shocking pink," yet even this is not as "loud" as the vibrant orange-red or the "shrieking" red of high saturation. The addition of white made pink more "feminine," as compared with the more aggressive variants of blood-red.[6] To be *in the pink* means to be in perfect health in colloquial English, as in the "flush of youth," or "rose of May." Shakespeare says: "Nay, I am the very pink of courtesy," meaning the embodiment of excellence. It is the pink color of the cheeks which evoked these figurative expressions. The color of the complexion, in the West and North, as well as the Near East, is supposed to be "pink," a mixture of red and white, *rosy*, which is best approached by the skin color of youth and perfect blood pressure. Shakespeare said: "How now my love? Why is your cheek so pale? How chance the roses there do fade so fast?" In the Old Testament, reflecting the culture of the Near East, this "pink" color is

---

* See pp. 179, 219.

termed *adom* in Hebrew. The noun *Adam* means "man," characterized by his ruddy complexion. This gives the concept of "rose" its specific charm. Shakespeare spoke of "beauty's rose," "rose of youth," or of a "maid yet rosed over with the virgin crimson of modesty." In the temporal dimension "women are as roses whose fair flower being once displayed, doth fall that very hour."

The word *pink*, for "rosy," projects upon the screen of language very repressed unconscious fantasies. The color name and its identity with "rosy" is generally agreed upon, but what about the flower-plant of "rose"? Roses have thorns, and thorns may prick and cause bleeding. The adjective *pink*, denoting this light or pale red color with a light purple tinge, has a parallel verbal form *to pink* or to be *pinked;* it is somewhat similar to the more popular *to pinch* or to be *pinched.* *To pink* means "to make holes, to prick, thrust, stab," or in the transitive, "to pierce, prick or stab with any pointed weapon or instrument." This refers to the eternal symbolism of the rose and the thorn which is used in depicting, in flower language, "defloration." The Shakespeare version of it says: "Prick not your fingers as you pluck it off lest bleeding you do paint the white rose red." The generally known literary illustration is Goethe's "Heideröslein," which has the pointed dialogue of the boy and the rose. "I prick you and you will ever remember me."

5. Blue

Objects with bluish coloring were known since ages when no general term for "blue" existed. This abstract color adjective belongs to a rather late development of language and thinking.[7] The English *blue* originally meant "livid," but did not refer, as did the corresponding Latin *lividus,* to the bluish color of the metal lead, but to the discoloring of the skin in consequence of cold or injury. It is sometimes identified with green and yellow, or specified as black-blue, purple-blue, reddish blue, or even with dark ash-gray. The primary point of reference is suggested by the phonemic relationship of *blue* and *blow.* The Old English *blaw* means "blue" and "blow." The skin reaction to a blow or a boil may show many colors.

6. Yellow

Yellow, as perceived by our languages, was rather on the green side, therefore, "yellow" and "green" are denoted by identical terms, as in many other pre-literate languages. By the same token, "green" was also perceived as "yellowish," as in the Greek *chlōros*, "greenish yellow." Obviously this greenish yellow or yellowish green was observed with great interest in antiquity. One may suppose that the gradual change in colors during the ripening of fruits and corn was perceived as *one* process with the "constancy" of colors. Painters like Vincent van Gogh know too well that, for instance, a "white" paper is never white, but gray, yellow, or many other possible colors. Yellow sunflowers, depending on light, may appear as yellow, blue, red, violet, or gray. Color discrimination was very important, for instance, for the Greek people in dealing with wine. Many variations of yellow were properly discriminated in reference to wine. The brightest wine was called *leukos oinos*, "white wine," even though the "white" wine is not "white" at all. The darker variety of wine was called *xanthos oinos*, "yellow wine"; and even more dark was the *kirros oinos*, a tawny, orange-yellow wine. The darkest wine was called *melas oinos*, properly "black wine." This was not a black wine, as the "white" wine was not a white-colored wine; "black" simply means "dark-colored." The interest in wine, not "codability," is reflected by this discrimination of yellow colors.

In English, *yellow* and *yolk* are related words, as in other languages, but the color perceived in objects seldom reached the yellow of the ripe citron or lemon, the *lemon-yellow* called *kitrinos*, from *kitron*, "citron," in Greek. In most cases this color was approximated, permitting many different tints or shades.

The identification of yellow with the brilliance of gold or sunshine is reflected in the symbolism of this color. Gold was not found on the surface of nature; therefore it served, as did the aerial blue, for the expression of transcendence, as in the golden mosaic background of Byzantine saints. In reference to the body, yellow is used for the description of hair color with the symbolic connotation of "beauty." In English, *fair* originally denoted, as in other relative languages, a concept which is the opposite of "foul." "Foul" spots are dark. "Fair" means "bright" whitish yellow. *Blond* hair is fair; it admits a shade of auburn. The ideal beauty in Western antiquity was of the "fair" or "blond" type with flaxen-yellow or dark blond hair, white skin, bright gray or bluish or even dark eyes, rosy cheeks—all the opposite of the sunburned dark taint, dark hair and eyes of the neighboring people. However, this is the beauty of the woman. In man this "fairness" carries an effeminate accent. The Greek *xanthos*, "yellow," originally referred exclusively to the color of the hair, as did the English *blond*. Shakespeare says: "Her hair is auburn, mine is perfect yellow." In an extended sense the Greek *xanthos* is the color of ripe corn, specifically the brilliance of gold and of the *xantho-phanēs*, "golden-gleaming" sun. The Homeric heroes, Achilles and Odysseus, are *xanthos*, "yellow-haired," as is Apollo and other representatives of youthful beauty. Dionysus is called *chruso-komos*, "golden-haired." "Golden" and "yellow" are used with the same meaning, although the color of gold, like the rays of the sun, may be *chruso-ruthros*, "golden-red." In such cases yellow-orange-red are fused into one concept.

The yellow color carries a different connotation in the East. In the Hebrew of the Old Testament, one term is *yerek*, "yellow," *yārāk*, "green." The primary body reference is recognizable because these words derive from the primary *yārak*, "to spit." Another term definitely refers to "gold"; *tsāhōb*, "yellow," from *tsāhab*, "golden, to glitter," but this yellow is not an attribute of beauty, but a symptom of sickness. The "yellow thin hair" of scall was considered as a sure sign of leprosy, but "if the scall be spread in the skin, the priest shall not seek for yellow hair; he is unclean" (Leviticus 13:36).

The reaction of the skin is registered also in the English *fallow*, an old Germanic term, the German *fahl* and *falb*, which described the yellow shading into gray. The word is related to the Latin *pallidus*, "pale"; the now obsolete *to fallow* means "to grow pale and yellow, to blanch and to wither, to blanch." It describes the effect of fear and anxiety upon the color of the skin, also the effect of age, as opposed to the healthy rosy cheeks. The related Greek *polios* means "gray." More complicated is the human reaction which may explain the Spanish *amarillo*, "yellow." It originally meant "bitter." The secretion of the bile, in specific conditions, may be perceived as yellow and bitter at the same time. Such words suggest that the color yellow was associated in unconscious fantasies with bitterness, envy, jealousy, fear, and anxiety. The word *yellow*, Old English *geolu*, is phonemically related to the Old English *gealla, gall*, as in gall bladder, bile, which still describes bitterness and exasperation on the emotional level. A "yellow streak" indicates fearfulness and cowardice. Shakespeare knows about the "green and yellow melancholy," a symbolic reference to the secretion of the bile. He also says: "not black in my mind though yellow in my legs," or "I will possess him with yellowness for the revolt of mine is dangerous." This psychological interpretation of "yellowness" is derived primarily from the reaction of the skin to anxiety and old age—it is the opposite of courage, health, youth, and vigor.

7. Green

Among all color names, "green" is the most transparent through its phonemic relationship to *grow* and *grass*. Plants seem to be the primary objects of reference. This explains the symbolic function of the green color. It means "growth," "youth," sometimes with an accent of immaturity. The green fruits or grapes are not ripe. Shakespeare said, with this in mind, "green virginity," "green is the color of lovers," or "green boy," "fancies too green and idle for girls of mine."

Another meaning of "green" is derived from its closeness to "yellow." Then it is not a sign of youth, but is indicative of old age, anemia, sometimes called "green sickness." "To look so green and pale," Shakespeare said. Jealousy is also called "green jealousy," in Shakespeare's language. The secretion of the bile, the "bitterness" of subjective experience, is the source of this body symbolism.

FIRE

"Fire" is an outstanding example which may stand for other elementary phenomena of life. It is a physico-chemical process of combustion as perceived by sense perception, but beyond that it means something not present in combustion, but projected upon it and enacted in myth and religion. The objectively perceived fire of the outside world and the subjective fire within, which grew out of unconscious fantasies, might be two different concepts in principle. They are in fact one. There exists in our languages a differentiation between two competitive genuine concepts: one remained preserved in the Greek *pur*, "fire," the other in the Latin *ignis*, "fire." It has been supposed (by Meillet) that the Greek *pur* type of fire is mostly neuter and referred to "household fire," while the Latin *ignis*, "fire," is masculine and refers to the sacral fire.[8] Meillet, the great French linguist, was not aware perhaps that in French the two genders (*le, la*) reduce the three genders (*he, she, it*) to two categories, identifying the feminine with the neuter, which is an age-old *mater-ial* concept of the woman. In other words, this means that the reality experience of "fire" was originally a female-neuter concept, differentiated from the subjective phenomenological experience of "fire." It might be that the Greek *pur*, to which the English *fire*, the German *Feuer* belong, did not carry the sacral implications of the Latin *ignis* type of fire; yet there can be little doubt that libidinous fantasies have been perceived, understood, depicted, and denoted in both images. The household fire on the fireplace, however realistic this concept might be, is a feminine concept, while the imaginary inside fire, the sacral-religious

312

"Fire," the god of fire, is definitely masculine. One can observe that the realistic household fire on the hearth became rekindled from the ashes kept on the fireplace. It was customary to do so in Greek, Roman, and Germanic antiquity. In the Germanic languages this rekindling from the ashes was called "quickening" because fire was equated with life. If ashes could not be set on fire, people did not take the trouble to "rub" or "drill" or "bore" fire or use flint. They simply brought the fresh fire from a neighbor. Such custom is attested by Homer (*Odyssey* 5:488).

The sacral fire is different in kind. For sacral purposes fire had to be made anew. This custom has been described for Greek, Roman, and German rituals. The same holds true for the Old English or Sanskrit-Vedic religion. The sacral fire must be a virgin fire. Once a year, in the temple of Vesta, in observance of the feast of the virginal goddess who was the guardian of the hearth, the home and the family, the sacral fire was kindled anew. It is obvious that the making of fire, not the fire as such, was the significant action of the ritual.

The difference between the feminine, realistic concept of fire identified with the hearth and the masculine, internalized fire with sexual connotations can still be observed in the whole area of associations in our languages. The feminine fire has oral connotations. This fire is *devouring, consuming,* and the flames have tongues. "The flames *licked up* everything in their path."[9] In German the flames lick with "little tongues," *züngeln,* when the corresponding English says the "flames leap." (The identification of "fire" and "tongue" was described in connection with "tongue," p. 247.)

The masculine inside fire is loaded with genital generative fantasies. These fantasies may also refer to the hearth or fireplace. For instance, in Old Slavic language the "husband" is called *ogniscaninu,* which properly means "owner of the fireplace."* According to these fantasies, the fire is "generated" or *kindled.* This verb *to kindle* means "to set fire," "to inflame with passion," "to make ardent," on the one hand, and "to generate offspring" on the other hand. The latter is now said mainly of the brood of animals, but the corresponding German *Kind,* "child," refers to the human. Our good dic-

---

* See p. 136.

tionaries try to separate these two kinds of *kindlings*, but the meanings were not so neatly separated in the minds of the speakers as in dictionaries. In English, *heat* denotes the physiological condition of animals at breeding time. In English dialects *spunk* means the "spark" that sets the touchwood on fire, but it denotes "semen" also. *To spunk* means to kindle fire and to emit semen. In German, the verb *brennen* means "to burn," the noun *Brunst* means "fire" and "libido," and *brunzen* means "to urinate." The term *to quicken* is used in many languages with the double reference: to the beginning of life, and to the kindling of fire.

> The naïve sexualization of fire is, for instance, supposed when it is said in the Bible that King David grew old and "gat no heat." His servants brought to him a young virgin: "let her stand before the king, and let her cherish him, and let her lie in thy bosom, that my lord the king may get heat . . . the damsel was very fair, and cherished the king, and ministered to him: but the king knew her not" (I Kings 1:1–4).

Unconscious fantasies implicated in "kindling fire" found their best-known mythological elaboration in the Greek myth of Prometheus. He was the Titan who stole the fire from the father-god Zeus and revealed to mankind the secret of generating fire. He also taught man the somehow related secrets of domestication of animals and of agriculture. These doings also imply human interference in the natural process of fertilization. He also tried the worst, the prohibited act: to fashion man from clay, that is, to generate human life. His deeds were considered as revolt and sin by the father-god Zeus. The kindling of fire and the fertilization of the Mother Earth were the prerogatives of the Father who dominates the order of Nature. Human interference in any natural process carried the seed of sin and guilt. Yet the essential human drive for self-assertion and freedom wanted nothing more than just this: to make man free from the bondage of natural laws and dominate or subjugate the forces of Nature. This is the progress of human development. Thus, Prometheus became the leading symbol in the ages of humanism and enlightenment.

The name itself is perhaps the result of the Greek reinterpretation or secondary rationalization of an old verb meaning "rubbing fire." It was understood as being associated with *pro-mēthēs*, "fore-thinking," from *pro*, "before," and *mathein*, "to learn." This is the implication of the word *mathēma*, "that which is learned, learning, knowledge," especially the predictive mathematical sciences. Abstract thinking means, for the practical Greek mind, "thinking ahead," thus *pro-mēthēs* means "fore-thinking, provident, cautious," as in the Greek verb *pro-mētheomai*, "to take care beforehand." This notion of thinking ahead does not justify the punishment which the great pioneer of human striving for independence received from Father Zeus. Zeus chained this rebellious son to a rock in the Caucasus and each day sent a vulture to eat away his liver (the liver was considered to be the seat of "fore-thinking"), but it was restored each night. In Sanskrit, the name of the fire-drill is *pramantha*.

It is difficult to know whether or not some prehistoric connection exists between the Sanskrit name of the fire-drill and the Greek Titan who brought the secret of making fire to man. One will ask again: Why was the invention of making fire a sin, why did fire have to be stolen from heaven for the benefit of mankind? The small child surely learns to make fire as an act of disobedience. "Don't do it" is impressed upon his mind, and he learns that it burns, yet he will do it nevertheless. Thus, it might be that "making fire" was charged with the meaning of prohibition; to do it nevertheless meant disobedience, rebellion, bad conscience, guilt, and sin.

The "fire" has held a specific fascination since the beginning of human history. Its introduction brought about a radical change in food habits and sacrifice; its impact upon unconscious fantasies is still strongly felt by children and adults alike. If "fire" would be simply what is said about combustion in our excellent dictionaries, there would not be pyromaniacs or so many cases of arson. Obviously, there is something more to it which is not implied in the reality definition of fire. If one wants to know what ideas are connected with this inside, divine fire, one should look into the language of the Bible, especially of the Hebrew Old Testament, or into the language of Shakespeare.

Shakespeare's language is descriptive concerning this inside, subjective phenomenological experience of "fire." He speaks about the "golden fire," the hot-burning, growing, flashing, spritely, sweet fire, about the fire of life, of love, of lust, of passion, also of rage and youth. He knows the raging, climbing, fierce, never-quenching, wrathful fire, "the true Promethean fire." "O, who can hold a fire in his hand, By thinking on the frosty Caucasus." This may describe the subjective, inside experience of fire. The divine fire personified in the old Hindu religion is the god *Agni;* he is also the god of speech. He is represented in the Old Testament by the "flame of fire out of the midst of a bush . . . the bush burned with fire, and the bush was not consumed" (Exodus 3:2). The Lord appears to his chosen people as a pillar of fire. His fire comes down from heaven and consumes the burnt offering (II Chronicles 7:1). His fire is a purifying agency; everything is "clean" that goes through the fire (Numbers 31:23). One will understand that this internalized fire is the symbolic representant of the life process, it is "kindled," it burns, consumes itself until it changes into coals and ashes. One does not sit around a well-heated radiator in the same pensive mood as one watches a log on the fireplace slowly burning up. The fire inspired the pre-Socratic Greek philosophy, the beginning of modern thinking. Heraclitus declared that "Fire" is the essence of life. Of course, he meant the symbolic fire and was not accused of pan-sexualism. The fire of his philosophy was not an object, but "burning," the process of transsubstantiation, of eternal birth and dying which is "becoming." Empedocles perceived the burning process, like the Old Testament, as purification, but it was not yet called catharsis at that time. Because fire meant this purifying transsubstantiation, he threw himself into the volcano of Etna. Such purifying fantasies are still alive in the rituals of incineration. The disposing of the dead corpses through fire on the funeral pyre, as practiced in Homeric ages and in the Old English *Beowulf,* still perceives life as a process of burning, and dying as the extinguishing of fire, as the transformation of the living substance into coals and ashes. It is not by chance that "old" and "cold" are related concepts.

No other subject has been investigated more thoroughly, as far as unconscious fantasies were concerned, than the terms and the myths about the origin of fire. The pioneer work done by Adalbert Kuhn might have brought about a new era of psychological understanding of language (1859) had it not been discredited and ridiculed for other than scientific reasons. The storm raised by moral indignation was led by anthropologists (Edward B. Taylor), orientalists (Paul de Lagarde), linguists (Georg Curtius), and classicists (M. Gilbert) for identifying the making of fire with "making love."* What is accepted as a matter of fact today was not so a hundred years ago. However, despite all the moral indignation, it has been demonstrated (by C. G. Jung) that, in the literature, alchemy clearly defined the sexual symbolism of fire. The pre-scientific literature on fire (investigated by Gaston Bachelard)[10] does not leave any doubt about the psychological implications which caused such vehement indignation when they were raised by Adalbert Kuhn. It is beside the point whether or not the Greek name *Prometheus,* "fore-thinker," is connected with the Sanskrit *pramantha,* the tool for making fire. "Thinking ahead" was surely a more appealing concept than making fire. Yet, punishing his son out of proportion for simply "thinking ahead" cast the shadow of paranoia upon Father Zeus. Despite all arguments to the contrary, there is no denying that the oldest document of Indo-European history, the Sanskrit *Rigveda* (III 29:1-3), describes in unequivocal terms the process of kindling fire, calling the boring piece of wood "generator," the other wood which is to be bored, "mistress of the house" (*vicpatnī*). The

---

* A pioneer work in linguistic prehistory is Adalbert Kuhn, *Die Herabkunft des Feuers und des Göttertranks: Ein Beitrag zur Vergleichenden Mythologie des Indogermanischen* (Berlin: Dümler, 1859). He came to a clear insight into the underlying unconscious fantasies of drilling and rubbing fire. It is rather interesting to observe the resistance against A. Kuhn's insight into verbal fantasies. The loudest protest came from historians and anthropologists who were unprepared to accept as a matter of fact even the obvious psychological realities. See Paul de Lagarde, *Gegen die Zote vom Feuerreiben,* Nachrichten der Königlichen Gesellschaft (Göttingen, 1881); also Sir James George Frazer, *Myth of the Origin of Fire* (London: Macmillan & Co., Ltd., 1930). Georg Curtius, *Grundzüge der griechischen Etymologie,* Vierte Auflage (Leipzig: Trübner, 1873), p. 337. W. H. Roscher, *Ausführliches Lexikon der Griechischen und Römischen Mythologie* (Leipzig: Trübner, 1909), s.v. *Prometheus,* pp. 3031–3167.

fire, *ātavedas,* is hidden in both woods like the fetus is in the pregnant woman. In other parts of the Vedic literature the "kindling" is described in even more explicit terms.

One early expert in Sanskrit language and literature was the great linguist Friedrich Max Müller. When he wrote about the origin of fire in the middle of the past century, Freud was still a child. Müller said that the fire was "the *son* of two pieces of wood," and "no sooner had it been born, than it devoured its *father* and *mother,* that is to say the two pieces of wood from which it has sprung." This is a most condensed dream fantasy about the oedipus complex.

LIGHT

Light, in psychology, is not the same as the light waves of physics which are measurable by their frequency and intensity. Nor is it the light which, in physiology, is one of the conditions of seeing. In psychology, the "light" means something altogether different. Light, in its physical or physiological qualities, is not perceived at all. Man does not perceive "light waves" or the play of these light waves upon the retina in the form of a miniature reversed picture, but rather sees objects which emanate or reflect light.[11] Objectless light does not exist for human perception, just as the Euclidian space or abstract time is beyond perception. The concept of "light," as expressed in languages, is inseparable from the things which can be seen, which appear, "stand out," exist, shine, beam, glow, glisten, in the visual field.

Seeing is dominant among the senses. It opens up the perception of space. "To see the light" means "to be alive." Man's world is primarily the visual world. In some languages this world is simply called "light." The Old Slavic *svetu* means "light" and "world"; and the same is true of the Hungarian *világ*, "light" and "world." This is the daylight world, the realm of Apollo. It is also the world of "en-lightenment," of intellect, order, and clear definitions. Yet it is also true that this visual world remains restricted to the appearance of things which are not always congruent with reality. Man sees only the surface of things; his visual perception remains "superficial." He perceives the outlines, shapes, edges, contours, colors, textures, distances, but vision cannot penetrate, as taste can, to intrinsic qualities. No wonder that in many lan-

319

guages the "appearance" became discredited as the outside aspect which covers up the inside essence. Man learned, however, to appreciate things not as what they are, but as what they pretend to be. The outside look became important more often than the inside. The appearance somehow reflects that which is inside. Deceptive optical illusions are rather exceptional. The subjective factor remains ineradicable and present in all perception. Man sees what he expects to see. His perception is stereotyped, selective, generalizing, far from objective exactness. Man projects and perceives things and meaning in one act. From this consideration follows that the meaning of "light" absorbed many of the apparent qualities of things.

The word *light* is prominent in vocabulary, just as seeing and light are prominent in perception. The sound pattern developed an array of disparate meanings which raise questions that are rather difficult to answer. One *light* is the opposite of darkness; another *light* is opposed to heaviness, also "swift, fickle" as opposed to slow, dull; and a third *light*, mainly in the plural *lights*, means the "lungs." To simply number these meanings as "light 1, 2, 3," as some dictionaries do, begs the question. To register these words as chance "homophonies," as other dictionaries do, also evades the question. It can happen that two words with disparate meanings assume, by mere chance, the same phonemic pattern, but before resorting to this emergency explanation, especially in the case of such an important word, it will be appropriate to look into the background of the phonetic form as well as of the meanings in English and other related languages.

The sound form *light* belongs, beyond doubt, to an inherited old stock with the meaning of "shining, white," which is the description of the emitted or reflected light. This meaning is implied in the Greek *leukos*, "shining, white," and the same is true in many related languages, such as the Latin *lūx* or *lūmen*, "light," *lūna*, "moon," *lūcidus*, "bright," and so on. The Old English form is *lēoht*; the Old German *lioht*, continued in German *Licht*, "light." Old English *lēohtan* means "to shine"; the same as German *leuchtēn*, "to shine." This "light" is the opposite of darkness.

Day and night, light and darkness are primary, universal experiences. Their verbal denotation is also direct, nonsymbolic, and universal. Yet, one cannot be sure even in this case that the qualities of luminous objects became projected upon man or the other way, that the subjective experience of seeing, perceiving visual things, the emerging of consciousness was projected upon the daylight. One must suppose that the perception of the external visual things was simultaneous with the subjective experience of the "inner light," called consciousness. However naïve the biblical account might be, it starts creation with the "let there be light." Light is created out of darkness; the day is separated from the night, never the darkness from the day and light. The mother of Apollo, god of light, was Lēto, the goddess of night. "And God *saw* the light, that it was good" (Genesis 1:4). This sentence indicates the subjective moral evaluation of the light as good, darkness as bad. The light became the symbol of consciousness and of the good conscience, while to hide in darkness became the indication of evil. The internalized symbolic light made man radiant, shining. This light-emanating capacity was the distinctive feature of divine persons. The "illumination" was considered, in religious experience, the sure sign of contact with the divine. "Splendor" radiated from "enlightened" persons. The glory of the halo was shining from the saints. Intellectual qualities were also described in terms of "brightness" and "clarity" of thinking. This symbolic light is the opposition of darkness: "the light shineth in darkness; and the darkness comprehended it not" (John 1:5).

The adjective *light* opposes not "dark," but the notion of "heavy," with all its attached connotations. It means "easy," especially "easygoing," "swift." In Old English there is no phonemic difference between these two *lights*, both are *lēoht*, but in other related languages, for instance in German, a differentiation took place: *leicht*, "easy," from the former *līht*; the noun is *Licht*, "light," from the former *lioht*. As far as the phonemic forms are concerned, it can be stated that these two words were formerly more separated than they appear today. However, this differentiation does not apply to the Old English. The characteristic diphthong, which appears in the German noun *Licht* from *lioht*, is present in the Old English *lēoht*, "easy." "My burden is light" (Matthew 11:30) is translated, in Old English, as *myn byrden is lēoht*. If there is a chance homophony, it existed already in Old English because *lēoht* means both "bright, shining," and "easy, not heavy."

The third *light*, plural *lights*, meaning "lungs," is supposed to be the same as the adjective. It is generally assumed that the lungs were called "lights" because they are not heavy. This might be true, and it is supported by the word *lungs* itself. This word, in Indo-European prehistory, carried the meaning of "light," but the reference to "little weight" seems to miss the essential point.

The phonemic separation of three different "lights" is contradicted by the meanings which indicate that they developed from one unitary fantasy. The light shining in the darkness was beyond reasonable doubt the basic idea, but this light of early fantasies was much like the photon—a very substantial thing—just as was the darkness which "can be cut." Because it could not be perceived in itself, it was supposed to have no weight and be very fast: *light* is *light*. The meanings of "bright," "shining," "fast," and "easy" are closely connected in unconscious fantasies and the pertinent words also must have developed from a common root meaning. The primary object of light is the sun. The sun appears, in the earliest records, with the attributes of speed and swiftness. The sun and the dawn were depicted in Sanskrit (Vedic) poetry as winged racing horses; thus the Sanskrit *ashvā* means "mare" and "dawn." The sun and the dawn were imagined as being carried in an easy-running chariot. "The Dawn with her jewels shone forth in all the corners of the sky, she, the bright (*devi*) opened the dark cloth ("can be cut"). She who awakens us, comes near, Ushas, with her red horses, on her swift car" (*Rigveda* 1:113). This is the perfect mythological illustration of "light is light." The Greek mythology is even more elaborate about the swiftness of light. Fire and light belong to Father Helios. This attribute is the chariot drawn by four horses. He struck down his son *Phaeton* (this name from the Greek verb *phaetein*, "to shine") with a thunderbolt for speeding, because he set almost the whole world on fire. However naïve these mythological rationalizations are, they prove that "light" and "speed" were identified with one another. The pictogram of the sun as a "winged wheel" has generally been understood as "speed" until the present. This is, of course, an absurd delusion. This blending of a wheel with wings might be a dream image or a schizophrenic fantasy, yet this nonsensical picture has meaning. It belongs to the prehistoric lore of our culture.

The "lungs" are related to speed. I do not believe that the objective measurement of the lungs as "not heavy" explains their name. In the light of all the other terms which derive their primary meaning from the subjective embodiment of the self, it seems to be more probable that "speed," "swift," were perceived as running fast, and this by the increased respiratory rate. Speed, meaning "running," was perceived in the subjective experience to be related to the "lungs," just as, for instance, "anger" was to the bile. Speed was generally symbolized by wings. Hermes, the messenger of the Olympians, had winged shoes.

To be winged, "light," weightless, swift, may have some bearing on the understanding of the so-called flying dreams. It is a characteristic of these dreams that they are almost universal, thus they refer to a common human experience. A century ago the German Scherner recognized that the "flying dreams" must have their origin in the somatic sensation of the lungs. Scherner followed, unconsciously, the suggestion of the German language which—perhaps, not by mere chance—called the two "lobes" of the lungs the "wings" (*Lungenflügel,* "lung-wings"). Scherner was severely criticized for this assumption by the great authority in this field, Wilhelm Wundt. In the light of verbal fantasies, one can see the merit of Scherner's somatic interpretation. Freud also noticed the somatic implication, especially of universal, repetitious dreams. He attributed to Strümpell the interpretation that, in sleep, the rising and sinking of the lobes of the lungs produce the feeling of floating in the air. Freud rejected this interpretation, but confessed that he had no better explanation.[12] The German language elaborated the mythology of the "winged lungs" even further by associating these lungs with fire. The German term for pneumonia is *Lungen-entzündung,* properly "lung-inflammation." This is everyday mythology which found its expression in the German language as well as in the Greek or Sanskrit mythology. It can, however, prompted by some unknown power, suddenly emerge in the mind of an English-speaking child. A patient of Jacob Arlow, who, when he was enrolled in public school at the age of six, was asked about his mother, said that her lungs caught fire and she died.[13]

The light is so important in the symbol language of fantasies because it came to represent the distinctive human qualities of man. The separation of day and night, of light and darkness, represents in cosmic projection the human process of the emerging consciousness out of nonconscious existence. Creation supposes light. An elementary and universal experience holds that things which can be seen truly exist, they are therefore true. The world of light opens up the reality of existing things, of "being," while darkness suggests "non-being" and the basic anxiety of nonexistence, the fear of death. Darkness is opposed to light in still another sense. Things which can be seen exist and are true, therefore "truth" also became equated with light. This is perhaps the most significant symbolism of light. The optimistic belief that truth will finally prevail is not often substantiated by empirical evidences, but it draws its convincing power from the popular equation of truth and light. Because light is emanating and spreading in all directions, it is supposed that truth will do the same. Truth is supposed to "radiate" as a power which can penetrate and dissipate that which is not true. Truth and light have according to this belief the immanent power to manifest themselves, to show things in distinctive clarity, in their true shapes, forms, and colors, in their relationship to one another. This clarity of thinking is supposed to break through the darkness of ignorance and prejudice and bring about the triumph of "insight" and "enlightenment" which is the specific human quality of existence. For this reason "to see the light" is the highest gift bestowed upon man. Sophocles' Ajax before committing suicide first says good-bye three times to light and only after that turns to his nearest kin, house, and home. Light is in the Greek conception the true house and home in which man lives.

NUMBERS

The number is inherent in perception, as are space and time. Everything that exists in space-time also exists in number.[14] "Everything is number," Pythagoras said.[15] The number refers either to the quantity of things in space or to the duration or repetition of events in time.

Things in space are counted if they exist simultaneously together in time. They must also have something in common. One does not count a fly and a tree together, even though they may appear together in the visual field (or in a test), because they are not perceived together by any similarity. The word *count* says just that. It is derived from the Latin *com-putō, -āre*, which means "to reckon together." In order to count, one has first to "gather" things. *To-gether* properly means "to-gather." Counting supposes putting things into the same category because they are perceived in their similarity as belonging together. They become *item-s*, within the category. This word, from the Latin *item*, means "just the same, in just the like manner." The "pair," "couple," is most readily perceived as a categorical unity because its two parts are almost the same and they complement one another. Counting supposes unification, on the one hand, and itemization, on the other. It considers *all* together and *each* separately at the same time, detached from one another. It supposes, in one act, two opposite functions, synthesis and analysis, perceiving the totality and also the parts which constitute it. The counting of quantities, however, does not result in qualitative discrimination.

Numbers share with time the serial quality. They may describe duration in time, just as they may describe expansion in space. A "while" can be short or long, as can a stick, or any distance. Thus, numbers unite spatial and temporal qualities. They are something in between space and time. They may also account for the repetition in time. In this case the English language refers to time by saying *third time, fourth time.* In German the same is said as *drei-mal, vier-mal,* properly "three-meal, four-meal."

Duration and repetition remember events which existed or happened before. This is sometimes represented by sound symbolism called reduplication. As in the nouns *ma-ma, pa-pa,* instead of the simple *ma* or *pa,* reduplication also occurs in verbal forms. This was a characteristic of early ages, but it faded out as a grammatical function in modern languages. A residue in English is *did,* the past of *to do,* in Old English *dide.* The corresponding Sanskrit *da-dhāmi,* Greek *ti-ṭhē-mi,* "I did," still reveal the reduplicative feature.

Once, the Germanic languages, such as the Gothic language, made frequent use of reduplication: Gothic *haldan,* "hold," *hai-hald,* "held," or *slēpan,* "sleep," *sai-slēp,* "slept." Some pre-literate languages make such frequent use of reduplication that they impressed an outsider as a language of stutterers.

The geometrical space and the abstract time developed out of the spatial existence of the body-self. The same holds true for the mathematical concept of numbers. The number, as the logical category of quantity, emerged out of the matrix of the subjective perception of the own body. It is true that arithmetic broke away from language and created its own system of signs. However, this sign system is an abbreviated visual substitute for verbal counting. Counting was once inseparable from speaking. *To tell,* from the Old English *tellan,* means both "to count" and "to say." The *teller* is the narrator and he "who counts." The Old English *talu* denotes the numerical series and the *tale,* "account"; the corresponding German noun is *Zahl,* "number"; the verb *zählen* means "count," *er-zählen,* "narrate." It is a remarkable fact that the numerals belong to the oldest, perhaps most time-resistant stock of the Indo-European languages. They developed as an articulate decimal system, reaching until "thousand" by verbal means in an age when people lived on a pre-literate stage without figures and letters. In early inscriptions the numbers are written in words.

Even though the Indo-European decimal system is inherited and analysis cannot proceed much beyond it, one may try a glimpse into the psychological conditions which made this numerical system possible.

Language and communication suppose the duality of the one who says something and the other who understands it. Without that, there would be no *dia-logue, dia-lect, dia-lectic;* there would be no language at all. How and when did this duality emerge? When did the primordial unity split into two? When did the *one* emerge from the *other?* In another context I advanced the idea that this great event, which is the foundation of all numerical perception, is rooted in the mother-child relationship. The creative act became reality in the pregnant mother. The *one* became *two.** This first split of the one and the other is still far from the arithmetical sequence of "one" and "two." It is still a concrete personal relationship of flesh and blood.

If the first numerical differentiation grew out in this way, it follows that the personal pronouns best reflect the primary meanings of numbers. The mother-child relationship sets the pattern for the "first" and "second" person, the *I* and the *thou.* It is a relationship of nearness and togetherness. It is clearly differentiated from the "third" person, the *he, she, it,* which imply distance.

The split of the "one" into "two" results in the concept of the *half.* This word is not a numeral and is altogether different from *third, fourth* part of something. The concept, in the related languages, refers to "cut," supposedly in the middle. The symmetry of the body-self also suggested the category, the existence in pairs, the idea of "two" and "half." The progenitors of the human race are often pictured in mythological fantasies as dual unities. The primary human beings were thought of as a male-female organism. The body fantasies of the small child are also thought of in this way. The primordial unity became split into two halves, and according to Plato, the two separated halves have longed for reunification ever since. The Germanic progenitor is the god *Tuisco;*

---

* See *The Subconscious Language,* pp. 15–19.

his name contains a reference to "two." The division accounts
for the body symmetry. The two sides of the body were the
halves; thus *half* originally meant "side," obviously the side of
the body. According to these early fantasies, the woman is
"the half" of man. In Hungarian, the name of the "wife" is still
"the half" (*fele-ség*). She is one half of a supposed unity; she
is on *be-half* of the man, as the child is on "behalf" of the
mother. Both complement one another. This word, from the
former name of "two," does not belong to the numeral system,
but applies to the unity of the two halves. The body parts,
which appear in "pairs," are still perceived as "both," as a
unity, as they are perceived in Hungarian. Thus, the perception of unity prevails over the perception of itemization. Two
hands, eyes, ears, feet, are referred to in the singular, so that
one hand, eye, ear, or foot is called "half-hand," "half-eye,"
"half-ear," "half-foot."

The *One* is the basic unit of the numerical system. It is an
old inherited word, corresponding to the Greek *oin-os*, the
Latin *ūn-us*, the Gothic *ain-s*. It functions not only as a numeral, but as a noun, pronoun, and adjective. The word seems
to have grown out of a prefixed demonstrative pronoun, thus,
the "one" was that which could be pointed out as "this," "this
one." The Greek language, for some reason, replaced this
word by *eis* which refers to "the same together." According to
the underlying unity of mother and child, the *one* assumed
the meaning of "whole, wholeness, healthy, holy," all interrelated concepts denoted by related phonetic patterns. The
emphatic form of *one* is *alone*, from *all-one*, and *lonely*. These
are definitely not arithmetic concepts. The newly born babe
has been eagerly inspected, since ancient ages, to determine
whether it is whole, healthy, complete, or a broken "fraction."
Without the mother, it was alone and lonely. The full implication of newly emerging unity is best expounded by the
pronomen *oneself* or *one's self*. This is the definition of the
"first person." "Number one" is still an overcharged word,
having many connotations in colloquial usage. The whole
significance of "number one" unfolds in the biblical term the
"Holy One of Israel." "Holy" and "One" mean the same. The
term translated either the Hebrew *echād*, properly "to be
united," from the verb *āchad*, "to unify"; or it translated the
Hebrew *anā*, from *ākōnī*, the pronoun "I." Thus, the "Holy

One" properly means the "Holy I," the first person. Not arithmetic or logic, but primary experiences shaped the numeral "one." This is also indicated by the ordinal *first*, once again, an altogether different word, not belonging to the numerical system. It is a superlative, related to the German *Fürst*, "prince." The "first" and the "prince" is the "firstborn" son in patristic society. It was his birthright to be the "first" in rank and social position.

It can be understood that the *One* became emotionally charged, therefore avoided and never pronounced in vain. The consequence of avoidance was, however, as in other similar cases, repression and meaningless repetition. Thus, we have *some-one, any-one, every-one, no one, none*. It can even stand as an indefinite plural for everything as "the big ones." Finally, the once avoided Holy One became the indefinite article *a, an,* a grammatical function without specific meaning used most frequently. It does not point out "this specific one" anymore, but simply says "one out of the many." However, early thinking is still specific. Whereas the Bible translates "and there came *a* lion, and *a* bear, and took *a* lamb out of the flock" (I Samuel 17:34), the Hebrew original says *the* lion, *the* bear, *the* kid—the definite article being a demonstrative pronoun, properly meaning this one.

Two is a numeral, not a pronoun, but it replaced the pronominal *other*. The "other day" formerly meant the "second day." It pointed out the separation and the difference from the "one." The "other country" can mean both the "second country" or the "different country."

There are people whose arithmetical span is on the level of a one-year-old child. They distinguish *one* hand from the *other* and they put *both* together, thus, they have a vague numerical concept of "two." However, beyond that, the indefinite plurality of the "few," "a lot," "many" begins. Even in English a *couple* can mean a "pair" or a few more. In German *ent-zwei*, properly "in-two," can mean many more fragments of a broken whole. An unspecified small quantity is meant, in Hebrew, when it is said "whether it were two days, or a month, or a year" (Numbers 9:22).

In many of our languages this primary "two" is expanded until "three," but it is seldom stretched until "four" and never beyond this limit. In reference to time, one says *once, twice,* but *thrice* is already obsolete and has been replaced by *three times*.

The number *three* represents a great step forward in quantitative thinking. It is the first number that goes beyond the dual unity of the two sides of the body. The *I-thou* affiliation is necessarily singular and qualitative. If a third enters the *I-you* relationship, it means the end of the pair, of "both halves," and of the absolute nearness and intimate closeness which go with it. More than one person cannot stand at the same place nearest to the "one"; they have to "stand apart," as is implied by the word *di-stance*. The "third person," *he, she, it*, indicates an even more remote position from the *one*. In the plural they remove the addressed person even further from the speaker. In German, the intimacy of the *ich-du*, "I-thou," dialogue is qualitatively separated from the cool and aloof *ich-Sie*, "I-you," properly "I-they" relationship.

The same qualitative differentiation took place between the dual and the plural as a grammatical distinction. Once, the dual was frequently used, but now it has faded out almost completely. The modern utilitarian-minded linguists feel that "the dual number was long ago given up as of insignificant practical value," (Whitney)[16] or, as the wisest of modern linguists put it, "In my own view of linguistic development . . . any discarding of old superfluous distinctions is progressive" (Jespersen).[17] Modern speakers who lost the subtle emotional discreetness of *thou* and *you*, German *du* and *Sie*, in address, do not feel any necessity to differentiate either the "pair" from the "many," the dual from the plural, the "two" or "both" from the "three" and more.*

The "three" represents the first plurality detached from one's own body. It appears first as an uncounted approximation of quantity, not exactly "three." "Two or three" in children's language means "a lot"; it can also mean a "few" or "quite a few," that is, a *lot* more than two. In such instances the "two or three" means a small quantity, not numbers. "Two or

---

* A clear distinction still exists between the "two" and the "many" as between the comparative which refers to two, and the superlative which refers to the "many." In Latin, for instance, *alter* means "one of two, the other," and *alius*, "one in relation to more than two, to many." The *alter* survived in the French *autre*, Italian *altro*, while *alius* vanished from the language.

three" is used in the Bible, especially in reference to witnessing: "two or three" witnesses are enough to put someone to death (Deuteronomy 17:6). However, even in this case, some unconscious reference to the body may be implied. The Latin *testis*, "witness," derives from a former *ter-stis*, "a third party standing by." The diminutive *testiculus*, in the plural, denotes the testicles. The *two* shares with *three*, but with no other number, the pronominal quality of displaying a masculine, feminine, and neuter form. It is surely not a mere accident, but a psychologically significant fact that, from the Old English masculine *twegen*, feminine *twa*, and neuter *tu*, the masculine form survived as *twain*, but became obsolete, and the feminine *twa* developed into the general form of *two*. I would not put too great an emphasis on the feminine quality of the "two," as Pythagoras and the Pythagorean numerologists did, because the *three*, which was supposed to be masculine, shows the same phenomenon. It derives from the feminine Old English *thrēo*, while the masculine *thrī* disappeared. The reason for this might simply be the fact that the feminine was also used as neuter. This means that the women were more likely to be depersonalized into numerable items than men. However, the claim of the Pythagorean numerology that the number "three" is masculine, in distinction to the feminine two, should not be completely rejected because the *three* also developed from a feminine-neuter gender. The feminine *even* number "two" is opposed by the *odd* "three." This *odd* derives from a Scandinavian word which refers to the "triangle." The "triangle" is, since the Stone Age, the symbol of the feminine. Thus, in English, the *odd man* is the "triangle man," the effeminate outcast of society with all the blemishes of castration fantasies. He still shares some qualities of the mythological complete unity—male-female in *One*.

People who can grasp the idea of the "pair," the "two-ness" of the parts of the body forming an obvious category, still do not extend the number concept of "two" to "three."[18] They do not see in the "three" the belonging together and the separatedness of its parts. If they say "three," this does not mean 2 + 1 or 1 + 1 + 1, but a hazy idea of a small plurality; it can mean more than three, it might be four or more. In biblical language the "three" still often means "not much," a small quantity. When Joseph interprets the dream of the "three branches" of vine: "The three branches are three days" (Genesis 40:12); or, when Moses was hid by his mother for "three months" (Exodus 2:2), this does not mean an exact numeral, but the approximation of a few days or a few months. This is significant because the Old Testament has no concept of the holy "trinity." In the Hebrew tradition "seven" is the holy number, not "three."

The emotional significance of the "three" seems to be rooted in the family situation. Pythagoras also saw the symbolic representation of the *one* for the father, *two* for the mother, and *three* for the child. The patristic family structure was based upon the unity of father, son, and the spirit of the grandfather if he was not alive. The "three" still meant a closely knit unity of a few, sometimes including the "four." With the personal pronouns, one stays, as it were, within the limits of a narrow family circle. The "few" belong together by a close personal relationship. That persons, not things, originally formed the concept of this "few" is indicated, for instance, by the German *wenig*, "few." It developed from the verb *weinen*, "to cry, weep." One may suppose that the "few" were primarily a "few crying children." More difficult is the case of the French *beau-coup*, "much, many." It originally meant a "beautiful thrust, blow, stroke."[19] The underlying idea must have been an uncounted repetitious action which could be termed "much, many," but also must imply the meaning of "beautiful." Perhaps it will not be far from the truth that this concept is also rooted in bodily fantasies and the intimacy of the *I-thou* relationship.

It can be observed that, to the Roman people, the concept of "child" hardly existed in the singular. Only the plural *liberi*, "children," is used. Within this plurality, the first three or four children were called by individual names; beyond the first four, they were simply numbered by ordinals: *Quintus, Sextus, Septimius, Octavus, Decimus*. Similar numbering occurred with the naming of the ten months of the Roman year. The Roman year started with March. The first four months were named with the name of the god whose festival was in this month, but beyond "four" they began numbering *Quinctīlis*, the "fifth," and *Sextīlis*, the "sixth." These two names were later replaced by *July* and *August* in honor of

Julius Caesar and Augustus. The other names—*September, October, November, December*—are simply ordinal numerals. This proves that, for the Roman mind, numbering begins really with "five." The first four numbers denoted individual qualities rather than quantities. The four limbs set the limit of body reference.

From all these observations, one will come to the conclusion that the primary numerical system was founded on the concept of the "pair" and started as a binary system. This made "four" an important limit. It was the "other pair," either $2 + 2$ or 2×2. It follows that the number "eight" also was perceived as a duality and a limit. The Old English *eahta*, Gothic *ahtau*, Greek, *oktō*, Latin *octō*, Sanskrit *ashtau*, clearly indicate that the name was a dual, and thus implied "twice" the four. It was also a limit because the following number *nine* shows, in all related languages, a connection with *new*, as in Latin *nov-em*, "nine," and *nov-us*, "new," or German *neun*, "nine," and *neu* "new." Eight days made the week, and the "nine" started the new week.

Counting, at this stage, was primarily counting the fingers.[20] Originally, the "four fingers" measured the handbreadth. The thumb, as its name indicates, was not a finger. In the Old Testament the "four fingers" were still the normal measure. The "five" and "ten" emerged later—a new system of counting the thumb among the fingers. The number *five* and the word *finger* and *fist* show an old prehistoric relationship. The number *ten*, in Latin *de-cem*, Gothic *tai-hun*, is a compound of *de*, "two," and the second part of the word is also present in *hand*, thus, "ten" originally said "two hands." The ten fingers became the bodily foundation of the decimal numerical system. It is a known symptom that children sometimes develop, at an early age, a strange aversion to numbers and arithmetic simply because counting refers to repetitious actions, which are considered bad, and the feeling of guilt is transferred to the fingers, and from the fingers to the basic ten numbers.

The Indo-European decimal system became upset and transformed once more by the revolutionary ideas of Babylonian astrology. It separated the concept of numbers from the human body, from fingers and toes, and opened the door for the logical symbolic progression of counting. Their primary concern was not the human body, but the starry sky. True, their interest was still astrology, not astronomy; it was still the magic *in-flux* or *influence* of heavenly bodies upon man. They wanted to decipher the horoscope upon which human life and fate depended. Its effect was the liberation of the narrow numerical concepts from their bodily fixation. Their central number became 60, and its division in 48, 24, 12, 6, set different meanings upon the older decimal system. Our division of *time* still follows the Babylonian system; it also changed the ten-month year into twelve months. Its influence upon the decimal system shows in the names of *eleven* and *twelve,* which remained distinguished from the following *thirteen* and subsequent numbers. The superstition of "thirteen" seems to be the consequence of its new position; it was the first number out of the order of the duodecimal system of 12.

While the new world of science followed the abstract mathematical number system which is void of any concretistic sense perception, the pre-scientific magical numerology still persists as a relic of prehistoric and infantile thinking in superstitions, astrology, in compulsive gambling, and many other forms of mental regression and deterioration.* Numerology is still a frequent occurrence in the records of mental patients.[21]

---

* The "numbering" of people was a magic procedure, therefore prohibited by the Lord of the Old Testament. David ordered "to number Israel" but is aware of his sin: "I have sinned greatly in that I have done" (II Samuel 24, and I Chronicles 21). See the excellent exposition by Theodore Reik, "The Sin of the Census," in *Dogma and Compulsion: Psychoanalytical Studies of Religion and Myths* (New York: International Universities Press, 1951), pp. 259–264.

SOUND SYMBOLISM

It is the thesis of behavioristic psychology and linguistics that once upon a time things became "labeled." This means that a sound pattern became attached to a thing. It became attached by conditioning, pairing, or reinforcement, just as the sound of a metronome or the red light might become attached to the perception of food by a laboratory-trained dog. This is the thesis, discussed previously in Plato's dialogue "Kratylos." Since Plato, it has been argued many times in its favor that one sound pattern may carry very different meanings in different languages, just as one identical thing is called by many different names by many different languages. The animal called *dog* in English is called *canis* in Latin, *chien* in French, *cane* in Italian, *perro* in Spanish, *Hund* in German, *sobaka* in Russian, *kutya* in Hungarian, and so on. How could such different sound patterns have any intrinsic connection with one identical concept which they all denote? If sound and meaning were connected with one another, it is argued, *one* thing would be named by *one* word through all the languages on the earth.

Popular as this "labeling" theory might be, it avoids the very stumbling blocks which require psychological explanations. It is an empirical fact, felt by many speakers, that some sound patterns of their native language truly describe and represent meaning. For the English speaker, verbs such as *clash, tap, trap, crack, split, bang, hit, hitch, dump, bump, boom, stop,* or words like *pin-prick* are felt to have some descriptive value; while to a German speaker the word *spitz,* "pointed," or *Blitz,* "lightning," are felt to be descriptive of an atmospheric explosion—more so than equivalent English terms. There is no denying that such empirical facts can be observed in all vocabularies of all languages.[22] This strange congruence of sound and meaning cannot be eliminated by stating that these are unfounded superficial associations, devoid of any linguistic value, or deceptive chance happenings. An example of this could be the compound *monotonous*, which is felt to be more descriptive in English than the German equivalent *eintönig*. True, sometimes just the opposite of the expected sound-meaning co-relationship strikes us. For instance, *big* and *small* should represent just the opposite of their expected meaning. The short vowel *i* is rather descriptive of *little, brittle, tiny, jiffy* things; whereas the long *a* fits the large objects.

Despite such objections, sound patterns speak for themselves in defiance of linguistic theories. For instance, the English verb *to murmur* has parallel forms in the German *murmeln*, the Latin *murmur*, the Greek *mormuro*, "roar, boil," said of water, the Hungarian *mormog*, and so on. Such terms as *clang, clangor, twang, clank, clink* appear in Greek as *klangē*, "twang," Latin *clangor*, "clang," German *klingen*, "to sound," *Klang*, "clang," and the same in many other instances.

The coherence of sound and meaning is indeed paradoxical from a logical viewpoint. How can a sound, produced by speech organs, represent "meaning" which is a nonphysical experience? How can objective auditory qualities represent intangible, inside events? Similar questions were raised in objection to psychosomatic medicine, too. The question was asked: How can a bodily symptom, a duodenal ulcer, be expressive of some emotional tension, or just why is trembling characteristic of anxiety? The coherence of body and mind, of the sound produced and the meaning implied, is still a mystery, but just these indescribable floating feelings raise challenging questions for psychological investigation.

Man perceives primarily by seeing, not by hearing. Blind people orient themselves by sound. Language is also blind in this respect; it is restricted to the world of sound. It can imitate and reproduce directly only auditory impressions. However, hearing can develop into a very sensitive discriminator, as in auscultation with a stethoscope in medical practice. Just so, the individual voice is often felt to be a more indicative personal characteristic than visual appearance. "The voice is Jacob's voice, but the hands are the hands of Esau" is said in the Bible (Genesis 27:22). The term *per-sona* properly means "per-sound" even in case the word was originally a loan word. It shows that the unalienable qualities of an individual voice reveal the very essence of a personality. The masks may fit various assumed roles of an actor, but the voice coming out behind the mask exposes the personality of the actor himself. There is always a difference between the voice of a man, a woman, or a child.

The small child, surrounded by the noises of the world, tries to imitate these sounds out of his vocal resources. Deaf children are handicapped; they cannot develop echo-words (onomatopoeia) in response to the noisy world.[23] Some of the infantile echo-words survive in the adult language. The infantile *baa*, imitating the bleating of a "baa-lamb," penetrated into the adult language. "He is a lamb indeed that baes like a bear," Shakespeare said. In Greek *bēbēn* means "sheep."

It is well known that children, and illiterate people in general, do not differentiate words and deeds, sound and meaning, in the same way as seems to be obvious to the developed adult mind. The thing and the word denoting it appear, to the infantile perception, as one thing, as a unity (called "nominal realism" by Piaget).[24] These infantile echo-words, however, do not simply imitate. They try the impossible. They try to reproduce through the human voice the inarticulate noises produced by animals and things, thus they translate the perceived sound into the phonemic system of a given language. In infantile language the dog is called by imitating its barking, but how can one imitate the barking of a dog? English children bark *bow-wow*, Germans *wau-wau*, Dutch *waf-waf*, and French children *oua-oua*. The cock, which might, in the English infantile language, be called *cock-a-doodle-doo* is called *kikeriki* in German and *coquelico* in French. The English cuckoo bird was once called by the Old English term *gēac*, but this old term was crowded out by the imitative name which is *kokkux* in Greek, *cucūlus* in Latin, *Kuckuk* in German, *cucu* in French, *kakuk* in Hungarian. The emphasis on sound imitation was so strongly felt in Germanic languages that the word defied and resisted all rules of phonemic changes.

Vocal imitations succeed best in reproducing human sounds. Such words as *fizz, hum, buzz, smack, grunt, blurb, snort, snap, sneer* refer to man-made noises. The verb to sneeze was *fnēozan* in Old English; the related Greek form is *ptarnumai,* and the Latin is *stērnuit,* from the previous *psterneuts*—all expressive of the explosive release of air. An age-old imitative name is *barbar,* a word used by Greeks in mocking imitation of not understood foreign languages. In Sanskrit *barbara* means "stammering." *Barbaros,* in Greek, and *barbarus,* in Latin, are descriptive of the neighboring people; the Arabic tribe was called *berber.* The original mocking intention became lost in the name of *Barbara.*

Sound symbolism really begins when non-auditory sensations are depicted by phonemic patterns. In such cases the human voice has to translate into the auditory field visual, tactile, or motor sensations. This implies the creativity of true symbolism. How is such a transposition from one sense organ to another possible at all? The answer is given by the developmental psychology of perception. The early perception of children, just as is often found in regressive mental states, is syncretic, that is, sense perceptions are not differentiated.[25] Seeing and hearing, touch, smell, taste, and movement are all fused into one synaesthetic unity. One can hear colors, one can feel a voice as soft as the touch of velvet, but taste also can be felt as soft. There are of course transitory stages. For instance, the "watch" or "clock" is called *tic-toc* in infantile language. This word looks like a sound imitation, but it is a far cry from the noise made by a watch. The word somehow depicts the monotonous, rhythmic oscillation of a pendulum. The *knock* on the door might be imitative; but the *snack,* denoting a hurried meal, like *to snatch* or *to catch* (perhaps from the late Latin *captiāre*), *to crash, to smash,* or a *nap,* however old these terms are, are still felt to be symbolic by their sound patterns. The vocabulary of colloquial language is colored through and through by such descriptive terms. The more slangish the style of expression, the greater is the influx of descriptive sound symbolism. The normal adult mind separates the sound pattern from the meaning and keeps the proper distance between sound and meaning, yet

Italian *miniatura,* denoting, primarily, a small painting, then anything in a diminished, very small scale. The word properly derives from the name of the *minium,* which was an Iberian loan word in Latin because the red cinnabar was imported from Spain. Thus, the verb *miniare* meant to "rubricate," "paint with red minimum." However, the two *i*-s and the nearness of such Latin words as *minimus, minimum,* "smallest," have "diminished" the meaning of red paint into the idea of smallness.

Associations by sound, however superficial or infantile, are a characteristic feature of primitive, pre-conscious mental activities. They crop up in puns, in dream pictures, as well as in the rhymes of poetry. They defy and cut across all phonetic rules and expectations of the linguists, but this is no reason to deny their existence.[27] Natural languages, spoken by untold generations all over the earth, are a "satisfactory demonstration" of existence, more so than laboratory experiments with nonsense syllables.

TASTE AND SMELL

Eating and drinking are biological processes. There is no difference in this respect between animal and man. The difference consists in the production of food (agriculture) and in its preparation. The preparation of food by fire seems especially to be the distinctive feature separating man from animal. However, it has been observed that no such distinction exists on the lowest level of human culture. The consumption of raw food once may have been a general human characteristic. The sense perception of taste and smell developed under such conditions as the dominant capacity of selecting the proper food. Repressed fantasies intrude perhaps in no other field so conspicuously as on the delicate matters of taste and smell. The logic of taste and smell is subjective and unpredictable. It is as personal as is, for instance, sexual appeal.

Taste is a sensitive index for group identification, and by the same token the dislike or rejection of people is often expressed by the disgust felt for their specific food. For this reason religious groups are bound together and differentiated by their food habits. The old religions are all food-religions. Social discrimination means food discrimination, just as individual antagonism makes one sensitive to the specific odor of the other person.

Language is in this case particularly indicative because it preserved long-forgotten, deeply repressed memories of the human race.[28] The verbal categories also show that primarily infantile experiences are instrumental in discriminating between the food which appeals as palatable and that which is rejected as disgusting.[29] The alimentary canal is more responsive to the picture language of fantasies than to the reasoning of conscious thinking. One and the same food product may appear as an appetizing delicacy in one community and be rejected as loathsome in another. What may be the reason for such differentiation? This question is the more intriguing because it has been observed that even primitive food-gatherers are seldom satisfied with the fruits, seeds, or roots which they find in their own habitat. They search mostly for some specifics which are scarce and appeal to them as exquisite or dainty.

Modern man may display in similar fashion his sophistication and freedom from prejudice by enjoying the strange food of a group alien to his own. In the general sense, however, the small child learns by identification and internalization to accept the taste and smell which are idiomatic with his own group. The reason for this might be utterly unconscious for the individual concerned. He simply accepted the food habits of the community in which he grew up. However, the statement, as repeated over and over in the pertinent literature, that smell and taste are socially conditioned does not explain anything. There are of course personal idiosyncrasies which have grown out of infantile experiences, and thus can be explained only in the individual way, yet analysis is interested primarily in those motives which have reached general social acceptance and are consequently reflected in the pertinent verbal forms.

Taste and smell, being qualities of objects, are never perceived in themselves but always as the taste or the smell of an object with which man came in contact. It is the task of the linguistic analyst to find out with some probability the primary object of reference. If one succeeds in such investigations, one may be able to shed some light upon the prehistory of taste and smell. The relics found by archaeology cannot furnish such information.

Man is far behind the animal in the perception of taste and smell. Our smell perception cannot be compared with the scent of a bloodhound. One must suppose that prehistoric man, especially the gatherers of food, developed an acuity and capacity of discrimination which modern man cannot achieve. These facts are corroborated by linguistic observations. Our languages developed no terminology of taste or smell which could match the differentiated terms for the visual or audial perception. But this holds true only for our language group. It does not apply to languages of a more primitive culture. For instance, the Totomac, a language of Mexico, distinguishes eight basic varieties of smell, but by making grammatical differences using suffixes, they are able to denote about twenty subclasses of smell.[30] Our languages denote taste and smell mostly by a reference to the object, as *salty*, in the same way as *rosy* or *violet* refers to the color perception of the objects *rose* or *violet*.

As far as categorical differences are concerned, our languages lump together all "good" smells or tastes, also all the "bad" ones. It is significant that taste and smell are distinguished by moral qualities. Even the term "evil" is used, a term one would not apply in reference to colors. There exists but one old genuine term for taste: this is *sweet* as the taste of honey. This is essentially the "good" taste, while smell has equally only one genuine term: *stink, stench*, the according German *Ge-stank*, denoting the "evil" smell. The food taken in, especially the milk of the mother, is "good" and "sweet," excrements are "bad." This polarization is conspicuous because otherwise taste is inseparable from smell. It is so physiologically and man perceives the "good smell" often as "good taste" or the "bad" taste as offensive odor. The verbal expressions exhibit this close interrelatedness. For instance, the German verb *schmecken*, "to taste," and the noun *Ge-schmack*, "taste," referred originally not only to the "good taste" but to the "good smell."

The term *sweet* is related to the Greek phonetic equivalent *hēdus* and to the Latin *suāvis* (from *suadw-is*). These words do not refer specifically to the taste but denote in a more general sense "delight, pleasure." For the infant "sweet" and "pleasure" are inseparable. The kind of pleasure referred to is primarily the tactile one, the feeling of "smoothness" of the breast of the mother, then as the English *suave* suggests, "easy and frictionless social intercourse," in distinction to the word *urbane* which implies much worldly experience and an ability to deal "with ticklish situations in soothingly agreeable manner." The Latin *suavior* means "to kiss," *suavium*, "a mouth puckered up to be kissed." The infantile emphasis on "sweetness" is still active in such words as *sweet-heart* and in the extensive use of "sweet" in various slang expressions.

Besides *sweet,* languages developed only a few specific denotations of other taste qualities, such as *bitter* and *sour.* Closer inspection shows that *bitter* did not refer originally to taste. It is a derivative of the verb *to bite.* The word *sour* referred primarily to the "unripe" quality of fruits or to the "raw" state of meat, not to their taste. Despite this seeming poverty of genuine verbal expressions, the sense perception of taste is capable of subtle discrimination. It holds even a priority over vision and hearing. It gives the babe, like touch and warmth, the first and primary orientation to the outside reality. For this reason "taste" is often blended with the tactile perception. The English verb *to taste* and the corresponding German *tasten,* "to touch," from the Latin *taxō, -āre,* illustrate well this physiological phenomenon. In the same way, the Latin *libō, -āre* and *de-gustō, -āre* mean "to taste" as well as "to touch slightly." To taste something presupposes, of course, to touch it first not only with the hands but with the mouth, but "touch" refers only to the sensation of the surface; taste reveals an intrinsic quality. The biblical words about the prohibited apple make this difference between the internal and the external contact very clear by saying: "Ye shall not eat of it, neither shall ye touch it" (Genesis 3:3).

The suckling infant tastes and smells the mother. He perceives especially the nipple in one act by touching it with the mouth, tasting the milk and smelling it at the same time. No wonder that these sense perceptions became charged with emotions, and the pertinent words drifted in the course of cultural development a long way from their primary concrete reference, from tasting food, toward highly abstract and spiritual concepts. Tasting, touching, trying, selecting, enjoying the good taste and rejecting the bad one are primary functions which even the primitive food-gatherer practiced. It is a characteristic feature of the words of taste that their meaning is often blended with the idea of "to try" or "to choose." The same word which is used in one language for denoting "taste" (as the German verb *kosten*) developed also the meaning "to enjoy," obviously the good taste, in other languages (so the Latin *gustō, -āre* with all its derivatives such as the French *goûter,* the Italian *gustare*), "to make a trial, to try" (as the Old English *costian,* the Old High German *koston,* the Gothic *kiusan*), or "to select," "to choose" (the German verb *kiesen,* the English *choose,* the French *choisir*), or "to like, to enjoy the chosen one, to love" (so in Sanskrit, much like the German *er findet Geschmack an ihr,* "he likes her"). It seems to be, as reflected by these words, a primary pattern of experience to sniffle around, put something in the mouth, taste it, try to eat it, to choose the food, enjoy the "good" taste and smell and reject the "bad"—all this is perceived to be essentially one act. The free selection of food may be an appetizing motive by itself.

I quote a literary example for this "selective taste" as it was experienced by a writer:

"The person who has set his teeth into a kind of fruit new to him, is usually as eager as he is unable to tell you how it tastes. It is not enough for him to be munching away on it with relish. No, he must twist his tongue trying to get its strange new flavor into words, which never yet had power to capture colors and tastes. 'It's not like a peach,' you hear him say, biting out another mouthful from the oddly colored and oddly shaped thing, and chewing thoughtfully, 'nor yet like a pear. Perhaps like a dead-ripe pineapple' . . . With some such nonsensical combination of impossibles do we all try to describe something—book or food—that has given us a new sensation. As if it were possible to suggest in words any sensation except those already known to everybody! Of course the only sensible thing to say is, 'Take a taste yourself. You'll eat it to the core, if you do.' "[31]

Besides "dung, excrements," the bad odor may be associated with the idea of putrefaction, to be foul, rotten, or with the notion of emitting "steam, smoke." The German verb *riechen,* "smell," and *rauchen,* "fume," are related in this way, perceiving the smell as steam. The English *steam* also referred primarily to the bodily "perspiration" and expanded this notion to "vapor, smoke, and smell."

The colloquial language refers to taste and smell if it wants to point out the unconscious motivation of likes and dislikes. The most subtle emotional discrimination for which no rational reason is found is expressed by such formulas as *I can't stomach it, digest, imbibe* or *assimilate it*, or the German *er kann ihn nicht riechen,* "he can't smell him," meaning "he dislikes him."

The Latin *gustō, -āre* is also used with the meaning "to become acquainted with," and the Latin verb *sapiō, -ere* means besides "to taste" and "to smell" also "to have insight of," "to understand" it. The noun *sapientia* which originally referred to taste and smell became the term for the highest level of insight which we call "wisdom." This word is fraught with emotions; it almost replaced in the Romance languages the old verb *sciō,* meaning "to know." Thus the French *savoir,* the Italian *sapere,* the Spanish *saber* have all developed from the late Latin *sapēre,* this from the Latin *sapiō, -ere,* "to taste, to smell." The Hebrew *tāʾam* means "to taste, perceive," the noun *tāʾam,* "taste and perception," also implies "intelligence," "a judicial sentence." Thus *tēʾem* means "flavor" on the one hand, "judgment" on the other. The Latin *ē-mungō, -ere* means "to wipe or clear the nose," but when Phaedrus said about Aesop that he was a *naris emunctae senex,* it means that he had a keen, delicate mind. The Latin *homo emunctioris naso,* properly "a man with a cleared nose," means a man with a discerning mind. The Italians still say: *aver buon naso,* "having a good nose," which means "to be clever."

A similar phenomenon can be observed within the Germanic languages: they used the same word which denoted in Old English *syntan,* "to clear the nose" (in German *schneuzen*), as the proper term for the high quality of wisdom and prudence in the Gothic *snutr-s,* the Old English *snotor,* the Old High German *snottar.* The clear nose meant clear thinking.

One may surmise from this preliminary survey of the pertinent terms that three focal points stand out in one's food fantasies. One focal point is the early experience of the sweet, warm, white milk of the mother. It represents the good taste and smell. It is associated with love, "sweet" home, security and the "milk and honey" of the Golden Age of infancy. The other focus of food fantasies is related to excrements. The association might be established by form, color, or smell perception. This does not mean that such associations are necessarily accompanied by disgust. The infant knows nothing about this disgust, but often displays coprophagous tendencies. Coprophagous fantasies became vehemently rejected in our culture. However repressed, they still exist and are implied in food habits.

The third focal point is represented by the taste quality *sour* which originally referred to the consumption of raw meat and fruit. The polarity of meat and milk was strongly felt and perceived in differentiating babe and adult.[32]

> Paul scolds those who "have need of milk, and not of strong meat. For everyone that useth milk is unskilful in the word of righteousness: for he is a babe. But strong meat belongeth to them that are of full age, even those who by reason of use have their senses exercised to discern both good and evil" (Hebrews 5:12-14).

Some categorical difference can be made between animal and man in respect to eating and drinking. Man does not simply feed like animals do, but bestows meaning upon the acquisition, consumption, and elimination of food. Man spiritualized the biological processes. He implied in alimentation fantasies which reach far beyond the necessities of body chemistry.

The fantasies implied may refer either to the act of eating or drinking itself or to the kind of food taken in. These unconscious components of normal eating habits become ostensible in the extreme cases of insatiable appetite (bulimia) and loss of any appetite (anorexia nervosa). In such cases nothing is wrong with the food or with eating as such, but the disturbance lies in the fantasies about food and eating. The disturbance may manifest itself either in the quantity or the quality of eating. In such cases the food idiosyncrasies display obsessional and compulsive features. The food taken in might be equated in fantasies with milk, the breast, the genitals; it may be considered as poison, feces, human flesh, and the act of eating may assume the meaning of cannibalism, destroying, castrating, but it equally can stand for love, intercourse, impregnation; it may absorb many other functions of instinctual gratification, lust and guilt.[33]

> A schizophrenic patient said: "At bottom everything, reading, going to the theatre, paying a call, is like eating.

First you expect a lot, then you are disappointed. When I come to analysis, I eat your furniture, clothes, words. You eat my words, clothes, money. If you work, your employer eats you up. But at the same time you do some eating yourself. At times I am very hungry, then once again I can eat nothing."[34]

Eating is such a sensitive indicator of unconscious fantasies because the earliest mother-child relationship is based on feeding, thus the food as well as the process itself may absorb emotions like love and hatred, appetite and disgust, acceptance and rejection, attraction and avoidance, satiety and deprivation, reward and punishment.

Just these implied unconscious motivations made the difference between the "good" and the "bad" taste and smell. The meaning implied separated the fruits, as we are told in the biblical story, which are "good for food" from the prohibited apple. The original sin was committed by transgression of a food taboo, thus the transgression of a food prohibition appeared to the early men as the archetype of all sins. The taste and smell of the prohibited apple must have been "bad" and "evil" indeed.

It seems to be probable that the separation of "clean" and "unclean" meats, which might or might not be eaten according to the Mosaic law, depends upon unconscious motivation. Otherwise the rule does not make sense: "Whatsoever parteth the hoof, and is clovenfooted, and cheweth the cud, among the beasts, that shall ye eat" (Leviticus 11:3). One cannot understand on rational grounds why just the parted hoof or the cloven foot should be the criterion of edibility. In the same way one does not understand why fish are classified in "good" and "bad" categories depending upon the distinction of whether they have fins or not. Religious commandments and prohibitions cannot be simply translated into sanitary regulations. The food laws of Leviticus or of the *Zend-Avesta* or of other religious source books cannot be reduced to a set of rational, utilitarian practices. It is an essential part of religion "to make a difference between . . . the beast that may be eaten and the beast that may not be eaten" (Leviticus 11:47). Our food habits are essentially religious in origin.

One can best approach the irrational elements that are involved in the daily preparation and consumption of food by observing the techniques used in sacrifice. It was the belief, primitive indeed, to suppose that the departed souls and divine spirits depend upon human needs and wants; thus they are in need of food, and eat and drink just as we do. The gods have hunger and thirst, according to this naïve conviction, and have to be fed. It is consistent with this conviction that the best food which man liked most became set apart for the gods. The sacral offering from the daily food, however, meant on the reverse side that man did not feed himself as animals do. By sharing the food with the gods he introduced a spiritual element in his daily routine of eating and drinking. He projected upon eating his deeply repressed fantasies. He performed the sacrifice much as he prepared his daily food. If there is a discrepancy between the performance on the altar and the preparation made on the hearth, then the sacral ritual presents the archaic type out of which the daily food habits developed.

If the community depended primarily on raising cattle or sheep and these animals served mainly as nourishment, they also served as the main victims of sacrifice. When agriculture developed and the food was produced mainly by the tilling of the ground, the "first fruits" prevailed also in the offering. However, it can well be observed even in the biblical account that "the fruit of the ground" offered by Cain was first not so well accepted as "the firstlings of his flock and of the fat thereof" offered by Abel. "And the Lord had respect unto Abel and to his offering: But unto Cain and to his offering he had not respect" (Genesis 4:4-5).

The fire perceived as burning inside the body reflects upon the burnt offering upon the altar and upon the preparation of food at the fireplace. The basic difference between the consumption of the raw meat and the cooked food consists in the act of *preparation,* "making ready." One will ask: "making ready" for what? It prepares the food for the inside metabolism which will take place through the inside fire. It is in line with infantile fantasies to project and dramatize on the hearth the very process which is invisible and is supposed to go on inside the body. Something uncanny was implied in this mysterious process of decomposition of the "good" taste into "bad" smell. The naïve projection of internal bodily fantasies upon the fireplace hits upon a physiological truth. The elaborate performance may stimulate or block the digestive process, may be "mouthwatering," because the autonomous nervous system regulating the alimentary tract is responsive to the dramatization of the invisible inside process. It "prepares," that is, makes ready not only the meal but the alimentary canal for digestion. The metabolism of digestion properly starts in the fireplace.

This may be one of the reasons why the fantasies referring to the inside fire are closely associated with the picture language of digestion. In English the fire is "fed," the flames "consume," "devour," the flames have "tongues" and "lick" as if they would digest gustatory food.[35] The Hebrew *ā kal* means "to eat, burn up, consume, devour, dine, feed."

This infantile philosophy of digestion is well illustrated by the Greek and Latin key words for "cooking" which denote at the same time "digestion." Whether meat or cereals are "prepared" on the hearth or not, the end is to produce a crushed, ground soft pulp in anticipation of the digestive process or to make raw materials through roasting, broiling, frying, baking on fire or dry heat, ready to be consumed by the inside fire.

The alimentary process begins with the mastication of food. The boiling, stewing, or seething of materials outside the body depict the process that will go on inside the body. The Latin *macerō, -āre* means "to soften, assuage"; the term *macēries* significantly denotes another internal process, meaning "worry, anxiety." This emotional condition, difficult to describe, is thus depicted by the alimentary process, obviously meant as "self-consuming." The same holds true for the Latin verb *mordeō*, "to chew," which carries the implication known as *remorse*.

The Greek key word for boiling, stewing, seething is the verb *pessō*, and the according noun *pepsis* applies to the cooking as well as to digestion. Various derivatives of this verb are *popanon*, "a round cake used at sacrifice" (in Latin called *popanum*); *arto-kopos* (from former *-pokos*) meaning "cook." Another Greek term, *tēkō*, "to melt, melt down of metals, to thaw, to wash away," shows that the digestive process of dissolution became equated with consuming oneself by worries and anxieties. The same meaning is expressed by the corresponding Latin words; *coquō, -ere* (from *quoquō*, "to cook") applies equally to cooking and to digestion. It can also mean "to ripen the fruit by the sun." The Greek *pessō*, "to soften, ripen by means of heat, ferment," is also used in reference to fruits. This means that the Greek and Latin mind perceived as one identical act the concepts which we differentiate by three words: to cook, to digest, and to ripen through the heat of the sun. A fourth meaning is also implied; this is "anxiety, worrying." So the Latin *con-coctiō* denotes the "cooked meal," "digestion," and "anxiety." Other derivatives of the word are *popanum*, "sacrificial cake," *popa*, "kitchen," and *popa*, "assistant in sacrifice," this being the parallel form of the Greek *arto-kopos*, "cook." Once more the notion of the kitchen and the cook is almost interchangeable with the place of sacrifice and the priest performing the sacrifice. These, and many other affiliated words, prove the thesis that to the Greek and Latin mind the "cooking" on fire and digestion are one and the same process. The process of transformation of food inside the body which is called metabolism became enacted on the altar as the spiritualization of the victim animal, and finally, this inside fire is used symbolically to depict the self-consuming anxiety.

In Germanic languages the terms referring to the preparation of food reveal a somewhat different realm of associations. The Germanic terms referring to this "preparation" by heat show more distinctly that this "making ready" is a cover word for something repressed which should not be mentioned overtly by its name. The process of metabolism through fire was after all a mystery. In Old English *gearu* means "ready, prepared, complete," and is continued in the obsolete English *yare*, "ready." The verb "to make ready," "prepare," is *gearw-ian*, and the noun "preparation" is *gearw-ung*. These words survived also in German. The German *gar*, from former *garo*, means "ready, complete." The corresponding verbal form *gären*, "to ferment," originally meant "to boil, surge up." The original point of reference still remained preserved in the compound forms *Gar-küche*, "kitchen," and *Gar-koch*, "cook," now used especially in reference to public restaurants. The verb "to make ready," former *garawen*, remained preserved in the German verb *gerben*, referring now specifically to the preparation of leather. The noun "preparation" appears in the obsolete German as *gerwung*; by an extension of the meaning it came to denote the "dressing," "adornment," not of food but of cloth; it was used also for the vestment of the clergy. Thus *gerwe-hūs* means "vestry, sacristy." Once again the place of preparation for the sacral performance is called by the parallel term *garküche*, the kitchen for public service. All these words referring to the use of fire became strangely obsolete in the modern language because they were loaded with some uncanny meaning. Even the genuine Latin term, *formus*, "hot," which is present in *fornication*, faded out and became replaced by *callidus*. The English *yare* became obsolete, but the German *gar* distinctly displays the work of repression. Once the meaning was repressed, the word became a matter of meaningless repetition like the other intensifiers; thus it can be added to other words; for instance: *nicht*, "not," or *gar nicht*, "not at all"; *kein*, "no," or *gar kein, ganz* or *ganz und gar*, "totally," *so gar*, "even." It adds emotional intensity to the word with which it is associated. This is a sign that a significant meaning has become repressed.

It is a common observation that to look at the preparation of food may have an appetizing effect. Some people like to watch the roasting or broiling, it affects their salivary glands like those of Pavlov's famous dog. The fantasies anticipate the digestive process.

It is illustrative in this respect to consider some cooking utensils of primitive people. The trough for kneading the bread, for instance, might be made and shaped in imitation of the open belly of a woman, holding up her opened abdomen by the hands and feet (the Smithsonian Museum in Washington, D. C., has such a remarkable piece on display). Such cooking utensils suggest the identity of the outside preparation of food and its internal consumption.

The German term for "to digest" is *ver-dauen*. It compares the internal metabolism with the "melting, smelting" by heat; in German *dauen* means "to melt," to change into liquid. The use of the English *liquidate* in reference to "business" demonstrates once more that digestive fantasies have shaped the business language. The "liquidation" of an opponent, an expression of Russian origin, corresponds to the Greek verb *cheō*, "to melt," and to the Old English *sweltan*, Gothic *swiltan,* "to die." The English word cluster *melt – smelt – smell* displays the same interrelatedness in meaning, keeping in mind the transmutation of the good taste into bad odor. A parallel development can be observed in the Greek *tekō* meaning "smelt, consume," which also refers to the self-consuming "worry," "to be anxious." It developed the forms of the verb *takerō,* "to boil soft," and the adjective *takeros,* "tender, melting in the mouth." These forms obviously referred to the good food. The other forms—*takōn,* "a kind of sausage," and *tilos,* "stercum liquidum, as in diarrhea"—developed with the idea of excrement.

> "Wasting away by melting into liquid may emerge in pathological fantasies. Laura, a severe borderline case with pathological weeping, says, 'The danger was of being liquefied, washed away. I would weep a river,' she said, 'and disappear down the drain.' This 'melting process,' as Laura called it, proceeded under the analytic lamp, as indicated in the dream."[36]
>
> In infantile fantasies the oral and the anal pole were not so opposed to one another as they appear in adult life. This confusion of oral and anal fantasies may account for eating disturbances and anorexia nervosa. Such is the famous case of Ellen West, analyzed by Binswanger. Her feeding on laxatives and eating in strict privacy show such a marked confusion of the fantasies about eating and digesting.[37]

The English *flavor* originally referred to the hue or color, not to taste or smell. Milton says of the wine, "the flavor or the smell or taste that cheers the hearts of Gods or men." This word and this original meaning derive from the Latin *flāvus a - um,* "golden yellow, blond." Yet the English *flavor* appears also in the meaning of "stench." This meaning developed under the influence of the Old French *flairer,* "to exhale an odor," or under the influence of the Latin *flātus.*

Taste and smell fantasies have been utilized commercially by the perfume industry. It is known that a grain of offensive odors added to perfume may result in an appealing fragrance. The trade names of perfumes do not hesitate to evoke "sweet-smelling" associations.

The food fads of children,[38] which appear in eating disturbances, reveal the repressed fantasies about excrement. The association may be established by the color and appearance of spinach, chocolate, brown mushy food, as some cereals or odorous cheeses. The disgust with undercooked egg-white may derive its force from the association with bodily excrements such as pus or mucus. The idiosyncrasy against mustard or ketchup indicates that repellent fantasies entered the taste and smell perception. Some children consider spaghetti or macaroni as worms; their association is substantiated by the Italian *vermicelli*, which is the diminutive of *verme*, from Latin *vermis*, "worm."

> A college student girl cannot eat soft-boiled eggs because, she says, "It reminds me of the runny nose of my little brother." A patient, female, twenty-five, displays a "frequent inability to eat eggs because living things come from them."[39] A Hindu student despised people for eating "chicken embryos," etc.

Because languages reveal the same association between the preparation of food on the hearth and the digestion in the alimentary canal, the terms denoting "intestines" and "stomach" are often used to denote qualities of food. In such cases the stomach was not eaten but was eating, symbolizing the digestive process. The Greek *gastēr*, which means "paunch, belly" and "womb," denotes at the same time "the paunch stuffed with mincemeat, a black pudding, sausage, haggis." Its diminutive is *gastrion*, properly "little paunch," meaning "sausage, a kind of cake." It would be difficult to uphold the explanation that this black pudding, sausage, or cake was so called because it was made of the "paunch." The opposite statement would be more correct: the paunch was imagined to be stuffed with such sausage. The word *ga-stēr*, if it is a compound, says exactly this: "containing" the *genta, entera*, "inwards." Another Greek term is *phuskē*, denoting "the large intestine, especially as stuffed with pudding, a sausage or black pudding."

The Latin term *botulus* also denotes both the "intestines" and the "sausage." Its diminutive *botellus* also covers both meanings. It denotes a "small sausage" but is continued in the

356

English *bowel* and the French *boyau*, "intestine." The English *pudding* is the term for "a piece of intestine stuffed with seasoned, minced meat and boiled," "a dessert of milk, eggs, rice, sago, sugar, spices, flour or some cereal." This may be a description of infantile fantasies about the contents of the intestines. Linguistic instances permit no doubt about the original location of this pudding. An instance of the early usage of this word says: "the fox . . . did bite and scratch the young man so sore, that his puddings gushed out of his side (1673)."[40] In the figurative sense, "pudding" means the realistic substantial matter in contrast to the empty words, as "solid pudding against empty praise (1728)."

> This repressed meaning of "pudding" is borne out in child analysis. Children are familiar with the repressed meaning which adults can learn only from dictionaries. I quote as clinical example the dream of a child: "He was standing beside his mother at a table on which lay a bowl of *chocolate pudding.* It was a postulate of the dream situation that he was starving, and that there was no food available apart from the pudding. He knew, therefore, that if he would not partake of the pudding, he would die of starvation; but he also knew that the pudding was poisoned, and that if he ate it, he would likewise die."[41]
> This "pudding" seems to be the same as what another boy, seven, when asked what the thick paint was like, explained: "The pudding that my mother won't cook."[42]

The English word *haggis* to which reference was made as a translation of the Greek *gastēr* is explained to be a "pudding consisting of the heart, liver and lungs of the sheep or calf, minced with suet, onions, oatmeal, seasoned with salt, pepper, onions and boiled like a large sausage in the stomach of the animal." The preparation of the food consists in this case in the anticipation of digestion by the inside fire; the stomach of the animal consumed stands for the stomach of the consumer. The "stuffing" of the animal exhibits in another way that appetizing fantasies anticipate the digestive process. The Latin verb *farciō, farsi, fartum* means "to stuff, cram, fill full," also to "fatten"; the noun *fartum* or *farctum* refers to "stuffing, filling"; *farcimen* means a "sausage" and "intestinal worm." These terms developed into the English *farce*, "stuffing as used in dressing a fowl," and into *force meat*, properly *farce-meat*, "a meat or fish chopped fine and highly spiced and seasoned; either served as garnish or used as stuffing, farce." In this idea of "farce" a food fantasy was involved which had to be repressed, indeed, while eating. An indication of repression is using the word in a more abstract sense, mostly for a text or a play releasing aggressive laughter. *To farce* means "to stuff with forcemeat, herbs, spices, to cram with food, to overlay thickly, padding or seasoning." As a noun it denotes a satirical or humorous show or mockery. The comic seasoning effect derives from the unconscious layer of fantasies. It is the same with *sarcasm* which originally meant in the Greek *sarkadzō*, "to tear the flesh asunder."

The sausage and pudding consisting mainly of hashed meat have a corresponding counterpart in the *cake*. This word originates from the Old Norse *kaka* and means a sweetened dough of flour, eggs, milk, fruits, nuts, flavorings, sometimes unleavened, baked; also hashed meat, fish, mashed potatoes, packed into a flattened mass and baked. The best expert in German etymology, after having explained the phonemic pattern of Germanic *kaka, koka,* says with some resignation as to the meaning: "it makes the impression of a reduplicative word of the infantile language."[43] One may add to this interpretation that not only the phonemic pattern is infantile in character but the meaning, too. The small child does not know what disgust is. He has to be taught disgust, especially in reference to his excrement. He likes to play with dirt and wet mud, to fingerpaint, and to put things in his mouth which are loathsome to the adult. But childish fantasies remain buried somewhere in the adult mind. If it were not so, if such fantasies did not exist, they could not crop up time and again in imprecation and symbolic speech as found in the Bible.* The Greek god Asclepios is called *skato-phagos*, "dung-eater," which should be an allusion to a medical practice of Hippocrates[44] but rather seems to be the mythological expression

---

* ". . . that they may eat their own dung, and drink their own piss with you" (II Kings 18:27).

of an infantile desire which is also implied in the food fantasies of sausage, pudding, haggis, and farce.

The "second harvest," the eating of one's excrement, is the symbolic expression of avarice, sometimes depicted in dreams. It is also demonstrated by clinical evidences, significant of the separation from the lost love object in melancholia. Homer tells us: "When Hector died, his father Priam rolls in dung, and gathering it up, smears his head and neck with it and stays in this stench for twelve days" (Iliad 22:414, 24:31, 163). Mental hospitals are familiar with this repressed behavior in patients.[45]

The German Hans-wurst (former Hans-mist) and his English alter-ego Jack Pudding appear as the modern representants of the same old idea.

> The equation of "sausage" and "excrement" is sometimes suggested on the verbal level of nursery language. Children's food fantasies might be influenced by calling their excrement "little sausages" or by asking "Did you move your cukies?" meaning "Did you move your bowels?"[46]
>
> Children grasp this association between "sausage" and "excrement" without much repression.
>
> Once when he was given some small sausages for supper, a two-year-old boy with chronic constipation was delighted, and said: "Mother dear, because I make such nice little sausages I get a good sausage for supper."[47]
>
> A boy of seven years . . . had abdominal pain after eating frankfurters, which he regarded "as a long red bowel movement."[48]

Besides the oral food fantasies (milk and honey) and anal association (sausage, cake, pudding), one may discern a third layer, the genital one. Just as in the use of obscene words the coprophagous vocabulary of infancy becomes overshadowed by genital obscenities of the adults, the same phenomenon can be observed in the repressed obscenities of the food language. There one also can find the transition from the oral-anal stage to the genital one. The "mask of sanity" may cover up genital strivings. By the same token, primary oral cravings may seek a genital outlet.

The obvious genital associations with *asparagus* are implied in verbal forms. The Greek word is the derivative of the verb *spargaō*, "to be full to bursting," "to swell with humors," "to swell with desire or passion." This permits little doubt about the primary implication which may also grow out in color-taste synaesthesia ("asparagus taste violet").

The "obscenities" of such fantasies may come to the surface of language in some trade names of *per-fumes* (from *fūmus*, "smoke") but also may appear in a more or less transparent form in recent food terms.

I refer as an example to the word *hot dog*, "wiener-wurst or frankfurter, placed *in a split roll*" served with mustard, ketchup, relish. How does the idea of a "dog" enter this picture? Children react spontaneously: "Joey," a seven-year-old boy said, "girls have a *bun*, and boys a *wiener* that goes in the bun."[49] It is generally known that baked goods since Greek and Roman antiquity were formed in the simulacra of male and female fertility symbols, the "split roll" is specifically female. The *dough-nut* is a compound form, *nut* "perforated block wormed with an internal, or female, screw, used to make a bolt or *screw* fast." The dough-nut is a female concept.

SPACE

The notion of "space," as reflected in languages, is not the
abstract "space" of philosophy. It has nothing to do with
geometry. Nor is it the outer space, but, on the contrary, it
is the "inner space" such as one has in mind when one says
"narrow space."[50] This describes the limited space of everyday experience. This space is "here" and "now," and is known
by concrete qualities, loaded with emotions and filled with
memories. This is not the infinite space of physics and mathematics.

Nothing proves more convincingly that the body-self is the
primary reality than spatial orientation. The body is the
center of space. It is the point of orientation from whence
one decides what is before or behind, what is above or below,
near or far, right or left. One does not perceive "space," but
perceives only things with spatial qualities. One cannot think
of nonmaterial phenomena like sleep, dream, memory, emotions, pain, or pleasure otherwise than in spatial terms. This
is a common characteristic of all languages. The terms referring to space represent the primary layer of sense perception,
while spatial terms applied to time and other nonmaterial
events are of secondary symbolic nature. One can *under-stand,
grasp, gather* facts, *for-get, per-ceive, con-ceive* mental experiences. One can *fall* asleep, the sleep can be *deep*, emotions can *break through* or remain *shallow, superficial*. One
thinks, in symbolic terms, that the mind is within the body,
even though the nonmaterial has no relationship with ma-
terial-spatial qualities such as "inside" or "outside." Psychology abounds with topological-spatial terms. One cannot

speak otherwise about psychological facts, yet one must remain aware that the topology of the mind does not mean "reification," neither verbalism nor verbal fetishism. It is, by necessity, nothing but metaphor, symbolic language.

The word *space* derives, through French, from the Latin *spatium*, which primarily denoted "room," a limited space. The word is a derivative of an old verb meaning "to span," "to stretch," like the verb *ex-tendō, -ere,* "to extend," from *ex,* "out," and *tendō, -ere,* "to stretch." It is used with the meaning "to stretch out," extend in space. In English a *stretch* still means a limited distance. "Space," as a "stretch," implies a dynamic action, an effort. The primary space is the "inner space," as for the infant, when the "inside" and the "outside" are still one. To the fetus the inner space is the womb, a matter of bodily contact, how far the body can stretch. This first stretch becomes, in time, ever wider and more abstract. Beyond the first narrow stretch reaches the "walk"; thus the Latin *spatium* came to mean "a walk, a promenade," then "a town's square," finally a racetrack like the corresponding Greek *spadion* or *stadion.* The Latin verb *spatior,* Italian *spaziare,* and late German *spazieren* mean "to take a walk, to walk about, to promenade."

In English this concrete life-space is generally called *room* or *place.* The English *place* derives from the French *place,* as does the German *Platz,* "place." The source of these words is the Latin *platea,* "a broad way in the city," within the house the "courtyard." Its derivative is the Italian *piazza,* "square." This is once more the oriented space, the experienced room filled with action.

This qualified space implies body postures as standing erect, sitting or setting down, even lying or laid down for orientation, either along the vertical or the horizontal line. The concept of stand and stay is implied in the obsolete *stead* as in *home-stead, in-stead,* meaning originally a place to stand or to stay; the place name *Stow* also carries this meaning. In English one can "place" something by "setting" or "laying" it down. The sitting place is implied in the Spanish *sitio,* "place," in the Latin verb *situāre,* continued in the French *situer,* "to place (it) in the proper position."

The orientation in space reveals even more characteristic qualities of body symbolism. Nonliterate people are known to

be very specific while we use general terms in our languages.
If they speak about another person, they have to indicate
whether this person is present or distant; if distant, whether
he is visible or not; if visible, whether he is standing, walking
or lying; whether he is alive or dead. In our language usage,
all such situational details are supposed to be supplemented
by the hearer from the understanding of the total situation.

The English adverbs and prepositions which refer to spatial
relations still sometimes describe body parts. One can *face* in
front of something, it can be near *at hand*, or can be done
beforehand, on the *one hand* or the other as *right* and *left*
generally refer to the hands. Such body references were in
early ages, for instance in the Babylonian language, more concrete. In the Hungarian language everything "in front" is said
to be in the eye (*szem* "eye"—*szemben* "in front"); everything "beside" still refers to the breast (*mell*, "breast"—
mellett, "beside"); everything "up" refers to the "head" (*fö*,
"head"—*föl*, "up"); everything "in" or "within" refers to the
"intestines" (*bél*, "intestine"—*be, bele, belsö*, "in, inside").
The Greek *pleurai*, "side," is the plural of the noun *pleura*,
"rib." The same reference to the "rib" is implied in the French
côté, Spanish *costado*, English *coast*, from the Latin *costa*,
"rib." Such words show which parts of the body served for
spatial orientation.

The famous proposition of Protagoras stating: "Man is the
measure of all things" (*pantōn mētrōn ho anthrōpos*), applies
specifically to man's spatial orientation. The human anatomy
provided the primitive measurements. The smallest unit was
the "finger." In Greek this unit is the *daktulos*, "finger," in
Latin *digitūs*, "finger." Four "fingers" made a handbreadth,
four "handbreadths" made a *foot*. "Behold, thou hast made
my days as an handbreadth" (Hebrew *tōpach*), the Psalmist
said (39:5). In Hebrew this "handbreadth" is sometimes
called "four fingers," for instance: "the thickness thereof was
four fingers" (Jeremiah 52:21). A somewhat larger unit than
the "finger" was the "thumb," as the French *pouce*, from the
Latin *pollex*, "thumb." The thumb, as a measure, was once
used in English and German also. It later was replaced
by the *inch*, from the Latin *uncia;* in German by the word
Zoll, "inch." A larger unit was the nine-inch *span* from the
tip of the extended thumb to the tip of the extended little

finger. The next larger unit was the *cubit*, about twenty inches, from the Latin *cubitus*, "elbow." In Greek *pugō* denotes this unit, generally measured from the tip of the middle finger to the "elbow." It is also equated with six "palms" or "handbreadths" or twenty-four fingers, not including the thumb. This measure was called, in Old English, *eln*, later *all*. It remained preserved in the Old English *eln-boga*, properly "fore-arm-bending," *el-bow*. It still measures a limited space of action as indicated by the term *elbow-room*. A larger arm measure was the *fathom*, Old English *faethm*. It measures the length man can extend his two arms. The primary meaning of space as a "stretch" is still implied, but the "open" arms or extended hands carry emotional, symbolic meanings derived from the gesture language.

The *foot* was formerly also generally used for measuring distance. The larger unit was the "foot-stretch," "step," or "pace." The term *pace*, which, as a verb, means measuring by large steps, derives from the Latin *passus*, "step." The Roman *passus* is larger than the English *pace*.

Greater distances were measured by larger units, always implying human action. Such distance was the "stone throw," how far a man could throw a stone or hurl a spear. Homer describes the "curtain of mist" by saying: "a man can see no further than he can throw a stone" (*Iliad* 3:12); or "the son of Peleus darted away a spear's throw from him" (*Iliad* 21:251). Another measure of distance was the human voice. For instance, a garden was "as far from the town as a man's voice will carry" (*Odyssey* 6:294). All these instances define the subjective quality of the space as distinguished from the objective measurement of abstract distances. The ever-growing distances gradually approach the abstract concept of space. The large distances were still filled with action, as "far *away*," measured as "walking distance." Caesar said that the Germanic people have no other measure for large distances than a day's march (*De Bello Gallico* 6:25). Thus, the large distance is still the outreach of action. It is the symbol of the Way. The Way implies direction, intention, a progressive action; it has a goal, it begins with the first step and ends with the last. These spatial qualities made the "Way" most appropriate for symbolizing the progressive experience of time and life. The

Way became the "way of life." Lao-tse's *Tao* means in Chinese, "the way."

The terms for spatial orientation, such as *near* and *far*, *up* and *down*, *high* and *low*, *over* and *under*, *above* and *below*, *front* and *behind*, do not derive their meaning only from bodily references, but grew out of the experience of the symbolic inner space. They are loaded with personal, moral, and emotional connotations. This is most obvious in the case of *right* and *left* vs. *right* and *wrong*. The same holds true for spatial adverbs and prepositions. They denote not a specific spatial position, but a direction, an intention toward a goal in the symbolic space. Thus, "near" and "far" describe personal relationships. The word *di-stance* supposes the standing position, from the Latin *di-*, "apart," and *stō, -āre*, "to stand"; thus, it refers to persons standing apart. It depends on the individual and the cultural situation as to what is considered the proper "di-stance" between two persons in specific situations. It is a rather delicate question not to come too near nor stay away too far. "Nearness" supposes the opposite of distance. Its direction is toward close bodily contact and unification. It is evident that not objects, but speaking persons are in mind in such expressions as *near at hand*. The Greek *enggus*, "nearby," is a compound of *en*, "in," and *guion*, "dual," *guia*, "hand," thus, properly says, "in the hands." One knows in English the meaning of "hand in hand." Milton says of Adam and Eve: "They hand in hand with wandering steps, and slow, through Eden took their solitary way." Nearness in space means emotional closeness and intimacy. The Greek verb *engguaō* translates this personal closeness into the idea "to pledge, to *hand over* as a pledge," especially "to have a woman plighted, betrothed." *Enguētē gunē* is the "wedded woman." This nearness supposes emotional closeness and security; it cannot be quantified as an objective space measure.

The Latin term for "near" is *prope;* its superlative is *proximus*. The English *proper*, from the Latin comparative *proprius*, describes with the term of "nearness," not simply the personal properties but also propriety, fitting to a mostly unwritten code of personal relationship. Proximity in space supposes propinquity in human relationship. The English *approach*, from the late Latin *appropiāre*, means "to come nearer," from *ad-*, "to," and *propius*, "nearer." Another Latin term for "near" is *juxta*. This word is even more outspoken concerning the close human relationship. It derives from the verb *jungō, -ere,* "to join, to be yoked together," as in marriage. The French *près,* "near," and the Italian *presso,* "near," derive from the late Latin *pressē,* "with pressure, violently," this from the verb *premō, -ere,* "to press heavily." This pressure symbolizes the highest degree of proximity.

The English *nigh-near-next* gradation shows that *near* is a comparative, meaning properly "nearer," like the German *näher.* It points in the direction of the superlative, to draw nearer and ever more nearer until it reaches the point of violent pressure as indicated by the French *près* or Italian *presso.* The same holds true for other spatial adverbs and prepositions like the Latin *prope-propius-proximus,* "near-nearer-next." These words denoted originally not fixed spatial positions, but a direction, a tendency which means an intention in the symbolism of space. The goal of this direction is the eliminating of the distance which is still implied in the comparative *near.* The superlative means immediacy and intimacy. The "immediacy" suggests that there should be nothing in between dividing the partners "in the middle." The word derives from the Latin *medium,* "middle." The word *intimacy* describes the final end in the direction of nearness. It derives from the Latin *intimus,* which is the superlative of *intus,* "within"; thus intimacy means to be in the innermost of the other person.

The intentional content can be observed in other spatial adverbs. The English *up* meant, as can also be observed in related languages, the *up-ward* direction from "below," *de profundis.* In words like *uphill, uplift, upset, uproar,* the fantasy as coming from deep down is still implied. This explains that the "up" could also refer to the "low bottom, under, down," from where the motion started. If somebody wants to come "up," he is in fact "down." The "upward" direction, in German *auf-wärts,* is, in Old English *ufe-waerd,* properly "turned toward up"; its phonemic equivalent is the Greek *hypo-,* meaning "under"; the corresponding Latin form is *sub,* "under"; but the comparative *super* and *superior* mean "over." The intentional character of these words is reflected in their relativity. Rather complicated is the body reference in the Latin *altus,* which can mean "high" and "deep." The

word developed into the Italian and Spanish *alto*, "high." This
adjective derives from the verb *alō, -ere*, "to feed, to nourish,"
with the connotation of the English "to bring up." The related
words are *ad-oleō*, "to bring up," *ad-olescō*, "to grow up," or
prōlēs, from *pro-olēs*, meaning "child," properly "who has
been brought up." Like the Latin *super*, from *sub*, the English
over from (ab)*ove*, or *upper* from *up*, with the superlative
uppermost, all show this direction—the grammatical expression of which is the comparative. The comparative describes
the relativity as depending on what we compare. This relativity supposes that the "here" can be everywhere; that the
I just happens to be; the "there" is where the I is not. The
"nearness" is expressed in the pronominal form by the *I-thou*
relationship. Greater distance from the speaker is implied in
he, she, it; nearness in *we;* distance in *they.* The English
usage has generally given up the subtle differentiation between the *thou* and *you* address. This is in accordance with
the simple spatial dichotomy of *here* and *there.* The German
language kept alive the *du*, "thou," and *er, sie*, "he, she"
differentiation and also, accordingly, the spatial terms, the
gradation of *hier*, "here," *da*, "near there," and *dort*, "far
there." The conspicuous vowel sequence of *i, a, o*, representing distance, returns in many related and unrelated languages.
As in the English *this-that*, the French *ci-là*, "here-there"
make use of sound symbolism for expressing spatial distance,
as does the German *dies*, "this" – *das*, "that," or the Hungarian *itt, emitt*, "here" – *ott, amott*, "there." How and why
this sound symbolism developed is one of the many secrets
of our languages.

It is generally understood that the symbolized space of
nearness and separatedness grew out of human relationship.
There is an old Latin saying: the greatest hardship is to live
far from those who are near and stay near among those who
are far. This refers to the conflict of the inside and outside
spatial relationship. It does not need much comment to demonstrate that the normal visual space is very different from the
space perceived by the blind. If a person with paranoid
tendencies says "they" it may mean distanciation in the dimension of suspicion or aggression. A person suffering from agora-
phobia, from fear of open places, must have a different relationship to space than has the claustrophobic, who cannot

tolerate closed doors or closed windows because he feels he will suffocate in a closed room. The psychological space is not homogeneous, not three-dimensional and isotropic like the Euclidean space of geometry. We do not perceive "space" as such, but perceive only the continuous background of persons and things with spatial qualities and relationship to one another. The psychological space is attuned with colors, it has specific atmosphere, temperature, it is filled with sounds, light or darkness, and first of all, it is filled with persons, objects, memories, and expectations. The concrete space is also "filled" with the personal experience of time. Some people's inner space developed the original meaning of "to stretch" into the feeling of "ex-pansion." They speak loud as over long distance. These are the *ex-ulting* type—this word derives from *ex-saltare*, "to jump out frequently"; they are the *ex-uberants*, and this word derives from *ex*, "out," and *uberāre*, "to bring forth in abundance"; *uber* means the large and full udder as of a cow. They are *out-going* people who are turned *out-ward*, they *out-do*, *out-flow*, *outcry*, *outburst*, or *outrage* others. They obviously need more life-space because they are the *pro-sperous* ones, of good *speed*. This word, Old English *spaed*, meant "wealth, power, success." The corresponding Sanskrit term *spāyatē* simply says "grow fat," thus to occupy much space. Other people prefer little space. They developed from the basal meaning "to stretch" the idea, to bind fast, ever tighter. They are *re-strictive*. This word derives from *re-stringō, -ere*, from *re-*, "back," and *stringō, -ere*, "to draw tight." They *with-draw, re-tract*. The *with* preserved, in this case, the old meaning of Old English *wither*, "against, in opposition."

It is to the credit of psychoanalysts and existentialists[51] that they discovered the all-out importance of the "inner space." If the life-space is perceived as a sterile, arid vacuum, this describes the inner "emptiness" and "loneliness." Absolute emptiness also means spacelessness. T. S. Eliot gave an adequate phenomenological description of the "waste land" as experienced by the "hollow men." French thinkers were fascinated by the emptiness of the inner space, the *"sentiment du vide"* as it was called by Janet. This inner emptiness takes the image of the *a-byss*, from *a-byssos*, "bottomless" pit, which always suggests the "fall," the direction down and the darkness of the pit. Baudelaire said about Pascal, in describing the inner abyss: "Pascal kept his abyss with him while moving around, Alas! everything is abyss—action, desire, dream, word . . . above, below, everywhere the depth of the shores, silence, space frightful and captivating . . . I fear sleep as a fear of a great hole, all filled with vague horror, leading no one knows where. I see nothing but the infinite through all the windows . . ."[52]

The English *vain* illustrates best the subjective feeling of emptiness. It derives from the Latin *vanus*, "empty"; it is related to *wan*, Old English *wann*, "dark," meaning "sickly pale"; and also related to *want*, which suggests deficiency. The inner emptiness of the abyss suggests the idea of "dark," and the color of the skin of the depressed "sickly pale." The other terms also describe the symptoms of depression and depersonalization.[53] The English *idle*, Old English *idel*, meant "empty." It developed, out of the inside emptiness, the idea of worthlessness. To the depressed, everything is *in vain* and worthless; the despair is the deep, dark abyss. The Latin *vacuus*, "empty," is the basic meaning of such words as *evacuation* or *vacant*, *vacate*, and *vacation*. The depressed man does not work, his idleness is the expression of the inside vacation. The "hollow man" is the empty man. The Gothic *laus*, "empty," the Old English *leas*, "void, loose, weak," are descriptive of the general "I can't" attitude of the depressed. Illustrative is the Dutch expression *een loze noot*, "a hollow nut." The German language developed the concept of "empty," *ledig*, into the idea "not married," thus inactive from a marital viewpoint. The Slavic languages evoked the idea of being empty in the feminine concept of not being pregnant; *prazdinu* means "empty" and *ne-prazdina*, "not empty, pregnant." Biological sterility is implied in these cases.

Man feels secure only in his familiar setting where the space is "filled" with meaningful persons and objects, when he feels the solid ground under his feet. In this setting he can orient himself, feel related and happy. Disorientation in space might be an indication of mental disturbance. The routine question of the psychiatrist to his patient at the first encounter is usually: "Do you know where you are?" The answer sometimes is: "I am mixed up." The orientation follows visual cues, but sometimes memories of a voice or of a fragrance are understood better than visual impressions. The basic inside orientation can distinguish between the "ups and downs," between "high" aspirations, "high" respect, "high" values, everything *ex-alting*, on the one hand, and the "low" degrading, diminishing forces in the morale and value of life. The *de-pressed* is "*down*hearted," as if he would carry an invisible "millstone around his neck," as said in the Bible. The infinite is properly spaceless emptiness; its only content is the hollow I. The Sanskrit *Upanishads* say: "Where one sees nothing else, hears nothing else, understands nothing else, that is the infinite. But where one sees something else, hears something else, understands something else, that is the small (the finite) . . . That (infinite) indeed is below. It is above. It is behind. It is in front. It is to the South, it is to the North . . . I, indeed, am below. I am above. I am behind. I am in front. I am to the South. I am to the North. I am, indeed, all this." (7:25).[54] To the apostles, true being is the being of the Lord and of Christ, "of his fullness have we all received" (John 1:16).

The opposite of the Greek *plērōma*, "fullness," is *kenōnis*, "emptiness." The related Greek *kenotēs* means "empty space" and also "vanity"; the *keno-pathēma* denotes the sensation of non-reality. This is the negative aspect of "being." It belongs to the category of non-being. While the eternity of the return is described as "from eon to eon," "for ever and evermore," this negative aspect of emptiness would say "from Nothing to Nothing" or "for never and nevermore." This is the expression of despair.

TIME

The perception of time is inseparable from the perception of space. It is always "space-time." The differentiation in verbal expressions consists in the fact that spatial terms refer to an outside, three-dimensional reality, whereas one can speak of time only in symbolic terms as an inner experience of continuous events which are progressive and irreversible. Two events can "take place" simultaneously, but they cannot occupy the same place "at the same time." The subjective perception of time is just as concrete and dynamic as that of space. The life-time is related to the progressive historical process, but has no relationship with the abstract concept of time in physics. As far as language is concerned, time is a psychological reality which has little in common with the homogeneous time of abstract mathematical measurement.[55]

The psychological reality of time experience refers to the "moment," the "hour," the appointed time of longer or shorter duration, the unique "opportunity" for action which never returns. This limited concept of time is described in spatial terms. The Latin term *tempus*, "time," originally denoted a "stretch," a short period filled with specific action.

This concretistic idea of "time" will be better understood if one keeps in mind that the term refers to the idea "to stretch" and also means the "temples" of the head. How do *tempus*, "time," and the dual *tempora*, "temples," hang together? The idea "to stretch," which was also used for denoting "space," implies not only the limitation, but also the consequences of stretching. Stretching makes the material thin, smooth, and weak. The temples were considered as the thin, vulnerable spots of the head. In Old English the "temples" were called *thun-wang*, properly "thin-cheeks." Similar denotations are used in other Germanic languages. In Greek the temples are called *ta kairia*, properly the "vital parts," the fatal spots where man can be hurt. The parallel Hebrew term *raggāh*, "temples," properly means "thinness." This explains the fantasy which is described in the biblical story: "Then Jael Heber's wife took a nail of the tent, and took a hammer in her hand, and went softly unto him (Sisera), and smote the nail into his temples, and fastened it into the ground" (Judges 4:21). The smoothness is described when it is said: "Thy temples are like a piece of a pomegranate" (Song of Solomon 4:3).

The German term *die Schläfe*, "temple," injects a new concept into this context. The word is the plural of *Schlaf*, "sleep," also related to *schlaff*, "flabby, flaccid, limp." The usual interpretation, stating that the temples are related to sleep because "one sleeps on the temples," is in the light of verbal fantasies obviously a naïve rationalization. However, there exists, indeed, a connection between the concept of "sleep" and the arterial pulse which can be felt on the temples.

For instance, the two *carotid* arteries of the neck, which supply the head with blood, are called *karōtides* in Greek, from *karos*, "heavy sleep, torpor"; *karōtikos* means "stupefying, soporific." Thus, the carotid arteries properly indicate the "sleepy" spots of the neck, as in German, the temples of the head. These terms translate the time of sleep into symbolic spatial concepts. Sleep is the defenseless section of the time which otherwise is spent mostly in alert wakefulness. "Time" is, according to these fantasies, within the "stretch" the weakest spot where the life-time can be cut most easily. We still say: "cut the time." The Greek term *kairos*, dual *kairia*, "temple," derives from the verb *kairō*, "to cut." Homer uses the term *kairos* several times and always uses it to point out the specific spot where the weapon can best penetrate the body and "cut off" the life-time. Odysseus as well as the archers in their shooting contest were aiming at the *kairos*, the vulnerable spot. In the symbolism of "time," this spot represents the unique "opportunity," thus the Greek *kairos* and the Latin *tempus* also mean "opportunity." This critical point of time is called the "nick of time" in English. It is said in an old (1681) text: "The wisdom of God . . . hits the very nick of time for his application."[56] The noun *nick* denotes a notch, while *neck* denotes the ridge. The verb *to nick* means to hit exactly at the critical moment. All these instances, and many more in the other related languages, prove that the original concept of time denoted a short span, a unique opportunity for action. Its dynamic aspect is best pointed out by the term *moment*. It derives from the Latin *momentum*, originally *movimentum*, "movement."

This concept of "time" will explain the not always understood coherence of *tempus*, "time," and *temptation*. "Temptation" is a time concept, therefore, it is said in the Bible "the hour of temptation," "the day of temptation," or "the time of temptation." Translating it into bodily expression, it is said: "temptation . . . was in my flesh" (Galatians 4:14). In spatial terms one "enters" it, or one is "led into it." Once again, time is perceived as an individualized moment when the "flesh is weak" and vulnerable.

It is consistent with these fantasies that the life-time is represented by a thin thread, the "thread of life" which can be cut easily. This is the most general symbol of the life-time which man is "winding up." Ancient mythologies elaborate these fantasies in many personifications, but it is always the woman whose work it is to spin the thread of life. In Greek fantasies it is also a woman who uses the fatal scissors. "What is the time?" is asked in Greek by *pēnika?* This is an interrogative adverb from *pēnē*, "the woof, the thread on the spool in weaving"; *pēnidzomai* means "to wind thread of a reel for the woof." *Pēnelopē*, the wife of Odysseus, properly means "Spinster." She is gaining time by spinning. "My days are swifter than a weaver's shuttle, and are spent without hope," Job said (7:6).

Besides the "thread of life," three other images were generally used for describing the inner experience of time. One image is the "way," another evokes "liquid, flowing," like a "river." A third image of time is the rotating "wheel."

The symbol of the "Way" describes, in spatial terms, the progressive direction of time, but "time" is strictly a "one way" on which one must proceed ahead, with no return. It has a beginning and an end. The orientation in time depends on the here and now where the person just happens to be on his way. This spatial relationship supposes that the future is "ahead," the stretch left behind is the past. The word *past* derives from the Latin *passus*, "step." "It *came to pass* at that time" (Genesis 38:1) is an obsolete formula, but it describes well the experience of someone walking along the way. Looking back, even in the picture language of dreams and the Bible, means remembering the past, that someone had "passed away." "Short" and "long," "*near*" and "far *away*," are spatial terms applicable to time. "Everywhere" means, in temporal language, *al-ways*, Old English *eallne waeg*, "all ways." The same image is used in obsolete German—*allewege*, "always." One can observe in the Hebrew Old Testament language how the spatial and temporal concepts flow together in this case: "The Lord shall preserve thy going out and thy coming in from this time forth, and even for evermore" (Psalms 121:8). When it is said: "I am the way, the truth, and the life," it means, in our sentence structure: "I am the true way of life." The experience of "stumbling," "going astray," "falling" along the long way of life became charged with moral implications.

The "river" is, in some respects, even more expressive for the progressive one-way direction of time. Heraclitus' saying: "One cannot step twice in the same river" expresses this subjective time experience. The orientation in relation to the river, however, is not so clear as it is while proceeding on the road. It depends whether the speaker is floating along in the river or standing on the shore and observing the stream flowing by. We generally suppose, from our "present" point of view, that we stand facing toward the oncoming stream, from "where" it comes, thus the future is "coming" toward us, the past is "going" away, ever farther away. However, this position is not necessarily universal. There are languages which show that the speaker, in his orientation, stands facing the past and turns his back toward the oncoming future. One can observe such cases of "reversed" time in pathological disorientation. The reason for such a stand is obviously the inner experience of time. One knows and sees only that which became past, fading away in ever greater distances, while the future is unknown, unseen like all things which approach us from behind.

One can also shift, in fantasy, the present position into the past, thus anticipating the past and speaking about it as future "before" us ("what he had written before"). It is more difficult to look at the oncoming future as already past; we do it mostly in the negative ("he shall not yet have written"). In such a case one speaks about the *after*-world as the distant future or *after-time,* the time anticipated *after* the present moment, as still future. The shift from the present stand into the anticipated past or future may contradict the spatial orientation of "before" and "behind, after." This is apparent in Greek: *opisō* means "backward, behind, after" in space, but in time the things to come.

We prefer our position facing the future because the time experience of the healthy person is "filled" with expectations, hopes, planning, futurity. It is a characteristic of the English language that the *now* is perceived as *new;* similar relationships exist between the Latin *nunc,* "now," and *novus,* "new." This means that the actual is perceived in contrast to the old as something not existing before.

While walking on the way, some goal is anticipated, even though the end of the action might be unconscious. The river never flows backward, nor stands still. It is, however, a well-known symptom of mental disturbance which results in the feeling that the inner time-clock has stopped, and time stands still, even flows back. The time experience, which cannot flow ahead because the future is blocked, frustrated, reverses its course and turns into the negative of "becoming." It represents decay, decomposition, it is an agency of hostility and destruction. This might be the heart of the idea called "return of the repressed." The pertinent verbal expression of this hostility is the preposition *against,* from the adverb *again.* What comes "again" returns from the past. It comes against the stream of time and approaches us, if the face is turned toward the future, from behind, "*back* again." This experience of hostility is expressed in many languages. The Greek *palin* means, of space "backward, returning"; of time, "again," and also "contrariwise, in opposition"; and as the English *gain-say,* "contradict," it is used for denoting hostility, malignancy. In Latin *rursus* means "turned backward," "on the contrary," "against," and "back again." In German *wieder* means "again," *wider* "against." The phonemically corresponding word of *a-gain* is *gegen,* "against." The noun *Gegen-stand,* "object," properly "against-stand," has a synonym, *Wider-stand,* meaning "resistance." The German adjective *gegen-wärtig*, "present," properly "turned against," developed the parallel form *wider-wärtig*, "disgusting." It is obviously a deeply rooted and very general fear of hostility of the "return" because it is incorporated in various languages. Even in Hungarian *ellen* means "against," *ellenség*, "enemy," *vissza*, "back, return," and *visz-ály*, "fight, hostility." The French call an embarrassing event a *contre-temps*, "against-time." Such instances can be multiplied. They all prove the wisdom that the return of the past is generally feared as a destructive power.

If the steady flow of time is so to say "frozen," it becomes a dead sequence of things which can be counted. It has been observed in clinical practice that, with the loss of futurity, the neurotic feeling of incapacity overcomes the patient. "I can't" is the stereotyped expression of such stagnation. Potentiality is directed toward the future. With the loss of the perspective into the future, the depressed prefers to leave every task unfinished, leave the door open, because every finished act leads to a new task in the process of time, each end is also the beginning of something new. Another not infrequent symptom of such patients who say they have no hope, no future, is the compulsion to count. For instance, they count the stairs, the steps because their walking is no longer a spontaneous action. The spontaneous function broke down in their perception to little segments, one after another. The flow of time became fragmented and resulted in compulsive counting. The sequence of numbers offers a mechanized substitute for the living time experience. Time becomes arithmetic, the expression for multiplication. Then, one can say *two times, three times*, and so forth. Time, in the plural *many times*, is just the negation of the thesis of Heraclitus that time is the irreversible unique moment of presence which never returns.

Time becomes stagnant or turns back its course if the fear of death has blocked out the outlook into the future. The symbols of the Way and of the River serve as a solace for the basic frustration of life because they foster the illusion that time is not a short "stretch." The Way and the River suggest a rather long distance in a wide space, as if the Way will never come to an end. If, however, the end is in sight, then time is "running out," as the sand runs out of the hourglass, which is an age-old attribute of the personified Death. In such case the feeling of despair emerges, of having missed the "opportunity" of life, the right moment for action, and now it is *late*, too late for doing anything. The result is passivity, inactivity, the feeling of hopeless helplessness. It is not worth-*while*, anymore, to start anew. The English *late* significantly assumed the meaning of "dead." The expression *to kill time* is a euphemism. It is one's own life-time which is killed. The hopeless attitude toward the future may spoil the potentialities of the present moment and always raises the question: "How long will it last?"

The verb *to last*, to persist in the stream of time, opens up a new aspect. This verbal form is related to *late, latest, at last*, which means at the end. The symbolism of the Way, although repressed, is in the background of these words. The noun *last*, Old English *laest*, remained preserved in the shoemaker's *last*. It referred to the "footstep"; as a verb, it meant "to follow the footsteps," the track, or the passway. To be everlasting does not mean to resist the flux of time, but on the contrary, it meant to be always on the go until the end. The corresponding German verb *leisten* speaks more clearly, by its meaning "to accomplish, to be able to do," about the unceasing activity which makes life worth living.

The opposite of the stagnant time is the accelerated flux of time, implying haste and hurry. The awareness that the lost moment never can be retrieved may become painful. The conscious or unconscious fear of the inexorable end may motivate the faster and ever-faster drive and accomplishment. The famous dictum of Heraclitus: *panta rhei*, "everything is flowing," may turn into a neurotic feeling that time is *running* much too fast. To *run* properly applies to the flowing liquid, but it came to be used for the accelerated gait of man. The ever-present threat of "too late" does not result, in this case, in paralyzed inactivity, but in restless overactivity. The term *speed*, Old English *spaed*, originally meant "wealth, power, success"; the corresponding verbal form *spowan* meant "to prosper, to succeed." Thus, "speed" on the road might be motivated by the drive for wealth, power, and success. This old meaning remained preserved in *Godspeed*, a wish for success.

Fugit irreparabile tempus, the Romans once said: "time is escaping for *good*." In English, "for good" means "forever" because the "good" moment is completely "fulfilled," and therefore, it is, as Goethe's Faust knows, remaining, everlasting. The reaction to the "futility" of time is the natural desire to take hold of the present moment, to grasp it and transform the inside event, by some creative act, into a lasting, objective reality. Man, who is aware of the limitation of life-time, will try to transcend it and strive to create something which will survive. Such a creative transformation of the flux of time does not simply want to achieve a petrified memory, which stands out of the stream of history as a dead monument like a rock standing out of the live stream, but wants to remain active and productive in shaping the future. It does not want to remain in the past; its ideal goal is eternal presence. It is the yearning of the time-conscious man "to be" fulfilling completely the present moment and at the same time "becoming" to grow into the unknown future. In the early Greek philosophy Parmenides stated "being" is opposed to "becoming," as Heraclitus perceived the world. Today, it is still the foundation of the healthy personality to be aware of the fact that man is ever the same and ever another. Subjectively one better perceives the constancy, while objectively one observes the change in the outside world, how generations grow up and fade away. Heraclitus saw first, in the conflict of these opposite tendencies, the conflict and the harmony in the cosmic process of "becoming."

The symbol of harmony between the "being" in present and "becoming" of the future is the "wheel of time," the universal idea of the eternal return. The measuring of the never-returning psychological time is, in itself, a paradox. It is based upon the observation of the constancy in the return. The "seasons" mark a permanence in the flux of time, a point of rest in the "running away" time. The psychological time is not measurable, as St. Augustine has expounded first in the famous passage of his *Confessions*. He said, man measures time "from that therefore, which is not, yet through that, which has no space, into that, which now is not . . . It is measured while passing, but when it shall have passed, it is not measured, for there will be nothing to be measured."[57] It is a psychological observation that the "fulfilled" time flies away fast, while the "empty" time, which produces the feeling of boredom, lasts relatively very long. One says, in English, "have a good time." This refers to the eventful, fulfilled time, while in German "boredom" is called *Lang-weile*, properly "long-while."

The circular motion of the eternal return of the "wheel of time" is implied in the term *period*, from the Greek *peri*, "round about," and *hodos*, "way, road." Periodicity is the basis for measuring time. The English *while*, like the German *Weile*, originally meant a "period" of time. This word characteristically means, in the related Scandinavian languages, "resting place, bed"; its phonemic equivalent in Latin is *quiēs*, "rest." There is an old Greek saying: *spende bradeōs*; the same in Latin *festina lente*, "hurry slowly." One says, in English: *take your time*. Paradoxical as it may sound, it is the maxim of the healthy, harmonious life. The English *while* was conceived in this idea. The corresponding German verb *weilen* means "to stay, remain."

The English *time*, and *tide*, the German *Zeit*, "time," denoted time as a returning event. For this reason *tide* became the term for the regular, periodic rise and fall of the water-level on the seashore. In this respect it is significant to notice that, for the early ages of the Western world, the measuring constant was not the sun, but primarily the moon, not the daytime, but the nighttime; the year was not counted by summers, but by winters. The *moon* and the *month* derive, in most of our languages, from an identical form, which implied, as it is supposed, the meaning of the "measurer." The moon-month was their measure of time. The immediate reference to the human organism is apparent even in this case. Pregnancy was formerly counted not as a nine-month but as a ten-month period. The normal child at birth is called *dasha-masya* in Sanskrit, a "ten-month" one. In early Greece the pregnancy year was also ten months. Herodotus reports that a Spartan mother explained about foreign women to her son Demaratus: "they bear at nine or seven months and not all go through the full ten months," which she considered as normal (6:69). The same was true for the Romans. The ten-month pregnancy year gradually changed, under Babylonian influence, into the twelve-month sun year. The changing "mood" of women is called *Laune* in German. This word derives from the Latin *luna*, "moon," and attributes to the moon the change of *mensis*, "month."

Man's early relationship to time was altogether different

from ours. "Time" once meant a specific qualified event set by some heavenly agency for each individual, each season and each hour of the day. Man was the passive recipient of the time measured out to him. The same moment can mean luck for one and disaster for another. Time was accepted as fate, destiny. This concept of time still emerges sometimes in neurotic regression. It survives best under normal conditions in astrology. The horoscope predicts by *con-sidering* the "stars together"; in Latin *con-* means "together" and *sidus, sideris,* "star." This *con-stellation* of heavenly bodies is supposed to decide the happenings on earth. Shakespeare says: "Heaven so speed me in my time to come." The Greek Penelope says to the stranger, in whom she does not recognize her returned husband Odysseus: "Heaven has appointed us dwellers on earth a time for all things" (19). Such appointed time is the weather depending on heavenly meteorology; man cannot do anything against it. In French, one still says for "it is a bad weather," *il fait mauvais temps,* properly "it makes bad time." Formerly, one thought that the gods made the bad time for men. In English, the weather can be *inclement.* Not that the weather is "not merciful, harsh," but the higher powers who ordained the weather-time are harsh. In Latin, one can observe man's passive acquiescence in the appointed time. A derivative word from *tempus,* "time," is *tempestas;* its primary meaning is "a portion or point of time, season, period, weather," and in a specialized sense, "bad or stormy weather, tempest." A further derivative is *tempestivitas,* "the right and proper time, timeliness," but *tempestuosus* means "stormy, turbulent." The word *temperatura,* which developed from the primary meaning "due measure, proportion," also means *temperament,* "a mixing in due proportion"; in reference to body fluids, it refers to "disposition, constitution." Astrologers still seek to interpret the human constitution in terms of constellations of stars at a given time. In this case time is the ordained fate of man conceived as liquid. *Temperantia* derives from the verb *temperō, -āre,* "to combine or compound properly." One can observe in all these terms, which derive their meaning from *tempus,* "time," that the decisions of higher powers were measured out by mixing in due proportion and proper combination. Man accepted it, like the weather and temperature, as the manifestation of a higher will. The Germanic languages developed the concept of *weather* from the rather "inclement" will of the heavenly powers; the Nordic climate made the people aware of merciless weather conditions. The meaning of English *weather* is clarified by its relationship to *wither,* properly "to weather," which was considered as a sign of the approaching death.

The changing weather conditions of the ever-turning time were not abstract quantities, but indefinite periods. *Summer* or *winter* could mean half-a-year; *spring* or *fall* had no clear-cut definitions. There were all kinds of seasons. In Old English, for instance, there was a *sol-monadh,* "sun-month," about February; a *hlyd-monadh,* "stormy-month," about March; *tri-milchi-monadh,* "three-milk-month," about May when the cows were milked three times a day; *sear-monadh,* "dry month," about June; *masd-monadh,* "harvest-month," about September; *blod-monadh,* "blood-month," about November; *mid-winter-monadh,* "mid-winter-month," about December. These terms show how the year, divided in "moons," was not quantified, but perceived in the concrete reality of weather conditions and seasonal human activities. In the Old Testament we read about the "month of *Abib*" (Exodus 13:4), which is the month of "ripening ears"; the "month of *Zif* (I Kings 6:1), which is the month of "flowers"; the "month of *Ethanim*" (I Kings 8:2), which is the month of "perennial streams"; the "month of *Bul*" (I Kings 6:38), which is the month of "rain." There was also a "time that the cattle conceived" (Genesis 31:10), a "time of the firstripe grapes" (Numbers 13:20), a "time of figs" (Mark 11:13), or an hour when the cock crows (Mark 14:72).

The word *season* developed its meaning from this concept of the "appointed" proper time for action. Seasons return infinitely, as does everything in the "wheel of time." The word derives from the Latin *satiō,* "sowing"; it is the proper time for planting, thus the springtime in the restricted sense. The English *meal* also originally meant the "proper time," especially the proper time for eating. It lost the overt reference to time; therefore, it is added again in *meal-time.* While in English one counts *two times, three times,* in German the same is *zweimal, dreimal,* properly "two meals, three meals." The "Days and Work," as Hesiod said, encompassed the periods of the human life-time. They represent the everlasting sameness, harmony, and constancy beyond all the struggle, haste, and running of the irretrievable time, in the final end, the higher order in life and world. The prophet says: "To everything there is a season, and a time to every purpose under the heaven: a time to be born and a time to die" (Ecclesiastes 3:1, 2).

The opposite of the limited, "lived time" is timelessness and eternity. It was felt to be the temporal equivalent of the infinite space. The Sanskrit *Upanishads* say: "Verily, the infinite is the same as the immortal, the finite is the same as the mortal" (7:24).[58] The idea of eternity cannot be grasped other than in terms of the finite human life space-time. Time and life became identified. There is no other time experienced than the experience of being alive. Death means timelessness, but one cannot speak of death either, except in terms of life. For this reason the words for "eternity" developed necessarily out of the concepts of human life experiences.

The Greek *aiōn*, the Latin *saeculum* both originally meant the normal human life-time, which was quite short in ancient calculations. Then, it meant the continuity of life in the father-son succession, thus it absorbed the meaning of procreation. How can the idea of "eternity" be represented by the symbol language of "life-time"? The Greek fantasies grasped the "stream" of time, its liquid quality, and related it, as indicated by the Latin term *temperamentum*, to body fluids. The life-time is "running out" when the body fluids *wither*, when liquids issue from the body. Tears and sweat discharge the life-time substance; death meant the final "withering," the drying up of the body. Among all body fluids discharged, the discharge of the generative organs was most suited to represent the "everlasting" in the limited life-time. We still speak of *generations* in reference to the succession in time. The periodicity of the female organism suggested, as did the *season*, the "sowing time," the eternal return and continuity. There is "a time to plant, and a time to pluck up that which is planted . . . a time to embrace, and a time to refrain from embracing" (Ecclesiastes 3:2-5). The Latin term *saeculum*, "life-time, generation," is generally referred to the verb *serō, -ere*, "to sow"; it also denotes "sex." The semen appeared to those early ages which were still close to nature as the vehicle of eternity. It was transferred from fathers to sons, since time immemorial, and will be so for future ages. The biblical language recalls this continuity of generations by saying "the seed of Abraham," "the seed of David." In the Gothic language the whole "world" was called *mana-sēths*, properly "man-seed." Representing the world as "semen" is, of course, a patristic conception, different from matristic fantasies, which consider the navel cord as an infinite continuity which connects mothers and daughters since timeless ages.

Other primitive ideas about procreation considered the bone marrow, especially the spinal marrow, to be the seat of virility. Shakespeare had such fantasies in mind when he said "spending his manly marrow in her arms." Because, in this primitive understanding, the spinal marrow was the seat of procreative power, it became the physical representation of "eternity." Time, as well as space, was visualized in the image of the human body and bodily functions. Thus, the Greek *aiōn*, from *aiw-ōn*, "life-time," "eternity," derives its meaning from "spinal marrow." This equation of "eternity" with "spinal marrow" may sound puzzling to some interpreters, yet it is logical and consistent with verbal fantasies.

"Eternity" is experienced in three forms. One is the eternal return in the rotation of the "wheel of time," a second form experiences existence in the fulfillment of the present moment as if the time-clock had come to a stop, when there is no more "before" and "after," no past or future, only the present existence fulfilled in the *now*. A third form experiences timelessness as nonexistence, as the temporal expression of the infinite vacuum. It represents "emptiness" in time. In order to differentiate these experiences, which are not always separated in verbal fantasies, in the following the term "eternity" will be restricted to the meaning of eternal return; its adverbs are *always, ever*. The timelessness of the *now* could be termed "fulfillment." The timelessness of the void and abyss is characterized by chaos, disorientation; its typical adverbial form is negative, *never*. Heraclitus conceived "eternity" in terms of the return. Parmenides grasped the full meaning of existence in the present moment; it "was not before, it will not be in the future," it is not becoming, nor passed away because existence is perfect and complete in itself (Fragment 8:1-6). Verbal fantasies reflect the idea of Heraclitus, of Parmenides, as well as of "nothingness."

The Greek *aiōn* describes "eternity" as materialized here on earth in the life-time of man.* It appears in the cosmic order of the ever-changing sequence of generations. Almost the same idea is expressed by the prophet: "One generation passeth away, and another generation cometh: but the earth abideth for ever" (Ecclesiastes 1:4). In an even more earthly way, it is said "for dust thou art and unto dust shalt thou *return*" (Genesis 3:19). In body symbolism it is said, "Naked came I out of my mother's womb, and naked shall I *return thither*" (Job 1:21). Death was generally symbolized as the return, the reunification with the mother. Freud expanded the idea of regression later into the eternal return of all organic life into nonorganic matter, thus interpreted in terms of Heraclitus, the eternal struggle of the two principles—life and death. "From food are born all creatures that live on earth; afterwards they live on food, and in the end they return to it."[59]

The Greek *aiōn*, continued in the English *aeon, aeonian,* describes well the recurring turns of the "wheel of time" by the form "from *aiōn* to *aiōn*, which properly means from one life-time to the other, "from aeon to aeon." The modern languages lost the full substantial meaning of "eternity" as disclosed by the Greek *aiōn*.

The strong reference to the human life-time in this life space is emphasized by the word *world,* Old English *werold.* The first part *wer-* meant "man," as in *wer-wulf;* the second part, Old English *yldu, yld,* "age, aetas, saeculum"; thus the compound properly means "man-age." Thus, when the modern translator of the Bible says "for *ever* and *ever*," the Old English still has *fram worulde on worulde,* "from world to world" (Psalms 48:14). The adverbial form is the colorless equivalent of the original nominal meaning. The New Testament Greek still sometimes uses *aiōn*, with the concrete meaning of "world," but it means "worldliness," this world as opposed to the "after-world" or "after-life," which is to follow the life-time, or it could also refer to the "afore-time," the "before-life" which preceded the life-time.

The Greek *aiōn*, former *aiw-ōn*, has a corresponding word

---

* See *The Subconscious Language,* pp. 191–192, 332. Also E. Benveniste, "Expression indo-européenne de l'éternité," in *Bulletin de la Société de Linguistique de Paris* (1937), 38:103–112.

in Latin, *aev-um*. It also denotes primarily the human life-time, and in symbolic transposition, "age" and "eternity." Derivative forms are *aetas*, from *aevitas*, "age." The English *age* continues the Latin *aetaticum*; *eternity* and *eternal* do not derive directly from the noun *aevum*, but from its adverbial derivative *aeternus*, from the former *aeviternus*, "eternal." It is characteristic for the modern languages that they turned the basic substantial meaning of *aiōn, aevum*, first into adjectival forms, then even preferred adverbial derivatives, like the Latin *semper*, "always," into *sempiternus*, "sempiternal." The English *ever* is the adverbial residue of the once substantial meaning of "eternity." The Old English language still had the noun *awa*; the Gothic language had *aiws* with the meaning of *aiōn*, but these nouns gradually disappeared from the Germanic languages and were replaced by adverbial forms such as the German *ew-ig*, "eternal," *Ew-igkeit*, "eternity."

The Germanic languages disclose, in another way, the meaning of "eternity" as cosmic order and harmony. The Old English *aew* also means "law" in the sense that we speak of "natural laws." Law, in its original meaning, was not some human statute, but a timeless order, the "divine law" implied in all existing things. The law was considered exclusively as such divine law down until the age of Hugo Grotius. Human laws were interpreted as applications and elaborations of the basic principles which reflected the cosmic order and harmony. Human laws are arbitrary and may change, but the divine law is everlasting. The biblical formula for law is therefore "statute for ever" or "ordinance for ever" (Exodus 27:21; 28:43; 29:28; 30:21). The Old English *aew, ae* also meant "wedlock, marriage," "spouse, wife." Marriage and wedlock are thus conceived within the framework of divine or natural laws, of the periodic change of generations, therefore, marriage of man and wife represents "eternity" here on earth. In German *Ehe*, former *ē* meant "law," "marriage"; *ē-haft*, "law-ful," continued in *echt*, "true, real," or Dutch *echt*, "marriage," from *ēhaft*, "lawful." The eternal return of the *seasons* as sowing time or the pronouncement "they shall be one flesh" is a divine ordinance which represents "eternity" in the concrete life situation.

Another aspect of existence without or beyond time is the

idea of "fulfillment" in the everlasting present moment. It suggests the sensation of time having come to a stop. This is rather an exceptional experience in normal life, a unique "peek experience" (Maslow), a "starry hour" (*Sternstunde*, Stefan Zweig); it is the moment of "illumination" in the religious soul-searching of the mystics. It can be a rare moment of creative *extasis;* it may appear in pathological conditions as manic elation. From a psychological viewpoint it seems to be probable that this *ex-stasis*, "stepping out" from the bondage of time, is the repetition of early infantile experiences. The image of "fulfillment" still refers to the liquid quality of time. Only an empty space can be fulfilled, filled full. The separation of mother and child at birth may result in the feeling of emptiness in both; then their reunification in the nursing situation may be experienced by the child as "fulfilling." Various forms of regression tend to re-experience this first happiness. One must keep in mind that time is a personal experience, thus man cannot speak or think of timeless existence, but the fetus in the womb alive and the newborn babe are still on the borderline of time and timelessness. Shakespeare grasped this marginal experience when he wrote: "When crouching marrow in the bearer strong cries of itself 'No more.'" The child, when entering life, is "being" here and now, he "fulfills" now a hitherto empty space. To the Greek mind, everything had its appointed space (*chōra*), just as it had its appointed time. "To be," in the true sense of the word, means to "fulfill" perfectly and completely the present occupied space and time. The word *com-plete*, from the Latin *com-pletus*, means to be "filled up," from the verb *plerō, -ere*, "to fill." The true being is such a satiated being in itself, when there is nothing to hope for because all hopes are "fulfilled," no future, no past, no becoming because everything is *accomplished*—this from the Latin *ad-*, "to," and *complēre*, "to fill up." In German this perfection of being is called V*oll-endung*, "full-ending," the end of time in fullness.

Religious language grasped this fullness of time as timeless perfection. In Greek this fullness is called *plērōma*, from the verb *pleroō*, "to fill." The true existence is the being in fullness, in the presence of the Lord, "the fulness of him that filleth all in all (Ephesians 1:23).

WRITING

The verb *to write* originally denoted something different from the rather complacent activity which it came to mean in our age.[60] The original meaning is still transparent in the closest related languages. The corresponding German word is *reissen, riss*, "to tear apart," from the former *rizan*, "to cut, tear, split"; in Old Saxon *writan* still means "to injure, cut"; in the more distant past the meaning seems to have been even more aggressive: Sanskrit *vardh*, "to cut," *vrana-h*, "wound," and *vrika*, "wulf," meaning the "sarcastic" animal. This word is derived from *sarkadzein*, "to tear flesh apart like dogs." In Greek the term *graphō*, "to write," carried similar implications. It meant "to encarve"; *graptus* means a cut on the skin. The Latin verb *scribō, -ere* also denoted originally "to engrave, scratch in." The question will be raised: What is the origin of this aggressive component in the notion of "writing"? Material explanations are at hand. It is said that writing was originally epigraphy carved into hard material—stone, metal, wood—thus the letters had to be engraved by force and violence. The missing link of this appealing interpretation is the psychological motivation which emanates from the reality of the human body. It hardly could be maintained that such primary references as "to wound," "cut the skin," "scar," "wulf," referred to stone material. Rather, the whole group of words indicates that the primary material of "writing" was the human skin.

It is true that plain white surfaces invite people to scratch in some letters or magic signs, often with aggressive intent, even in our age; but this age-old propensity can hardly be considered to be the final motivation in the development of writing. Rather, the verbal forms indicate a more violent activity than "writing" is in reality. One must start in this case, as in many others, not from physical realities, but from repressed bodily fantasies. Not the pen or the pencil, but the hammer and chisel were the proper tools for engraving the characters on hard material. Such notions had to undergo a transformation until they became fitting to the work with pen and pencil, which was painting rather than chiseling.

The fantasies involving "writing" come from another source. This is indicated by the symbolic equation of "writing" and "plowing." It is in accordance with verbal fantasies that the "pen-man" calls himself *Arator* in Latin, or *Plowman* in early English literature. "My pen is my plowshare," the German *Ackermann*, "plowman," said. One has no difficulty in understanding when Cicero wrote to Atticus: *Hoc litterularum exaravi*—"I plowed out this little letter." The pen "plows" the paper. In fact, this is the proper idiom in Hungarian. It is in accordance with these fantasies that the written lines were called "furrows." In Latin the lines were called *versus*, in English, *verse*, properly something "turned over," from the verb *vertō, -ere, versum* "to turn." One can even observe that the "furrow-lines" were running from the left to the right and then from the right to the left in early literacy—a strange way of writing which must have had some motivation. Its Greek denotation gives the answer: it was called *bou-strophedon*, properly "oxen-turn," equating the lines with the furrows of plowing.

Why did "writing" become equated with "plowing"? Obviously, because it was perceived in the image of "plowing." "Writing" and "plowing" have little in common on the level of object realities. It is not realistic to state that writing looks like plowing, that the pen looks like a plowshare, or the lines on the paper are like the furrows of the plowland. There must be a common element, not apparent on the level of object realities, which brought about the standard association between "writing" and "plowing." "Farming is easy," Stevenson once said during an election speech, "when the pen is the plowshare" (October 26, 1956). To the physiognomic perception, there must be something alike, a syncretic fantasy which connects these two disparate meanings. Such an association can be verified seldom in itself. The word "writing" does not exist alone, as it stands in dictionaries, but it is connected by unconscious fantasies to the field of literacy. It belongs to a whole group of words which all refer in some hidden way to the same underground of fantasies. This field is a system of cross references: one word is but an element in the total context of fantasies. If one wants to entangle the meanings implied in "writing," one finds oneself entangled in a complicated network of cross references. One will find that the concept of "writing" is inseparable from fantasies implied in reading and speaking, with the tools and materials as pen, pencil, book, and even with such distant fantasies as plowing and sowing. An interpretation becomes plausible only within the framework of the total field to which it belongs. In this case the field is literacy, which was something strange and new in the sight of nonliterate people when the words were shaped.

The equation between writing and plowing is a first step in understanding all the violence, the cutting, splitting, tearing apart which are implied in writing. It introduced "writing" to the minds of illiterate, agricultural people. The plowshare better served the aggressive purpose than did the pen and pencil. It has been demonstrated that the act of plowing and sowing, with all their implements, in early ages belonged to the magic-religious rituals, fertilizing the Mother Earth. The early husbandry did not make any difference between the seed of plants and the "seed of Abraham," or between the fruit of a tree and the "fruit of the womb." The human body and its functions assert their primacy once more in the perception of reality. It would be an offense against the reader's intelligence to translate plowing and sowing into physiological terms. It is understood without comment when Lucretius, the Roman naturalist, said, "pliant movements are of no use whatever to wives . . . for she turnes the share clean away from the furrow and makes the seed fail of its place."[61] It belongs to the understanding of such figurative speech that "word" and "seed" were also identified with one another.*

---

* See p. 86. Plato's Socrates said that the writer uses his pen "to sow words" and to "sow his seed in literary gardens." *Phaedrus* 276.

The reference to "plowing" injects a sexual accent into the act of writing. It still does not explain the obvious violence, inflicting wounds, cutting the skin which are present in the meaning. Unconscious fantasies connect the first recognition of the other sex with castration fear and images of the primal scene into a diffuse overall idea. The female organ is perceived by these fantasies as the "furrow," an incision, therefore the idea of a "blunt knife" carries sexual connotations in most of our languages, especially in vulgar and infantile speech. Aristophanes uses the most common and vulgar term *bīnein*, "coire." This word is a derivative of *bīa*, "violence," *biadzō*, "overpower," like the Latin *stuprāre*, "violate, beat, strike, torment, knock." The more vulgar these terms are, the more they reveal the sadistic component of infantile sex-fantasies, which became repressed. The Latin *sexus*, "sex," is the nominal component of the verb *secō, -āre*, "to cut." In German "sex" means *Ge-schlecht*. The word is derived from *schlagen*, "to hit, beat." These fantasies partly explain the aggressive concept of writing. As the plowshare violently cuts open and tears apart the surface of the Mother Earth, in the same way the work of the pen and pencil on paper was perceived as violence by early fantasies.

Remaining within the field of early literacy, the tool for writing, the word *pencil*, becomes significant. The pencil is just a "pencil" to the normal mind, and nothing else. Because its material might be chalk, it is called *crayon* in French, which comes from the Latin *crēta*, "chalk." It can be made of lead, thus it is called *Blei-stift*, in German, "lead-stick." Such denotations remain within the boundaries of sound common sense. However, the word *pencil* deviates from this normal perception. In schizophrenic fantasies the object appears not simply as a tool for drawing or writing, but as something imbued with the magical power of the body, fused with the image of the male organ, charged with awe and anxiety. This genitalization of a practical instrument is the result of the same mental process which identified "writing" with "plowing," or "seed" with "word." It is the product of nonsensical fantasies, which the normal speaker will reject and feel repugnant to his standard of taste and thinking. This word may serve as a good example, illustrating that the original meaning has to be obliterated first, before the present, correct meaning "pencil" could be established. One does not associate *pencil* with *penicillum*, "little penis," anymore. If this background of the word is called to one's attention, it will perhaps be asserted that such an association never was in one's normal mind, or that it exists only in dictionaries.

Does the forgotten meaning of *pencil* not exist anymore in the mind of the sober, normal speaker? I am not as sure as some interpreters seem to be in trusting in the "functional autonomy" of motivation. There exists a strange identification of the writer with his pencil. There are also almost ritualistic customs in presenting a pen or a pencil to the adept of initiation ceremonies as a symbol of having grown up to adulthood.[62] Perhaps it was a misuse of motivation research to call a fountain pen by the trade name of "Papermate," with two hearts as a trademark and other additionally conspicuous features, but there are many good reasons to justify the clinical truth concerning the "writer's cramp." Freud pronounced it a long time ago when he stated that, if writing assumed "the symbolic meaning of coitus," it will be charged with the anxiety and guilt which properly belong to the forbidden sexual behavior.[63]

Our good dictionaries avoid the unpleasant association in this case by resorting to the original meaning of the Latin *penis* which was "tail"; this continued in *penicillum* or *peniculum*, which properly meant "little tail." A little tail is a brush for painting, and from the notion of paintbrush, the English *pencil* developed. Thus, there is nothing reprehensible in the background of the word. It developed along the line of "tail"– "little tail"–"paintbrush"–"pencil." This whole change of meaning is supported by the fact that writing was considered to be painting in early literacy. The Gothic word *mēljan*, "to paint," translates the Greek *graphein*, "to write." Chaucer said: "With subtil pensil peinted was this storie." The Chinese write with a little paintbrush even in our day. It seems to be evident that the word *pencil* never had anything to do with the repudiated meaning which supposedly has become repressed. The corresponding German word *Pinsel*, "paintbrush," also underlines the idea that "writing" was originally equated with "painting" and the pencil with the brush, and nothing else. Yet, one never can be absolutely sure about the unpleasant meaning which supposedly does not exist.

Let us consider, as a test example, the German term *Ein-falts-pinsel,* properly "sim-plex-little paintbrush"; now it means "simpleton." The trouble starts with the first part of the compound, which properly means "one-fold." The Latin *sim-plex,* like *du-plex* or *sim-plus, du-plus, tri-plus,* refers to "folding" once, twice, or three times. The same is true of the Greek *haploos, diploos, triploos.* This folding belongs to the field of weaving, and it carries many symbolic meanings, as is indicated by such verbs as *ap-plicate, com-plicate, ex-plicate* (properly *un-folding*), *du-plicate, im-plicate, re-plicate.* Within this context, the Greek *haploos,* or the Latin *simplus, simplex,* holds the most respectable qualities as "plain, unmixed, pure, sincere, free from risk and complications, without dissimulation, open, frank, straightforward, direct, guileless, honest, ingenuous, blunt, natural, upright," and so on. The noun *simplicitas* means "of the noblest honesty, candor." This word is contrasted to the Greek *diploos,* "two-fold," which assumed the moral qualities of "doubtful, double-minded, treacherous." The noun *di-plōma* means "twice as much of a thing, a folded paper, letters of license or privilege." The Latin *du-plex* means, in addition to "two-fold, double," to be "ambiguous, double-tongued, double-faced, false, deceitful." This polarity of simple and double is best exposed by Christ's teaching: "if thine eye be single" as against "if thine eye be evil" (Matthew 6:22-23). The English *duplicity, double-minded, double-cross, double-dealing* describe the original contrast to simplicity. In German, *Zwei-fel,* "doubt," properly means "two-fold."

Some strange thing happened with the idea of "one-fold," *sim-plex,* that it came to denote, in both English and German, the feeble-minded simpleton who is silly, foolish, easily deceived, stupid, good-for-nothing. The same was true of the German *ein-fältig,* "one-folded," meaning "stupid, imbecile." Some authorities suggest that these two concepts—"the noblest honesty" and "stupidity"—are very close to one another. One should be skeptical toward such common-sense explanations and should be alerted by the fact that these words—*simpleton, simplex, simplicius, simplicissimus*—come from a slangish background and carry some humorous overtones. The humor implied becomes apparent by the German *Einfalts-pinsel*, "simpleton," which occurred first as a student slang expression. In this language the "simpleton" describes, as many similar terms do, the stereotype of the castrated "odd man," generally identified as stupid, imbecile, good-for-nothing. Thus, one may readily doubt whether this "one-fold-little paintbrush" is not rather a "one-fold-little penis." Some interpreters perceive the improbability of their common-sense explanation and resort to a radically new idea: in the case of *Ein-falts-pinsel*, the word *pinsel* does not denote "paintbrush," but little "pin-sole," the wooden pegs which the shoemakers use for pinning the soles. This interpretation does not fit, but rather contradicts the notion of "one-fold." The noun *pin* originally denoted an "erect point, peg." Its diminutive in English is *pintel*, the "bolt" which is to be put in the socket, and it is derived from the Old English *pintil*, "penis." Thus, one may interpret the word *simplex*, *ein-falt*, as not being expressive enough for the castrated type; therefore, they added *pinsel* to make the hidden implication better understood. The unpleasant meaning of *pencil*, German *Pinsel*, "paintbrush," could be perfectly repressed and forgotten if the word stood in an independent position alone, but this repressed meaning looms to the surface if the word enters a dependent position as a compound form, sheltered by other associations.

It could be pointed out, in contradiction to these assumptions, that this *penis-pencil* complex is just a phonemic association; the equation of meanings is not valid even for *pen*, from the Latin *penna*, "feather," nor valid for the Italian *lapis*, "pencil," or the German *Blei-stift*, "lead-stick." For the German form it will be asked again: Why is *-stift* added to "lead"? This *stift* means a "piece of wood," a "boy"; it is related to *steif*, English *stiff*. It suggests just the opposite of the odd man *Einfaltspinsel*. The sexualization of writing-plowing, pencil-penis is not an isolated phenomenon. It can be observed in nonrelated languages in which the phonetic pattern of "pencil" does not derive from *penicillum*. In the Hungarian language any interference of these terms is out of the question. Yet there are many telling instances in Hungarian folklore in which the notion of "pencil" is equated with "penis" without embarrassment. These instances, not quotable here,[64] permit no doubt about the fact that the two concepts supplement one another in unconscious fantasies, not because they hang together by similar phonemic patterns, but, on the contrary, they became equated in phonemics because they were equated previously in the meaning.

If the concept of "pencil" became infused with the meaning of the male, the "ink-pot" may appear as its female complement. A Hindu proverb says: "No man abstains from writing for fear of falling into the ink-pot."[65] This appears again as schizophrenic nonsense, yet "to fall into the ink-pot" is just as contrary to reason, within the field of writing, as is the biblical "return in the mother's womb," or to till, plow, and sow into "mother's holy field," which was the crime of Oedipus.

Unconscious fantasies permeated the field of early literacy and spread the mystery of magic upon the hitherto unknown art of spelling. According to early mythological fantasies, writing was invented by gods as divine magic. Reading was, too. Orpheus and Cadmus were the originators of writing in the Greek tradition. The words *spell, spelling,* originally denoted such charm, or magical incantation, later on, the recital of a text. This meaning remained preserved in *gospel,* from the former *gōd-spell.* It is the characteristic feature of the pre-literate verbal tradition that the text, whether magic ritual, law, or report, has to be reproduced verbatim. Not one syllable could be missed or changed; it had to be exact and correct. This quality of the magic spell became transferred to writing. Writing originally was "spelling" out the letters aloud and setting them into the proper order. The words *spell, spell-bound* still kept the magic connotation. In terms of developmental psychology, the magic implied expresses the awe and anxiety which the small child may feel toward the writing and reading of adults. He considers it a privilege of the father. He approaches it with fear and fantasies of intruding into a prohibited activity.

Difficulties in spelling are sometimes rooted in this infantile layer of unconscious apprehension of magic.

It is consistent with these infantile fantasies, which became repressed by the adult mind, that the classic book "roll" was called, in Latin, *liber*, plural *libra*, "books"; the plural *liberi* means "children." The book-roll is sometimes termed *penis* in Latin; the knob of the roll is called *omphalos* in Greek and *umbilicus*, "navel," in Latin.[66] The clerical writers wrote *homiletics*, but the Greek verb *homileō* means primarily "to be intimate with," "to consort with," "intercourse," whether verbal, social, or sexual. When writing became a "book," it was called, in Latin, *cōdex* or *caudex*, in the diminutive *cōdicillum*, but all these terms are in a close relationship to *cauda*, "tail," "penis." The "little paintbrush" idea is not injected here. If the *liber*, as a result of writing, became printed, it was called *in-cunabula*, properly "swaddling clothes," which are *in* the *cunabula*, "cradle." Such terms, and many other similar ones, betray fantasies which were also revealed through psychoanalytical studies of children.

Children may develop inhibitions in writing certain letters and numbers because they perceive these letters to be infused with the magical spell, and that disturbs them. The letters of the alphabet were not learned as meaningless, abstract signs of sounds, but they assumed some very concrete, often frightening, meanings; for instance, "the C is biting." The old names of the letters suggest some concrete meaning. The Greek *alpha*, from the Hebrew *aleph*, meant "ox, bull," the symbol of the father. The Greek *bēta*, from the Hebrew *bēyth*, meant "house," the symbol of the mother. *Gamma*, from the Hebrew *gīymel*, meant "camel"; *delta*, the sign of the triangle, from the Hebrew *dāleth*, "entrance" of the "house-mother"; the meaning "cunnus" remained preserved in Greek; and so on. How easily anxiety and feelings of guilt may enter the field of writing can be demonstrated best by analyzing, from this point of view, many of our children's alphabets. The classic New England's *Primer* starts with "A like apple," the symbol of the mother; "B like bull," the symbol of the father; "C like cat," the symbol of the girl; "D like dog," the symbol of the boy, and so on. The commenting verses start with: "In Adam's fall, we sinned all."

The proliferation of unconscious fantasies can be pursued

until the insignificant punctuation marks. As an illustrative example, I chose the word *point*. What kind of fantasies have determined the naming of this most simple sign? Starting from the English, the remark to the word point, "two, or perhaps three words," shows the embarrassment of the interpreters in front of the great variety of meanings as there are listed in dictionaries. *Point* did not primarily mean the "dot," but the instrument by which a surface was perforated, thus, it means "the sharp, tapering end of a thing," i.e., the gradual "diminishing in thickness in an elongated object," as "to the fine taper fingers' end (1821)." One would like to have a more concrete substantiation of this meaning. It seems rather disturbing that the verbal form *to point out* does not refer to the perforating needle's prick, but to the index finger. It is even more difficult to understand why this "point" also means the most prominent, salient feature of a story or joke. This usage obviously corresponds to the Latin *punctum saliens,* and the German *springender Punkt,* properly "jumping point." This pointed object, equated with the index finger, sometimes called "jumping," being at the same time the most important feature, also means in archaic usage "a feat of arms, a deed of valour, an exploit"—obviously a peak experience of life. This *peak* refers once more to the "tapering pointed end" of a projecting thing. The vigorous state of body and mind can be disclosed by the related synonyms of *pointed, piquant, pungent, poignant;* while, on the opposite side, *pointless* suggests "to be stupid, dull, without sense or force"—all characteristics of physical and mental impotency.

This preliminary sketch of the meaning complex will take on a more concrete shape if the Greek and Latin antecedents are also brought into the picture. The Latin *punctum* derives from the verb *pungō, -ere,* "to prick, puncture; to pierce into, penetrate, enter; to affect sensibly, to sting; to vex, grieve, trouble, mortify, annoy." In Romance languages *punctum* denotes "the place where the colts become castrated." The original sense of the Latin word, with the connotation of a painful effect, remained preserved in another English word: *punch,* through the French, from *punctum,* meaning either a tool for piercing and penetrating a surface or a blow with the fist. As a verb, *to punch* means either to perforate, to make a hole with a punch, or to strike with a blow. These two meanings—to perforate with a tool and to strike with the fist—are not very consistent. Some dictionaries want to avoid the difficulty by supposing that two different words are behind the sound-form *punch,* but even so, it does not change the fact that both words mean "to perforate," and both derive from the Latin *pungō, -ere, punctum.* However, closer inspection of this Latin verb also reveals the same inconsistency. From this verb, meaning "to pierce, perforate," derive also *pugnus,* "fist," *pugnō, -āre,* "to fight," and *pugna,* "fight." The strange connection between "fist"–"fight"–"perforate" is reflected in the pertinent French words. While *point, pointe, pointiller* evoke the idea of acuteness and the "point" pierced by such instruments, *poign, poigne,* "fist," and *poignard,* "dagger," from *pugnalis,* properly "belonging to the fist," once again show the same connection between piercing an object and the fist. The French word, loaded with late Latin connotations, lost its meaning and became a functional element for negation, *ne—point.* As such, it is void of any lexical meaning. The word became relegated from the vocabulary to the grammar. The reason for it must be in some repugnant connotation which motivated its repression. Some strange fantasies must have been implied in the idea of a "punch." In French, a punch is called "beautiful," and it developed the meaning of "much, many" in *beau-coup*—obviously for an uncounted, repetitious action. We shall come nearer to this repressed meaning by considering the pertinent Greek terms. In Greek, *pux* means "with the fist," equivalent to our box; *pugmē* is the term for "fist" and for the "fight" with the fists; *pugmachos* or *puk-tēs* is the "boxer." Through these words it becomes increasingly evident that the primary notion of the Latin *pungō, -ere, punctum,* "to pierce, to hurt, to penetrate," refers to the hand or fist. There is a good reason why our *point out* has something to do with the index finger. Latin lexicographers have trouble in harmonizing the notion of "to perforate" and "boxing"; they want us to believe that boxing is essentially "perforating" because the fight with fists was carried out with an outstretched middle finger. There obviously exists a great gap between *punch,* as boxing with the fists, and *to punch* a hole. One cannot identify the one with the other unless the middle finger is considered as the dagger or the piercing instrument. Languages are, at this point, very outspoken.* They reveal the fantasies which have been connected in various speech communities with the "middle finger." The verbal instances make it quite clear why just the stretched-out middle finger became equated with a perforating tool in the language of fantasies. The meaning was repellent and became repressed, yet it remained the common point of reference through which the various lexical meanings of *point* hang together.

As an illustration of the etymological analysis of the "point," I would like to refer to a not always understood example taken from Greek mythology. It is the case of *Pygmalion*, who is represented by G. B. Shaw as a linguist, but was a sculptor in the Greek legend. The name obviously has something in common with *pugmē*, "fist." It has been assimilated by this form and meaning in the Greek language, thus it is from this viewpoint of little interest whether or not the Greek name covers up another foreign name, a Phoenician one of unknown origin, as some authorities pretend. However, it is hard to believe, as these authorities argue, that the name of this sculptor contains a reference to the "boxing fist." Pygmalion is, by all signs, the favorite of Aphrodite, thus he is a great lover, as he is a great sculptor. His *pugmē*, "fist" (still with the connotation of "piercing, perforating"), must be understood in this context. He fashioned the image of a woman and fell in love with the work of his hands. Arnobius and Ovid, who related his story, considered his love for the ivory statue as a sex relation worse than idolatry, incest, or sodomy. Arnobius said that Pygmalion, "in his madness, just as if he were dealing with his wife, raised (the image of) the deity to his bed to copulate with her by embraces and *mouth*, and to do other things enrapted by the foolish imagination of empty libido." Ovid is even more descriptive; he relates how beautifully Pygmalion adorned his love object, but "no less beautiful is the statue undressed. He lays it on a bed, calls it the consort of his couch (*appellatque tori sociam*), he kisses it and thinks his kisses are returned, he speaks to it, he

---

* See p. 272.

grasps it and *seems to feel his fingers penetrate* into the members when he touches them (*tenetque et credit tactis digitos insidere membris*)"; then he fears he has hurt "lest he leave marks of bruises on them" (*Metamorphoses* 10:240–297). Ovid, without any linguistic pretense, shows a perfect understanding of the unconscious implication of *pugmē*. The ivory image of the woman has been called, by a later tradition, *Galatea,* a significant name, related to *galateia,* "milk-white." The ivory statue was milk-white, indeed. The name, however, may have been suggested by another association, too. Some authorities hold that this name is not related to *gala,* "milk," but derives from *galēnē,* "calm of the sea." It is interrelated with an old cluster of words grouping around *gela-,* "to freeze," or to *gelaō,* "to laugh." All these meanings can emerge in modern poetry. The "Sinngedicht" by the German poet Logau, elaborated by Gottfried Keller, says: "How will you make white lilies to change into red roses? Kiss a white Galatea—blushing she will laugh." The Greek *gelandron* means "cold, frigid, sterile," and also refers to the clotted blood. Whatever might be the right etymology of the name Galatea, the sphere of its association remains the same. It suggests either "white virginity" or "cold frigidity." In Hungarian, for instance, the milk "goes to sleep" or "is sleeping," while in English it becomes "sour." Of the frigid woman, it is said in Hungarian: "milk is in her veins instead of blood." In any case, Ovid displays a great understanding for the miracle of the white ivory Galatea, who became alive through the touch of the *pugmē* of her lover.

It would mean an incomplete understanding of verbal forms if the interpretation were restricted to the lexical realities as "fist fighting" or "boxing." The change of meanings which took place must be understood on the level of unconscious fantasies. The "pointing tool" and the result of it, the hole, the "point" appear, in the light of fantasies, infused with body references, just as the "pencil" does, or "writing." Even the study of the history of boxing will not elucidate the meanings implied. Realities are not of great relevancy when fantasies are at work. Not the objective aspect, but the infantile fantasies, loaded with anxiety, shaped these words. This can be demonstrated best by a control test asking: What kind are the most general associations referring to the male organ, as it is denoted in infantile and colloquial languages? In answer to this question, one will find that the idea of "piercing into," "stab," "wound," "sting" are all inherent in the meanings attached to it. It is called *prick* in low colloquial English, from the Old English *prica*, "penis," and a mark made by a pointed instrument, "a point," also a "sharp pain." As a verb, *to prick* means to perforate with a pointed instrument, also, as in *prick up*, "to rise erect, to point up." It also means "to thrust or stick a pointed object into something." A similar low colloquial English term is *pintle*, Old English *pintel*, meaning "penis" and "a pin or a bolt, especially one on which some other part turns," an upright pivot. The *pintle-fish* is also called *yard* or *shame-fish*. The same holds true for the English word *tip* which, on the lexical level, means a small gratuity, but the original meaning is the "pointed tapering, or rounded end of something long"; it also means a light or sharp blow or pain. One will better understand the English term by its nasalized variants, such as the German *Zumpf* and the Dutch *tump*, "penis." This may explain the strange fact that the verbal form not only suggests secrecy, as the colloquial "give a tip," but also it means to upset, overturn, to slant into a tipped position. I refer to these instances, which are collected in the excellent work of C. D. Buck, for no other reason than to show that the lexical meanings, as described in our best dictionaries, for instance, in Webster, can be understood only against the background of repressed fantasies implicated, which are, of course, not listed in Webster. The psychological interpretation, however, is interested in the forgotten language of fantasies which lies hidden or below the manifest surface of language. The various abstract, objective meanings, which are listed incoherently in dictionaries, turn out to be offshoots of just the one meaning not listed in the dictionary.

No other part of the body-self has stirred up more traumatic fantasies than the male and female genitals, not by their anatomical reality, but by subjective delusions connected with them. The male organ is called, in Old English, *waepon*, "weapon"; *waepned* is the general term for "male"; it is also called "sting," "sword," "dart," "spear"; in Irish "nail"; and in Russian "needle." In Spanish *carajo,* from the late Latin *caracium, caraculum,* from the Greek *charakion,* "a little pointed stake," shows the original meaning in the speaker's mind. The relative Greek verb *charassō* means, accordingly, "to make pointed." This applies to the male as well as to the female; it means "to encarve, make an incision." The noun *charadra* denotes a "ravine" or "gully," a little valley made by running water. The character, the name of the encarved "letter" refers, in the final analysis, to these imageries. The analysis of the punctuation mark "point," which started from the pointed instrument and led to the notion of "to point out" as "to make a little hole," arrived at a repressed bodily fantasy which disappeared from the surface of lexical language. Goethe's Mephisto knows about the medical advice to cure all the pains and aches of women, they are thousands—"at *one* point."

This investigation on the repressed meaning of the word *point* could be completed by the analysis of the names denoting other punctuation marks, but the sphere of association would remain the same. For instance, the Latin *virga,* French *verge,* properly means "rod," just as *penis* means "tail"; but the equation with "penis" is general in all our languages, so that no one can say that the one meaning was original, the other metaphorical. The diminutive of the Latin *virga* is *virgula;* it assumed the meaning of "comma." The word *comma* shows the following already known associations: the Greek *komma,* "incision," *koptō,* "to thrust, strike, beat"; *kopos,* "stroke" and "weariness, fatigue"; *kopadzō,* "to become weary"; *kopis,* "knife"; *kopens,* "chisel"; *kōphos,* "blunt"; *kopas,* "castrated"; *kapōn,* like the Latin *capus, capō,* "capon"; and a large group of words referring, either in a concealing or an unmasking way, to castration fantasies. The same holds true for the English *dash.* Considering only the present usage, the following meanings are listed in dictionaries: "to strike with violence so as to shatter, to knock, splash, frustrate"; as a noun "a violent blow, splash, a small portion of something thrown into something else with violence, bespatter, to ruin, frustrate, put to shame, to adulterate." Considering these and other words in the field of writing, the pencil is no innocent "little paintbrush" in the language of unconscious fantasies.

REFERENCE NOTES
STANDARD DICTIONARIES
SELECTIVE BIBLIOGRAPHY

NOTES FOR INTRODUCTION
Facts and Theories

[1] A classic introduction to these considerations is Susan K. Langer, *Philosophy in a New Key: A Study in the Symbolism of Reason, Rite, and Art* (New York: Mentor Books, Thirteenth Printing, 1964).

[2] For a short survey history of the science of linguistics, see Otto Jespersen, *Language: Its Nature, Development and Origin* (New York: The Macmillan Company, 1922, reprinted 1949) and also Louis H. Gray, *Foundation of Language* (New York: The Macmillan Company, 1939). For a more elaborate description of the early days of scientific linguistics, see Berthold Delbrück, *Introduction to the Study of Language—A Critical Survey of the History and Methods of Comparative Philology of Indo-European Languages* (London: Trübner, 1882).

[3] This estrangement started at the beginning of the century. Wilhelm Wundt, *Völkerpsychologie. Eine Untersuchung der Entwicklungsgesetze der Sprache, Mythus und Sitte* (Leipzig: Engelmann, 1900, 2nd ed., 1904). Volume I and II of this monumental work deal with the psychology of language. The opposition of linguists to Wundt's psychological approach was almost general. It has been voiced most distinctly by Berthold Delbrück, *Grundfragen der Sprachforschung: Mit Rücksicht auf W. Wundts Sprachpsychologie Erörtert* (Strassburg: Trübner, 1901). The reply by Wundt: *Sprachgeschichte und Sprachpsychologie. Mit Rücksicht auf B. Delbrücks Grundfragen der Sprachforschung* (Leipzig: Engelmann, 1901). This early rift separating the science of psychology from the science of language at the beginning of our century became, as the years went by, wider and deeper. A rather understanding attitude found expression in the works of anthropologists. See Franz Boas, *The Mind of Primitive Man* (New York:

403

The Macmillan Company, 1938); *Race, Language and Culture* (New York: The Macmillan Company, 1949); *Handbook of American Indian Languages* (Washington: Government Printing Office, 1911) and A. L. Kroeber, *Anthropology, Race, Language, Culture, Psychology, Prehistory* (New York: Harcourt, Brace & Co., 1923). The work of Edward Sapir will be discussed later.

[4] The mathematical-technical information theory of language has been developed by Norbert Wiener, *Cybernetics* (New York: John Wiley & Sons, 1948); also his *The Human Use of Human Beings: Cybernetics and Society* (Garden City, N. Y.: Doubleday, Anchor Books, 1950)—see especially the chapter on "Mechanism and History of Language." See also *Cybernetics—Circular Causal and Feedback Mechanism in Biological and Social Systems*. Transaction of the Seventh Conference (New York: Josiah Macy, Jr., Foundation, 1950). "As object of scientific inquiry humans do not differ from machines," is said in Arturo Rosenblueth and Norbert Wiener, "Purposeful and Non-Purposeful Behavior," *Philosophy of Science*, 18:326. The philosophical-mathematical formulation of neurology is put forth in W. Ross Ashby, *Design for a Brain* (New York: John Wiley & Sons, 1952). Of special interest are G. A. Miller, *Language and Communication* (New York: McGraw-Hill Book Company, 1951) and *Machine Translations of Languages*, edited by William N. Locke and A. Donald Booth (New York: John Wiley & Sons, 1955).

[5] A short survey of behavioral-linguistic problems is given by Hobart Mowrer, "The Psychologist Looks at Language," *The American Psychologist* (1954), pp. 659–695. Similar viewpoints prevail in *Psycholinguistics—A Survey of Theory and Research Problems*, edited by Charles E. Osgood and Thomas A. Sebeok, with bibliography (Bloomington, Ind.: Indiana University Press, 1965). Part 2, 1954. The same: Sol Saporta and Jarvis R. Bastian, *Psycholinguistics: A Book of Readings* (New York: Holt, Rinehart & Winston, Inc., 1961).

[6] Joseph Breuer and Sigmund Freud, *Studies in Hysteria*, translated by A. A. Brill (Boston: Beacon Press, 1937). Sigmund Freud, "On the History of the Psychoanalytic Movement," 1914, *Standard Edition* 14:7–66. Sigmund Freud, *Zur Auffassung der Aphasien*, 1891, English translation: *On Aphasia* (London and New York: International Universities Press, 1953). S. Bernfeld, "Freud's Earliest Theories and the School of Helmholtz," *Psychoanalytic Quarterly* (1944), 13:28–49. Ernst Kris, "The Significance

of Freud's Earliest Discoveries," *International Journal of Psycho-Analysis* (1951), 31:108–116. Rainer Spehlmann, *Sigmund Freuds Neurologische Schriften. Eine Untersuchung zur Vorgeschichte der Psychoanalyse* (Heidelberg: Springer, 1953).

[7] Sigmund Freud, "Introductory Lectures on Psycho-Analysis," 1916, *Standard Edition* 15:28. *A General Introduction to Psycho-Analysis* (New York: Washington Square Press, Inc.), p. 32.

[8] *Standard Edition* 15:28, p. 20, pp. 24–25.

[9] Sigmund Freud, "The Antithetical Meaning of Primal Words," 1910, *Standard Edition* 11:161.

NOTES FOR PART ONE
The Linguistic Approach

[1] B. F. Skinner, *Verbal Behavior* (New York: Appleton-Century-Crofts, 1957), p. 11.

[2] Charles E. Osgood, "The Nature and Measurement of Meaning," *The Psychological Bulletin* (1952), 49:197–237. Charles E. Osgood, G. Suco and P. Tannenbaum, *The Measurement of Meaning* (Urbana, Ill.: University of Chicago Press, 1957).

[3] B. F. Skinner, *Verbal Behavior, loc. cit.*

[4] Jean Piaget, "Verbal Understanding," in *The Language and Thought of the Child* (New York: Meridian Books, 1955), pp. 141–170.

[5] This is the basic contention of Husserl and the phenomenological philosophy. See also: Alice Ambrose, "Linguistic Approaches to Philosophical Problems," *The Journal of Philosophy* (1952), 49:289–301. The author says: "I suspect it is nonsense to speak, as Berkeley did, of taking ideas bare and naked into one's view. . . ." (p. 293). See also: J. O. Wisdom, *The Unconscious Origin of Berkeley's Philosophy*, International Psycho-Analytic Library No. 47 (London: The Hogarth Press, 1953). Also: J. O.

Wisdom, *Philosophy and Psycho-Analysis* (Oxford: B. Blackwell, 1953). Norman O. Brown, *Life Against Death: The Psychoanalytical Meaning of History* (New York: Random House, Inc., Modern Library Paperbacks, 1959).

[6] Leonard Bloomfield, the protagonist of behavioral linguistics, in his *Language* (New York: Holt and Rinehart, 1933), surely had protested against any assumptions which suspect the interference of unconscious fantasies with his stimulus-response linguistics, but it is unfailingly the apple which is to demonstrate the "practical" event: "she gets the apple into her grasp and eats it," pp. 22–25. Indeed, "people very often utter a word like *apple* when no apple at all is present," p. 141. Skinner, while stating that ideas, meanings "have little relevance to the practical control of verbal behavior," asserts that "an English-speaking subject, unaware of the point of the experiment, is to be made to emit a common response, say, *pencil*." *Verbal Behavior, loc. cit.,* p. 253.

[7] Lee J. Cronbach, "Processes Affecting Scores on Understanding Others and Assumed Similarity," *Psychological Bulletin* (1955), 52:177–193.

[8] Theodore Thass-Thienemann, "Left-handed Writing: A Study in the Psychoanalysis of Language," *Psychoanalytic Review* (1955), 42:239–261; "Oedipus and the Sphinx: The Linguistic Approach to Unconscious Fantasies," *Psychoanalytic Review* (1957), 44:40–73; "The Talking Teapot: A Note on Psycho-Linguistics," *Comprehensive Psychiatry* (1960), 1:199–200; "Psychotherapy and Psycholinguistics," *Topical Problems of Psychotherapy* (1963), 4:37–45. *The Subconscious Language* (New York: Washington Square Press, Inc., 1967).

[9] An introduction to the basic concepts: Ernst Cassirer, *An Essay on Man: An Introduction to a Philosophy of Human Culture* (Garden City, N. Y.: Doubleday, Anchor Books, 1953). W. N. Urban, *Language and Reality: The Philosophy of Language and the Principles of Symbolism* (New York: The Macmillan Company, 1939). The elaborate presentation of these concepts by Ernst Cassirer, *The Philosophy of Symbolic Forms,* three vols.—Volume one: *Language,* Volume two: *Myth* (New Haven, Conn.: Yale University Press, 1953). A comprehensive presentation: the developmental-holistic experimental studies of Heinz Werner and Bernard Kaplan, *Symbol Formation: An Organismic-Developmental Approach to Language and the Expression of Thought* (New York: John Wiley & Sons, 1963).

[10] Joseph R. Royce, "Psychology at the Crossroads between the Sciences and the Humanities," in *Psychology and the Symbol: An Interdisciplinary Symposium*, edited by Joseph R. Royce (New York: Random House, Inc., 1965), pp. 16–23.

[11] For the proper understanding of the relationship of the sound form and symbolic meaning, see Heinz Werner and Bernard Kaplan, *Symbol Formation: An Organismic-Developmental Approach to Language and the Expression of Thought* (New York: John Wiley & Sons, 1963), pp. 100, 104, 218.

[12] "Whereof one cannot speak, thereof one must be silent." Ludwig Wittgenstein, *Tractatus Logico-Philosophicus* (New York: Harcourt, Brace & Co., 1922), p. 189.

[13] Jean Piaget: "The Meaning and Origin of Child Artificialism," in *The Child's Conception of the World* (Paterson, N. J.: Littlefield, Adams & Company, 1963), pp. 350–388.

[14] Ernest Jones, *Papers on Psycho-Analysis*. 1912, 5th ed. (Baltimore, Md.: Williams & Wilkins, 1948; Boston: Beacon Press, Beacon Paperback, 1961), p. 102.

[15] Lawrence S. Kubie, "Body Symbolization and Development of Language," *Psychoanalytic Quarterly* (1934), 3:430–444. Reprinted in *Cybernetics: Circular Causal and Feedback Mechanism in Biological and Social Systems*. Transactions of the Seventh Conference. (New York: Josiah Macy, Jr., Foundation, 1950), pp. 237–249.

[16] B. F. Skinner, *Verbal Behavior*, *loc. cit.*, p. 10.

[17] *Psychology and the Symbol: An Interdisciplinary Symposium*, edited by Joseph R. Royce (New York: Random House, Inc., 1965), pp. 103–104, also p. 4.

[18] Charles M. Solley and Gardner Murphy, *Development of the Perceptual World* (New York: Basic Books, Inc., 1960), p. 288.

[19] C. C. Fries, "Meaning and Linguistic Analysis," *Language* (1954), 30:57–68.

[20] Floyd H. Allport, *Theories of Perception and the Concept of Structure* (New York: John Wiley & Sons, 1955), p. 575.

[21] Hervey Cleckley, *The Mask of Sanity* (St. Louis, Mo.: The C. V. Mosby Co., 1955), pp. 428–429 on semantic aphasia.

[22] A promising approach is Edward S. Tauber and Maurice R. Green, *Prelogical Experience: An Inquiry into Dreams and Other Creative Processes* (New York: Basic Books, Inc., 1959).

[23] Lauretta Bender and Allison Montague, "Psychotherapy through Art in a Negro Child," *College Art Journal* (1947), 7:12–17.

[24] Hanna Segal, "Note on Symbol Formation," *International Journal of Psycho-Analysis* (1957), 38:391–397.

[25] Marguerite A. Sechehaye, *Autobiography of a Schizophrenic Girl* (New York: Grune & Stratton, Inc., 1951), pp. 34–80.

[26] Theodore Thass-Thienemann, "The Talking Teapot: A Note on Psycho-Linguistics," *Comprehensive Psychiatry* (1960), 1:199–200.

[27] R. Andree, "Menschenschädel als Trinkgefässe" (Mit sechs Abbildungen), *Zeitschrift des Vereins für Volkskunde* (1912), 22:1–12; also O. Schrader, *Reallexikon der Indogermanischen Altertumskunde* (Berlin-Leipzig: Walter de Gruyter, 1917–1923), 1:355–369, with bibliography.

[28] Caroline Bedell Thomas, Donald C. Ross and Ellen S. Freed, *An Index of Rorschach Responses: Studies on the Psychological Characteristics of Medical Students* (Baltimore, Md.: The Johns Hopkins Press, 1964), p. 440.

[29] Marion Milner, "The Communication of Primary Sensual Experience," *International Journal of Psycho-Analysis* (1956), 37:278–281.

[30] Jean Piaget, *The Language and Thought of the Child* (New York: Meridian Books, 1955), p. 150.

[31] H. Flanders Dunbar, *Emotions and Bodily Changes: A Survey of Literature on Psychosomatic Interrelationship, 1910–1933* (New York: Columbia University Press, 1935). Also: *Psychosomatic Diagnosis* (New York: Paul B. Hoeber, 1948). Walter B. Cannon, *The Wisdom of the Body* (New York: W. W. Norton & Company, Inc., 1939). Also: *Bodily Changes in Pain, Hunger, Fear and Rage*, 2nd ed. (Boston, Mass.: Charles T. Branford Co., 1953). The excellent exposition of internal noncognitive bodily sensations by Russell E. Mason, *Internal Perception and Bodily Functioning* (New York: International Universities Press, 1961).

[32] Eduardo Weiss and O. Spurgeon English, *Psychosomatic*

Medicine: The Clinical Application of Psychopathology to General Medical Problems, 2nd ed. (Philadelphia and London: W. B. Saunders Co., 1949). Franz Alexander, *Psychosomatic Medicine* (New York: W. W. Norton & Company, Inc., 1950). *Advances in Psychosomatic Medicine,* edited by Arthur Jores and Hellmuth Freyberger (New York: Robert Brunner, 1961).

[33] René A. Spitz, *The First Year of Life* (New York: International Universities Press, 1965), pp. 81, 344.

[34] Charles Darwin, *The Expression of the Emotions in Man and Animals* (London: J. Murray, 1872). New edition with preface by Margaret Mead (New York: Philosophical Library, Inc., 1955).

[35] The distinction between "speech" and "language" is reflected in the strict separation of phonetics and phonemics which was fundamental for the development of structural linguistics. Basic in this respect is F. de Saussure, *Cours de Linguistique Général,* 4th ed., edited by C. Bally and M. Sechehaye (Paris: Payot, 1949). *Course in General Linguistics,* translated by Wade Baskin (New York: Philosophical Library, 1959). See also Alan H. Gardiner, *Speech and Language* (Oxford: Oxford University Press, 1932). N. S. Troubetzkoy, *Principes de Phonologie,* translated by I. Cantineau (Paris: La Société Linguistique de Paris, 1949). It should be remembered in this context that Wilhelm von Humboldt, one of the pioneers of modern linguistics, made at the very outset a clear-cut separation between the physical "voice-form" (*Lautform*) which corresponds to the subject matter of phonetics on the one hand, and the inside intended articulation (*Articulationssinn*) which is concerned with phonemics on the other. *Über die Kawi-Sprache auf der Insel Java. Nebst einer Einleitung über die Verschiedenheit des Menschlichen Sprachbaues* (Berlin: Akademie, 1836), Vol. I, p. cvii. The principles of structural linguistics prevail in Stephen Ullmann, *The Principles of Semantics: A Linguistic Approach to Meaning,* 2nd ed. (Oxford: B. Blackwell, 1957). The way for structural linguistics and semantics has been successfully prepared—in contradiction to Wilhelm Wundt—by Anton Marty. See especially his *Nachgelassene Schriften* (Herausg. Otto Funke) Vol. I—*Psyche und Sprachstruktur,* Vol. II—*Über den Wert und Methode einer beschreibenden Bedeutungslehre;* also *Satz und Wort* (Bern: Francke, 1950). See also Ludwig Landgrebe, *Nennfunktion und Wortbedeutung. Eine Studie über Martys Sprachphilosophie* (Halle: Akademie Verlag, 1934).

[36] Marguerite A. Sechehaye, *A New Psychotherapy in Schizo-*

phrenia: Relief of Frustrations by Symbolic Realization (New York: Grune & Stratton, Inc., 1956), pp. 18–19. Also: *Symbolic Realization: A New Method of Psychotherapy Applied to a Case of Schizophrenia* (New York, International Universities Press, 1951), pp. 48–66.

[37] The various techniques of primitive fire-making are described by Edward B. Taylor, *Researches into the Early History of Mankind and the Development of Civilization*, 2nd ed. (London: J. Murray, 1870), pp. 231–258.

[38] A thorough discussion of this topic can be found in *Thinking and Speaking: A Symposium*, edited by Géza Révész (Amsterdam: North Holland Publishing Co., 1954). A different approach is presented by L. S. Vygotsky, *Thought and Language*, edited and translated by Eugenia Hanfmann and Gertrude Vakar (Cambridge, Mass.: The M.I.T. Press, 1962).

[39] *Corpus Juris Secundum—The General Index* in five volumes since 1959 (Brooklyn, N. Y.: The American Law Book Company).

[40] Jacob A. Arlow, "Smug," *International Journal of Psycho-Analysis* (1957), 38:1–12.

[41] John B. Watson, "The Myth of the Unconscious," *Harper's* (1927), 155:503–507. He equated what is unconscious with that which has not been verbalized.

[42] John Wild, "Husserl's Critique of Psychologism: Its Historic Roots and Contemporary Relevance," in Marvin Farber, *Philosophical Essays in Memory of Eduard Husserl* (Cambridge: University Press, 1940), pp. 19–43.

[43] Margaret Mead's excellent chapter on "The Ethics of Insight-Giving" applies to the linguist as well as to all social scientists. See *Male and Female: A Study of the Sexes in a Changing World* (New York: Mentor Books, 1955), pp. 317–330.

[44] Gordon W. Allport, *Pattern and Growth of Personality* (New York: Holt, Rinehart & Winston, Inc., 1961), p. 227. Also: Chalmers L. Strachey and F. DeMartino, *Understanding Human Motivation* (Cleveland, Ohio: Howard Allen, 1958), p. 71.

[45] Karl Vossler, *The Spirit of Language in Civilization* (London: Routledge & Kegan Paul, Ltd., 1951), p. 228.

[46] L. D. Lewin: "Body as Phallus," *Psychoanalytic Quarterly* (1933), 2:24.

[47] John B. Watson, *Behaviorism* (Chicago, Ill.: University of Chicago Press, Phoenix Books, 1961), p. 18. Also: "The Myth of the Unconscious," *Harper's* (1927), 155:503–507. The opposite viewpoint, for instance: Geraldine Pedersen-Krag, "The Use of Metaphor in Analytic Thinking," *Psychoanalytic Quarterly* (1956), 25:66–71.

[48] Chapter IV, "Dynamics as Opposed to Machine Theory," in Wolfgang Köhler, *Gestalt Psychology* (New York: Mentor Books, 1959), pp. 60–79.

[49] C. G. Jung, "The Psychology of the Unconscious," in *Two Essays on Analytical Psychology* (New York: Pantheon Books, Bollingen Series 20, 1955), pp. 117–130. Also C. G. Jung and C. Kerényi, *Essays on a Scene of Mythology: Child and the Mysteries of Eleusis* (New York: Pantheon Books, Bollingen Series 22, 1949), p. 104.

[50] Italics are mine.

[51] *Loc. cit.*, pp. 209–210.

[52] Robert Fliess, "Phylogenetic vs. Ontogenetic Experience," *International Journal of Psycho-Analysis* (1956), 37:46–60.

[53] C. G. Jung, *Collected Works* (New York: Pantheon Books, Bollingen Series), 7:578. Also: *Two Essays, loc. cit.* (New York: Meridian Books, 1956), p. 76.

[54] Sigmund Freud, *Standard Edition*, 23:132, also *Moses and Monotheism* (New York: Knopf, Vintage Books), p. 170.

[55] Julian Huxley, *Man in the Modern World* (New York: Mentor Books, 1949), p. 9.

[56] An example of mythological analysis according to the principles of C. G. Jung is Erich Neumann, *The Origin and History of Consciousness* (New York: Pantheon Books, Bollingen Series, 1954).

[57] Roman Jacobson, the leader of structural linguistics, says: "The cognitive function, however, is not the sole function of language, and in jest, in rhetoric, in poetry, in dreams, in magic, in what I should call everyday verbal mythology the grammatical categories carry a high semantic import." Sol Tax, Loren C. Eiseley, Irving Rouse and Carl Voegelin, *An Appraisal of Anthropology Today* (Chicago, Ill.: University of Chicago Press, 1953), p. 280.

[58] C. G. Jung and C. Kerényi, *loc. cit.*, p. 105.

[59] Edward Sapir, *Culture, Language and Personality: Selected Essays* (Berkeley, Calif.: University of California Press, 1956), p. 149.

[60] Edward Sapir, *Language: An Introduction to the Study of Speech* (New York: Harcourt, Brace & Co., Harvest Book, 1949), p. 4. But E. Sapir also wrote "Why Cultural Anthropology Needs the Psychiatrist," *Psychiatry* (1938), 1:7–12. Quoted with the permission of the publisher.

[61] The primary importance of "body symbolism" in the development of language has been most clearly expounded by Lawrence S. Kubie, "Body Symbolization and Development of Language," *Psychoanalytic Quarterly* (1934), 3:430–444. Reprinted in *Cybernetics: Circular Causal and Feedback Mechanisms in Biological and Social Systems*. Transactions of the Seventh Conference (New York: Josiah Macy, Jr., Foundation, 1950), pp. 237–249.

[62] Andrew Curry, "The Revitalization of Language in Chronic Schizophrenia," *American Journal of Psychotherapy* (1963), 17:45–53.

[63] Clark E. Moustakas, *Children in Play Therapy: A Key to Understanding Normal and Disturbed Emotions* (New York: McGraw-Hill Book Company, 1953), p. 67.

[64] Even in Hitler's Auschwitz annihilation camp the place of massacre, the crematorium, "had the word *Bath* written over its doors." Victor E. Frankl, *From Death-Camp to Existentialism* (Boston: Beacon Press, 1959), p. 10. The same in *Man's Search for Meaning—An Introduction to Logotherapy* (New York: Washington Square Press, Inc., 1963).

NOTES FOR PART TWO
The Psychological Approach

[1] G. Herdan, *Language as Choice and Chance* (Groningen: Nordhoff N.V., 1956).

[2] Norbert Wiener, *The Human Use of Human Beings: Cybernetics and Society* (Garden City, N. Y.: Doubleday, Anchor Books, 1950), p. 11.

[3] Ludwig Binswanger, *Sigmund Freud: Reminiscences of a Friendship* (New York: Grune & Stratton, Inc., 1957). F. Schmidl, "Sigmund Freud and Ludwig Binswanger," *Psychoanalytic Quarterly* (1959), 28:40–58.

[4] Theodore Thass-Thienemann, "Oedipus and the Sphinx: The Linguistic Approach to Unconscious Fantasies," *Psychoanalytic Review* (1957), 44:40–73.

[5] Berkeley said the same concerning language: "Whatever ideas I consider, I shall endeavour to take them bare and naked into my view, keeping out of my thoughts so far as I am able, those names which long and constant use have so strictly united with them." *Treatise Concerning the Principles of Human Understanding*, 1710.

[6] "The Concept of a Normal Mind," in Ernest Jones, *Papers on Psycho-Analysis*, 1912, 5th ed. (Baltimore, Md.: Williams & Wilkins, 1948), pp. 201–217.

[7] E. E. Southard, "On the Application of Grammatical Categories to the Analysis of Delusions," *The Philosophical Review* (1916), 25:445–450; and "On Descriptive Analysis of Manifest Delusions from the Subject's Point of View," *The Journal of Abnormal Psychology* (1916), 11:189–202. The distinguished author wanted to shed light upon psychopathology with the help of grammar. What he really did was to shed light upon grammar with the help of psychopathology. His promising researches found no followers.

[8] Ralph R. Greenson, "The Psychology of Apathy," *Psychoanalytic Quarterly* (1949), 18:290–302.

[9] Sigmund Freud, "The Psychopathology of Everyday Life," 1901, *Standard Edition*, Vol. 6.

[10] *Language and Thought in Schizophrenia*, edited by J. S. Kasanin (Berkeley, Calif.: University of California Press, 1944). Alfred Storch, *The Primitive Archaic Forms of Inner Experiences and Thought in Schizophrenia* (New York and Washington: Nervous and Mental Disease Monograph Series, No. 36, 1924). The most comprehensive presentation now is J. Bobon, *Psychopathologie de l'Expression* (Paris: Masson, 1962).

[11] Eva Balken and Jules H. Masserman, "The Language of Phantasies of Patients with Conversion Hysteria, Anxiety State and Obsessive-Compulsive Neuroses," *The Journal of Psychology* (1940), 10:75–86. See also Jules H. Masserman, "Language Be-

havior and Dynamic Psychiatry," *International Journal of Psycho-Analysis* (1944), 25:1–8.

[12] Merton M. Gill and Margaret Brenman, *Hypnosis and Related States: Psychoanalytic Studies in Regression* (New York: International Universities Press, 1961), pp. 352–354.

[13] Marcel Proust, *Jean Santeuil* (New York: Dell Publishing Co., Inc., Laurel Editions, 1961), p. 467.

[14] Sándor Ferenczi, "The Further Development of an Active Therapy in Psychoanalysis, 1920," in *Further Contributions to the Theory and Technique of Psychoanalysis* (New York: Basic Books, Inc., 1960), p. 260.

[15] Joseph Breuer and Sigmund Freud, *Studies in Hysteria,* translated and edited by James Strachey and Anna Freud (New York: Basic Books, Inc., 1957; also Boston, Mass.: Beacon Press, 1950).

[16] Harry Stack Sullivan, *The Inter-Personal Theory of Psychiatry* (New York: W. W. Norton & Company, Inc., 1955).

[17] Mark Kanzer: "The Communicative Function of the Dream," *International Journal of Psycho-Analysis* (1955), 36:260–266.

[18] Ralph R. Greenson, "The Mother-Tongue and the Mother," *International Journal of Psycho-Analysis* (1950), 31:18–23.

[19] Joseph Breuer and Sigmund Freud, *Studies in Hysteria* (Boston, Mass.: Beacon Press, 1950), pp. 16–17.

[20] Erwin Stengel, "On Learning a New Language," *International Journal of Psycho-Analysis* (1939), 20:471–476; also Edith Buxbaum, "The Role of a Second Language in the Formation of Ego and Superego," *Psychoanalytic Quarterly* (1949), 18:279–289.

[21] Lawrence S. Kubie, "The Unconscious Levels of Symbolic Functions," in *Neurotic Distortion of the Creative Process* (New York: Farrar and Straus, Noonday Press, 1961), pp. 26–52.

[22] For one of the first insights into the psychology of repetition, see Søren Kierkegaard, *Repetition: An Essay in Experimental Psychology,* translated by Walter Lowrie (Princeton, N. J.: Princeton University Press, 1946).

[23] Phyllis Greenacre, "Experience of Awe in Childhood," *The Psychoanalytic Study of the Child* (1956), 11:9–30.

[24] Lawrence S. Kubie: "The Repetitive Core of Neurosis," *Psychoanalytic Quarterly* (1941), 10:24–43.

[25] Anton Marty, *Untersuchungen zur Grundlage der allgemeinen Grammatik und Sprachphilosophie*, Vol. I, 1908; Vol. II, *Nachgelassene Schriften*, Herausg. von Otto Funke (Bern: Francke, 1951).

[26] George Berkeley, *A New Theory of Vision and Other Writings* (New York: E. P. Dutton & Co., Inc., Everyman's Library, 1922).

[27] Erwin W. Straus, "The Upright Posture," *Psychiatric Quarterly* (1952), 26:529–561.

[28] Martin Heidegger, "On the Grammar and Etymology of the Word Being," in *An Introduction to Metaphysics* (Garden City, N. Y.: Doubleday, Anchor Books, 1961), pp. 43–77.

[29] Gabriel Marcel, *Being and Having* (London: Dacre, 1949). Another approach by Jean-Paul Sartre, "Doing and Having," in *Being and Nothingness: An Essay on Phenomenological Ontology* (New York: Washington Square Press, Inc., 1966), pp. 682–754.

[30] E. Mogk, "Freyr," in Johannes Hoops, *Reallexikon der Germanischen Altertumskunde* (Strassburg: Trübner, 1913), 2:91–93.

[31] The inscription reads: DEO MARTI THINGSO; see Otto Siebs, "Thins und die Alaisiagen," *Zeitschrift für deutsche Philologie* (1891), 24:433–456.

[32] Maurice Bloomfield, "On Adaptation of Suffixes in Congeneric Classes of Substantives," *American Journal of Philology* (1891), 12:1–29. Also: "On Assimilation and Adaptation in Congeneric Classes of Words," *American Journal of Philology* (1895), 14:409–434.

[33] Hanns Oertel and Edward P. Morris, "An Examination of Theories Regarding the Nature and Origin of Indo-European Inflection," *Harvard Studies in Classical Philology* (1905), 16:63–122.

[34] F. A. Woods, "Rime-Words and Rime-Ideas," *Indogermanische Forschungen* (1907), 12:133–171.

[35] Edmund D. Cressmann, *The Semantics of -mentum, -bulum, and -culum*, Bulletin of the University of Kansas, *Humanistic Studies*, Vol. I, No. 4 (Lawrence, Kansas: University of Kansas, 1915).

[36] Hermann Güntert, *Über Reimwortbildungen im Arischen und Altgriechischen: Eine Sprachwissenschaftliche Untersuchung* (Heidelberg: Winter, 1914).

37 Theodore Reik, *Ritual* (New York: Farrar, Straus, 1946).

38 Lawrence Abt and Leopold Bellak, *Projective Psychology: Clinical Approaches to the Total Personality* (New York: Alfred A. Knopf, Inc., 1950). Harold H. Anderson and Gladys L. Anderson, *An Introduction to Projective Techniques* (New York: Prentice-Hall, Inc., 1951).

39 Sigmund Freud's *The Interpretation of Dreams* appeared in 1900. First English translation by A. A. Brill (New York: The Macmillan Company, 1912); a new translation by James Strachey (New York: Basic Books, Inc., 1960), p. 608. See also *Standard Edition*, Vols. 4–5, same pagination. See also Robert Fliess, *The Revival of Interest in the Dream: A Critical Study of Post-Freudian Psychoanalytic Contributions* (New York: International Universities Press, 1953).

40 Otto Jespersen, *Language: Its Nature, Development and Origin* (New York: The Macmillan Company, 1949), p. 307.

41 C. D. Buck, *loc. cit.*, p. XIV.

42 Otto Jespersen, *loc. cit.*, p. 316.

43 Hanns Oertel, *Lectures on the Study of Language* (New York: Scribner's & Sons, 1901), p. 307.

44 "Interpretation of Dreams," *Standard Edition*, 4:530.

45 Selwyn Gurney Champion, *Racial Proverbs* (New York: The Macmillan Company, 1938), p. 213.

46 "Interpretation of Dreams," *loc. cit.*, p. 530.

47 Hanns Oertel, *Lectures on the Study of Language* (New York: Scribner's & Sons, 1901), p. 306.

48 C. G. Jung first published his word association studies in 1904 in German: *Diagnostische Assoziationsstudien* (Leipzig: Barth, 1904). English translation: *Studies in Word-Association*, authorized translation by M. D. Eder (New York: Moffat, Yard & Co., 1919). A further step was made by G. H. Kent and A. J. Rosanoff, "A Study of Association in Insanity," *American Journal of Insanity* (1910), 67:37–96, 317–390. See also Ludwig Binswanger, "On the Psycho-galvanic Phenomenon in Association Experiment," in Jung, *Studies in Word-Association*, pp. 446–530.

49 The significance of the rhyme as a formative element in the development of language was pointed out by Hermann Güntert,

Über Reimwortbildungen im Arischem und Altgriechischen: Eine Sprachwissenschaftliche Untersuchung (Heidelberg: Winter, 1914).

⁵⁰ Edward Sapir, "A Study in Phonetic Symbolism," *Journal of Experimental Psychology* (1929), 12:225–239. S. S. Newman, "Further Experiments in Phonemic Symbolism," *American Journal of Psychology* (1933), 45:53–75. L. K. Davis, "Sounds in Language," *Journal of Nervous and Mental Diseases* (1938), 88:491–500.

⁵¹ Emil Kraepelin, *Dementia Praecox and Paraphrenia*, translated by R. M. Barclay (Edinburgh, 1919), p. 63.

⁵² Martin Damstra, "The Phonetic Associative Element in Thought-Development and in Thought-Imagination in the Dream," *Psychiatric Quarterly* (1954), 28:24–26. Otto Isakower, "Spoken Words in Dreams, a Preliminary Communication," *Psychoanalytic Quarterly* (1954), 25:1–6.

⁵³ Ludwig Pfandl, "Der Narzissbegriff: Versuch einer Neuen Deutung," *Imago* (1935), 21:279–310. Also Géza Róheim, "Spiegelzauber," *Imago* (1917–1919), 5:63–120.

⁵⁴ A laboratory projective test on echo has been developed by B. F. Skinner, "The Verbal Summator and a Method for the Study of Latent Speech," *Journal of Psychology* (1936), 2:71–107.

⁵⁵ Henry Lanz, *The Physical Basis of Rime: An Essay on the Aesthetics of Sound* (Stanford, Calif.: Stanford University Press, 1931).

⁵⁶ "Interpretation of Dreams," *Standard Edition*, 4:277.

⁵⁷ Bertram D. Lewin, *Dreams and the Uses of Regression* (New York: International Universities Press, 1958), pp. 20–21. With permission of the author.

⁵⁸ Eduard Schwyzer, "Die Bezeichnung des Zahnfleisches in den Indogermanischen Sprachen," *Zeitschrift für Vergleichende Sprachforschung* (1929–1930), 57:256–275.

⁵⁹ "Interpretation of Dreams," *Standard Edition*, 5:373–377.

⁶⁰ "Interpretation of Dreams," *Standard Edition*, p. 241. See also Allan Roos, "Psychoanalytical Study of a Typical Dream," *Psychoanalytic Quarterly* (1960), 29:153–174.

⁶¹ "The Theme of the Three Caskets," 1913, *Collected Papers*, IV:244–256. *Standard Edition*, 12:291–301.

418

[62] This linguistic way of interpreting literature is not the usual procedure. A reference to such an interpretation is the remark by S. Ferenczi stating: "Finally I quote a verbal statement of the psychoanalyst Dr. Hanns Sachs according to which the words in which the poets clothe their ideas often indicate the deeper unconscious source of those ideas." *Further Contributions to the Theory and Technique of Psychoanalysis* (New York: Basic Books, Inc., 1960), (London: The International Psycho-Analytical Library, No. 11, 1926), p. 403. An approximation of this way of interpretation can be found in the studies of Leo Spitzer even though he is opposed in principle to psychoanalysis. Some of his papers were published in English: *Essays in Historical Semantics* (New York: S. F. Vanni, 1947); *A Method of Interpreting Literature* (Northampton, Mass.: Smith College, 1949); *Linguistics and Literary History: Essays in Stylistics* (Princeton, N. J.: Princeton University Press, 1948).

[63] K. R. Eisler, "Further Remarks on the Theme of the Three Caskets," in *The Psychiatrist and the Dying Patient* (New York: International Universities Press, 1955), pp. 16–29.

[64] Melanie Klein, *The Psychoanalysis of Children* (New York: Grove Press, 1960), p. 198.

NOTES FOR PART THREE
The Symbolism of the Body

[1] A general introduction to these problems: J. H. Van Den Berg, *The Phenomenological Approach to Psychiatry: An Introduction to Recent Phenomenological Psychopathology* (Springfield, Ill.: Charles C Thomas, 1955).

[2] Paul Schilder, *The Image and Appearance of the Human Body* (London: Kegan Paul, 1935; new ed.—New York: International Universities Press, 1950).

[3] L. C. Kolb, *The Painful Phantom: Psychology, Physiology and Treatment* (Springfield, Ill.: Charles C Thomas, 1954).

4 Mrs. Malcolm Peabody in New York *Herald Tribune,* June 16, 1964.

5 Arthur Burton, "The Quest for the Golden Mean—A Study in Schizophrenia," in *Psychotherapy of Psychoses,* edited by A. Burton (New York: Basic Books, Inc., 1961), pp. 172–207. See also: A. M. Ostfeld, L. F. Chapman, H. Goodell and H. G. Wolff, "Studies in Headache: Summary of Evidence Concerning a Noxious Agent Active Locally during Migraine Headache," *Psychosomatic Medicine* (1957), 19:199–208.

6 Paul Schilder, "Psychoanalysis of Space," *International Journal of Psycho-Analysis* (1935), 16:280.

7 Eric Wittkover and Brian Russell, *Emotional Factors in Skin Disease,* A Psychosomatic Medicine Monograph (New York: Paul B. Hoeber, Inc., 1954). A recent survey of literature in Russell E. Mason, *Internal Perception and Bodily Functioning* (New York: International Universities Press, 1961), pp. 195–203.

8 F. A. Pattie, "The Production of Blisters by Hypnotic Suggestion," *Journal of Abnormal and Social Psychology* (1947), 36:62–72.

9 Helen Merrell Lynd, *On Shame and the Search for Identity* (New York: Harcourt, Brace & World, Inc., 1958).

10 Felix Deutsch and William F. Murphy, *The Clinical Interview,* Vol. I. *Diagnosis* (New York: International Universities Press, 1955), pp. 257–319. See the chapter on "Atopic Dermatitis" with extensive bibliography.

11 L. M. Baker and W. M. Taylor, "An Apparatus for Recording Changes in Skin-Temperature," *American Journal of Psychology* (1953), 66:124–125.

12 M. Sulzberger, *Dermatologic Allergy* (Springfield, Ill.: Charles C Thomas, 1940); also Mason, *loc. cit.,* p. 202.

13 Pierre Lacombe, "A Special Mechanism of Pathological Weeping," *Psychoanalytic Quarterly* (1958), 27:246–251. Also Phyllis Greenacre, "Pathological Weeping," *Psychoanalytic Quarterly* (1945), 14:62–75.

14 Excellent interpretations of the various words referring to the Self in Richard Braxton Onians, *The Origins of European Thought about the Body, the Mind, the Soul, the World, Time and Fate— New Interpretations of Greek, Roman and Kindred Evidence also*

of Some Jewish and Christian Beliefs (Cambridge: University Press, 1954), p. 198.

[15] *Iliad* 6:211, also 20:241; *Odyssey* 16:300.

[16] Jules P. Miller, "The Psychology of Blushing," *International Journal of Psycho-Analysis* (1965), 46:188–199.

[17] Excellent treatment of the various implications of these words and concepts by Onians, *loc. cit.* See also: A. Feleky, "The Influence of Emotions on Respiration," *Journal of Experimental Psychology* (1916), 1:218–241.

[18] T. H. Holmes, H. Goodell, S. Wolf, and H. G. Wolff, *The Nose: An Experimental Study of Reactions Within the Nose in Human Subjects during Varying Life Experiences* (Springfield, Ill.: Charles C Thomas, 1950). On nasal hyperfunction, T. H. Holmes and H. G. Wolff, "Life Situations and Nasal Disease," *Psychosomatic Medicine* (1951), 13:71–82.

[19] The case of Ellen West in *Existence: A New Dimension in Psychiatry and Psychology*, edited by Rollo May, Ernest Angel and Henry F. Ellenberger (New York: Basic Books, Inc., 1958), pp. 237–364.

[20] Marion Milner, "Communication of Primary Sensual Experience," *International Journal of Psycho-Analysis* (1956), 37:278–281.

[21] *Odyssey* 17:539–547.

[22] In Greek, *epoikiston gemos*, for they were carrying their own *splangchna* in their hands.

[23] Herman Nunberg, "The Feeling of Guilt," *Psychoanalytic Quarterly* (1934), 3:591. See also his *Principles of Psychoanalysis: Their Application to the Neuroses* (New York: International Universities Press, 1955), p. 164.

[24] Franz Alexander, "The Influence of Psychologic Factors upon Gastro-Intestinal Disturbances," *Psychoanalytic Quarterly* (1934), 3:501–583; and Silvan S. Tomkins, *Contemporary Psychopathology: A Source Book* (Cambridge: University Press, 1947), pp. 122–149.

[25] W. C. Alvarez, *Nervousness, Indigestion and Pain* (New York: Paul B. Hoeber, Inc., 1934).

[26] Contradicting Alvarez see Franz Alexander, "Fundamental

Concepts of Psychosomatic Research: Psychogenesis, Conversion, Specificity," *Psychosomatic Medicine* (1934), 3:205–210; "Treatment of a Case of Peptic Ulcer and Personality Disorder," *Psychosomatic Medicine* (1947), 9:321–330.

[27] Walter Porzig, "Daimon," *Indogermanische Forschungen* (1923), 41:171–173.

[28] Angel Sarma, "On the Pathogenesis of Peptic Ulcer," *International Journal of Psycho-Analysis* (1950), 31:63.

[29] Freud in reporting on "butterfly dreams" did not point out the verbal fact that the Greek *psyche* means both "butterfly" and "soul." *Interpretation of Dreams, loc. cit.*, p. 254.

[30] The verbal instances were contradicted by clinical observations. See Eric Wittkover, "Studies on the Influence of Emotions on the Functions of the Organs," *Journal of Mental Sciences* (1935), 81:533–682. He observed that joy, sorrow, anxiety stimulate the secretion of the bile but anger almost inhibits it. See also, Mason, *loc. cit.*, p. 225.

[31] I. P. Stevenson and H. G. Wolff, "Life Situations and Bronchial Mucus," *Psychosomatic Medicine* (1949), 11:223–227.

[32] Christ Rogge, "Homerisch *phrēn, phrenes* und Verwandtes in neuer medizinischer und sprachpsychologischer Beleuchtung: Ein Stück aus der Urgeschichte menschlicher Denkanschauung," *Archiv für die gesamte Psychologie* (1927), 58:307–324.

[33] J. C. Flügel, "A Note on the Phallic Significance of the Tongue and of Speech," *International Journal of Psycho-Analysis* (1925), 6:209–215, emphasizes the equation of "tongue" and "speech" and "sexual power," consequently the equation of "dumbness" with "castration, impotence."

[34] Robert Plank, "Seeing the Salamander," *The Psychoanalytic Study of the Child* (1957), 12:379–398.

[35] Paul Schilder, "Psychoanalysis of Space," *International Journal of Psycho-Analysis* (1935), 16:280.

[36] Henry Harper Hart, "The Eye in Symbol and Symptom," *Psychoanalytic Review* (1949), 36:1–21. Daniel A. Huebsch, "Psychoanalysis of Eye Disturbances," *Psychoanalytic Review* (1931), 18:166–180.

[37] Lawrence S. Kubie, "Communication between Sane and Insane: Hypnosis," *Cybernetics, Circular Causal and Feedback*

Mechanism in Biological and Social Systems Transactions of the Seventh Conference. (New York: Josiah Macy, Jr., Foundation, 1950), pp. 92–133.

38 Sigmund Freud, "An Infantile Neurosis," 1918, *Collected Papers*, 3:505. *Standard Edition*, 17:34.

39 Marguerite A. Sechehaye, *Symbolic Realization: A New Method of Psychotherapy Applied to a Case of Schizophrenia* (New York: International Universities Press, 1951), p. 152.

40 Berta Bornstein, "Clinical Notes on Child Analysis," *The Psychoanalytic Study of the Child* (1945), 1:163.

41 Harries Glessner Creel, Chang Tsung-Ch'ien and R. C. Rudolph, *Literary Chinese by the Inductive Method* (Chicago, Ill.: University of Chicago Press, 1946), s.v. *jealousy*.

42 L. Scartazzini, *A Companion to Dante* (London: Macmillan & Co., Ltd., 1893), p. 201.

43 Henry J. Cadbury, "The Single Eye," *Harvard Theological Review* (1954), 47:69–74.

44 Frederick Thomas Elworthy, *The Evil Eye: An Account of the Ancient and Widespread Superstition* (London, J. Murray, 1895).

45 Theodore Thass-Thienemann, "The Single Eye," *Gordon Review* (1955), 1:19–23.

46 *Interpretation of Dreams*, loc. cit., p. 187.

47 *The Bestiary: A Book of Beasts* (Being a translation from a Latin bestiary of the twelfth century), edited by T. H. White. (New York: G. P. Putnam's Sons, 1954), pp. 105–107.

48 Hermann Junker, "Der Sehende und Blinde Gott," *Sitzungsberichte der Bayrischen Akademie der Wissenschaften*: Phil.-Hist. Abt. Vol. 7, München, 1942.

49 Rudolf Bultmann, "Zur Geschichte der Lichtsymbolik im Altertum," *Philologus* (1945), 97:1–35.

50 Karl Abraham, "Restriction and Transformation of Scoptophilia in Psycho-Neurotics with Remarks on Analogous Phenomena in Folk-Psychology," 1913, *Selected Papers* (New York: Basic Books, Inc., 1960), pp. 169–234. See also Sigmund Freud, "Psychogenic Visual Disturbance According to Psycho-Analytical Con-

ceptions," 1910, *Collected Papers* 2:105–112; *Standard Edition* 11:211–218. Sándor Ferenczi, "On Eye Symbolism," 1913, *Sex in Psychoanalysis* (New York: Basic Books, Inc., 1950), pp. 270–275.

[51] Sigmund Freud, "Psycho-Analysis: Notes upon an Autobiographical Account of a Case of Paranoia," *Collected Papers* 3:438–439; *Standard Edition* 12:53. Freud did not take into consideration the fact that Schreber was at this time in the *Sonnen-stein* Asylum.

[52] Berta Bornstein, "Analysis of a Phobic Child," *The Psychoanalytic Study of the Child* (1950–1953), 3–4:181–225, p. 193.

[53] Paul Schilder, *The Image and Appearance of the Human Body* (New York: International Universities Press, 1950). Otto Zauner, "Die Romanischen Namen der Körperteile," *Romanische Forschungen*, 14:339–430. W. Meyer-Lübke, "Neubenennungen von Körperteilen im Romanischen," *Wörter und Sachen* (1921), 12:1–16. W. T. Arnoldson, *Parts of the Body in Older Germanic* (Dissertation: University of Chicago, 1915).

[54] Otto Fenichel, "Outline of Clinical Psychoanalysis," *Psychoanalytic Quarterly* (1932), 1:309.

[55] H. Aigremont (pseudonym of Siegmar Baron von Schultze-Galléra), "Beiträge zur Hand und Finger Symbolik und Erotik," *Anthropophyteia* (1913), 10:314–329.

[56] Theodore Thass-Thienemann, "Left-handed Writing: A Study in the Psychoanalysis of Language," *Psychoanalytic Review* (1955), 42:239–261.

[57] The small child is ambidextrous. See the chapter "With both Hands," in Wolfgang Grozinger, *Scribbling, Drawing, Painting: The Early Forms of the Child's Pictorial Creativeness* (New York: Frederick A. Praeger, Inc., 1955), pp. 48–57. A. Gesell and L. B. Ames, "The Development of Handedness," *Journal of Genetic Psychology* (1947), 70:155–175.

[58] Konrad Blersch, "Die Rechts-links Theorie," in *Wesen und Entstehung des Sexus im Denken der Antike. Tübinger Beiträge zur Altertumwissenschaft,* Heft 29 (Stuttgart-Berlin: Kohlhammer, 1937), pp. 41–58.

[59] William F. Murphy, "Character, Trauma and Sensory Perception," *International Journal of Psycho-Analysis* (1958), 39:555–568.

[60] Sigmund Freud, "Leonardo da Vinci and a Memory of His

424

Childhood," 1910, *Standard Edition*, 9:71. The drawing is reproduced in *Standard Edition*, 11:71.

61 It is of psychological interest to observe the linguists in a test situation. They admit matters of fact reluctantly, hesitantly, if they do not like these facts opposed to their philosophy. So A. Meillet asks: "On se demande dès lors si le nom *genu* de 'genou' ne devrait pas être rapporté à la racine de *gignō*," Ernout-Meillet, s. v. *genu*. No answer is given to this question. Hermann Hirt says: "Wenn wir das Wort 'Knie' untersuchen, so bleibt ein Stamm *gen-*, und dieser bedeutet auch 'erzeugen, gebären.' Ein Zusammenhang scheint mir nicht vorzuliegen. Und doch ist er möglich." *Indogermanische Grammatik* (Heidelberg: Winter, 1921), Vol. I, p. 162. He does not explain either how this connection may be possible. H. Güntert says concerning the association between "knee" and "generation" that there must be a missing link, and the "node of the grass" (Knoten am Halm) was the transitory meaning (Zwischenbedeutung). "Weiteres zum Begriff Winckel im ursprünglichen Denken," *Wörter und Sachen* (Heidelberg: Winter, 1927), 10:124–142. J. B. Hofmann states that the connection between "beget" and "know" is possible but "knee" hardly can be brought in this context: "Dagegen ist *genu* in der Bedeutung kaum zu vermitteln." Walde-Hofmann, s.v. *gignō*. Hermann Stieglecker ("Zeugen, Wissen und Knie im Semitischen und Indogermanischen," *Anthropos* [1927], pp. 1000–1003), admits as a matter of fact that some coherence must exist. H. A. Bunker and B. D. Levin, "A Psychoanalytic Notation on the Root GN, KN, CN," in George B. Wilbur and Warren Muensterberg, *Psychoanalysis and Culture* (New York: International Universities Press, 1951), pp. 363–367. Excellent in philological data is the chapter written on "knee," by R. B. Onians, *The Origin of European Thought* (Cambridge, Mass.: University Press, 1954), pp. 174–186. Pertinent material is presented by J. Loth, "Le mot désignant le genou au sense de génération chez les Celtes, les Germains, les Slaves, les Assyriens," *Revue Celtique* (1923), 40:143–152. P. Thieme, "Über einige Benennungen des Nachkommen," *Kuhn's Zeitschrift für vergleichende Sprachforschung auf dem Gebiete der Indogermanischen Sprachen* (1939), 66:130–144.

62 Mortimer Ostow, "The Illusory Reduplication of Body Parts," *Psychoanalytic Quarterly* (1958), 17:98–100.

63 Hyman S. Lippman, "The Use of Dreams in Psychiatric Work

with Children," *The Psychoanalytic Study of the Child* (1945), 1:233–245.

[64] Albert J. Lubin, "A Feminine Moses," *International Journal of Psycho-Analysis* (1958), 39:535–546.

[65] Alfred M. Freedman and Lauretta Bender, "When the Childhood Schizophrenic Grows Up," *American Journal of Orthopsychiatry* (1957), 27:553–565.

[66] A somewhat different psychoanalytical interpretation is given by Theodore Reik, "Psychoanalytic Studies of the Bible: Exegesis I—The Wrestling of Jacob," in *Dogma and Compulsion: Psychoanalytic Studies of Myths and Religions* (New York: International Universities Press, 1957), pp. 229–251.

[67] The misunderstanding of unconscious fantasies is evident in Eduard Schwyzer, "Der Götter Knie—Abrahams Schoss," in *Antidoron: Festschrift für Jakob Wackernagel* (Göttingen: Van der Hoeck and Ruprecht, 1924), pp. 283–293.

[68] "Knee," *Wörter und Sachen* (1927), 10:123.

[69] Sándor Lorand and Sándor Feldman, "The Symbolism of Teeth in Dreams," *International Journal of Psycho-Analysis* (1955), 36:145–160.

[70] Sándor Lorand and Sándor Feldman, *loc. cit.*

NOTES FOR
Addenda

[1] R. M. Evans, *An Introduction to Color* (New York: John Wiley & Sons, 1948). The classic work on colors is still David Katz, *The World of Colours* (London: Kegan Paul, Trench, Trübner & Co., 1935).

[2] Birren Faber, *Color Psychology and Color Therapy* (New York: McGraw-Hill Book Company, 1950).

[3] Albert S. Gatschet, "Adjectives of Color in Indian Languages," *The American Naturalist* (1879), 13:475–485. Same: "Farben-

benennungen in Nordamerikanischen Sprachen," *Zeitschrift für Ethnologie* (1879), 11:295–302.

4 Roger W. Brown and Eric H. Lenneberg, "A Study in Language and Cognition," *The Journal of Abnormal and Social Psychology* (1954), 49:454–462.

5 Barbara Seward, *The Symbolic Rose* (New York: Columbia University Press, 1960).

6 Louis Cheskin, *Colors: What They Can Do for You* (New York: Liveright Publishing Corp., 1947).

7 K. E. Goetz, "Waren die Römer blaublind?" *Archiv für lateinische Lexikographie und Grammatik* (1906), 14:75–88.

8 A. Meillet, *Linguistique Historique et Linguistique Générale* (Paris: Champion, 1948).

9 *The Shorter Oxford Dictionary*, s.v. *lick*.

10 Gaston Bachelard, *The Psychoanalysis of Fire*, translated by Alan C. Ross (Boston, Mass.: Beacon Press, 1964).

11 James J. Gibson, *The Perception of the Visual World* (Boston, Mass.: Houghton Mifflin Company, 1950). Also, *The Senses Considered as Perceptual Systems* (Boston, Mass.: Houghton Mifflin Company, 1966).

12 *The Interpretation of Dreams*, *loc. cit.*, pp. 37 and 273. Scherner, *Das Leben des Traumes* (Berlin: Heinrich Schindler, 1861), long before Strümpell, clearly recognized that the "flying dreams" must have their origin in the somatic sensation of the lungs; they have two "wings." Scherner has been criticized for this interpretation by Wilhelm Wundt, *Grundzüge der Physiologischen Psychologie*, 4th ed. (Leipzig: Engelmann, 1893), p. 537.

13 Jacob A. Arlow, "Notes on Oral Symbolism," *Psychoanalytic Quarterly* (1955), 24:67.

14 Ernst Cassirer, "The Linguistic Development of the Concept of Number," in *The Philosophy of Symbolic Forms* (New Haven, Conn.: Yale University Press, 1953), 1:227–249.

15 Eric Temple Bell, *The Magic of Numbers* (New York: McGraw-Hill Book Company, 1946).

16 William Dwight Whitney, *Language and the Study of Language* (New York: Scribner & Co., 1868), p. 274.

[17] Otto Jespersen, *The Philosophy of Grammar* (New York: Henry Holt and Company, 1934), p. 208.

[18] W. J. McGee, *Primitive Numbers,* Bureau of American Ethnology—19th Annual Report, 1897–1898 (Washington: Government Printing Office, 1900), pp. 825–851.

[19] A. Rauschmaier, *Über den figürlichen Gebrauch der Zahlen im Altfranzösischen,* Münchener Beiträge zur Romanischen und Englischen Philologie III (Erlangen-Leipzig: Deichert-Böhme Verlag, 1892).

[20] M. Wertheimer, "Numbers and Numerical Concepts in Primitive Peoples," in *A Source Book of Gestalt Psychology,* edited by W. D. Ellis (New York: Humanities Press, 1950).

[21] George A. Miller, "The Magical Number Seven, Plus or Minus Two: Some Limits on Our Capacity for Processing Information," *The Psychological Review* (1956), 63:81–97. It is a study in information theory. In Latin *computātor* means "compulsive reckoner."

[22] Edward Sapir, "A Study in Phonetic Symbolism," *Journal of Experimental Psychology* (1929), 12:225–239. S. S. Newman, "Further Experiments in Phonetic Symbolism," *American Journal of Psychology* (1933), 45:53–75.

[23] Margareth Eberhardt, "A Study of Phonetic Symbolism of Deaf Children," *Psychological Monographs* (1940), 52:23–42.

[24] Jean Piaget, *The Child's Conception of the World* (Paterson, N. J.: Littlefield, Adams & Company, 1963), p. 126. See the chapter on "Nominal Realism," pp. 61–87.

[25] Heinz Werner and Bernard Kaplan, *Symbol Formation: An Organismic-Developmental Approach to Language and the Expression of Thought* (New York: John Wiley & Sons, 1963), pp. 100, 128, *passim.* H. Wissemann, *Untersuchungen zur Onomatopoiie. I. Teil: Die Sprachpsychologischen Versuche* (Heidelberg: Winter, 1954). H. Müller, *Experimentelle Beiträge zur Analyse des Verhältnisses von Laut und Sinn* (Berlin: Müller & Kiepenheuer, 1935).

[26] Otto Jespersen, "Sound Symbolism," in *Language: Its Nature, Development and Origin* (New York: The Macmillan Company, 1949), pp. 396–411. "Symbolic Value of the Vowel *i,*" in *Selected Writings* (London: George Allen & Unwin, 1962), pp. 557–577.

Also: M. Chastaing, "Le Symbolism des Voyelles: Significations des *i*," *Journal de Psychologie* (1958), 55:403–423, 461–483. On the symbolism of sound gemination: André Martinet, *La Gemination Consonantique d'Origin Expressive dans les Langues Germanique* (Copenhagen, Munksgaard, 1937).

27 Roger Brown, *Words and Things* (Glencoe, Ill.: Free Press, Inc., 1958), p. 129. Also Roger Brown, A. H. Black and A. E. Horowitz, "Phonetic Symbolism in Natural Languages," *The Journal of Abnormal and Social Psychology* (1955), 50:388–393.

28 Richard Payne Knight, *An Analytical Inquiry into the Principles of Taste*, 3d ed. (London, 1806).

29 A. A. Brill, "The Sense of Smell in Neurosis and Psychosis," *Psychoanalytic Quarterly* (1932), 1:7–42. John Pratt, "Notes on the Unconscious Significance of Perfume," *International Journal of Psycho-Analysis* (1942), 23:80–83. Paul Friedman, "The Nose: Some Psychological Reflections," *The American Imago* (1951), 8:337–350. Also: "Some Observations on the Sense of Smell," *Psychoanalytic Quarterly* (1959), 28:307–329. Leo Weisgerber, "Der Geruchsinn in unseren Sprachen." *Indogermanische Forschungen* (1928), 46:121–150.

30 E. Nida, *Morphology: The Descriptive Analysis of Words* (Ann Arbor, Mich.: University of Michigan Press, 1949), p. 158.

31 Isak Dinesen, *Seven Gothic Tales* (New York: Modern Library, 1934). The quotation is from the Introduction by Dorothy Canfield.

32 Otto Fenichel, "The Dread of Being Eaten," *The Collected Papers*, First Series (New York: W. W. Norton & Company, Inc., 1953), pp. 158–159. Gert Heilbrunn, "The Basic Fear," *Journal of the American Psychoanalytical Association* (1955), 3:447–466.

33 Eugen Falstein, Sherman Feinstein, and Ilse Judas, "Anorexia Nervosa in the Small Child," *American Journal of Orthopsychiatry* (1956), 26:751–772.

34 Melitta Schmideberg, "Intellectual Inhibition and Disturbances in Eating," *International Journal of Psycho-Analysis* (1938), 19:17–22.

35 Jacob A. Arlow, "Notes on Oral Symbolism," *Psychoanalytic Quarterly* (1955), 24:69.

[36] Pierre Lacombe, "A Special Mechanism of Pathological Weeping," *Psychoanalytic Quarterly* (1958), 27:246–251.

[37] Rollo May, E. Angel, and H. F. Ellenberger, *Existence: A New Dimension in Psychiatry and Psychology* (New York: Basic Books, Inc., 1958), pp. 237–364.

[38] A few basic studies on food fantasies: Lillian Malcove, "Bodily Mutilation and Learning to Eat," *Psychoanalytic Quarterly* (1933), 2:557–561. A. Conrad, "The Attitude toward Food," *American Journal of Orthopsychiatry* (1937), 7:360–367. Editha Sterba, "An Important Factor in Eating Disturbances in Childhood," *Psychoanalytic Quarterly* (1941), 10:365–372. O. R. Lurie, "Psychological Factors Associated with Eating Difficulties in Children," *American Journal of Orthopsychiatry* (1941), 11:452–467. Edward Lehman, "Feeding Problems of Psychogenic Origin," *The Psychoanalytic Study of the Child* (1950), 3–4:461–488. Lowell S. Selling, "Behavior Problems of Eating," *American Journal of Orthopsychiatry* (1946), 15:163–169. Melitta Sperling, "Food Allergies and Conversion Hysteria," *Psychoanalytic Quarterly* (1953), 22:525–538.

[39] Emanuel Klein, "Psychoanalytic Aspects of School Problems," *The Psychoanalytic Study of the Child* (1949), 34:383.

[40] *New English Dictionary*, s.v. *pudding*.

[41] W. Ronald Fairbairn, "Nature and Aims of Treatment," *International Journal of Psycho-Analysis* (1958), 39:374–385.

[42] Dorothy W. Baruch and Hyman Niller, "Developmental Needs and Conflicts Revealed in Children's Art," *American Journal of Orthopsychiatry* (1952), 22:186–203.

[43] Kluge, *Etymologisches Wörterbuch*, s.v. *Kuchen*.

[44] John G. Bourke, *Scatological Rites of all Nations* (Washington: W. H. Lowdermilk, 1891).

[45] For clinical examples of scatophagia as a symbolic expression of mourning see: Karl Abraham, *Selected Papers* (New York: Basic Books, Inc., 1960), pp. 444–446. Norman O. Brown: *Life Against Death: The Psychoanalytical Meaning of History* (Middletown, Conn.: Wesleyan University Press, 1959), p. 300.

[46] Arnold H. Modell, "The Theoretical Implications of Hallucinatory Experiences in Schizophrenia," *Journal of the American Psychoanalytical Association* (1958), 6:442–480.

[47] Editha Sterba, "Analysis of Psychogenic Constipation in a Two-year-old Child," *The Psychoanalytic Study of the Child* (1950–1953), 3–4:237.

[48] Edward Lehman, "Feeding Problems of Psychogenic Origin," *The Psychoanalytic Study of the Child* (1950–1953), 3–4:477.

[49] Briand Bird, "Bisexual Meaning of Foreskin," *Journal of the American Psychoanalytic Association* (1958), 6:287–304.

[50] Paul Schilder, "Psychoanalysis of Space," *International Journal of Psycho-Analysis* (1935), 16:274–295. Gaston Bachelard, *The Poetics of Space,* translated by Maria Foles, foreword by Etienne Gilson (New York: The Orion Press, 1964).

[51] Ludwig Binswanger, "Dream and Existence," in *Being-in-the-World—Selected Papers,* translated with a critical introduction to his existential psychoanalysis (New York: Basic Books, Inc., 1963), pp. 222–248.

[52] Charles Baudelaire, "Le Gouffre," in *Les Fleurs du Mal* (Paris: Limited Editions Club, 1940).

[53] V. E. von Gebsattel, "Zur Frage der Depersonalisation," in *Prolegomena einer medizinischen Anthropologie* (Berlin-Göttingen-Heidelberg: Springer, 1954), pp. 18–46.

[54] S. Radhakrishnan, *The Principal Upanishads* (New York: Harper Brothers, 1953), p. 486.

[55] Some samples of the expanded psychoanalytical literature on "time": Ernest Jones, "Anal-erotic Character Traits, 1918," in *Papers on Psychoanalysis* (London: Baillière, Tindall & Cox, 1948), pp. 413–437. (He pointed out the periodic tensions of digestion.) S. Harnik, "Die triebhaft-affektiven Momente im Zeitgefühl," *Imago* (1925), 11:32–57. (He also points to the digestive system. The "father" Chronos is the "devourer" of time.) Marie Bonaparte, "Time and the Unconscious," *International Journal of Psycho-Analysis* (1940), 21:427–468. L. Dooley, "The Concept of Time in Defense of Ego Integrity," *Psychiatry* (1941), 4:13–25. Clarence P. Oberndorf, "Time—Its Relation to Reality and Purpose," *Psychoanalytic Review* (1943), 28:139–155. A. M. Merloo, "Father Time," *Psychiatric Quarterly* (1948), 22:587–608. (The father interferes with oedipal gratification.) E. Bergler and Géza Róheim, "Psychology of Time Perception," *Psychoanalytic Quarterly* (1946), 15:190–206. (Periodic separation from the nursing mother.) K. R. Eisler, "Time Experience and the Mechanism of

Isolation," *Psychoanalytic Review* (1952), 39:1–22. F. S. Cohn, "Time and the Ego," *Psychoanalytic Quarterly* (1957), 26:168–189. (Fight against time measuring and the idea of death.) Shelley Orgel, "On Time and Timelessness," *Journal of the American Psychoanalytical Association* (1965), 13:102–121. Besides the psychoanalytical approach, the concept of "time" is basic for the thinking of phenomenologists and existentialists. Edmund Husserl, *Vorlesungen zur Phänomenologie des inneren Zeitbewusstseins*, edited by Martin Heidegger (Halle: Niemeyer, 1928). Johannes Volkelt, *Phänomenologie und Metaphysik der Zeit* (München: C. H. Beck, 1925). Martin Heidegger, *Sein und Zeit* (Halle: Niemeyer, 1928; new edition, Tübingen: Neumarius, 1949). Eugène Minkowski, *Le Temps Vécu: Etudes Phenomenologiques et Psychopathologiques* (Paris: J. L. L. D'Artrey, 1933). *The Voices of Time,* J. T. Fraser, ed. (New York: George Braziller, 1966).

[56] *The Shorter Oxford English Dictionary,* s.v. *nick.*

[57] *The Confessions of St. Augustine,* introduction by Harold C. Gardiner (New York: Washington Square Press, Inc., 1960), Book II, p. 229.

[58] S. Radhakrishnan, *loc. cit.*

[59] *The Sacred Books of the East*—A General Index, edited by F. Max Müller (Oxford: Clarendon Press, 1910), p. 212.

[60] Theodore Thass-Thienemann, "Left-handed Writing: A Study in the Psychoanalysis of Language," *Psychoanalytic Review* (1955), 42:239–261.

[61] Lucretius, *De Rerum Natura,* with an English translation by W. H. D. Rouse; The Loeb Classical Library (Cambridge: University Press, 1953), 4:1272–1273.

[62] R. R. McMurry conducted a study on people buying fountain pens. His results indicated that the pen has become the body image of men. This is the reason why buyers "will pay up to fifteen dollars for a pen with an image particularly satisfying them even though a cheaper one might write just as well." Vance Packard, *The Hidden Persuaders* (New York: Pocket Books, Inc., 1958), p. 73.

[63] Sigmund Freud, "Inhibitions, Symptoms and Anxiety," 1926, *Standard Edition,* 20:89–90.

[64] *Anthropophyteia* 1905, 2:131; 1906, 3:52; 1907, 4:13.

[65] Selwin Gurney Champion, *Racial Proverbs* (New York: The Macmillan Company, 1938), p. 423.

[66] Theodor Birt, *Das Antike Buchwesen* (Berlin: Hertz, 1882), p. 17.

STANDARD DICTIONARIES

FOR GENERAL REFERENCE

Carl Darling Buck. *A Dictionary of the Selected Synonyms in the Principal Indo-European Languages: A Contribution to the History of Ideas.* Chicago and London: University of Chicago Press, 1949. Second impression, 1965.

Otto Schrader. *Reallexikon der Indogermanischen Alterstumskunde: Grundzüge einer Kultur-und Völkergeschichte Alteuropas.* Zweite vermehrte und umgearbeitete Auflage. Herausg. A. Nehring. Berlin and Leipzig: Walter de Gruyter & Co., 1917–1923.

FOR OLD TESTAMENT HEBREW

James Strong. *The Exhaustive Concordance of the Bible: Dictionaries of the Hebrew and Greek Words of the Original.* New York and Nashville: Abingdon-Cokesbury Press, 1894. Seventeenth printing, 1947.

FOR THE SANSKRIT, OLD INDISH

Manfred Mayrhofer. *Kurzgefasstes Etymologisches Wörterbuch des Altindischen*: A Concise Etymological Sanskrit Dictionary. Heidelberg: Winter, 1962–1964.

FOR CLASSIC GREEK

Henry George Liddell and Robert Scott. *A Greek-English*

Lexicon. New York: Harper & Brothers (since 1882 many augmented and revised editions).

Émile Boisacq. *Dictionnaire Etymologique de la Langue Greque,* 4th ed. Heidelberg: Winter, 1950.

Hjalmar Frisk. *Griechisches Etymologisches Wörterbuch.* Heidelberg: Winter, since 1960.

J. B. Hofmann. *Etymologisches Wörterbuch des Griechischen.* München: R. Oldenburg, 1950.

FOR CLASSIC LATIN

Harper's Latin Dictionary. New York: Harper & Brothers. Since 1877 many "revised, enlarged and in great part rewritten" editions. Oxford: Clarendon Press, 1965.

Alfred Ernout and A. Meillet. *Dictionnaire Etymologique de la Langue Latine. Histoire des Mots.* Paris: C. Klincksieck, 1932.

A. Walde. *Lateinisches Etymologisches Wörterbuch.* 3. neubearbeitete Auflage von J. B. Hofmann. Heidelberg: Winter, 1938–1956.

FOR LATE LATIN

A. Meyer-Lübke. *Romanisches Etymologisches Wörterbuch,* 3rd ed. Heidelberg: Winter, 1935.

FOR FRENCH

Ernest Gamillscheg. *Etymologisches Wörterbuch der Französischen Sprache.* Heidelberg: Winter, 1928.

FOR GERMAN

Friedrich Kluge. *Etymologisches Wörterbuch der Deutschen Sprache,* 17th revised ed. by W. Mitzka. Berlin: Walter de Gruyter & Co., 1957.

Hermann Paul. *Deutsches Wörterbuch.* 4th revised ed. by Karl Euling. Halle: Niemeyer, 1934.

FOR GOTHIC

Sigmund Feist. *Vergleichendes Wörterbuch der Gotischen Sprache,* 3rd ed. Leiden: E. J. Brill, 1939.
F. Holthausen. *Gotisches Etymologisches Wörterbuch.* Heidelberg: Winter, 1934.

FOR SCANDINAVIAN

Hjalmar Falk and A. Torp. *Etymologisk Ordbog over det Norske Sprog.* Kristiania, 1906.

FOR ENGLISH

Joseph Bothworth and Northcott Toller. *An Anglo-Saxon Dictionary.* Two vols. Oxford: Clarendon Press, since 1887.
Friedrich Holthausen. *Altenglisches Etymologisches Wörterbuch.* Heidelberg: Winter, 1939.
Shermann M. Kuhn and John Reidy. *Middle-English Dictionary.* Ann Arbor: University of Michigan Press, since 1956.
New English Dictionary. Oxford: Clarendon Press, 10 vols. *The Shorter Oxford English Dictionary on Historical Principles.* Oxford: Clarendon Press, since 1933.
Webster's New World Dictionary of the American Language. Cleveland and New York: The World Publishing Company, since 1953.

CONCORDANCES

John Bartlett. *A New and Complete Concordance or Verbal Index to Words, Phrases, and Passages in the Dramatic Work of Shakespeare.* London: Macmillan & Co., Ltd., 1889.
D. C. Browning. *Dictionary of Shakespeare Quotations.* New York: E. P. Dutton & Co., Inc., 1963.
Charles Grosvenor Osgood. *A Concordance of the Poems of Edmund Spenser.* Washington: Carnegie Foundation, 1915.
Laura E. Lockwood. *Lexicon to the English Poetical Works*

of John Milton. New York: The Macmillan Company, 1907.

Homer Caroll Combe and Zay Rusk Sullen. *A Concordance to the English Poems of John Donne.* Chicago: Packard and Co., 1940.

Leslie N. Broughton and Benjamin F. Stelter. *A Concordance to the Poems of Robert Browning.* Two vols. New York: G. E. Stechert & Company, 1924.

SELECTIVE BIBLIOGRAPHY

ABRAHAM, KARL. "Restriction and Transformation of Scoptophilia in Psycho-Neurotics with Remarks in Analogous Phenomena in Folk-Psychology," (1913), *Selected Papers*. New York: Basic Books, Inc., 1960.

ABT, LAWRENCE, and LEOPOLD BELLAK. *Projective Psychology: Clinical Approaches to the Total Personality*. New York: Alfred A. Knopf, Inc., 1950.

AIGREMONT, H. (pseudonym of SIEGMAR BARON VON SCHULTZE-GALLÉRA). "Beiträge zur Hand und Finger Symbolik und Erotik," *Anthropophyteia* (1913), 10:314–329.

ALBRIGHT, WILLIAM FOXWELL. *From the Stone Age to Christianity: Monotheism and the Historical Process*. Garden City, N. Y.: Doubleday, Anchor Books, 1957.

ALEXANDER, FRANZ. "Fundamental Concepts of Psychosomatic Research: Psychogenesis, Conversion, Specificity," *Psychosomatic Medicine* (1934), 3:205–210.

———. "The Influence of Psychological Factors upon Gastro-Intestinal Disturbances," *Psychoanalytic Quarterly* (1934), 3:501–583.

———. "Treatment of a Case of Peptic Ulcer and Personality Disorder," *Psychosomatic Medicine* (1947), 9:321–330.

———. *Psychosomatic Medicine*. New York: W. W. Norton & Company, Inc., 1950.

ALLPORT, FLOYD H. *Theories of Perception and the Concept of Structure*. New York: John Wiley & Sons, 1955.

ALLPORT, GORDON W. *Pattern and Growth of Personality*. New York: Holt, Rinehart & Winston, Inc., 1961.

ALVAREZ, W. C. *Nervousness, Indigestion and Pain.* New York: Paul B. Hoeber, Inc., 1934.

AMACHER, PETER. "Freud's Neurological Education and Its Influence on Psychoanalytic Theory," *Psychological Issues* (New York: International Universities Press, 1965), Vol. 4.

AMBROSE, ALICE. "Linguistic Approaches to Philosophical Problems," *The Journal of Philosophy* (1952), 49:289–301.

ANDERSON, HAROLD H., and GLADYS L. ANDERSON. *An Introduction to Projective Techniques.* New York: Prentice-Hall, Inc., 1951.

ANDREE, R. "Menschenschädel als Trinkgefässe" (Mit sechs Abbildungen), *Zeitschrift des Vereins für Volkskunde* (1912), 22:1–12.

ARLOW, JACOB A. "Notes on Oral Symbolism," *Psychoanalytic Quarterly* (1955), 24:63–74.

————. "Smug," *International Journal of Psycho-Analysis* (1957), 38:1–12.

ARNOLDSON, W. T. *Parts of the Body in Older Germanic.* Dissertation: University of Chicago, 1915.

ASHBY, W. ROSS. *Design for a Brain.* New York: John Wiley & Sons, 1952.

AUGUSTINE. *The Confessions.* Introduction by Harold C. Gardiner. New York: Washington Square Press, Inc., 1960.

BACHELARD, GASTON. *The Psychoanalysis of Fire.* Translated by Alan C. Ross. Boston, Mass.: Beacon Press, 1964.

————. *The Poetics of Space.* Translated by Maria Foles. Foreword by Etienne Gilson. New York: The Orion Press, 1964.

BAKER, L. M., and W. M. TAYLOR. "An Apparatus for Recording Changes in Skin-Temperature," *American Journal of Psychology* (1953), 66:124–125.

BALKEN, EVA, and JULES H. MASSERMAN. "The Language of Phantasies of Patients with Conversion Hysteria, Anxiety State and Obsessive-Compulsive Neuroses," *The Journal of Psychology* (1940), 10:75–86.

BARUCH, DOROTHY W., and HYMAN NILLER. "Developmental Needs and Conflicts Revealed in Children's Art," *American Journal of Orthopsychiatry* (1952), 22:186–203.

BAUDELAIRE, CHARLES. *Les Fleurs du Mal.* Paris: Limited Editions Club, 1940.

―――. *Oeuvres Compètes.* Paris: M. Levy Frères, 1868–1870.

BELL, ERIC TEMPLE. *The Magic of Numbers.* New York: McGraw-Hill Book Company, 1946.

BENDER, LAURETTA, and ALLISON MONTAGUE. "Psychotherapy through Art in a Negro Child," *College Art Journal* (1947), 7:12–17.

BENVENISTE, E. "Expression indo-européenne de l'éternité," *Bulletin de la Société de Linguistique de Paris* (1937), 38:103–112.

BERGLER, E., and GÉZA RÓHEIM. "Psychology of Time Perception," *Psychoanalytic Quarterly* (1946), 15:190–306.

BERKELEY, GEORGE. *Treatise Concerning the Principles of Human Understanding,* 1710.

―――. *A New Theory of Vision and Other Writings.* New York: E. P. Dutton & Co., Inc., Everyman's Library, 1922.

BERNFELD, S. "Freud's Earliest Theories and the School of Helmholtz," *Psychoanalytic Quarterly* (1944), 13:28–49.

BINSWANGER, LUDWIG. "On the Psycho-galvanic Phenomenon in Association Experiment," in C. G. Jung: *Studies in Word-Association.* Authorized translation by M. D. Eder. New York: Moffat, Yard & Co., 1919, pp. 446–530.

―――. *Sigmund Freud: Reminiscences of a Friendship.* New York: Grune & Stratton, Inc., 1957.

―――. *Being–in–the–World—Selected Papers.* Translated with a critical introduction to his existential psychoanalysis. New York: Basic Books, Inc., 1963.

BIRD, BRIAND. "Bisexual Meaning of Foreskin," *Journal of the American Psychoanalytic Association* (1958) 6:287–304.

BIRT, THEODOR. *Das Antike Buchwesen.* Berlin: Hertz, 1882.

BLERSCH, KONRAD. *Wesen und Entstehung des Sexus im Denken der Antike. Tübinger Beiträge zur Altertumwissenschaft,* Heft 29. Stuttgart-Berlin: Kohlhammer, 1937.

BLOOMFIELD, LEONARD. *Language.* New York: Henry Holt and Company, 1933.

BLOOMFIELD, MAURICE. "On Adaptation of Suffixes in Congeneric Classes of Substantives," *American Journal of Philology* (1891), 12:1–29.

―――. "On Assimilation and Adaptation in Congeneric Classes of Words," *American Journal of Philology* (1895), 14:409–434.

BOAS, FRANZ. *Handbook of American Indian Languages.* Washington: Government Printing Office, 1911.

―――. *The Mind of Primitive Man.* New York: The Macmillan Company, 1938.

―――. *Race, Language and Culture.* New York: The Macmillan Company, 1949.

BOBON, J. *Psychopathologie de l'Expression.* Paris: Masson, 1962.

BOHM, DAVID. *Causality and Chance in Modern Physics* (Princeton: Van Nostrand, 1957).

BONAPARTE, MARIE. "Time and the Unconscious," *International Journal of Psycho-Analysis* (1940), 21:427–468.

BORNSTEIN, BERTA. "Clinical Notes on Child Analysis," *The Psychoanalytic Study of the Child* (1945), 1:15–166.

―――. "Analysis of a Phobic Child," *The Psychoanalytic Study of the Child* (1950–1953), 3–4:181–225.

BOURKE, JOHN G. *Scatological Rites of All Nations.* Washington: W. H. Lowdermilk, 1891.

BREUER, JOSEPH, and SIGMUND FREUD. *Studies in Hysteria.* Translated by A. A. Brill. Boston, Mass.: Beacon Press, 1950. Also translated and edited by James Strachey and Anna Freud. New York: Basic Books, Inc., 1957 and *Standard Edition,* Vol. 2.

BRILL, A. A. "The Sense of Smell in Neurosis and Psychosis," *Psychoanalytic Quarterly* (1932), 1:7–42.

BROWN, NORMAN O. *Life Against Death: The Psychoanalytical Meaning of History.* New York: Random House, Inc., Modern Library Paperbacks, 1959.

BROWN, ROGER. *Words and Things.* Glencoe, Ill.: Free Press, Inc., 1958.

―――, and ERIC H. LENNEBERG. "A Study in Language and Cognition," *The Journal of Abnormal and Social Psychology* (1954), 49:454–462.

―――, A. H. BLACK, and A. E. HOROWITZ. "Phonetic Symbolism in Natural Languages," *The Journal of Abnormal and Social Psychology* (1955), 50:388–393.

BULTMANN, RUDOLF. "Zur Geschichte der Lichtsymbolik im Altertum," *Philologus* (1945), 97:1–35.

BUNKER, H. A., and B. D. LEVIN. "A Psychoanalytic Notation on the Root GN, KN, CN," in George B. Wilbur and Warren Muensterberg: *Psychoanalysis and Culture.* New York: International Universities Press, 1951.

BURTON, ARTHUR. "The Quest for the Golden Mean—A Study in Schizophrenia," in *Psychotherapy of Psychoses,* edited by A. Burton. New York: Basic Books, Inc., 1961.

BUXBAUM, EDITH. "The Role of a Second Language in the Formation of Ego and Superego," *Psychoanalytic Quarterly* (1949), 18:279–289.

CADBURY, HENRY J. "The Single Eye," *Harvard Theological Review* (1954), 47:69–74.

CAMUS, ALBERT. *The Myth of Sisyphus,* translated by Justin O'Brien. New York: Random House, Inc., Vintage Books, 1959.

CANNON, WALTER B. *The Wisdom of the Body.* New York: W. W. Norton & Company, Inc., 1939.

———. *Bodily Changes in Pain, Hunger, Fear and Rage,* 2nd ed. Boston, Mass.: Charles T. Branford Co., 1953.

CASSIRER, ERNST. *An Essay on Man: An Introduction to a Philosophy of Human Culture.* Garden City, N. Y.: Doubleday, Anchor Books, 1953.

———. *The Philosophy of Symbolic Forms,* three vols. New Haven, Conn.: Yale University Press, 1953.

CHAMPION, SELWYN GURNEY. *Racial Proverbs.* New York: The Macmillan Company, 1938.

CHASTAING, M. "Le Symbolism des Voyelles: Significations des *i,*" *Journal de Psychologie* (1958), 55:403–423, 461–483.

CHESKIN, LOUIS. *Colors: What They Can Do for You.* New York: Liveright Publishing Corp., 1947.

CLECKLEY, HERVEY. *The Mask of Sanity.* St. Louis, Mo.: The C. V. Mosby Co., 1955.

COHN, F. S. "Time and the Ego," *Psychoanalytic Quarterly* (1957), 26:168–189.

CONRAD, A. "The Attitude toward Food," *American Journal of Orthopsychiatry* (1937), 7:360–367.

CORNFORD, FRANCIS M. *From Religion to Philosophy: A Study in the Origin of Western Speculation.* New York: Longmans, Green, 1912.

Corpus Juris Secundum—The General Index, five vols. since 1959. Brooklyn, N. Y.: The American Law Book Company.

CREEL, HARRIES G., CHANG TSUNG-CH'IEN and R. C. RUDOLPH. *Literary Chinese by the Inductive Method.* Chicago, Ill.: University of Chicago Press, 1948.

CRESSMANN, EDMUND D. *The Semantics of -mentum, -bulum, and -culum.* Bulletin of the University of Kansas. *Humanistic Studies,* Vol. I, No. 4. Lawrence, Kansas: University of Kansas, 1915.

CRONBACH, LEE J. "Processes Affecting Scores on Understanding Others and Assumed Similarity," *Psychological Bulletin* (1955), 52:177–193.

CURRY, ANDREW. "The Revitalization of Language in Chronic Schizophrenia," *American Journal of Psychotherapy* (1963), 17:45–53.

CURTIUS, GEORG. *Grundzüge der griechischen Etymologie,* Vierte Auflage. Leipzig: Trübner, 1873.

Cybernetics—Circular Causal and Feedback Mechanism in Biological and Social Systems. Transaction of the Seventh Conference. New York: Josiah Macy, Jr. Foundation, 1950.

DAMSTRA, MARTIN. "The Phonetic Associative Element in Thought-Development and in Thought-Imagination in the Dream," *Psychiatric Quarterly* (1954), 28:24–26.

DARLINGTON, H. S. "Ceremonial Behavior Respecting Houses and House Burials," *Psychoanalytic Review* (1931), 18:181–200.

DARWIN, CHARLES. *The Expression of the Emotions in Man and Animals.* London: J. Murray, 1872. New edition with preface by Margaret Mead. New York: Philosophical Library, Inc., 1955.

DAVIS, L. K. "Sound in Language," *Journal of Nervous and Mental Diseases* (1938), 88:491–500.

DELBRÜCK, BERTHOLD. *Introduction to the Study of Language—A Critical Survey of the History and Methods of*

Comparative Philology of Indo-European Languages. London: Trübner, 1882.

―――. *Grundfragen der Sprachforschung: Mit Rücksicht auf W. Wundts Sprachpsychologie Erörtert.* Strassburg: Trübner, 1901.

DEUTSCH, FELIX, and WILLIAM F. MURPHY. *The Clinical Interview.* New York: International Universities Press, 1955.

DINESEN, ISAK. *Seven Gothic Tales.* New York: Modern Library, 1934.

DOOLEY, L. "The Concept of Time in Defense of Ego Integrity," *Psychiatry* (1941), 4:13–25.

DUNBAR, H. FLANDERS. *Emotions and Bodily Changes: A Survey of Literature on Psychosomatic Interrelationship, 1910–1933.* New York: Columbia University Press, 1935.

―――. *Psychosomatic Diagnosis.* New York: Paul B. Hoeber, Inc., 1948.

DURKHEIM, ÉMILE. *The Elementary Forms of Religious Life,* translated by Joseph Ward Swain. New York: Collier, 1961.

EBERHARDT, MARGARETH. "A Study of Phonetic Symbolism of Deaf Children," *Psychological Monographs* (1940), 52:23–42.

EINSTEIN, ALBERT. *Ideas and Opinions.* New York: Crown Publishers, Inc., 1954.

EISLER, K. R. "Time Experience and the Mechanism of Isolation," *Psychoanalytic Review* (1952), 39:1–22.

―――. *The Psychiatrist and the Dying Patient.* New York: International Universities Press, 1955.

ELIADE, MIRCEA. *The Sacred and the Profane.* New York: Harper & Row Publishers, 1961.

ELWORTHY, FREDERICK THOMAS. *The Evil Eye: An Account of the Ancient and Widespread Superstition.* London: J. Murray, 1895.

EVANS, R. M. *An Introduction to Color.* New York: John Wiley & Sons, 1948.

FABER, BIRREN. *Color Psychology and Color Therapy.* New York: McGraw-Hill Book Company, 1950.

FAIRBAIRN, W. RONALD. "Nature and Aims of Treatment," *International Journal of Psycho-Analysis* (1958), 39:374–385.

444

FALSTEIN, EUGEN, SHERMAN FEINSTEIN, and ILSE JUDAS. "Anorexia Nervosa in the Small Child," *American Journal of Orthopsychiatry* (1956), 26:751–772.

FARBER, MARVIN, ed. *Philosophical Essays in Memory of Eduard Husserl.* Cambridge: University Press, 1940.

FELEKY, A. "The Influence of Emotions on Respiration," *Journal of Experimental Psychology* (1916), 1:218–241.

FENICHEL, OTTO. "Outline of Clinical Psychoanalysis," *Psychoanalytic Quarterly* (1932), 1:309.

———. *The Collected Papers,* First Series. New York: W. W. Norton & Company, Inc., 1953.

FERENCZI, SÁNDOR. "On Eye Symbolism," 1913, *Sex in Psychoanalysis.* New York: Basic Books, Inc., 1950.

———. *Further Contributions to the Theory and Technique of Psychoanalysis.* New York: Basic Books, Inc., 1960.

FLIESS, ROBERT. *The Revival of Interest in the Dream: A Critical Study of Post-Freudian Psychoanalytic Contributions.* New York: International Universities Press, 1953.

———. "Phylogenetic vs. Ontogenetic Experience," *International Journal of Psycho-Analysis* (1956), 37:46–60.

FLÜGEL, J. C. "A Note on the Phallic Significance of the Tongue and of Speech," *International Journal of Psycho-Analysis* (1925), 6:209–215.

FRANKL, VICTOR E. *Man's Search for Meaning—An Introduction to Logotherapy.* New York: Washington Square Press, Inc., 1963.

FRASER, J. T., ed. *The Voices of Time.* New York: George Braziller, 1968.

FRAZER, SIR JAMES GEORGE. *Myth of the Origin of Fire.* London: Macmillan & Co., Ltd., 1930.

FREEDMAN, ALFRED M., and LAURETTA BENDER. "When the Childhood Schizophrenic Grows Up," *American Journal of Orthopsychiatry* (1957), 27:553–565.

FREUD, SIGMUND. *Zur Auffassung der Aphasien,* 1891; English translation: *On Aphasia.* London and New York: International Universities Press, 1953.

———. *The Standard Edition of the Complete Psychological Works of Sigmund Freud.* Translated from the German under the general editorship of James Strachey, in collaboration with Anna Freud. London: The Hogarth Press, Ltd., and The Institution of Psycho-Analysis. First published in 1955.

———. *The Interpretation of Dreams*. Translated by A. A. Brill. New York: The Macmillan Company, Inc., 1912. Also translated by James Strachey. New York: Basic Books, Inc., 1960.

FRIEDMAN, PAUL. "The Nose: Some Psychological Reflections," *The American Imago* (1951), 8:337–350.

———. "Some Observations on the Sense of Smell," *Psychoanalytic Quarterly* (1959), 28:307–329.

FRIES, C. C. "Meaning and Linguistic Analysis," *Language* (1954), 30:57–68.

FROMM, ERICH. *The Forgotten Language: An Introduction to the Understanding of Dreams, Fairy Tales and Myths*. New York: Rinehart and Co., Inc., 1951. Also Grove Press, New York.

GARDINER, ALAN H. *Speech and Language*. Oxford: Oxford University Press, 1932.

GATSCHET, ALBERT S. "Adjectives of Color in Indian Languages," *The American Naturalist* (1879), 13:475–485.

———. "Farbenbenennungen in Nordamerikanischen Sprachen," *Zeitschrift für Ethnologie* (1879), 11:295–302.

GEBSATTEL, V. E. VON. *Prolegomena einer medizinischen Anthropologie*. Berlin–Göttingen–Heidelberg: Springer, 1954.

GESELL, A., and L. B. AMES. "The Development of Handedness," *Journal of Genetic Psychology* (1947), 70:155–175.

GIBSON, JAMES J. *The Perception of the Visual World*. Boston, Mass.: Houghton Mifflin Company, 1950.

———. *The Senses Considered as Perceptual Systems*. Boston, Mass.: Houghton Mifflin Company, 1966.

GILL, MERTON H., and MARGARET BRENMAN. *Hypnosis and Related States: Psychological Studies in Regression*. New York: International Universities Press, 1961.

GOETZ, K. E. "Waren die Römer blaublind?" *Archiv für lateinische Lexikographie und Grammatik* (1906), 14:75–88.

GRAY, LOUIS H. *Foundation of Language*. New York: The Macmillan Company, 1939.

446

GREENACRE, PHYLLIS. "Pathological Weeping," *Psychoanalytic Quarterly* (1945), 14:62–75.

———. "Experience of Awe in Childhood," *The Psychoanalytic Study of the Child* (1956), 11:9–30.

GREENSON, RALPH R. "The Psychology of Apathy," *Psychoanalytic Quarterly* (1949), 18:290–302.

———. "The Mother-Tongue and the Mother," *International Journal of Psycho-Analysis* (1950), 31:18–23.

GRODDECK, GEORG. *The Book of the It.* Introduction by Lawrence Durrell. New York: Random House, Inc., Vintage Books, 1961.

GROTJAHN, MARTIN. "Georg Groddeck and His Teaching about Man's Innate Need for Symbolization," *Psychoanalytic Review* (1945), 32:9–24.

GROZINGER, WOLFGANG. *Scribbling, Drawing, Painting: The Early Forms of the Child's Pictorial Creativeness.* New York: Frederick A. Praeger, Inc., 1955.

GÜNTERT, HERMANN. *Über Reimwortbildungen im Arischen und Altgriechischen: Eine Sprachwissenschaftliche Untersuchung.* Heidelberg: Winter, 1914.

———. "Weiteres zum Begriff Winckel im ursprünglichen Denken," *Wörter und Sachen.* Heidelberg: Winter, 1927. 10:124–142.

HALL, CALVIN S. *The Meaning of Dreams: Their Symbolism and Their Sexual Implications.* New York: Dell Publishing Co., Inc., 1959.

HARNIK, S. "Die triebhaft-affektiven Momente im Zeitgefühl," *Imago* (1925), 11:32–57.

HART, HENRY HARPER. "The Eye in Symbol and Symptom," *Psychoanalytic Review* (1949), 36:1–21.

HEGEL, GEORG WILHELM FRIEDRICH. *Lectures on the History of Philosophy.* Translated by E. S. Haldane and F. H. Simson. Three vols. London: Kegan Paul, Trench, Trübner & Co., 1895.

HEIDEGGER, MARTIN. *Sein und Zeit.* Halle: Niemeyer, 1928. New ed. Tübingen: Neomarius, 1949.

———. *An Introduction to Metaphysics.* Garden City, N. Y.: Doubleday, Anchor Books, 1961.

HEILBRUNN, GERT. "The Basic Fear," *Journal of the American Psychoanalytical Association* (1955), 3:447–466.

HERDAN, G. *Language as Choice and Chance.* Groningen: Nordhoff N.V., 1956.

HIRT, HERMANN. *Indogermanische Grammatik.* Heidelberg: Winter, 1921.

HOFMANN, ERICH. *Ausdrucksverstärkung. Untersuchungen zur etymologischen Verstärkung und zum Gebrauch der Steigerungsadverbia im Balto-Slavischen und in anderen indogermanischen Sprachen.* Göttingen: Vanderhoeck & Reprecht, 1930.

HOLMES, T. H., H. GOODELL, S. WOLF, and H. G. WOLFF. *The Nose: An Experimental Study of Reactions Within the Nose in Human Subjects during Varying Life Experiences.* Springfield, Ill.: Charles C Thomas, 1950.

———, and H. G. WOLFF. "Life Situations and Nasal Disease," *Psychosomatic Medicine* (1951), 13:71–82.

HOOPS, JOHANNES. *Reallexikon der Germanischen Altertumskunde.* Strassburg: Trübner, 1913, 2:91–93.

HUEBSCH, DANIEL A. "Psychoanalysis of Eye Disturbances," *Psychoanalytic Review* (1931), 18:166–180.

HUMBOLDT, WILHELM VON. *Über die Kawi-Sprache auf der Insel Java. Nebst einer Einleitung über die Verschiedenheit des Menschlichen Sprachbaues.* Three vols. Berlin: Akademie, 1836–1839.

HUSSERL, EDMUND. "Philosophie als strenge Wissenschaft," *Logos* (1910), 1:289–290.

———. *Vorlesungen zur Phänomenologie des inneren Zeitbewusstseins.* Edited by Martin Heidegger. Halle: Niemeyer, 1928.

HUXLEY, JULIAN. *Man in the Modern World.* New York: Mentor Books, 1949.

JESPERSEN, OTTO. *Language: Its Nature, Development and Origin.* New York: The Macmillan Company, 1922, reprinted 1949.

———. *The Philosophy of Grammar.* New York: Henry Holt and Company, 1934.

———. *Selected Writings.* London: George Allen & Unwin, 1962.

JONES, ERNEST. *Papers on Psycho-Analysis*, 1912, 5th ed. Baltimore, Md.: Williams & Wilkins, 1948. Boston, Mass.: Beacon Press, Beacon Paperback, 1961.

JORES, ARTHUR, and HELLMUTH FREYBERGER, eds. *Advances in Psychosomatic Medicine*. New York: Robert Brunner, 1961.

JUNG, CARL GUSTAV. *Studies in Word-Association*. Authorized translation by M. D. Eder. New York: Moffat, Yard & Co., 1919.

––––––. *Two Essays on Analytical Psychology*. New York: Pantheon Books, Bollingen Series 20, 1955.

––––––. *Modern Man in Search of a Soul*. New York: Harcourt, Brace & Co., Harvest Book, 1933.

––––––, and C. KERÉNYI. *Essays on a Scene of Mythology: Child and the Mysteries of Eleusis*. New York: Pantheon Books, Bollingen Series 22, 1949.

JUNKER, HERMANN. "Der Sehende und Blinde Gott," *Sitzungsberichte der Bayrischen Akademie der Wissenschaften*. Phil.–Hist. Abt., Vol. 7, München, 1942.

KANZER, MARK. "The Communicative Function of the Dream," *International Journal of Psycho-Analysis* (1955), 36:260–266.

KASININ, J. S., ed. *Language and Thought in Schizophrenia*. Berkeley, Calif.: University of California Press, 1944.

KATZ, DAVID. *The World of Colours*. London: Kegan Paul, Trench, Trübner & Co., 1935.

KENT, G. H., and A. J. ROSANOFF. "A Study of Association in Insanity," *American Journal of Insanity* (1910), 67:37–96, 317–390.

KIERKEGAARD, SØREN. *Repetition: An Essay in Experimental Psychology*. Translated by Walter Lowrie. Princeton, N. J.: Princeton University Press, 1946.

KLEIN, EMANUEL. "Psychoanalytic Aspects of School Problems," *The Psychoanalytic Study of the Child* (1949), 34:369–390.

KLEIN, MELANIE. *The Psychoanalysis of Children*. New York: Grove Press, 1960.

KLUGE, FRIEDRICH. *Nominale Stammbildungslehre der altgermanischen Dialekte*. Halle: Niemeyer, 1926.

KNIGHT, RICHARD PAYNE. *An Analytical Inquiry into the Principles of Taste,* 3rd ed., London: 1806.

KÖHLER, WOLFGANG. *Gestalt Psychology.* New York: Mentor Books, 1959.

KOLB, L. C. *The Painful Phantom: Psychology, Physiology and Treatment.* Springfield, Ill.: Charles C Thomas, 1954.

KRAEPELIN, EMIL. *Dementia Praecox and Paraphrenia.* Translated by R. M. Barclay. Edinburgh: 1919.

KRIS, ERNST. "The Significance of Freud's Earliest Discoveries," *International Journal of Psycho-Analysis* (1951), 31:108–116.

KROEBER, A. L. *Anthropology, Race, Language, Culture, Psychology, Prehistory.* New York: Harcourt, Brace & Co., 1923.

KUBIE, LAWRENCE S. "Communication between Sane and Insane: Hypnosis," *Cybernetics: Circular Causal and Feedback Mechanism in Biological and Social Systems.* Transactions of the Seventh Conference. New York: Josiah Macy, Jr., Foundation, 1950, pp. 92–133.

———. *Neurotic Distortion of the Creative Process.* New York: Farrar, Straus, Noonday Press, 1961.

———. "Body Symbolization and Development of Language," *Psychoanalytic Quarterly* (1934), 3:430–444. Reprinted in *Cybernetics: Circular Causal and Feedback Mechanism in Biological and Social Systems.* Transactions of the Seventh Conference. New York: Josiah Macy, Jr., Foundation, 1950, pp. 237–249.

KUHN, ADALBERT. *Die Herabkunft des Feuers und des Göttertranks: Ein Beitrag zur Vergleichenden Mythologie des Indogermanischen.* Berlin: Dümler, 1859.

KWANT, REMY C. *Phenomenology of Language.* Pittsburgh, Pa.: Duquesne University Press, 1965.

LACOMBE, PIERRE. "A Special Mechanism of Pathological Weeping," *Psychoanalytic Quarterly* (1958), 27:246–251.

LANDGREBE, LUDWIG. *Nennfunktion und Wortbedeutung. Eine Studie über Martys Sprachphilosophie.* Halle: Akademie Verlag, 1934.

LANGER, SUSAN K. *Philosophy in a New Key: A Study in the*

Symbolism of Reason, Rite, and Art. New York: Mentor Books, Thirteenth Printing, 1964.

LANZ, HENRY. *The Physical Basis of Rime: An Essay on the Aesthetics of Sound.* Stanford, Calif.: Stanford University Press, 1931.

LEHMAN, EDWARD. "Feeding Problems of Psychogenic Origin," *The Psychoanalytic Study of the Child* (1950–1953), 3–4:461–488.

LÉVY-BRUHL, LUCIEN. *How Natives Think.* London: George Allen & Unwin, Ltd., 1926.

———. *The Soul of the Primitive.* Translated by Lilia A. Claire. New York: Frederick A. Praeger, Inc., 1966.

LEWIN, BERTRAM D. *Dreams and the Uses of Regression.* New York: International Universities Press, 1958.

———. "Body as Phallus," *Psychoanalytic Quarterly* (1933), 2:24.

LIPPMAN, HYMAN S. "The Use of Dreams in Psychiatric Work with Children," *The Psychoanalytic Study of the Child* (1945), 1:233–245.

LITTLETON, C. SCOTT. *The New Comparative Mythology: An Anthropological Assessment of the Theories of Georges Dumézil.* Berkeley and Los Angeles: University of California Press, 1966.

LOCKE, WILLIAM N., and A. DONALD BOOTH, eds. *Machine Translations of Languages.* New York: John Wiley & Sons, 1955.

LORAND, SÁNDOR, and SÁNDOR FELDMAN. "The Symbolism of Teeth in Dreams," *International Journal of Psycho-Analysis* (1955), 36:145–160.

LOTH, J. "Le mot désignant le genou au sense de génération chez les Celtes, les Germains, les Slaves, les Assyriens," *Revue Celtique* (1923), 40:143–152.

LUBIN, ALBERT J. "A Feminine Moses," *International Journal of Psycho-Analysis* (1958), 39:535–546.

LURIE, O. R. "Psychological Factors Associated with Eating Difficulties in Children," *American Journal of Orthopsychiatry* (1941), 11:452–467.

LYND, HELEN MERRELL. *On Shame and the Search for Identity.* New York: Harcourt, Brace & World, 1958.

MALCOVE, LILLIAN. "Bodily Mutilation and Learning to Eat," *Psychoanalytic Quarterly* (1933), 2:557–561.

MALINOWSKI, BRONISLAV. *Magic, Science and Religion.* Garden City, N. Y.: Doubleday, Anchor Books, 1954.

MARCEL, GABRIEL. *Being and Having.* London: Dacre, 1949.

MARGENAU, HENRY. "Quantum Mechanics, Free Will and Determinism," *The Journal of Philosophy* (1967), 64:714–725.

MARTINET, ANDRÉ. *La Gemination Consonantique d'Origin Expressive dans les Langues Germanique.* Copenhagen: Munksgaard, 1937.

MARTY, ANTON. Vol. I: *Psyche und Sprachstruktur;* Vol. II: *Über den Wert und Methode einer beschreibenden Bedeutungslehre. Nachgelassene Schriften.* Herausg. von Otto Funke. Bern: Francke, 1950.

———. *Satz und Wort.* Bern: Francke, 1950.

———. *Untersuchungen zur Grundlage der allgemeinen Grammatik und Sprachphilosophie,* Vol. I, 1908; Vol. II: *Nachgelassene Schriften.* Herausg. von Otto Funke. Bern: Francke, 1951.

MASON, RUSSELL E. *Internal Perception and Bodily Functioning.* New York: International Universities Press, 1961.

MASSERMAN, JULES H. "The Language of Phantasies of Patients with Conversion Hysteria, Anxiety State and Obsessive-Compulsive Neuroses," *The Journal of Psychology* (1940), 10:75–86.

———. "Language Behavior and Dynamic Psychiatry," *International Journal of Psycho-Analysis* (1944), 25:1–8.

MAY, ROLLO, ERNEST ANGEL, and HENRY F. ELLENBERGER. *Existence: A New Dimension in Psychiatry and Psychology.* New York: Basic Books, Inc., 1958.

MCGEE, W. J. *Primitive Numbers.* Bureau of American Ethnology. 19th Annual Report, 1897–1898. Washington: Government Printing Office, 1900, pp. 825–851.

MEAD, MARGARET. *Male and Female: A Study of the Sexes in a Changing World.* New York: Mentor Books, 1955.

MEILLET, A. *Linguistique Historique et Linguistique Générale.* Paris: Champion, 1948.

MERLEAU-PONTY, MAURICE. *Signs.* Translated by Richard C.

McCleary. Evanston, Ill.: Northwestern University Press, 1964.

MERLOO, A. M. "Father Time," *Psychiatric Quarterly* (1948), 22:587–608.

MEYER-LÜBKE, W. "Neubenennungen von Körperteilen im Romanischen," *Wörter und Sachen* (1921), 12:1–16.

MILLER, GEORGE A. *Language and Communication.* New York: McGraw-Hill Book Company, 1951.

————. "The Magical Number Seven, Plus or Minus Two: Some Limits on Our Capacity for Processing Information," *The Psychological Review* (1956), 63:81–97.

MILLER, JULES P. "The Psychology of Blushing," *International Journal of Psycho-Analysis* (1965), 46:188–199.

MILNER, MARION. "The Communication of Primary Sensual Experience," *International Journal of Psycho-Analysis* (1956), 37:278–281.

MINKOWSKI, EUGÈNE. *Le Temps Vécu: Études Phénomenologiques et Psychopathologiques.* Paris: J. L. L. D'Artrey, 1933.

MODELL, ARNOLD H. "The Theoretical Implications of Hallucinatory Experiences in Schizophrenia," *Journal of the American Psychoanalytical Association* (1958), 6:442–480.

MOUSTAKAS, CLARK E. *Children in Play Therapy: A Key to Understanding Normal and Disturbed Emotions.* New York: McGraw-Hill Book Company, 1953.

MOWRER, HOBART. "The Psychologist Looks at Language," *The American Psychologist* (1954), pp. 659–695.

MÜLLER, F. MAX, ed. *The Sacred Books of the East.* A General Index. Oxford: Clarendon Press, 1910.

MÜLLER, H. *Experimentelle Beiträge zur Analyse des Verhältnisses von Laut und Sinn.* Berlin: Müller & Kiepenheuer, 1935.

MURPHY, WILLIAM F. "Character, Trauma and Sensory Perception," *International Journal of Psycho-Analysis* (1958), 39:555–568.

NEUMANN, ERICH. *The Origin and History of Consciousness.* New York: Pantheon Books, Bollingen Series, 1954.

NEWMAN, S. S. "Further Experiments in Phonetic Symbolism," *American Journal of Psychology* (1933), 45:53–75.

NIDA, E. *Morphology: The Descriptive Analysis of Words.* Ann Arbor, Mich.: University of Michigan Press, 1949.

NUNBERG, HERMAN. "The Feeling of Guilt," *Psychoanalytic Quarterly* (1934), 3:589–604.

———. "Transference and Reality," *International Journal of Psycho-Analysis* (1951), 32:1–9.

———. *Principles of Psychoanalysis: Their Application to the Neuroses.* New York: International Universities Press, 1955.

OBERNDORF, CLARENCE P. "Time—Its Relation to Reality and Purpose," *Psychoanalytic Review* (1943), 28:139–155.

OERTEL, HANNS. *Lectures on the Study of Language.* New York: Scribner & Sons, 1901.

———, and EDWARD P. MORRIS. "An Examination of Theories Regarding the Nature and Origin of Indo-European Inflection," *Harvard Studies in Classical Philology* (1905), 16:63–122.

OESTERLEY, HERMANN. *Gesta Romanorum.* Berlin: Weidmann, 1872.

ONIANS, RICHARD BRAXTON. *The Origins of European Thought about the Body, the Mind, the Soul, the World, Time and Fate—New Interpretations of Greek, Roman and Kindred Evidence also of Some Jewish and Christian Beliefs.* Cambridge: University Press, 1954.

ORGEL, SHELLEY. "On Time and Timelessness," *Journal of the American Psychoanalytical Association* (1965), 13:102–121.

OSGOOD, CHARLES E. "The Nature and Measurement of Meaning," *The Psychological Bulletin* (1952), 49:197–237.

———. SUCO, G. AND P. TANNENBAUM. *The Measurement of Meaning.* Urbana, Ill.: University of Chicago Press, 1957.

OSTFELD, A. M., L. F. CHAPMAN, H. GOODELL, and H. G. WOLFF. "Studies in Headache: Summary of Evidence Concerning a Noxious Agent Active Locally during Migraine Headache," *Psychosomatic Medicine* (1957), 19:199–208.

OSTOW, MORTIMER. "The Illusory Reduplication of Body Parts," *Psychoanalytic Quarterly* (1958), 17:98–100.

PATTIE, F. A. "The Production of Blisters by Hypnotic Suggestion," *Journal of Abnormal and Social Psychology* (1947), 36:62–72.

454

PAUL, HERMANN. *Prinzipien der Sprachwissenschaft*, 1st ed. Halle: Niemeyer, 1880. Translated as *Principles of the History of Language*, by A. Strong. London: Swan Sonnenschein, 1888.

PEDERSON-KRAG, GERALDINE. "The Use of Metaphor in Analytic Thinking," *Psychoanalytic Quarterly* (1956), 25:66–71.

PFANDL, LUDWIG. "Der Narzissbegriff: Versuch einer Neuen Deutung," *Imago* (1935), 21:279–310.

PIAGET, JEAN. *The Language and Thought of the Child.* New York: Meridian Books, 1955.

———. *The Child's Conception of the World.* Paterson, N. J.: Littlefield, Adams & Company, 1963.

PLANK, ROBERT. "Seeing the Salamander," *The Psychoanalytic Study of the Child* (1957), 12:379–398.

PORZIG, WALTER. "Daimon," *Indogermanische Forschungen* (1923), 41:171–173.

PRATT, JOHN. "Notes on the Unconscious Significance of Perfume," *International Journal of Psycho-Analysis* (1942), 23:80–83.

PROUST, MARCEL. *Jean Santeuil.* New York: Dell Publishing Co., Inc., Laurel Editions, 1961.

Psycholinguistics—A Survey of Theory and Research Problems. Edited by Charles E. Osgood and Thomas E. Sebeok. With extensive bibliography. Bloomington, Ind.: Indiana University Press, 1965.

RADHAKRISHNAN, S. *The Principal Upanishads.* New York: Harper Brothers, 1953.

RAUSCHMAIER, A. *Über den figürlichen Gebrauch der Zahlen im Altfranzösischen.* Münchener Beiträge zur Romanischen und Englischen Philologie III. Erlangen-Leipzig: Deichert-Böhme Verlag, 1892.

REIK, THEODORE. *Ritual.* New York: Farrar, Straus, 1946.

———. *Dogma and Compulsion: Psychoanalytic Studies of Myths and Religions.* New York: International Universities Press, 1957.

RESCHER, O. "Psychologisches im Arabischen Sprichwort," *Beiträge zur Kenntnis des Orients,* Hugo Grote, ed. (1911), 9:55–61.

RÉVÉSZ, GÉZA, ed. *Thinking and Speaking: A Symposium.* Amsterdam: North Holland Publishing Co., 1954.

ROGGE, CHRIST. "Homerisch *phrēn, phrenes* und Verwandtes in neuer medizinischer und sprachpsychologischer Beleuchtung: Ein Stück aus der Urgeschichte menschlicher Denkanschauung," *Archiv für die gesamte Psychologie* (1927), 58:307–324.

RÓHEIM, GÉZA. "Spiegelzauber," *Imago* (1917–1919), 5:63–120.

ROOS, ALAN. "Psychoanalytical Study of a Typical Dream," *Psychoanalytic Quarterly* (1960), 29:153–174.

ROSANOFF, A. J. "A Study of Association in Insanity," *American Journal of Insanity* (1910), 67:37–96, 317–390.

ROSCHER, W. H. *Ausführliches Lexikon der Griechischen und Römischen Mythologie.* Leipzig: Trübner, 1909.

ROYCE, JOSEPH R. "Psychology at the Crossroads between the Sciences and the Humanities," in *Psychology and the Symbol: An Interdisciplinary Symposium* edited by Joseph R. Royce. New York: Random House, Inc. 1965.

SAPIR, EDWARD. "A Study in Phonetic Symbolism," *Journal of Experimental Psychology* (1929), 12:225–239.

———. "Why Cultural Anthropology Needs the Psychiatrist," *Psychiatry* (1938), 1:7–12.

———. *Language: An Introduction to the Study of Speech.* New York: Harcourt, Brace & Co., Harvest Book, 1949.

———. *Culture, Language and Personality: Selected Essays.* Berkeley, Calif.: University of California Press, 1956.

SAPORTA, SOL, and JARVIS R. BASTIAN. *Psycholinguistics: A Book of Readings.* New York: Holt, Rinehart & Winston, Inc., 1961.

SARMA, ANGEL. "On the Pathogenesis of Peptic Ulcer," *International Journal of Psycho-Analysis* (1950), 31:53–72.

SARTRE, JEAN-PAUL. *Being and Nothingness: An Essay on Phenomenological Ontology.* New York: Washington Square Press, Inc., 1966.

SAUSSURE, F. DE. *Cours de Linguistique Général,* 4th ed. Edited by C. Bally and M. Sechehaye. Paris: Payot, 1949.

———. *Course in General Linguistics.* Translated by Wade Baskin. New York: Philosophical Library, 1959.

SCARTAZZINI, L. *A Companion to Dante.* London: Macmillan & Co., Ltd., 1893.

SCHILDER, PAUL. "Psychoanalysis of Space," *International Journal of Psycho-Analysis* (1935), 16:274–295.

———. *The Image and Appearance of the Human Body.* London: Kegan Paul, 1935. New edition: New York, International Universities Press, 1950.

SCHMIDEBERG, MELITTA. "Intellectual Inhibition and Disturbances in Eating," *International Journal of Psycho-Analysis* (1938), 19:17–22.

SCHMIDL, F. "Sigmund Freud and Ludwig Binswanger," *Psychoanalytic Quarterly* (1959), 28:40–58.

SCHRADER, OTTO. *Reallexikon der Indogermanischen Altertumskunde* (Berlin-Leipzig: Walter de Gruyter, 1917–1923), 1:355–369.

SCHULZE, WILHELM. *Der Tod des Kambyses.* Sitzungsberichte der konigl. Preussischen Akademie der Wissenschaften, Berlin, 1912.

SCHWYZER, EDUARD. "Der Götter Knie—Abrahams Schoss," in *Antidoron: Festschrift für Jakob Wackernagel.* Göttingen: Van der Hoeck and Ruprecht, 1924.

———. "Die Bezeichnung des Zahnfleisches in den Indogermanischen Sprachen," *Zeitschrift für Vergleichende Sprachforschung* (1929–1930), 57:256–275.

SECHEHAYE, MARGUERITE A. *Autobiography of a Schizophrenic Girl.* New York: Grune & Stratton, Inc., 1951.

———. *Symbolic Realization: A New Method of Psychotherapy Applied to a Case of Schizophrenia.* New York: International Universities Press, 1951.

———. *A New Psychotherapy in Schizophrenia: Relief of Frustrations by Symbolic Realization.* New York: Grune & Stratton, Inc., 1956.

SEGAL, HANNA. "Note on Symbol Formation," *International Journal of Psycho-Analysis* (1957), 38:391–397.

SELLING, LOWELL S. "Behavior Problems of Eating," *American Journal of Orthopsychiatry* (1946), 15:163–169.

SEWARD, BARBARA. *The Symbolic Rose.* New York: Columbia University Press, 1960.

SIEBENTHAL, W. V. *Die Wissenschaft vom Traum. Ergebnisse*

und Probleme. Eine Einführung in die Allgemeinen Grundlagen. Berlin-Göttingen: Springer, 1953.

SIEBS, OTTO. "Things und die Alaisiagen," *Zeitschrift für deutsche Philologie* (1891), 24:433–456.

SKINNER, B. F. "The Verbal Summator and a Method for the Study of Latent Speech," *Journal of Psychology* (1936), 2:71–107.

———. *Verbal Behavior.* New York: Appleton-Century-Crofts, 1957.

SOLLEY, CHARLES M., and GARDNER MURPHY. *Development of the Perceptual World.* New York: Basic Books, Inc., 1960.

SOUTHARD, E. E. "On Descriptive Analysis of Manifest Delusions from the Subject's Point of View," *The Journal of Abnormal Psychology* (1916), 11:189–202.

———. "On the Application of Grammatical Categories to the Analysis of Delusions," *The Philosophical Review* (1916), 25:445–450.

SPEHLMANN, RAINER. *Sigmund Freuds Neurologische Schriften. Eine Untersuchung zur Vorgeschichte der Psychoanalyse.* Heidelberg: Springer, 1953.

SPERLING, MELITTA. "Food Allergies and Conversion Hysteria," *Psychoanalytic Quarterly* (1953), 22:525–538.

SPITZ, RENÉ A. *The First Year of Life.* New York: International Universities Press, 1965.

SPITZER, LEO. *Essays in Historical Semantics.* New York: S. F. Vanni, 1947.

———. *Linguistics and Literary History: Essays in Stylistics.* Princeton, N. J.: Princeton University Press, 1948.

———. *A Method of Interpreting Literature.* Northampton, Mass.: Smith College, 1949.

STEINTHAL, HEYMANN. *Einleitung in die Psychologie und Sprachwissenschaft. Abriss der Sprachwissenschaft.* Berlin: 1888.

STENGEL, ERWIN. "On Learning a New Language," *International Journal of Psycho-Analysis* (1939), 20:471–476.

STERBA, EDITHA. "An Important Factor in Eating Disturbances in Childhood," *Psychoanalytic Quarterly* (1941), 10:365–372.

———. "Analysis of Psychogenic Constipation in a Two-year-old Child," *The Psychoanalytic Study of the Child* (1950–1953), 3–4:227–252.

STEVENSON, I. P., and H. G. WOLFF. "Life Situations and Bronchial Mucus," *Psychosomatic Medicine* (1949), 11:-223–227.

STIEGLECKER, HERMANN. "Zeugen, Wissen und Knie im Semitischen und Indogermanischen," *Anthropos* (1927), pp. 1000–1003.

STORCH, ALFRED. *The Primitive Archaic Forms of Inner Experiences and Thought in Schizophrenia.* New York and Washington: Nervous and Mental Disease Monograph Series, No. 36, 1924.

STRACHEY, CHALMERS L., and F. DEMARTINO. *Understanding Human Motivation.* Cleveland, Ohio: Howard Allen, 1958.

STRAUS, ERWIN W. "The Upright Posture," *Psychiatric Quarterly* (1952), 26:529–561.

SULLIVAN, HARRY STACK. *The Inter-Personal Theory of Psychiatry.* New York: W. W. Norton & Company, Inc., 1955.

SULZBERGER, M. *Dermatologic Allergy.* Springfield, Ill.: Charles C Thomas, 1940.

TAUBER, EDWARD S., and MAURICE R. GREEN. *Prelogical Experience: An Inquiry into Dreams and Other Creative Processes.* New York: Basic Books, Inc., 1959.

TAX, SOL, LOREN C. EISELEY, IRVING ROUSE, and CARL VOEGELIN. *An Appraisal of Anthropology Today.* Chicago, Ill.: University of Chicago Press, 1953.

TAYLOR, EDWARD B. *Researches into the Early History of Mankind and the Development of Civilization,* 2nd ed. London: J. Murray, 1870.

THASS-THIENEMANN, THEODORE. "Left-handed Writing: A Study in the Psychoanalysis of Language," *Psychoanalytic Review* (1955), 42:239–261.

———. "The Single Eye," *Gordon Review* (1955), 1:19–23.

———. "Oedipus and the Sphinx: The Linguistic Approach to Unconscious Fantasies," *Psychoanalytic Review* (1957), 44:40–73.

———. "The Talking Teapot: A Note on Psycho-Linguistics," *Comprehensive Psychiatry* (1960), 1:199–200.

————. "Psychotherapy and Psycholinguistics," *Topical Problems of Psychotherapy* (1963), 4:37–45.

————. *The Subconscious Language*. New York: Washington Square Press, Inc., 1967.

THIEME, P. "Über einige Benennungen des Nachkommen," *Kuhn's Zeitschrift für vergleichende Sprachforschung auf dem Gebiete der Indogermanischen Sprachen* (1939), 66:130–144.

THOMAS, CAROLINE BEDELL, DONALD C. ROSS, and ELLEN S. FREED. *An Index of Rorschach Responses: Studies on the Psychological Characteristics of Medical Students*. Baltimore, Md.: The Johns Hopkins Press, 1964.

TOMKINS, SILVAN S. *Contemporary Psychopathology: A Source Book*. Cambridge: University Press, 1947.

TROUBETZKOY, N. S. *Principes de Phonologie*. Translated by I. Cantineau. Paris: La Société Linguistique de Paris, 1949.

ULLMANN, STEPHEN. *The Principles of Semantics: A Linguistic Approach to Meaning*, 2nd ed. Oxford: B. Blackwell, 1957.

URBAN, W. N. *Language and Reality: The Philosophy of Language and the Principles of Symbolism*. New York: The Macmillan Company, 1939.

VAN DEN BERG, J. H. *The Phenomenological Approach to Psychiatry: An Introduction to Recent Phenomenological Psychopathology*. Springfield, Ill.: Charles C Thomas, 1955.

VOLKELT, JOHANNES. *Phänomenologie und Metaphysik der Zeit*. München: C. H. Beck, 1925.

VOSSLER, KARL. *The Spirit of Language in Civilization*. London: Routledge & Kegan Paul, Ltd., 1951.

VYGOTSKY, L. S. *Thought and Language*. With an introduction by Jerome S. Brunner. Edited and translated by Eugenia Hanfmann and Gertrude Vakar. Cambridge, Mass.: The M.I.T. Press, 1962.

WATSON, JOHN B. "The Myth of the Unconscious," *Harper's* (1927), 155:503–507.

————. *Behaviorism*. Chicago, Ill.: University of Chicago Press, Phoenix Books, 1961.

WEISGERBER, LEO. "Der Geruchsinn in unseren Sprachen," *Indogermanische Forschungen* (1928), 46:121–150.

WEISS, EDUARDO, and O. SPURGEON ENGLISH. *Psychosomatic*

Medicine: The Clinical Application of Psychopathology to General Medical Problems, 2nd ed. Philadelphia and London: W. B. Saunders Co., 1949.

WERNER, HEINZ, and BERNARD KAPLAN. *Symbol Formation: An Organismic–Developmental Approach to Language and the Expression of Thought.* New York: John Wiley & Sons, 1963.

WERTHEIMER, M. "Numbers and Numerical Concepts in Primitive Peoples," in *A Source Book of Gestalt Psychology*, edited by W. D. Ellis. New York: Humanities Press, 1950.

WHATMOUGH, JOSHUA. "The Neural Basis of Language and the Problem of the Root," *Harvard Studies in Classical Philology* (1941), pp. 52–133.

WHITE, T. H., ed. *The Bestiary: A Book of Beasts* (Being a translation from a Latin bestiary of the twelfth century). New York: G. P. Putnam's Sons, 1954.

WHITNEY, WILLIAM DWIGHT. *Language and the Study of Language.* New York: Scribner & Co., 1868.

WHORF, BENJAMIN LEE. *Language, Thought and Reality.* New York: John Wiley & Sons, 1956.

WIENER, NORBERT. *Cybernetics.* New York: John Wiley & Sons, 1948.

———. *The Human Use of Human Beings: Cybernetics and Society.* Garden City, N.Y.: Doubleday, Anchor Books, 1950.

WILD, JOHN. "Husserl's Critique of Psychologism: Its Historic Roots and Contemporary Relevance," in Marvin Farber: *Philosophical Essays in Memory of Eduard Husserl.* Cambridge: University Press, 1940.

WISDOM, J. O. *Philosophy and Psycho-Analysis.* Oxford: B. Blackwell, 1953.

———. *The Unconscious Origin of Berkeley's Philosophy.* International Psycho-Analytic Library No. 47. London: The Hogarth Press, 1953.

WISSEMANN, H. *Untersuchungen zur Onomatopoiie. I. Teil: Die Sprachpsychologischen Versuche.* Heidelberg: Winter, 1954.

WITTGENSTEIN, LUDWIG. *Tractatus Logico-Philosophicus.* New York: Harcourt, Brace & Co., 1922.

WITTKOVER, ERIC. "Studies on the Influence of Emotions on the Functions of Organs," *Journal of Mental Sciences* (1935), 81:533–682.

―――, and BRIAN RUSSELL. *Emotional Factors in Skin Disease*. A Psychosomatic Medicine Monograph. New York: Paul B. Hoeber, Inc., 1954.

WOODS, F. A. "Rime-Words and Rime-Ideas," *Indogermanische Forschungen* (1907), 12:133–171.

WUNDT, WILHELM. *Grundzüge der Physiologischen Psychologie*, 4th ed. Leipzig: Engelmann, 1893.

―――. *Sprachgeschichte und Sprachpsychologie. Mit Rücksicht auf B. Delbrücks Grundfragen der Sprachforschung*. Leipzig: Engelmann, 1901.

―――. *Völkerpsychologie. Eine Untersuchung der Entwicklungsgesetze der Sprache, Mythus und Sitte*, 2nd ed. Leipzig: Engelmann, 1904.

ZAUNER, OTTO. "Die Romanischen Namen der Körperteile," *Romanische Forschungen* (1903), 14:339–430.

INDEX OF NAMES

INDEX OF FOREIGN WORDS

AKKADIAN

ARABIC

BOHEMIAN

nevole, 191

sirka, 58

DANISH

maal, 53

tungemaal, 53

DUTCH

blaken, 302
echt, 384
een loze noot, 368
fniezen, 226
lichaam, 213

lucifer, 59, 62
praten, 48
taal, 54
tump, 399
waf-waf, 337

EGYPTIAN

khāt, 199

FRENCH

angoisse, 225
autre, 330
avoir, 142, 149, 150
beaucoup, 332, 396
besoin, 191
boyau, 356
casette, 199
chien, 335
choisir, 346
ci, 339, 366
coeur, 174
commencement, 180
contretemps, 375
coquelico, 337
côté, 362
crayon, 389
cucu, 337
demander, 51
par Dieu, 308
dire, 47
écoeurer, 233
entrailles, 231
été, 146
être, 142

faire la figue, 274
il fait mauvais temps, 379
ferblanc, 197
feu, 26
fi, 226
fleurs, 181
gauche, 268
gauchir, 268
goûter, 345
il est, 143
il faut, 191
il faut que je le fasse, 192
jalousie, 256
je suis, 143
jeter à la figure de, quelqu'un, 234
là, 339, 366
maintenant, 149
mal au coeur, 233
massacre, 104
mèche, 59–60, 61, 63
mort dieu, 308
ne . . . point, 396
or, 159

oua-oua, 337
parbleu, 308
parler, 47, 48
parole, 48
penser, 15
petit, 339
place, 361
plomb, 195
plonge, 195
poign, 396
poignard, 396
poigne, 396
poilu, 303
point, 396
pointe, 396

pointiller, 396
pouce, 362
près, 365
répondre, 52
Riviera, 118
savoir, 15, 347
sentiment du vide, 367
situer, 361
tête, 32
tête qui tourne, la, 204
tort, 271
traduire, 176
vermeil, 304
verge, 400
vertigo, 204

GERMAN

Ackermann, 387
Albrecht, 298
Angst, 224–225
auflesen, 90
aufwärts, 365
Auge, 210
auslesen, 90
auswerfen, 234
Backe, 207, 225
Backenbart, 207
Backenzahn, 207
Batzen, 170
Bedürfnis, 190
Bertha, 298
beten, 52
Bett, 170
bis in das dritte Glied, 282–283
bitten, 51, 52
blaken, 302–303
blau, 198, 293, 307
Blech, 197
blecken, 303
Blei, 197–198
bleich, 197
Bleistift, 389, 392
Bleiweiss, 197
Blitz, 335–336
Blut, 174, 182, 305
Blutbad, 104
Blüte, 182, 305
-brecht, 298
brennen, 34, 247–248, 314

Brunnen, 34
Brunst, 34, 247–248, 314
brunzen, 34, 247–248, 314
Butzen, 170
da, 366
darf, 190
das, 339, 366
dauen, 353
Daumen, 273
Däumlinge, 273, 274
dies, 339, 366
dort, 339, 366
Dreck, 170
drehen, 233
dreimal, 326, 380
du, 330, 366
du bist, 146, 148
dumm, 197
Dumme hat Glück, der, 197
dürfen, 190
echt, 384
Ehe, 384
Einfalt, 392
einfältig, 391
Einfaltspinsel, 391, 392
eintönig, 336
Enkel, 283
entstehen, 149
entzwei, 329
er, 366
er findet Geschmack an ihr, 346
er ist, 143

GOTHIC

GREEK

takerō, 354
takeros, 354
takōn, 354
Tartaros, 97
tekō, 351–352, 354
theon en gounasi kettai, 282
thesei, 26
thumos, 219, 223, 224
tilos, 354

tithēmi, 326
triploos, 391
triskelion, 277
Tuchē, 193
xanthophanēs, 310
xanthos, 310
xanthos oinos, 309
zēloō, 256
zetros, 256

HEBREW

*In transcription and Latin
alphabetical order*
ā kal, 351
Abib, 380
āchad, 328
ādhom, 294
adom, 306
aleph, 394
anā, 328
ākonī, 328
arab, 256
arubhah, 256
bāsār, 211
beten, 231
bēyth, 394
bōhen, 273
Bul, 380
chīydāh, 49
chūwd, 49
dāleth, 394
echād, 328
Ethanim, 380
gīymel, 394
jereq, 292
kal, 351

lāshan, 247
lāshōn, 45, 247
leshōnah, 45
malach, 54
māshāl, 49
me'im, 231, 232
nephesh, 222, 223
raggāh, 371
rebem, 234
ruach, 222–223, 231
sāphāh, 45
seor, 134, 135
shā'ar, 135
Sheol, 97
tā'am, 347
Techōm, 97
tē'em, 347
tekeleth, 308
tōpach, 362
tsāhab, 310
tsāhōb, 310
yārāk, 310
yerek, 310
Zif, 380

HITTITE

birku, 282

pat, 240

HUNGARIAN

amott, 366
be, 362
bél, 362
bele, 362
belsö, 362

ellen, 375
ellenség, 375
emészti magát, 235
emitt, 366
fakad, 182

IRISH

ITALIAN

JAPANESE

LATIN

Decimus, 332
dedicō, -āre, 54
degustō, -āre, 345
dentes pruriunt, 214
despicō, -ere, 257
dexter, 267
di-, 235, 364
dicō, -āre, 47, 54
dicō, -ere, 54
digitus, 272, 362
diligens, 90
diligō, -ere, 90
dingua, 247
dis-, from former duis, 90
duis-, 90
duplex, 391
duplus, 391
ego tu intus et in cute novi,
   213
elegans, 89–90
ēmungō, -ere, 347
est, 143
ex, 361, 367
exsaltō, -āre, 367
exsistō, -ere, 146
extendō, -ere, 361
fabula, 48
fābulor, -āri, 48, 49
facio, -ere, 72
fallit, 191
fallō, -ere, 191
falsum, 191
famosus, 272
farcimen, 357
farciō, farctum, fartum, 356-
   357
fāri, 47
farsi, 356
femur, 278
fermentum, 135
fermeō, ēre, 135
ferrō, ferre, 62, 193
ferveō, -ēre, 135
fervō, -ere, 135
fervor, 135
festina lente, 378
fieri, 148
fiō, fis, fit, fui, 148
flagrō, -āre, 302, 307
flātus, 225, 354
flāvus, 293, 307, 354
flectō, -ere, 170

fluor, 181–182
fore, 148
formus, 353
fors, 193
Fors Fortuna, 193, 194, 195
fragilis, 33
fu, 226
fufae, 226
fugit irreparabile tempus, 376
fulvus, 307
fūmus, 134, 223, 359
fuscus, 295
futurus, 148
galbinus, 292
gemō, -ere, 239
gena, 286
geni-, 283
genii, 239
genius, 239, 240, 241
genius indulgere, 240
genō, -ere, 275
genu, 275, 283, 285, 286, 424
genuini, 179
genuinus, 283, 285
genus, 179
gerō, -ere, 235
gignō, -ere, 89, 239, 275, 424
glaucus, 307
gratis, 72
grāvus, 296
gustō, -āre, 345, 347
habeō, -ēre, 150
habitō, āre, 150
habitudō, -inis, 150
habitus, -ūs, 150
Hannibal ante portas, 68
haruspex, 229, 230
hemicranium, 210
homo emunctioris naso, 347
hypochondria, 245
ignis, 18, 26, 312
impudicus, 217, 272
in, 147
in manu sua est, 268
in suspecto loco, 260
incunabula, 394
infāmis, 272
ingenuus, 283
ineō, -īre, 180
inserō, -ere, 92
intelligō, -ere, 90
interior, 230

LITHUANIAN

MIDDLE ENGLISH

NORDIC

OBSOLETE ENGLISH

farce, 357
farcemeat, 357
lucifer, 62
stead, 361

swart, 303
tongue, 249
wrong, 268
yare, 352, 353

OBSOLETE GERMAN

allewege, 373
Bad segnen, das, 104
ē, 384
ēhaft, 384
garküche, 353

gerwung, 353
Hansmist, 358
Kindes liegen, eines, 276
rizan, 386
Sterne schneuzen, die, 60

OLD ENGLISH

acsian, 51
ae, 384
aew, 384
andswarian, 52
awa, 384
axian, 51
beō, 143
beom, 146
beorht, 298
bera, 295
bernu, 295
blaw, 306, 307
blew, 181
blod, 181
blodisōjan, 104, 221
blodmonadh, 380
blōdsung, 221
blowan, 181
blown, 181
braeth, 225, 226
brōd, 136
cennan, 25
cild, 339
cneow, cneo, 275
costian, 346
dide, 326
eagduru, 253
eage, 209
eagthyrel, 253
eahta, 333
eallne waeg, 373
eln, 363

elnboga, 363
faethm, 363
fnēozan, 226, 338
fram worulde on worulde, 383
gall, 311
gamaecca, gemaca, 61
gēac, 337
gealla, 242, 311
gearu, 352
gearwian, 352
gearwung, 352
geolo, 242
geolu, 311
gerwehūs, 353
gōdspell, 50, 393
habbam laetran tungan, 45
haewe, 307
haewen, 307
heofon, 307
hlaefdige, 136
hlāf, 135
hlāford, 136
hlāfweard, 136
hlydmonadh, 380
hordweard, 136
idel, 368
kittle, 217
laest, 376
leas, 368
lēoht, 320, 321–322
lēohtan, 320

OLD FRENCH

OLD HIGH GERMAN

PERSIAN

PORTUGUESE

RUSSIAN

SANSKRIT

SLAVIC

SPANISH

SWEDISH